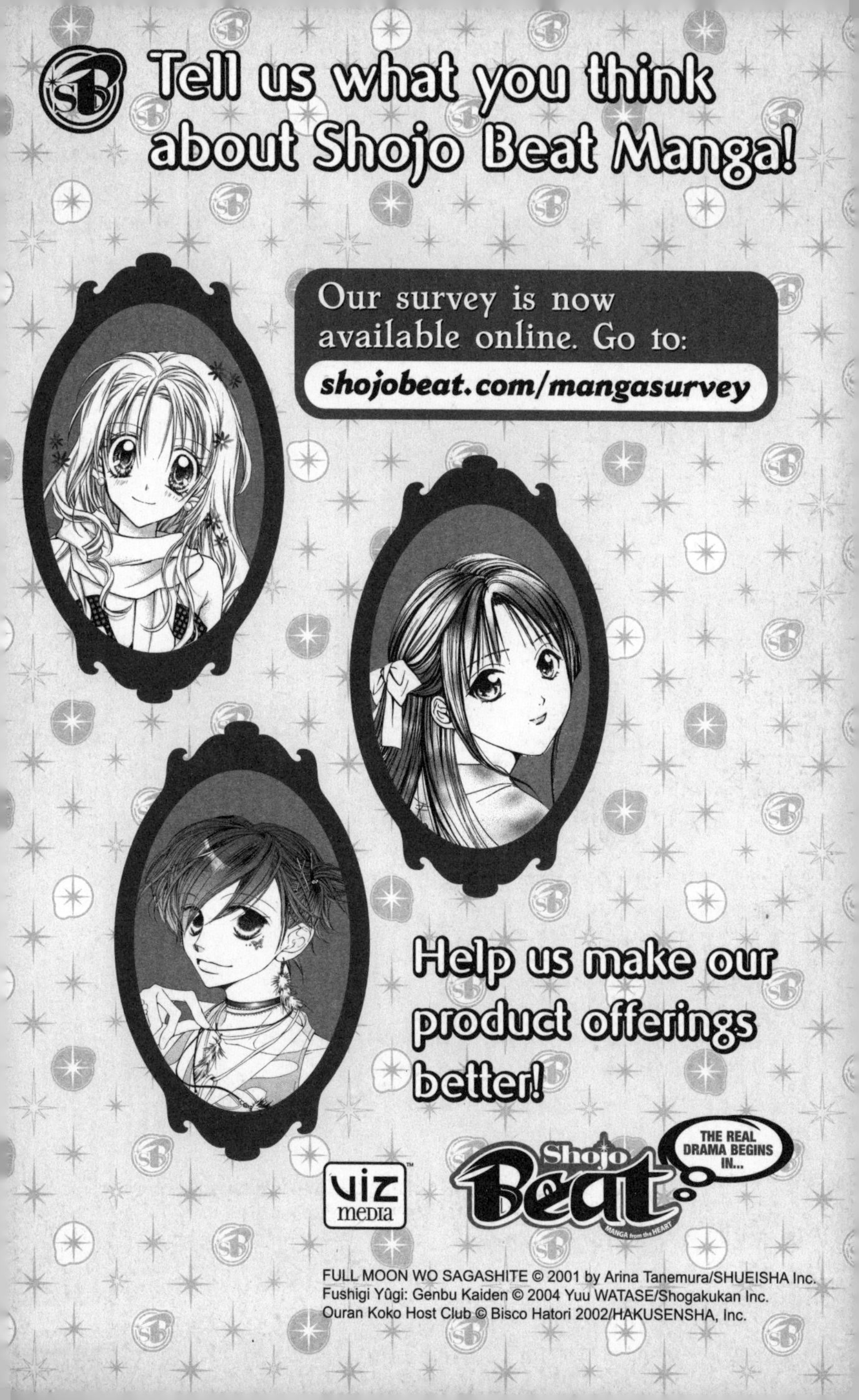
Tell us what you think about Shojo Beat Manga!
Our survey is now available online. Go to:
shojobeat.com/mangasurvey
Help us make our product offerings better!
viz media
Shojo Beat
MANGA from the HEART
THE REAL DRAMA BEGINS IN...
FULL MOON WO SAGASHITE © 2001 by Arina Tanemura/SHUEISHA Inc.
Fushigi Yûgi: Genbu Kaiden © 2004 Yuu WATASE/Shogakukan Inc.
Ouran Koko Host Club © Bisco Hatori 2002/HAKUSENSHA, Inc.

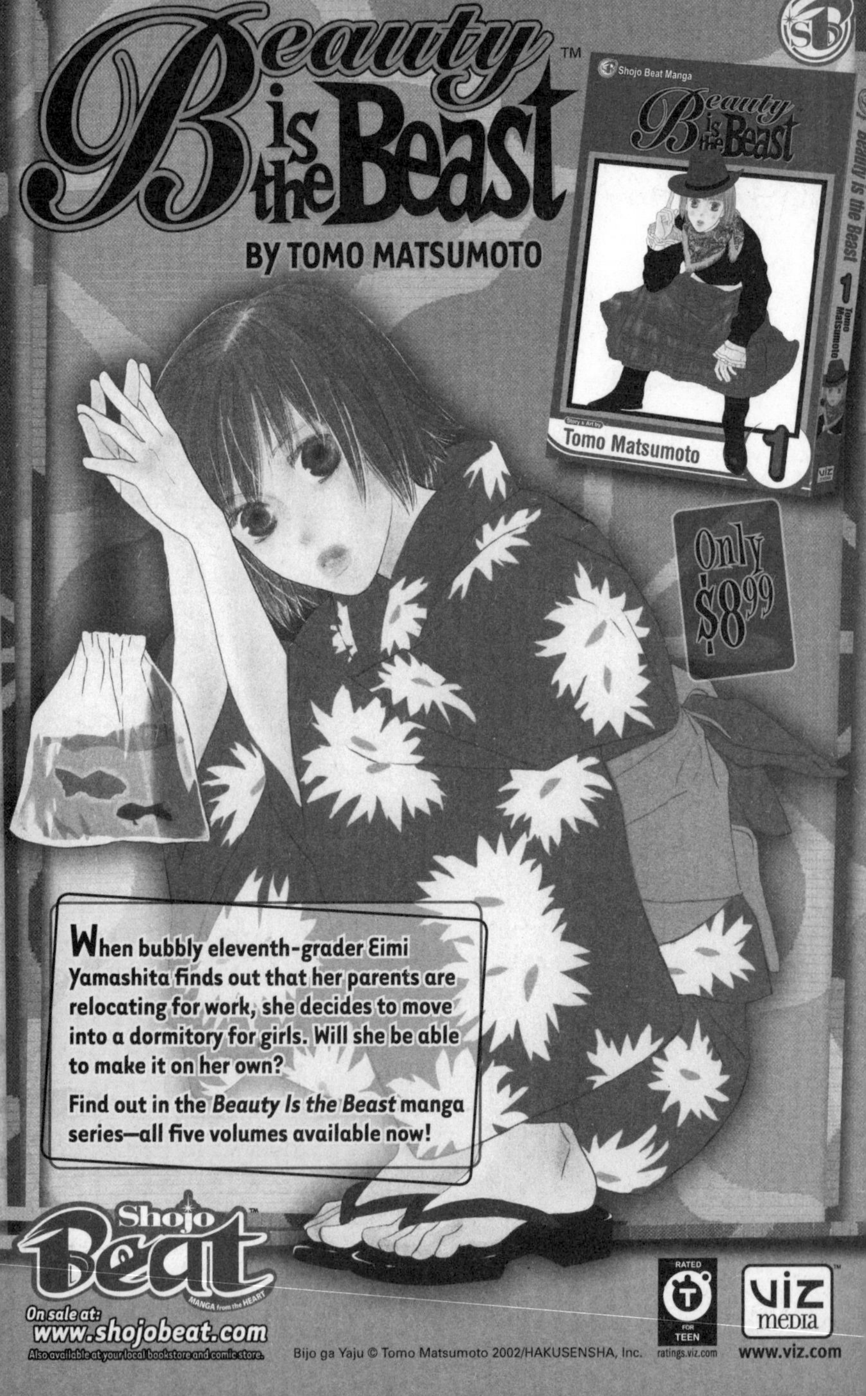

WILD ONES
VOL. 4
The Shojo Beat Manga Edition

STORY AND ART BY
KIYO FUJIWARA

Translation & Adaptation/Mai Ihara
Touch-up Art & Lettering/HudsonYards
Cover Design/Hidemi Dunn
Interior Design/Yuki Ameda
Editor/Jonathan Tarbox

Editor in Chief, Books/Alvin Lu
Editor in Chief, Magazines/Marc Weidenbaum
VP of Publishing Licensing/Rika Inouye
VP of Sales/Gonzalo Ferreyra
Sr. VP of Marketing/Liza Coppola
Publisher/Hyoe Narita

Arakure by Kiyo Fujiwara
© Kiyo Fujiwara 2006
All rights reserved.
First published in Japan in 2007 by HAKUSENSHA, Inc., Tokyo.
English language translation rights arranged with HAKUSENSHA, Inc., Tokyo. All
rights reserved. The stories, characters and incidents mentioned in this publication
are entirely fictional.

Printed in Canada

Published by VIZ Media, LLC
P.O. Box 77010
San Francisco, CA 94107

Shojo Beat Manga Edition
10 9 8 7 6 5 4 3 2 1
First printing, September 2008

www.viz.com

store.viz.com

Kiyo Fujiwara made her manga debut in 2000 in *Hana to Yume* magazine with *Bokuwane*. Her other works include *Hard Romantic-ker, Help!!* and *Gold Rush 21*. She comes from Akashi-shi in Hyogo Prefecture but currently lives in Tokyo. Her hobbies include playing drums and bass guitar and wearing kimono.

Wild Ones
アラクレ

Vol. 4

Story & Art by
Kiyo Fujiwara

YOU TOLD ME TO JUST WAIT A SECOND, RIGHT...?
AHHHH...!!
RIGHT?
TMP
TMP
TMP
TMP

Wild Ones アラクレ

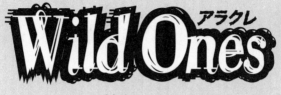

Volume 4

CONTENTS

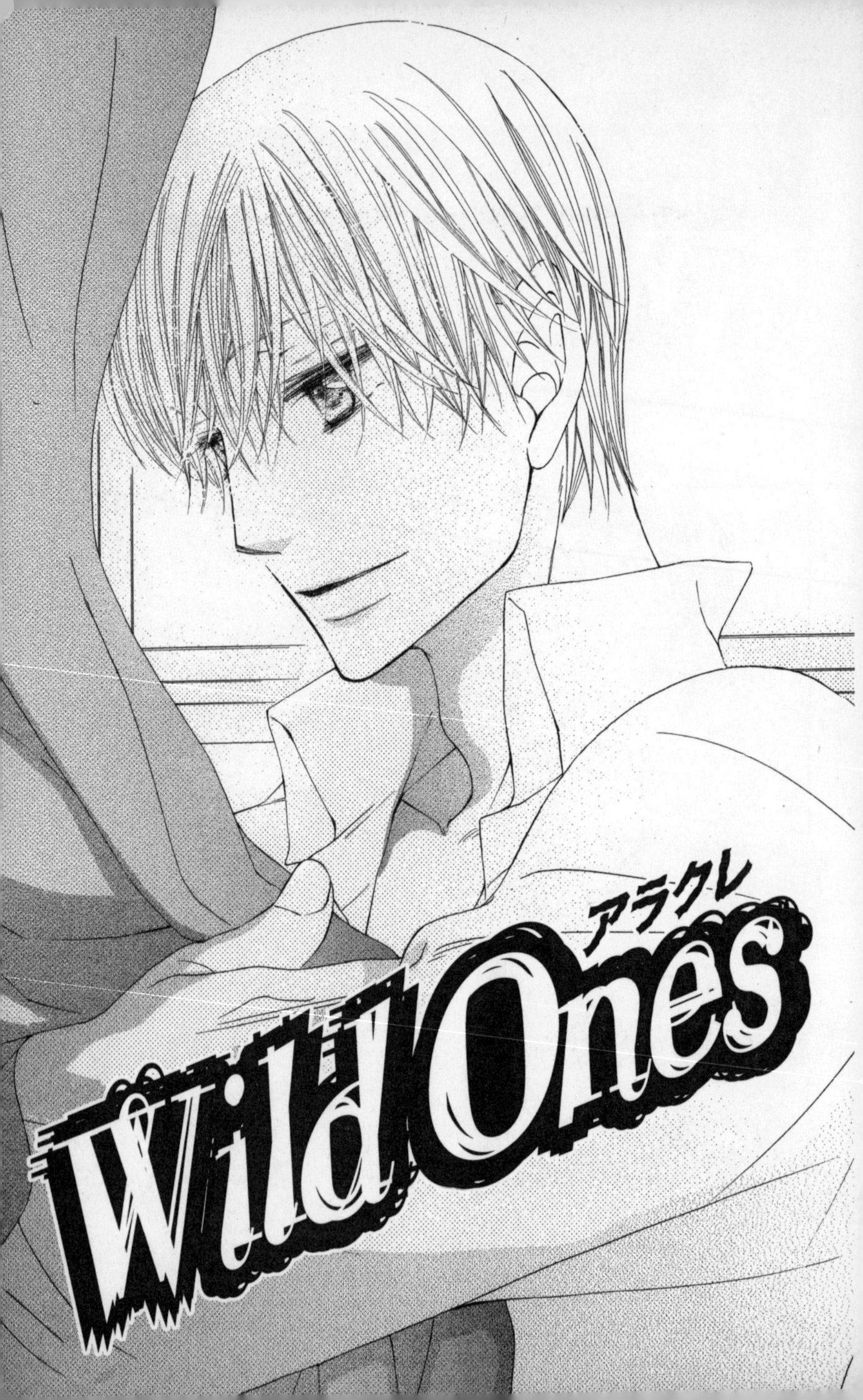

アラクレ
Wild Ones

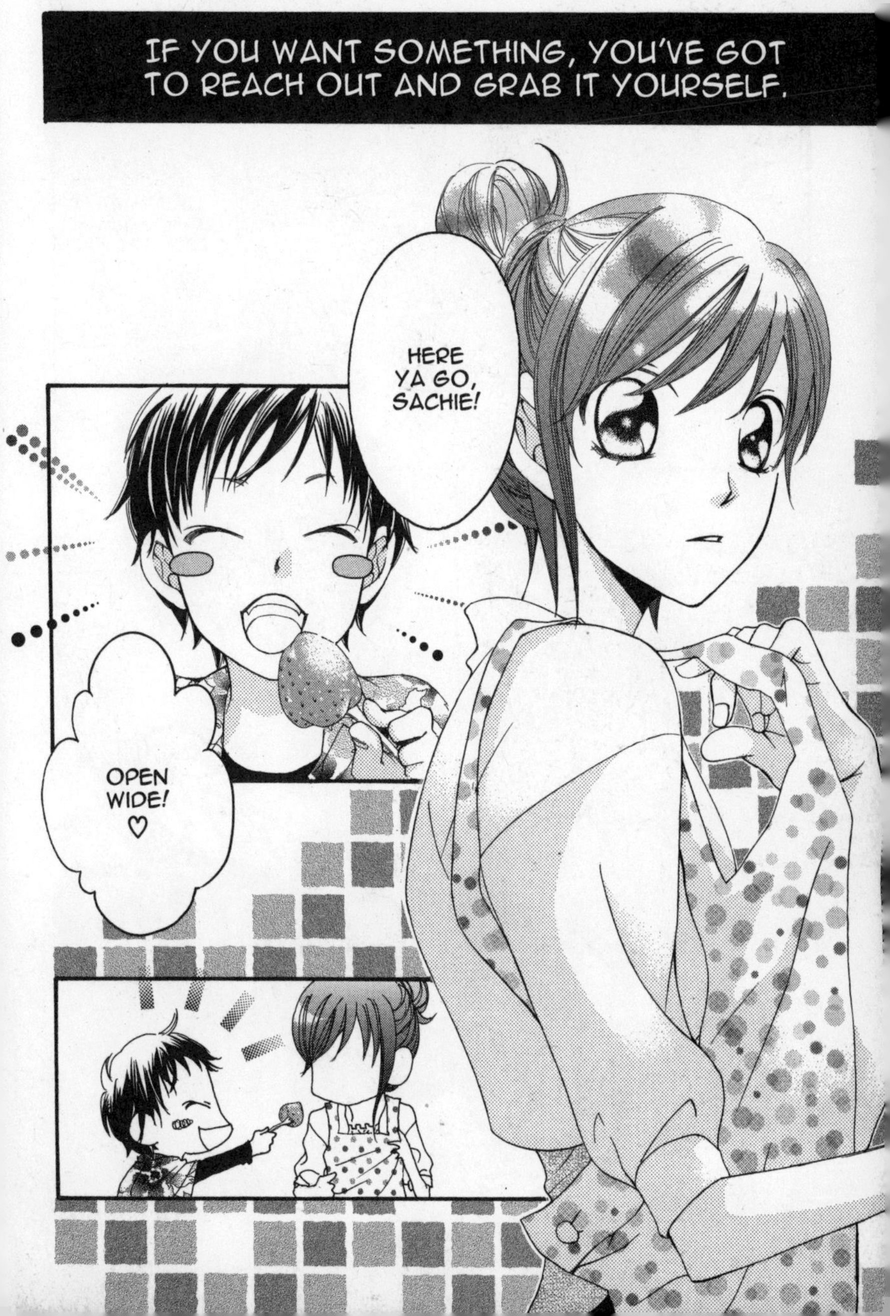
IF YOU WANT SOMETHING, YOU'VE GOT TO REACH OUT AND GRAB IT YOURSELF.
HERE YA GO, SACHIE!
OPEN WIDE! ♡

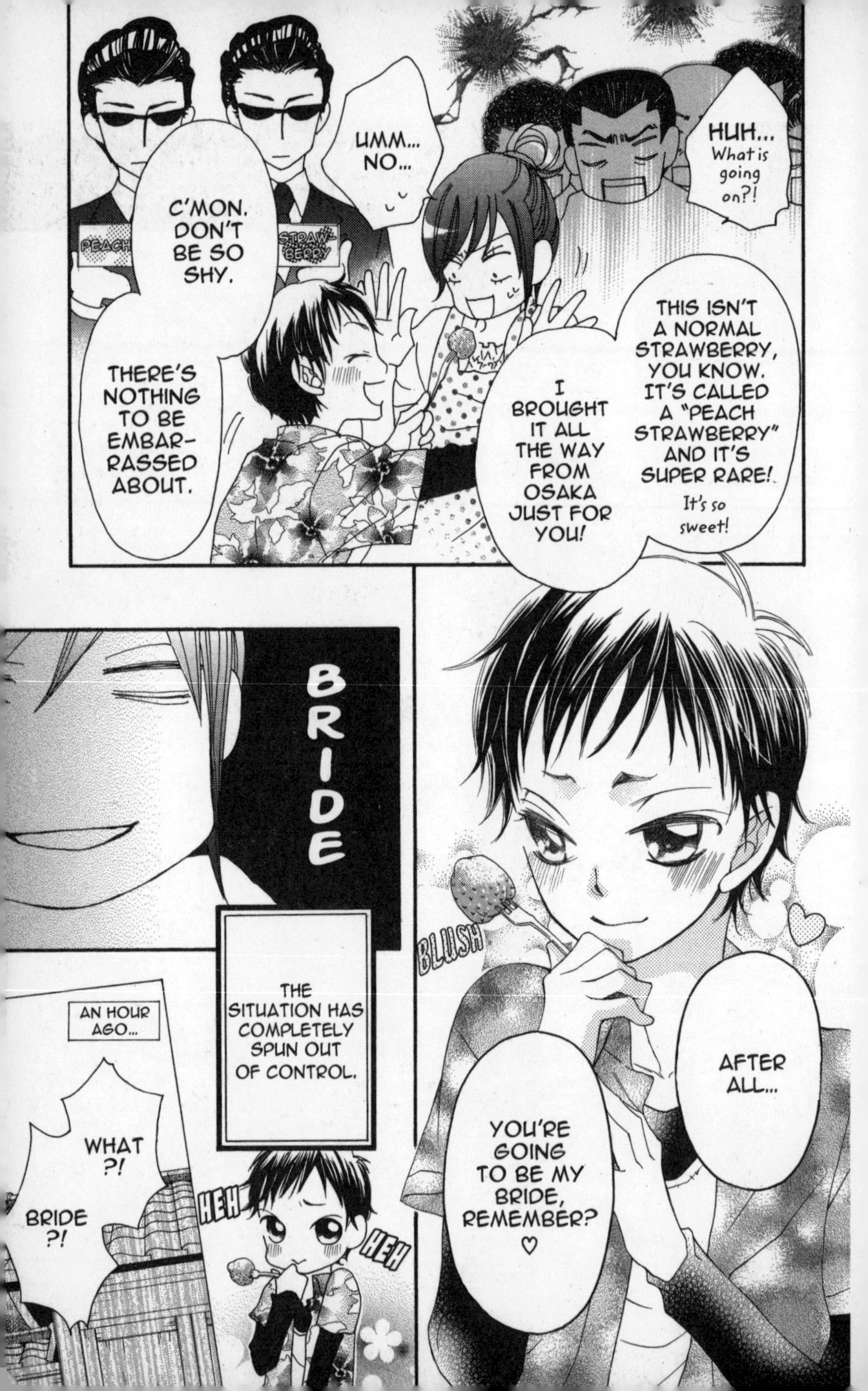
HUH... What is going on?!
UMM... NO...
C'MON. DON'T BE SO SHY.
STRAWBERRY
PEACH
THIS ISN'T A NORMAL STRAWBERRY, YOU KNOW. IT'S CALLED A "PEACH STRAWBERRY" AND IT'S SUPER RARE! It's so sweet!
I BROUGHT IT ALL THE WAY FROM OSAKA JUST FOR YOU!
THERE'S NOTHING TO BE EMBARRASSED ABOUT.
BLUSH
AFTER ALL...
YOU'RE GOING TO BE MY BRIDE, REMEMBER? ♡
BRIDE
THE SITUATION HAS COMPLETELY SPUN OUT OF CONTROL.
HEH
HEH
AN HOUR AGO...
WHAT?!
BRIDE?!

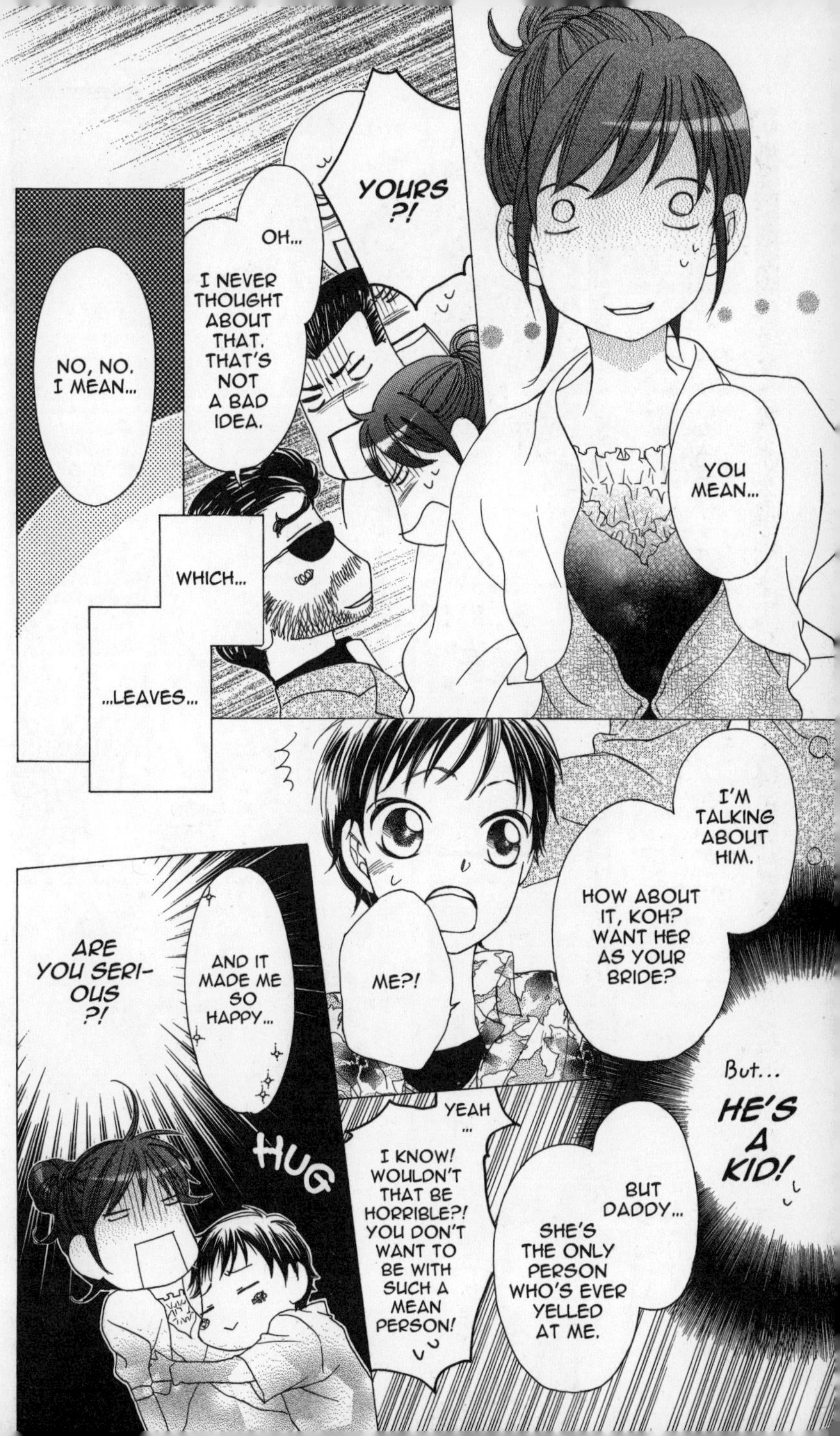
YOU MEAN...
YOURS ?!
OH...
I NEVER THOUGHT ABOUT THAT. THAT'S NOT A BAD IDEA.
NO, NO. I MEAN...
WHICH...
...LEAVES...
I'M TALKING ABOUT HIM.
HOW ABOUT IT, KOH? WANT HER AS YOUR BRIDE?
ME?!
But...
HE'S A KID!
BUT DADDY...
SHE'S THE ONLY PERSON WHO'S EVER YELLED AT ME.
YEAH...
I KNOW! WOULDN'T THAT BE HORRIBLE?! YOU DON'T WANT TO BE WITH SUCH A MEAN PERSON!
AND IT MADE ME SO HAPPY...
ARE YOU SERI-OUS ?!
HUG

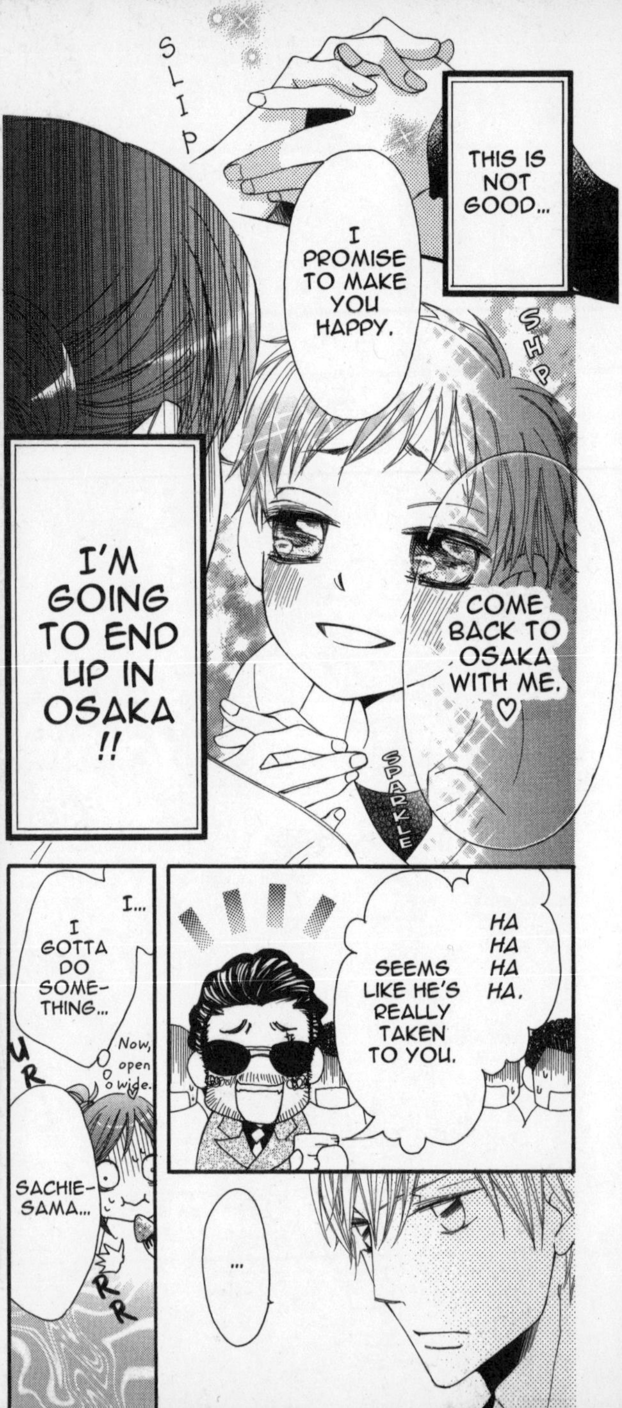
SLIP
THIS IS NOT GOOD...
I PROMISE TO MAKE YOU HAPPY.
SHP
COME BACK TO OSAKA WITH ME. ♡
SPARKLE
I'M GOING TO END UP IN OSAKA !!
HA HA HA HA.
SEEMS LIKE HE'S REALLY TAKEN TO YOU.
I...
I GOTTA DO SOMETHING...
Now, open wide.
URRRR
SACHIE-SAMA...
...

I MADE IT TO WILD ONES VOLUME 4!! THANK YOU SO MUCH!

IT ALL WENT BY SO QUICKLY. I CAN'T BELIEVE IT'S THE FOURTH ONE ALREADY.

I'VE EVEN BEEN ABLE TO PUBLISH ABROAD, AND I'VE BEEN GETTING LETTERS FROM OVERSEAS LATELY. IT MAKES ME VERY HAPPY.

I ALWAYS FEEL A BIT OVERWHELMED WHEN I GET LETTERS FROM ABROAD SAYING, "I THINK SACHIE'S REALLY CUTE," OR "I LOVE AKI." I WRITE THESE AS A JAPANESE COMIC, AND IT'S AMAZING TO HAVE PEOPLE PICK UP ON THE SAME NUANCES IN A DIFFERENT CULTURE. (ALTHOUGH I'M NOT REALLY SURE IF THAT'S WHAT'S REALLY HAPPENING....)

BUT THAT IS WHY I DRAW! IT'S AWESOME!!

I'M REALLY VERY HAPPY.

I REMEMBER I HAD A PEN PAL IN HONG KONG BACK IN THE DAY. I WASN'T DILIGENT ENOUGH TO KEEP IT GOING... I WISH I HAD BEEN, THOUGH.

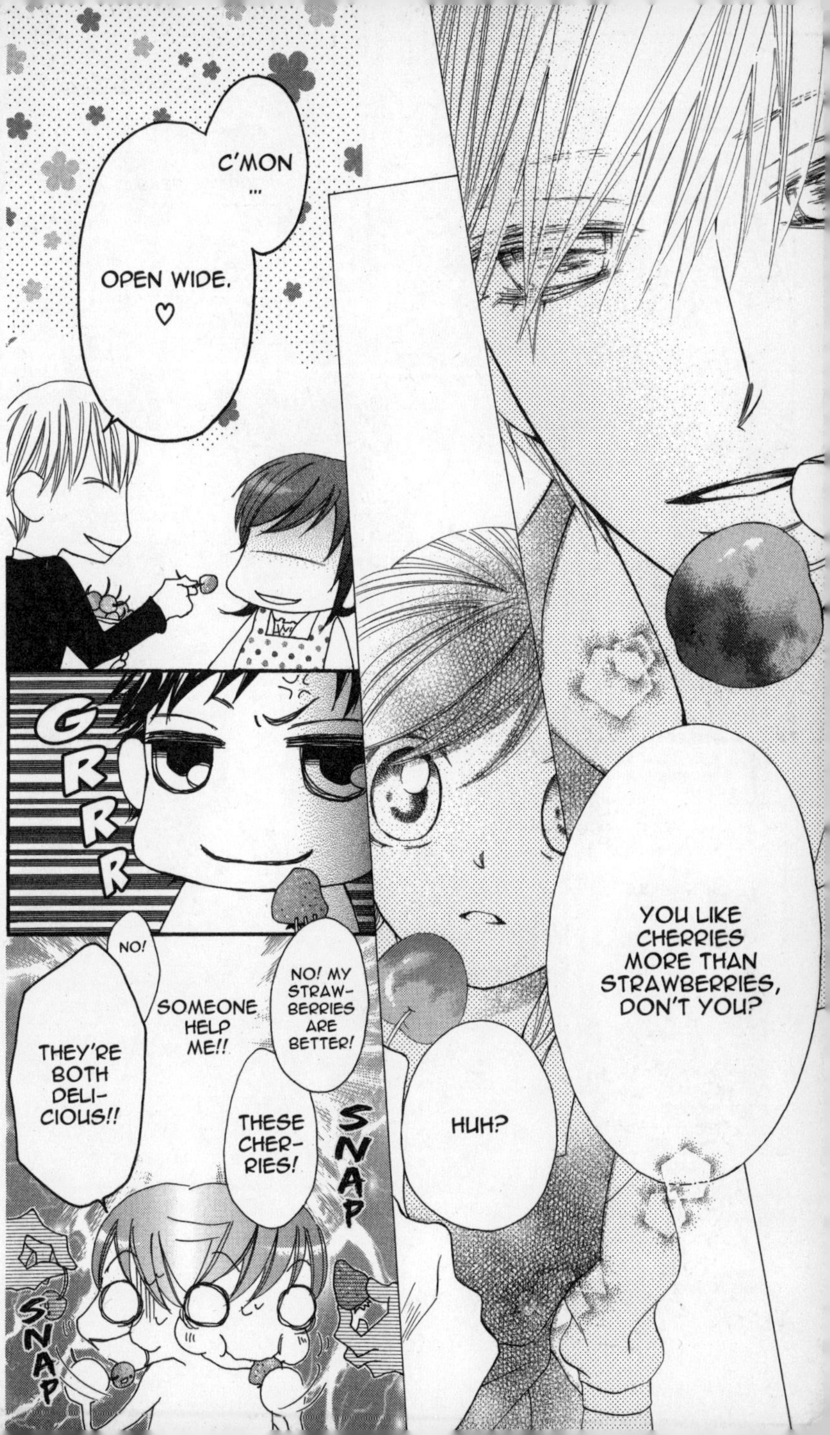
YOU LIKE CHERRIES MORE THAN STRAWBERRIES, DON'T YOU?
HUH?
C'MON ... OPEN WIDE. ♡
GRRR
NO! MY STRAW-BERRIES ARE BETTER!
SNAP
THESE CHER-RIES!
SOMEONE HELP ME!!
NO!
THEY'RE BOTH DELI-CIOUS!!
SNAP

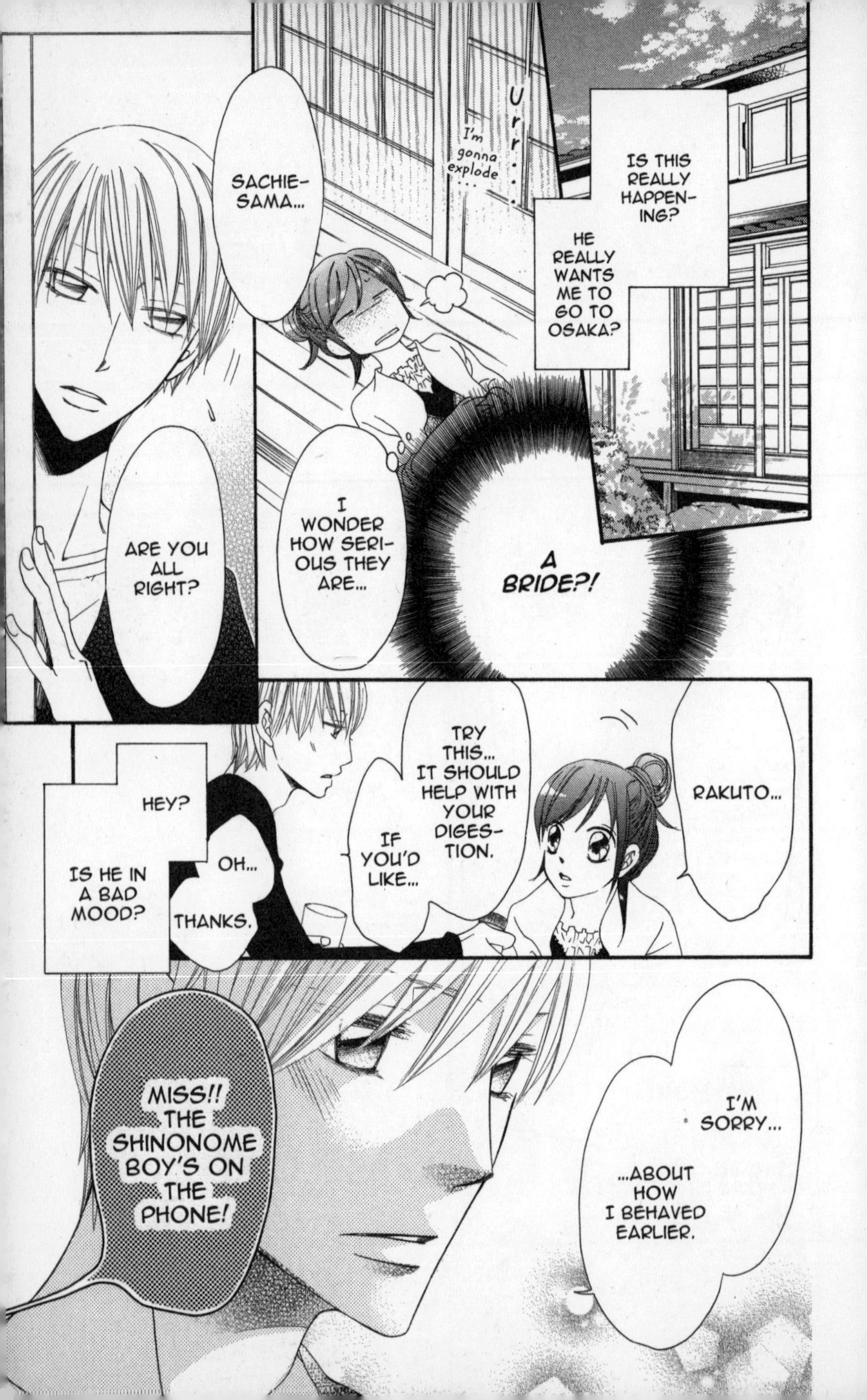
IS THIS REALLY HAPPENING?
HE REALLY WANTS ME TO GO TO OSAKA?
Urr...
I'm gonna explode...
A BRIDE?!
I WONDER HOW SERIOUS THEY ARE...
SACHIE-SAMA...
ARE YOU ALL RIGHT?
RAKUTO...
TRY THIS... IT SHOULD HELP WITH YOUR DIGESTION.
IF YOU'D LIKE...
OH... THANKS.
HEY?
IS HE IN A BAD MOOD?
I'M SORRY...
...ABOUT HOW I BEHAVED EARLIER.
MISS!! THE SHINONOME BOY'S ON THE PHONE!

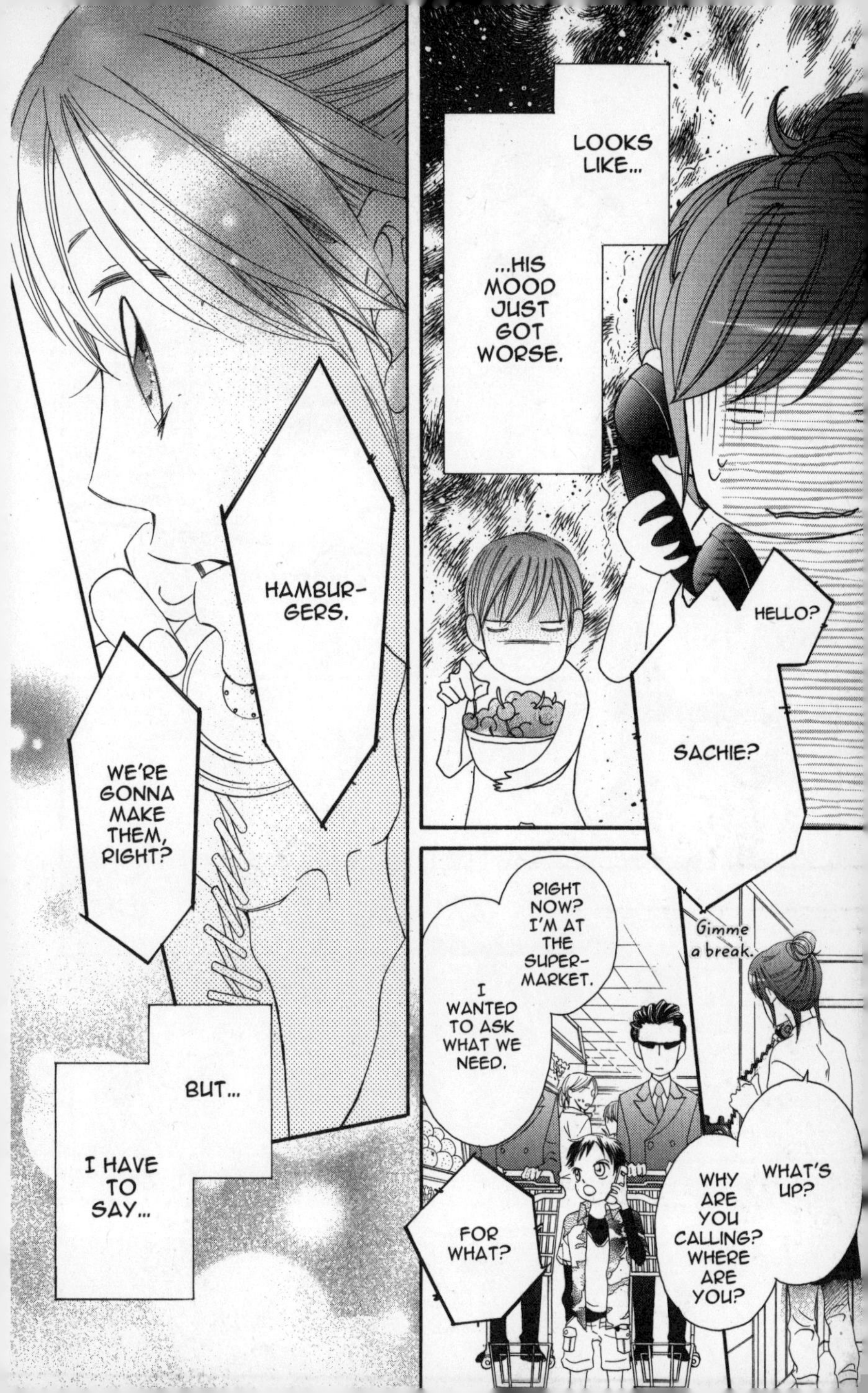
LOOKS LIKE...
...HIS MOOD JUST GOT WORSE.
HELLO?
SACHIE?
Gimme a break.
WHAT'S UP?
WHY ARE YOU CALLING? WHERE ARE YOU?
RIGHT NOW? I'M AT THE SUPER-MARKET.
I WANTED TO ASK WHAT WE NEED.
FOR WHAT?
HAMBURGERS.
WE'RE GONNA MAKE THEM, RIGHT?
BUT...
I HAVE TO SAY...

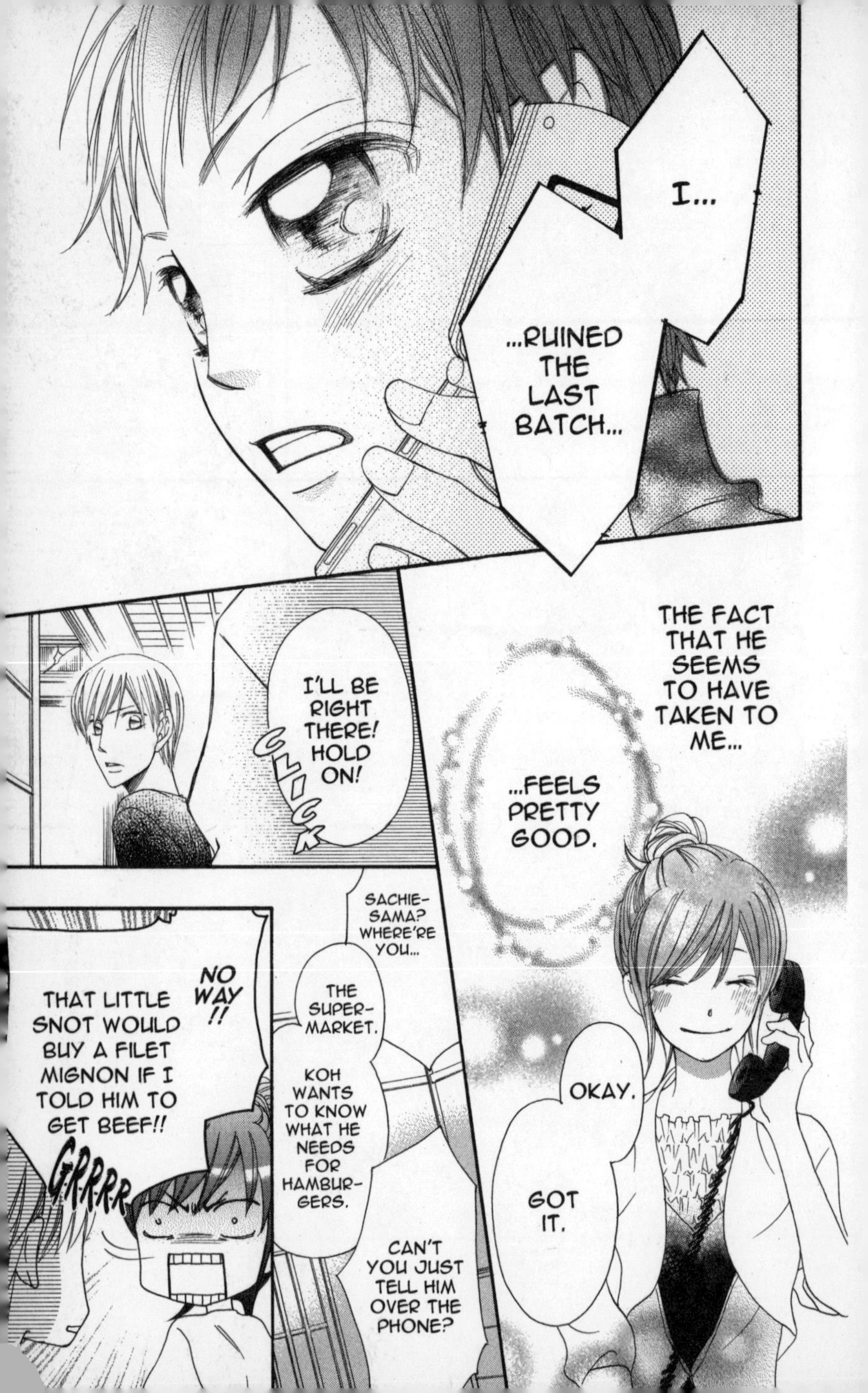
I...
...RUINED THE LAST BATCH...
THE FACT THAT HE SEEMS TO HAVE TAKEN TO ME...
...FEELS PRETTY GOOD.
OKAY.
GOT IT.
I'LL BE RIGHT THERE! HOLD ON!
CLICK
SACHIE-SAMA? WHERE'RE YOU...
THE SUPER-MARKET.
KOH WANTS TO KNOW WHAT HE NEEDS FOR HAMBUR-GERS.
CAN'T YOU JUST TELL HIM OVER THE PHONE?
NO WAY!!
THAT LITTLE SNOT WOULD BUY A FILET MIGNON IF I TOLD HIM TO GET BEEF!!
GRRRR

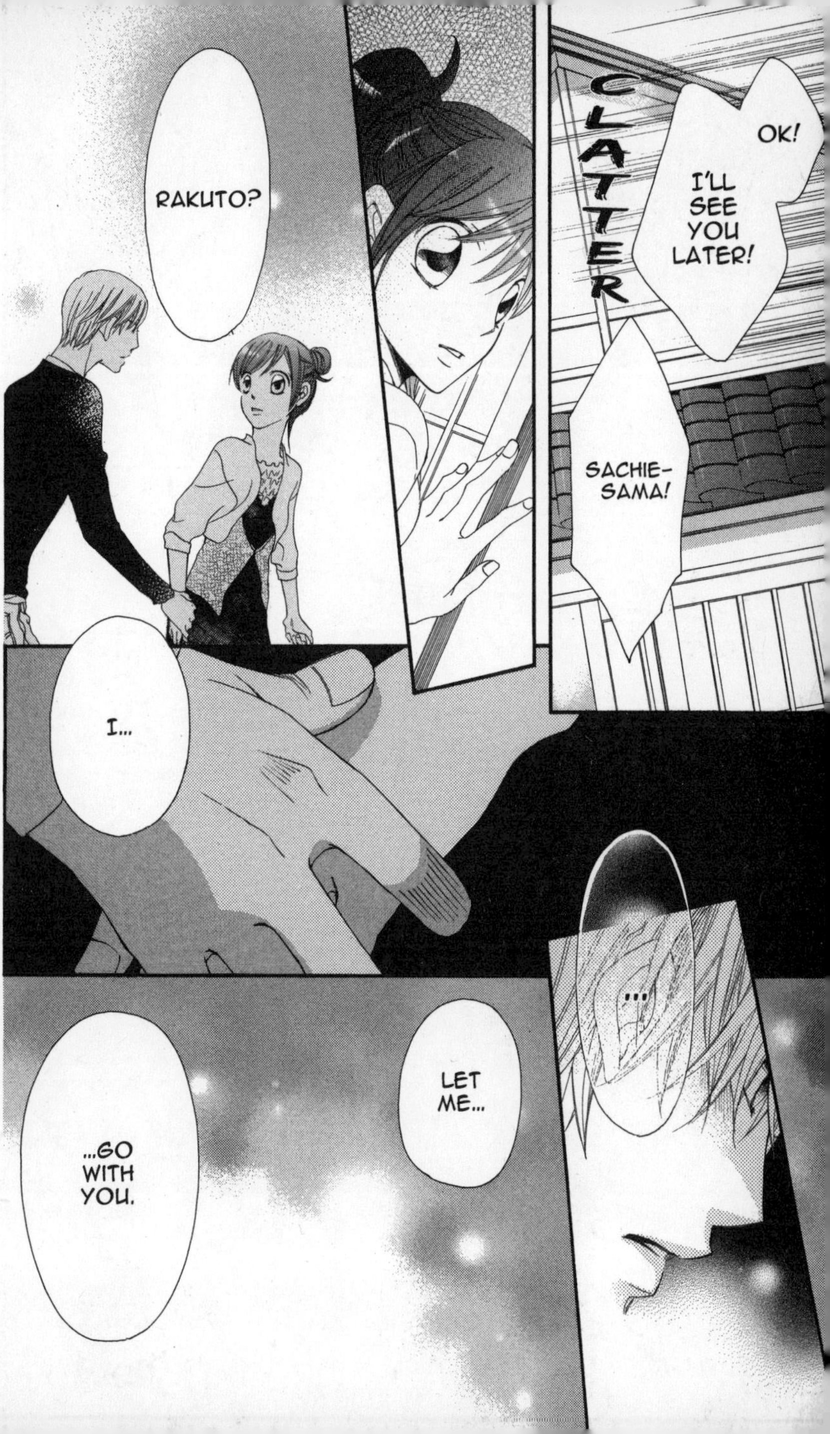
OK!
I'LL SEE YOU LATER!
CLATTER
SACHIE-SAMA!
RAKUTO?
I...
...
LET ME...
...GO WITH YOU.

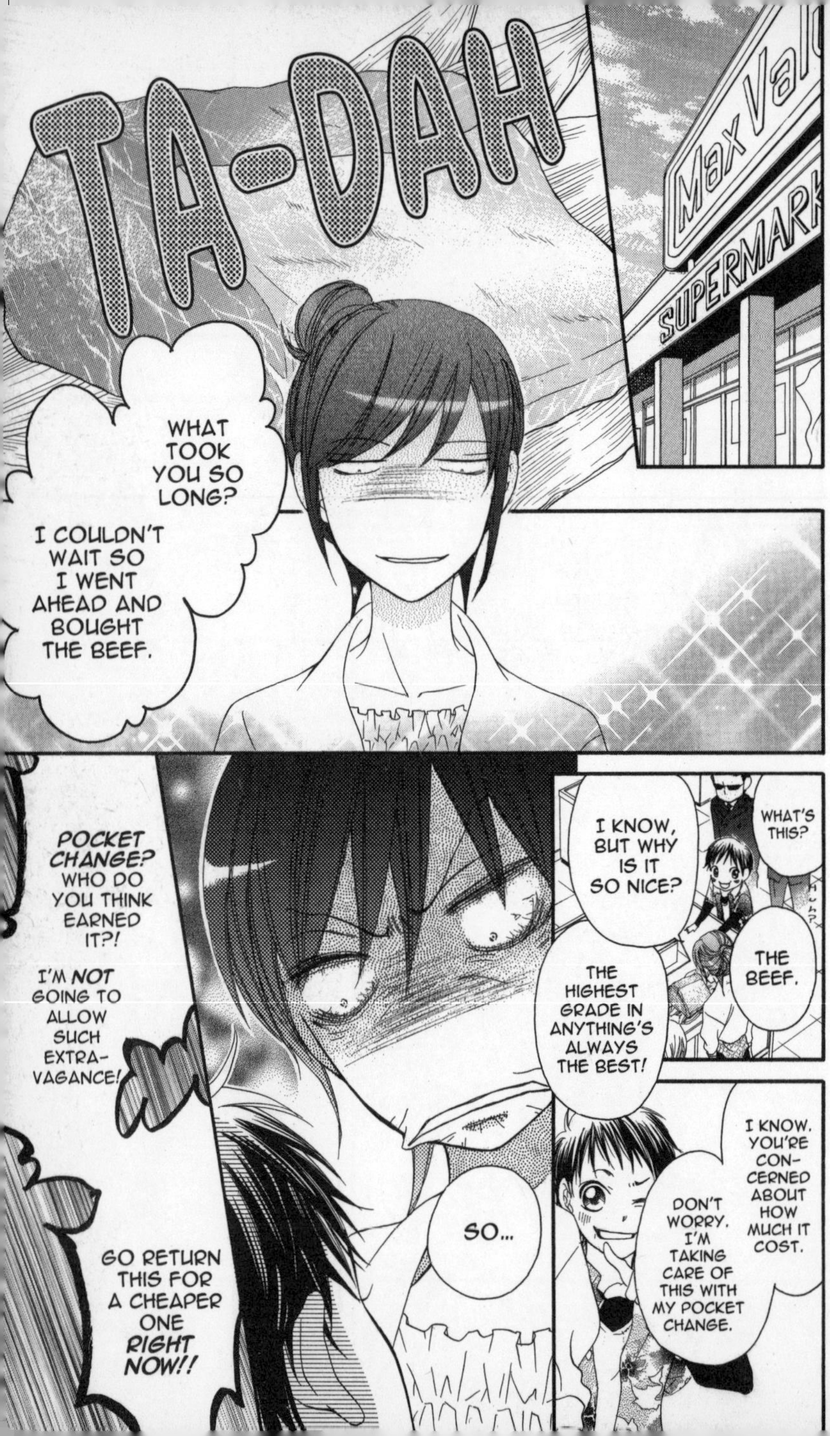
TA-DAH
WHAT TOOK YOU SO LONG?
I COULDN'T WAIT SO I WENT AHEAD AND BOUGHT THE BEEF.
WHAT'S THIS?
THE BEEF.
I KNOW, BUT WHY IS IT SO NICE?
THE HIGHEST GRADE IN ANYTHING'S ALWAYS THE BEST!
I KNOW. YOU'RE CON-CERNED ABOUT HOW MUCH IT COST.
DON'T WORRY. I'M TAKING CARE OF THIS WITH MY POCKET CHANGE.
SO...
POCKET CHANGE? WHO DO YOU THINK EARNED IT?!
I'M *NOT* GOING TO ALLOW SUCH EXTRA-VAGANCE!
GO RETURN THIS FOR A CHEAPER ONE *RIGHT NOW!!*

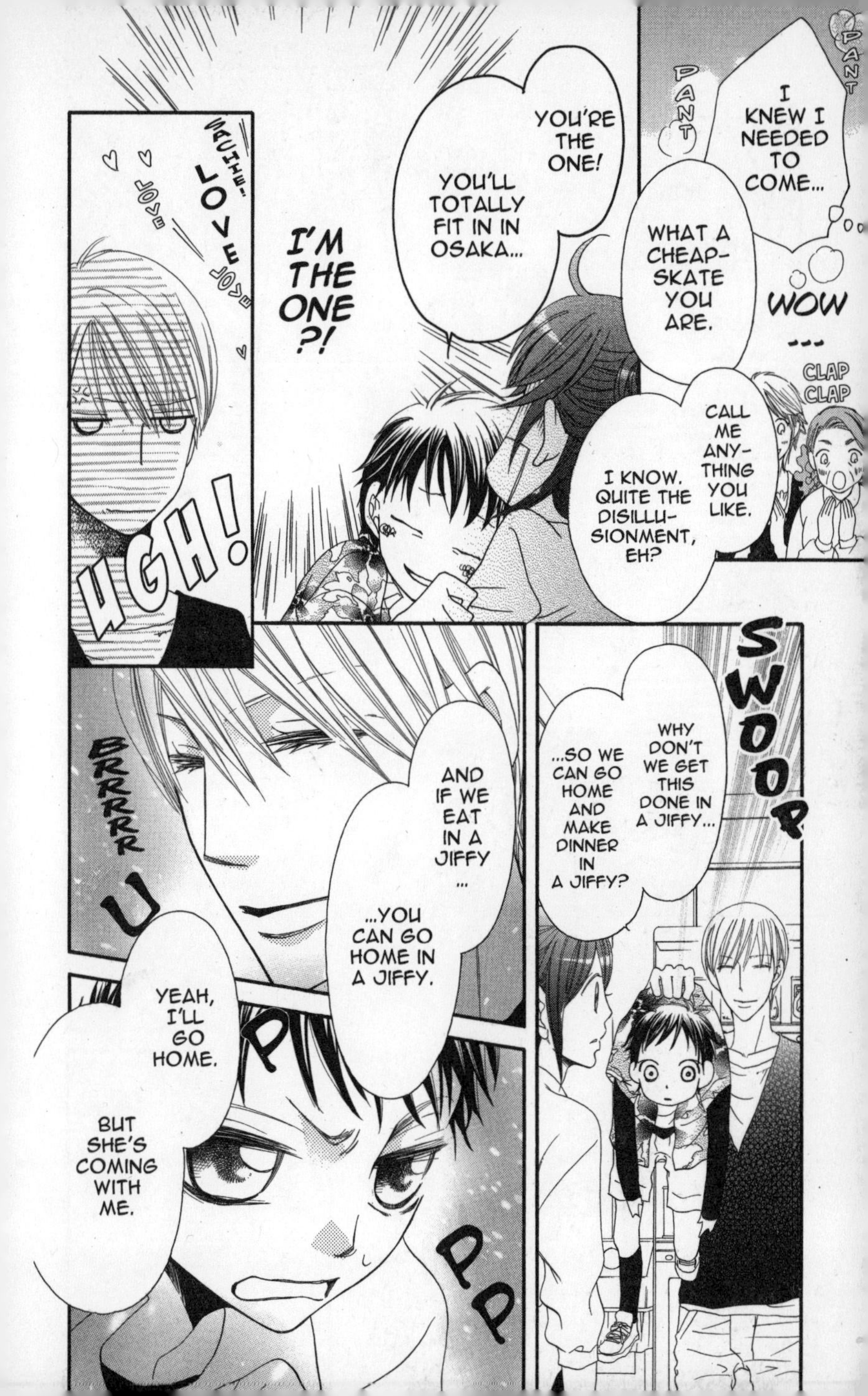
PANT
PANT
I KNEW I NEEDED TO COME...
WOW...
CLAP CLAP
YOU'RE THE ONE!
YOU'LL TOTALLY FIT IN IN OSAKA...
I'M THE ONE?!
WHAT A CHEAPSKATE YOU ARE.
CALL ME ANYTHING YOU LIKE.
I KNOW. QUITE THE DISILLUSIONMENT, EH?
SACHIE! LOVE LOVE LOVE
UGH!
SWOOP
WHY DON'T WE GET THIS DONE IN A JIFFY...
...SO WE CAN GO HOME AND MAKE DINNER IN A JIFFY?
BRRRRR
AND IF WE EAT IN A JIFFY...
...YOU CAN GO HOME IN A JIFFY.
UPPP
YEAH, I'LL GO HOME.
BUT SHE'S COMING WITH ME.

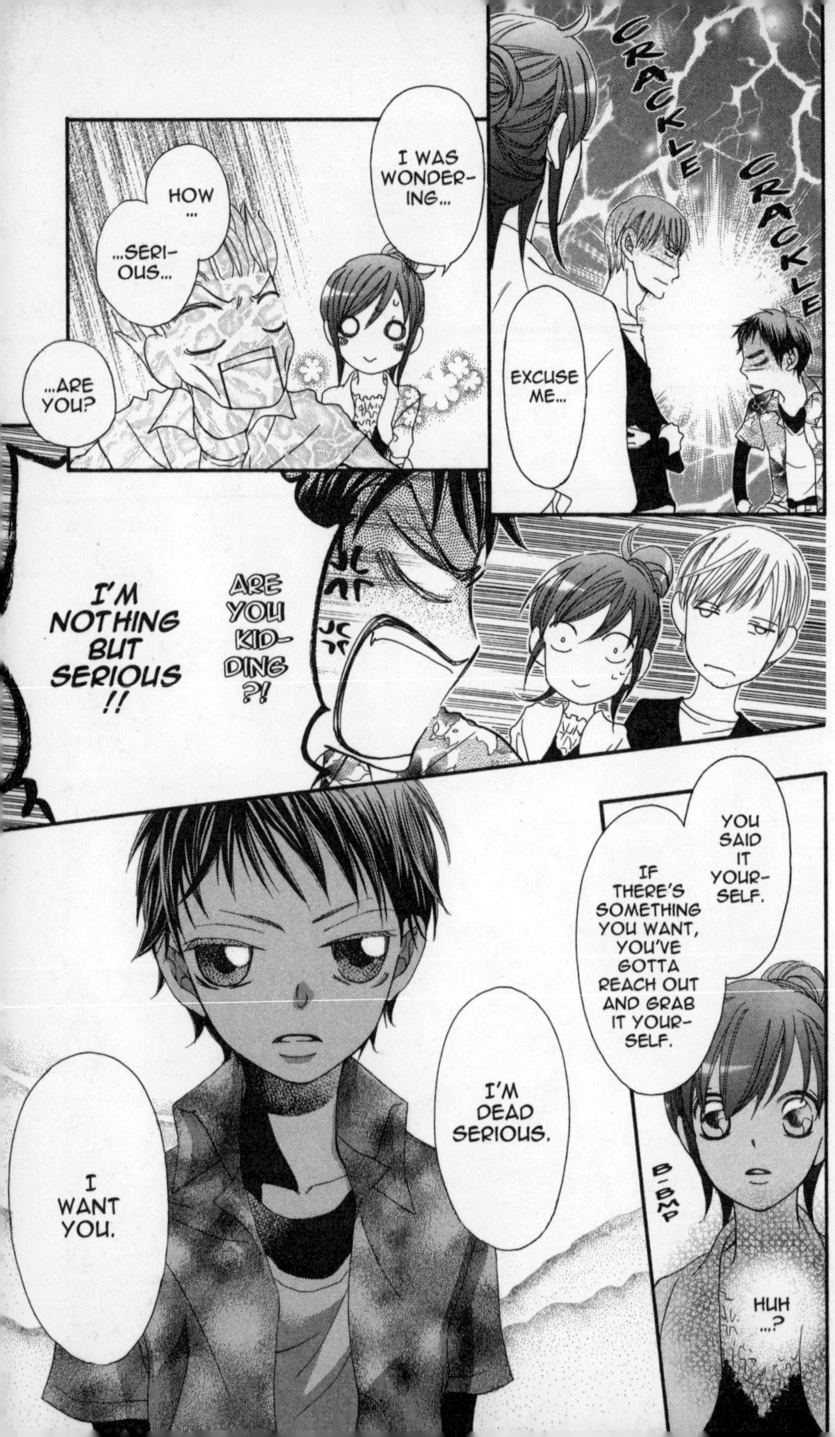
CRACKLE
CRACKLE
EXCUSE ME...
I WAS WONDERING...
HOW ...
...SERIOUS...
...ARE YOU?
ARE YOU KIDDING?!
I'M NOTHING BUT SERIOUS!!
YOU SAID IT YOURSELF.
IF THERE'S SOMETHING YOU WANT, YOU'VE GOTTA REACH OUT AND GRAB IT YOURSELF.
B-BMP
HUH ...?
I'M DEAD SERIOUS.
I WANT YOU.

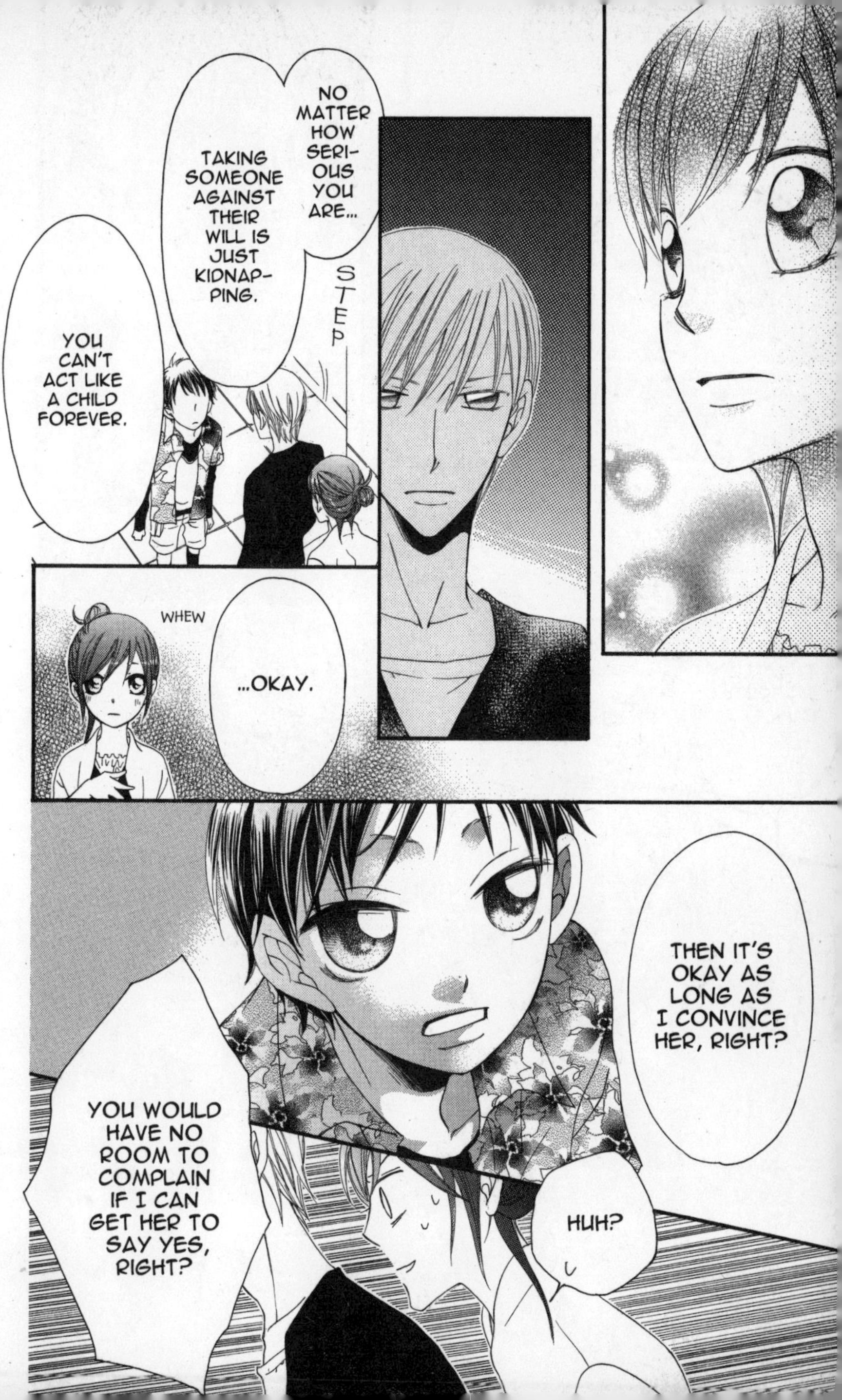

NO MATTER HOW SERIOUS YOU ARE...
TAKING SOMEONE AGAINST THEIR WILL IS JUST KIDNAPPING.
STEP
YOU CAN'T ACT LIKE A CHILD FOREVER.
...OKAY.
WHEW
THEN IT'S OKAY AS LONG AS I CONVINCE HER, RIGHT?
YOU WOULD HAVE NO ROOM TO COMPLAIN IF I CAN GET HER TO SAY YES, RIGHT?
HUH?

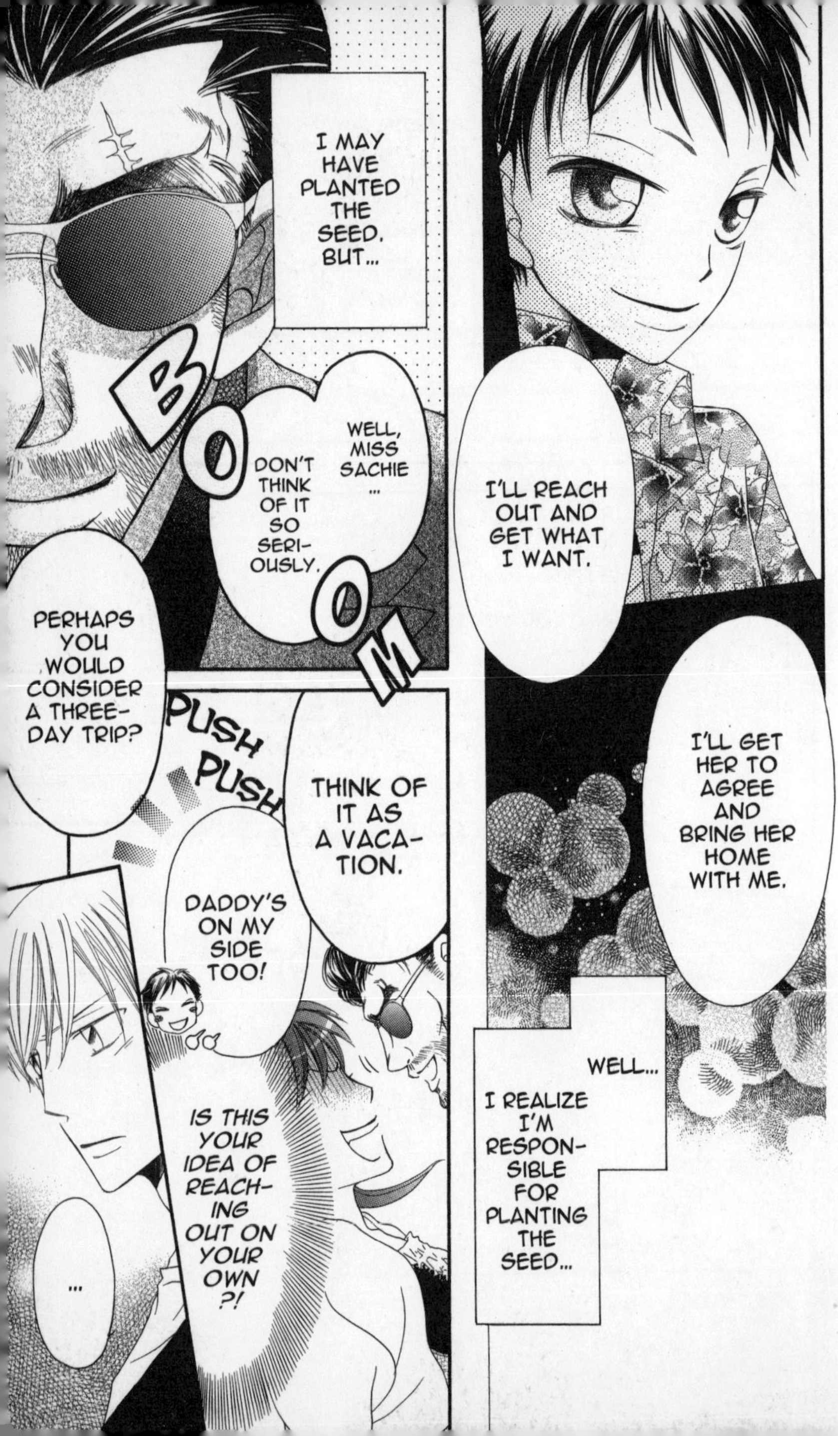

I'LL REACH OUT AND GET WHAT I WANT.
I'LL GET HER TO AGREE AND BRING HER HOME WITH ME.
WELL...
I REALIZE I'M RESPONSIBLE FOR PLANTING THE SEED...
I MAY HAVE PLANTED THE SEED. BUT...
WELL, MISS SACHIE...
DON'T THINK OF IT SO SERIOUSLY.
BOOM
PERHAPS YOU WOULD CONSIDER A THREE-DAY TRIP?
THINK OF IT AS A VACATION.
PUSH PUSH
DADDY'S ON MY SIDE TOO!
IS THIS YOUR IDEA OF REACHING OUT ON YOUR OWN?!
...

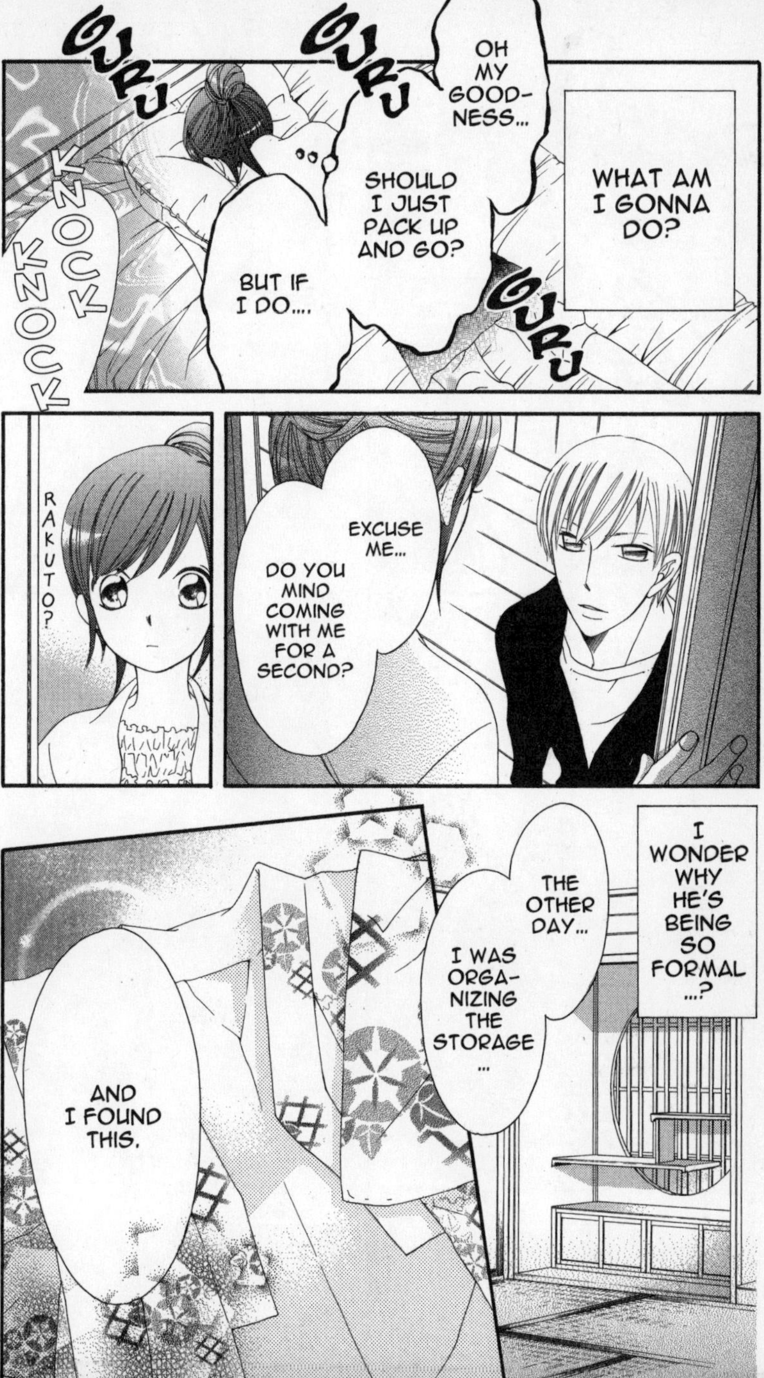
GURU
GURU
GURU
WHAT AM I GONNA DO?
OH MY GOODNESS...
SHOULD I JUST PACK UP AND GO?
BUT IF I DO....
KNOCK KNOCK
EXCUSE ME...
DO YOU MIND COMING WITH ME FOR A SECOND?
RAKUTO?
I WONDER WHY HE'S BEING SO FORMAL ...?
THE OTHER DAY...
I WAS ORGANIZING THE STORAGE ...
AND I FOUND THIS.

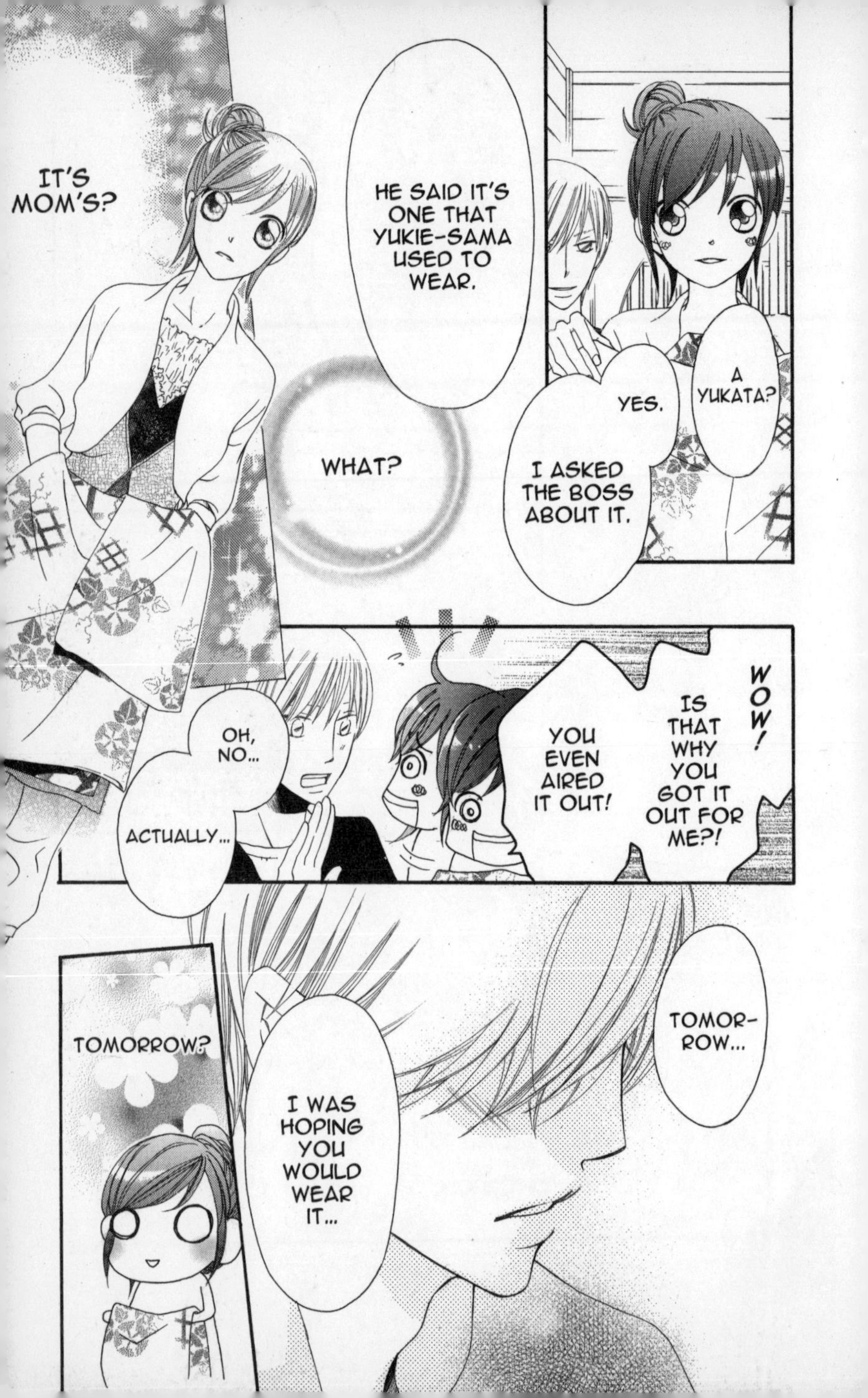
A YUKATA?
YES.
I ASKED THE BOSS ABOUT IT.
HE SAID IT'S ONE THAT YUKIE-SAMA USED TO WEAR.
WHAT?
IT'S MOM'S?
WOW!
IS THAT WHY YOU GOT IT OUT FOR ME?!
YOU EVEN AIRED IT OUT!
OH, NO...
ACTUALLY...
TOMOR-ROW...
I WAS HOPING YOU WOULD WEAR IT...
TOMORROW?

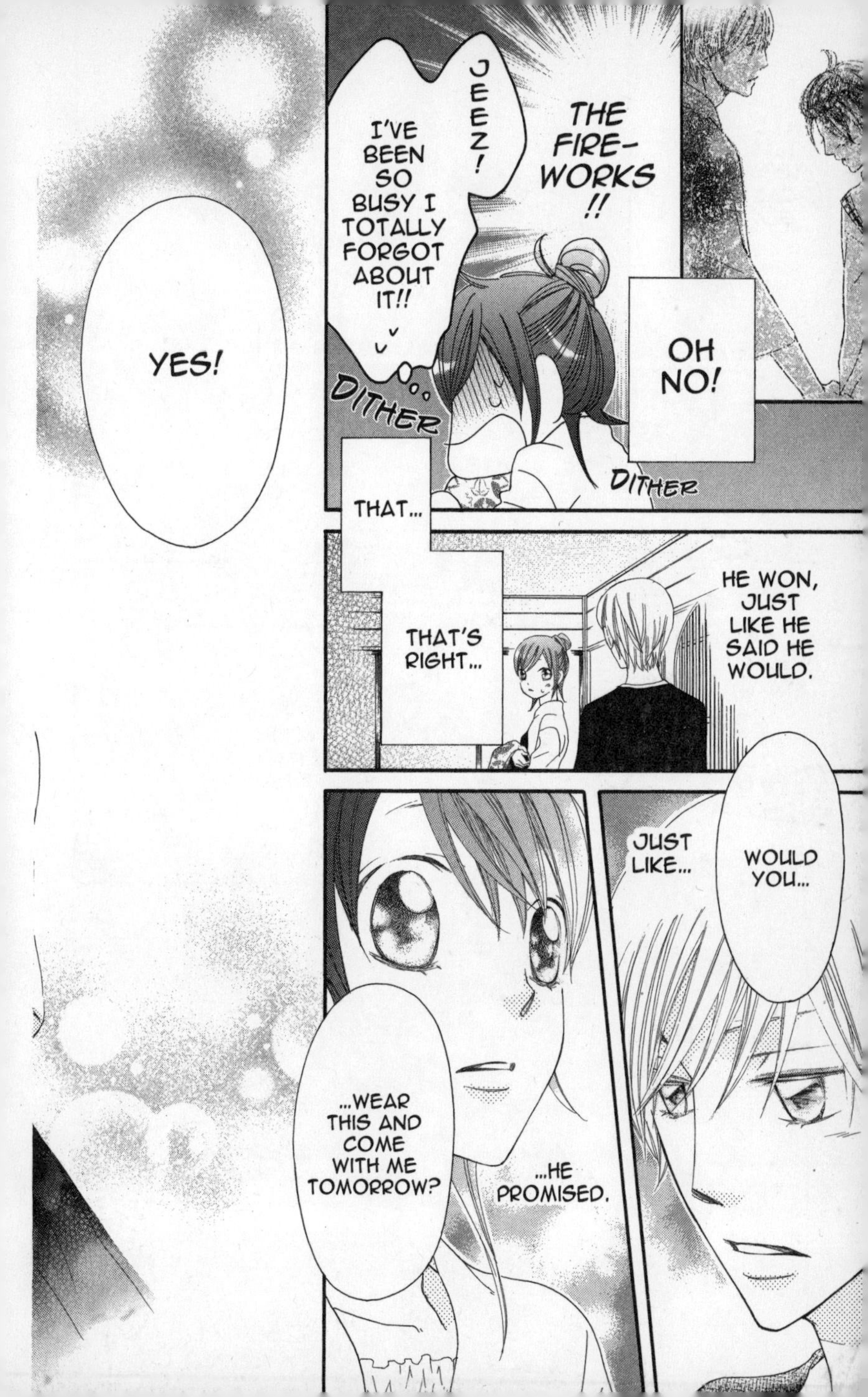
THE FIRE-WORKS!!
JEEZ! I'VE BEEN SO BUSY I TOTALLY FORGOT ABOUT IT!!
OH NO!
DITHER
DITHER
HE WON, JUST LIKE HE SAID HE WOULD.
THAT...
THAT'S RIGHT...
WOULD YOU...
JUST LIKE...
...WEAR THIS AND COME WITH ME TOMORROW?
...HE PROMISED.
YES!

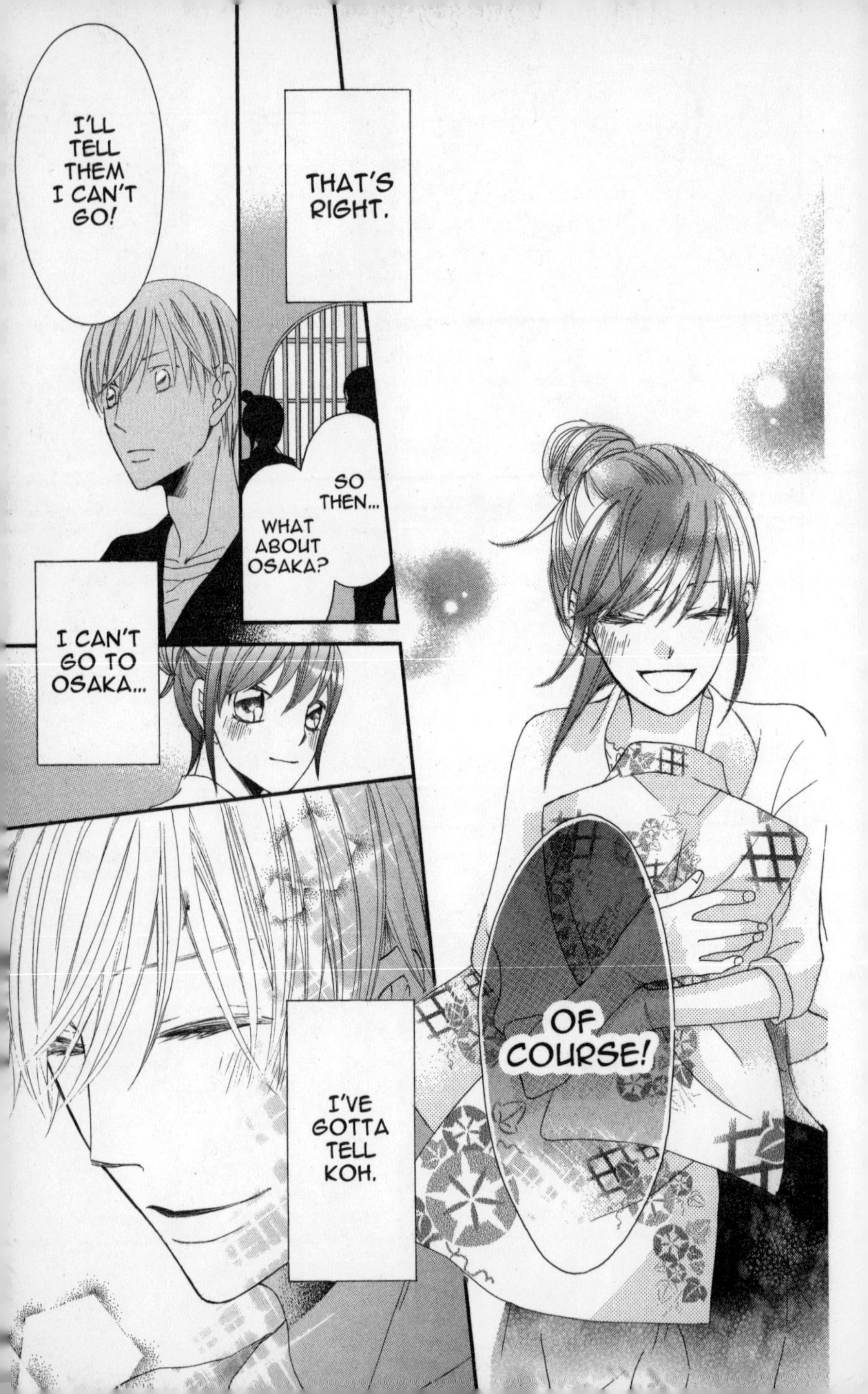
THAT'S RIGHT.
I'LL TELL THEM I CAN'T GO!
SO THEN... WHAT ABOUT OSAKA?
I CAN'T GO TO OSAKA...
OF COURSE!
I'VE GOTTA TELL KOH.

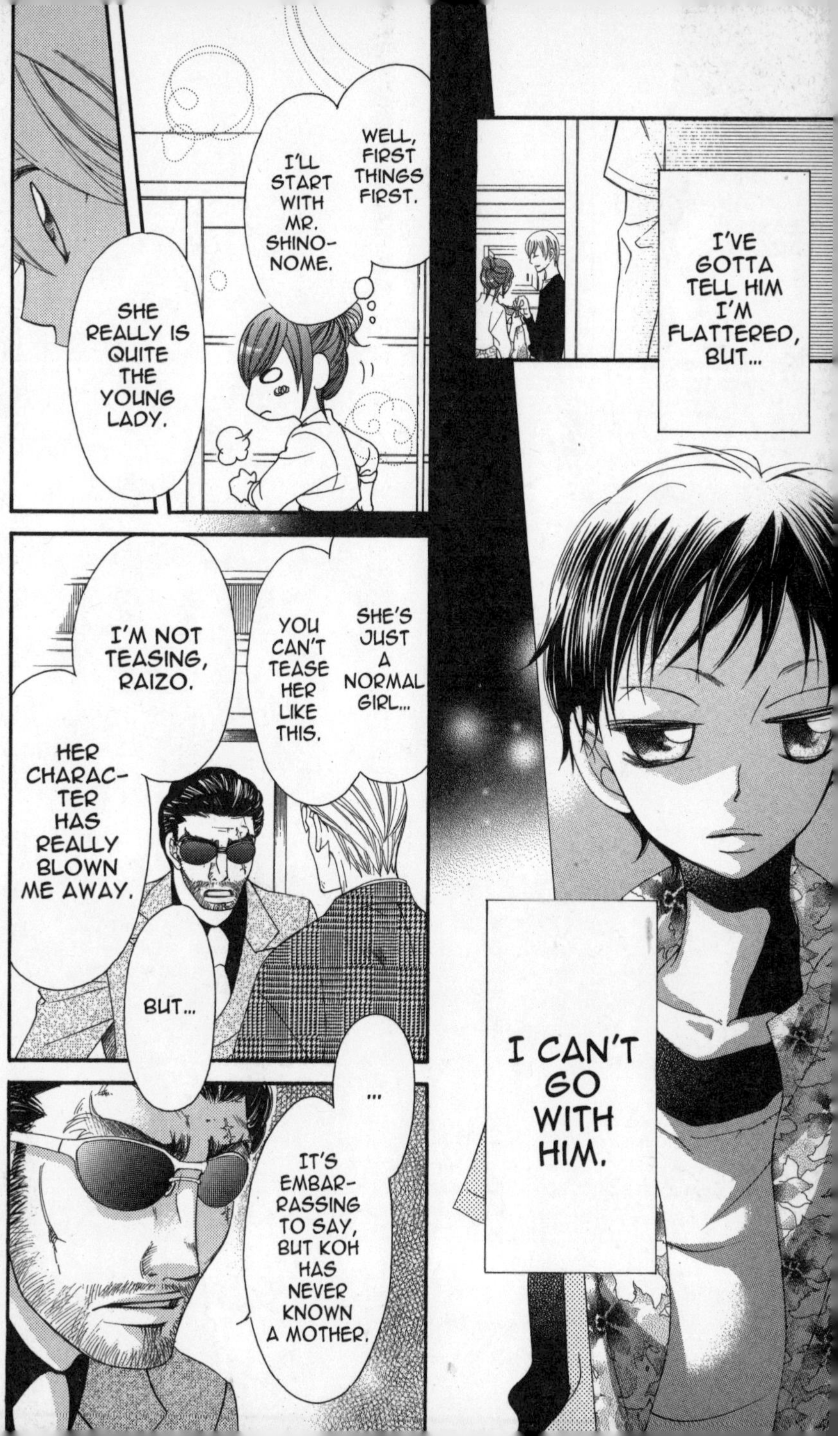
I'VE GOTTA TELL HIM I'M FLATTERED, BUT...
I CAN'T GO WITH HIM.
WELL, FIRST THINGS FIRST.
I'LL START WITH MR. SHINONOME.
SHE REALLY IS QUITE THE YOUNG LADY.
SHE'S JUST A NORMAL GIRL...
YOU CAN'T TEASE HER LIKE THIS.
I'M NOT TEASING, RAIZO.
HER CHARACTER HAS REALLY BLOWN ME AWAY.
BUT...
...
IT'S EMBARRASSING TO SAY, BUT KOH HAS NEVER KNOWN A MOTHER.

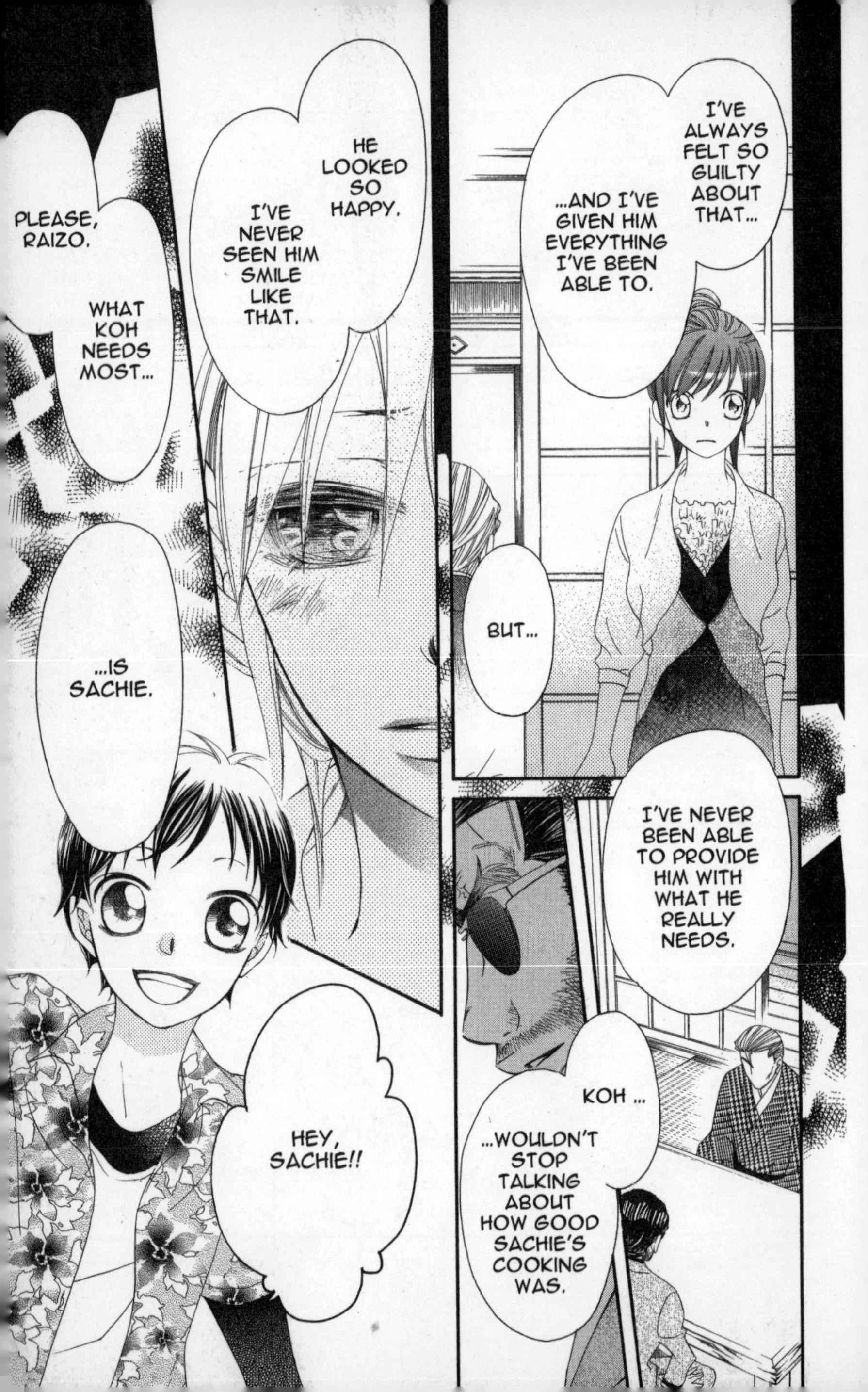
I'VE ALWAYS FELT SO GUILTY ABOUT THAT...
...AND I'VE GIVEN HIM EVERYTHING I'VE BEEN ABLE TO.
BUT...
I'VE NEVER BEEN ABLE TO PROVIDE HIM WITH WHAT HE REALLY NEEDS.
KOH ...
...WOULDN'T STOP TALKING ABOUT HOW GOOD SACHIE'S COOKING WAS.
HEY, SACHIE!!
HE LOOKED SO HAPPY.
I'VE NEVER SEEN HIM SMILE LIKE THAT.
PLEASE, RAIZO.
WHAT KOH NEEDS MOST...
...IS SACHIE.

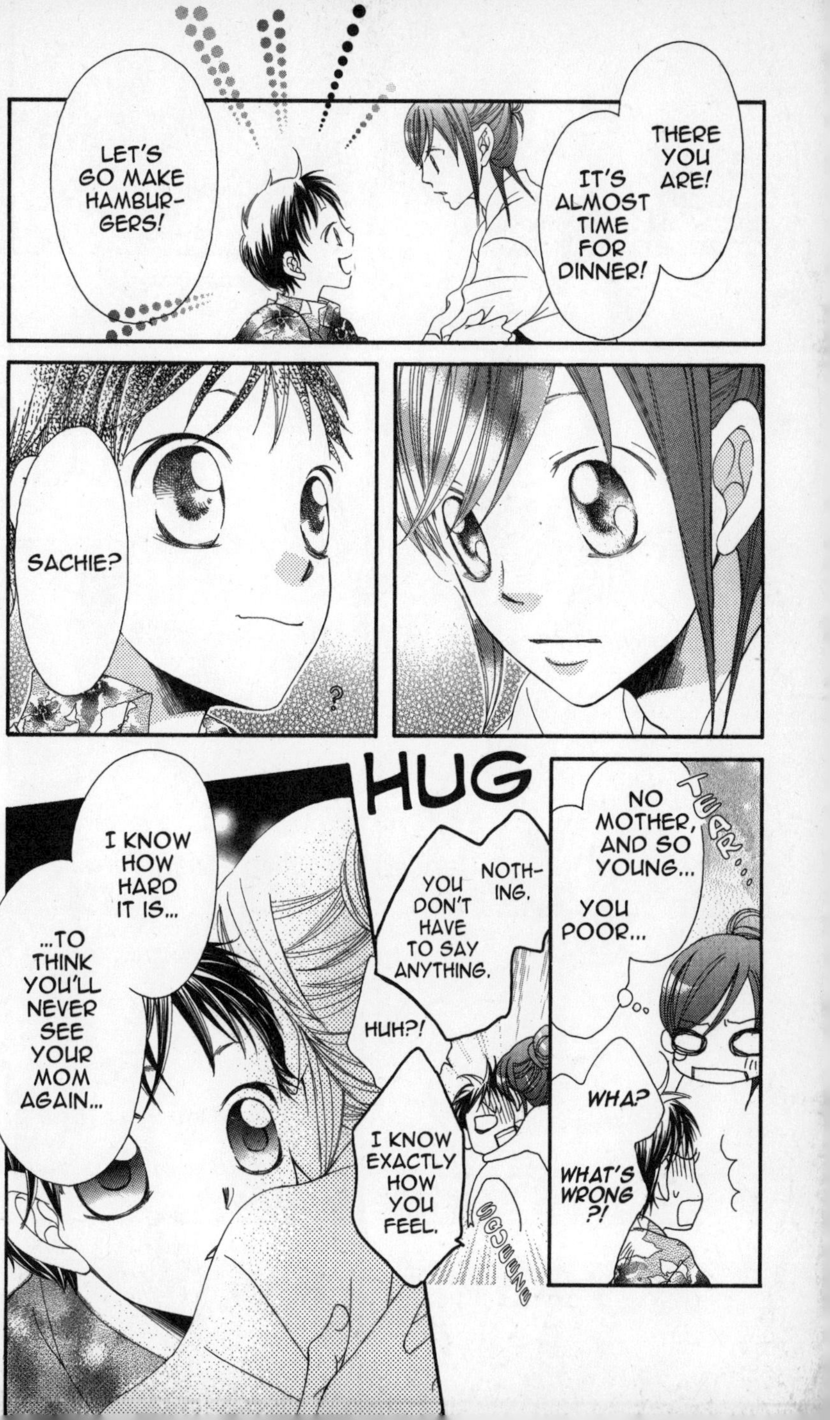
THERE YOU ARE! IT'S ALMOST TIME FOR DINNER!
LET'S GO MAKE HAMBURGERS!
SACHIE?
NO MOTHER, AND SO YOUNG... YOU POOR...
TEAR...
WHA?
WHAT'S WRONG?!
HUG
NOTHING. YOU DON'T HAVE TO SAY ANYTHING.
HUH?!
I KNOW HOW HARD IT IS...
...TO THINK YOU'LL NEVER SEE YOUR MOM AGAIN...
I KNOW EXACTLY HOW YOU FEEL.

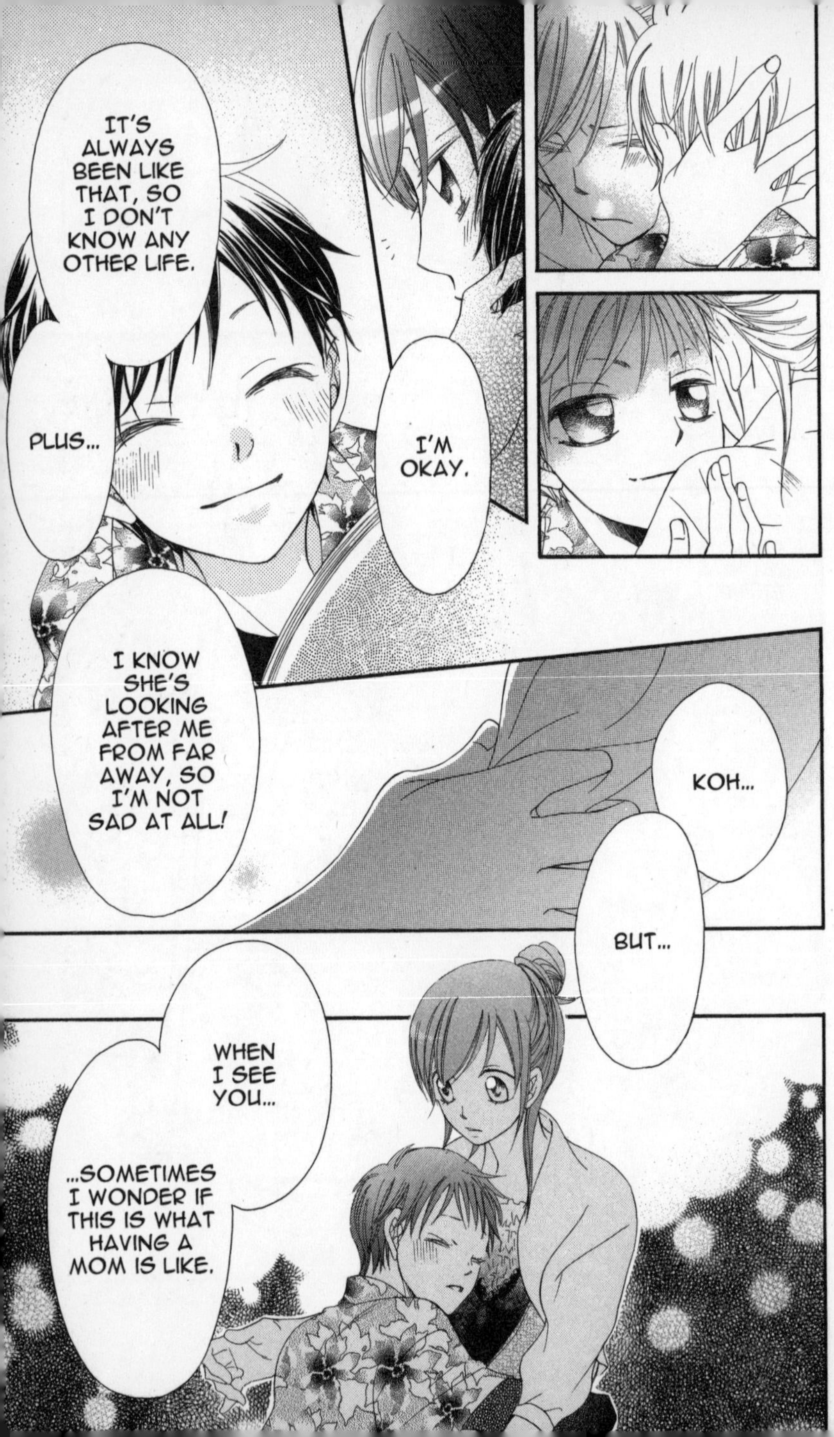
I'M OKAY.
IT'S ALWAYS BEEN LIKE THAT, SO I DON'T KNOW ANY OTHER LIFE.
PLUS...
I KNOW SHE'S LOOKING AFTER ME FROM FAR AWAY, SO I'M NOT SAD AT ALL!
KOH...
BUT...
WHEN I SEE YOU...
...SOMETIMES I WONDER IF THIS IS WHAT HAVING A MOM IS LIKE.

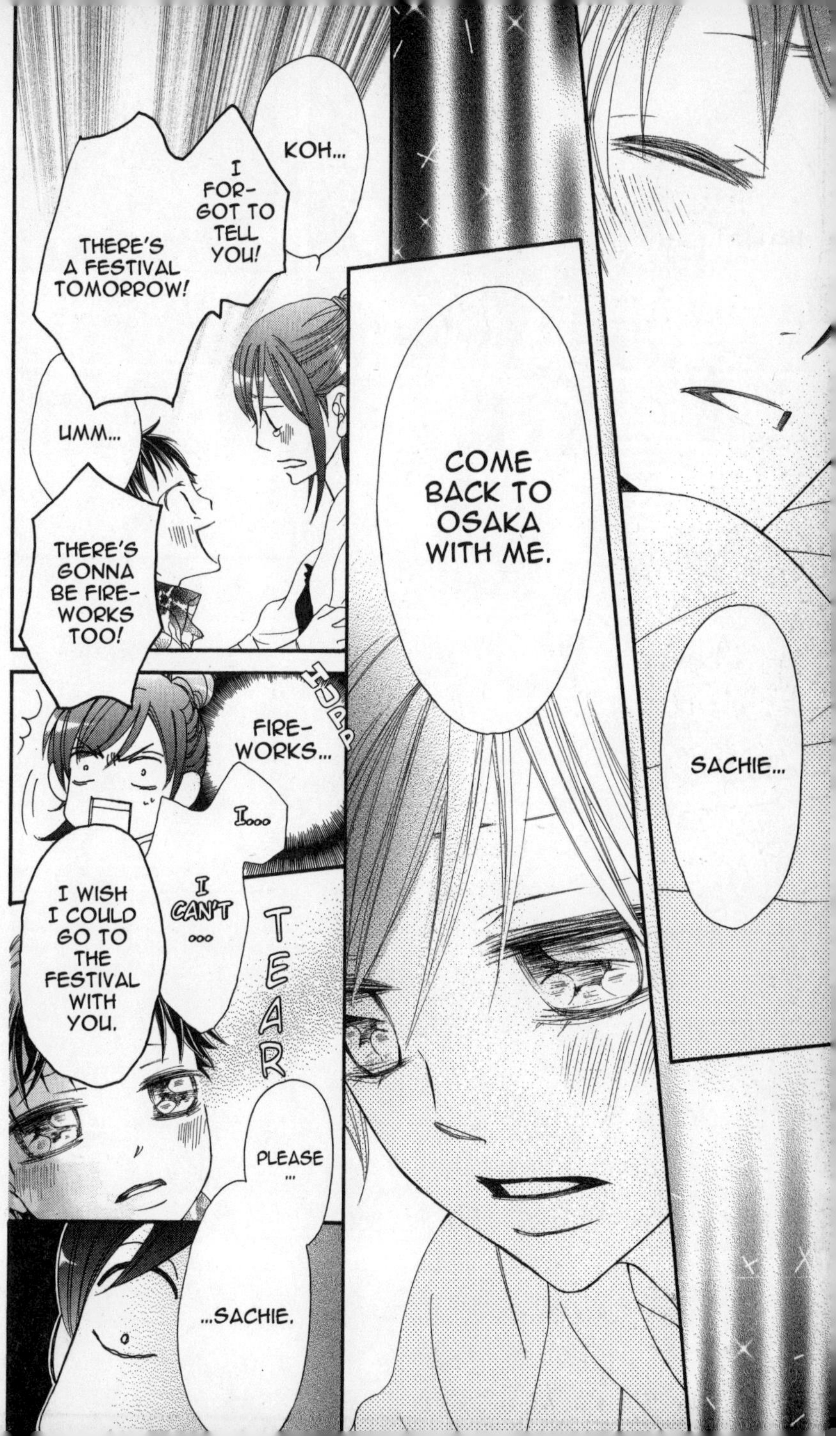
SACHIE...
COME BACK TO OSAKA WITH ME.
KOH...
I FOR-GOT TO TELL YOU!
THERE'S A FESTIVAL TOMORROW!
UMM...
THERE'S GONNA BE FIRE-WORKS TOO!
FIRE-WORKS...
I...
I CAN'T...
I WISH I COULD GO TO THE FESTIVAL WITH YOU.
TEAR
PLEASE...
...SACHIE.

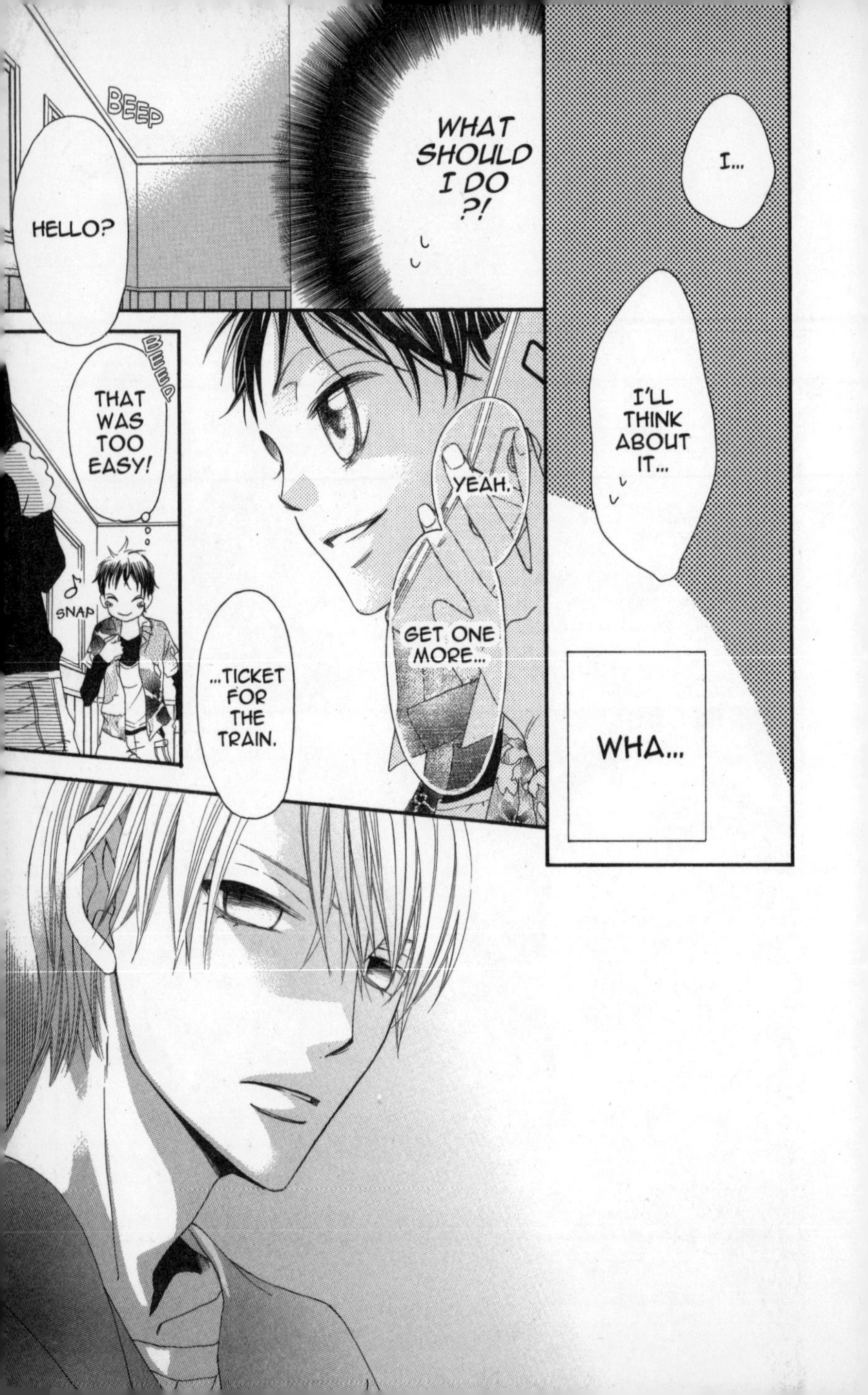
I...
I'LL THINK ABOUT IT...
WHA...
WHAT SHOULD I DO ?!
BEEP
HELLO?
YEAH.
GET ONE MORE...
...TICKET FOR THE TRAIN.
BEEP
THAT WAS TOO EASY!
SNAP

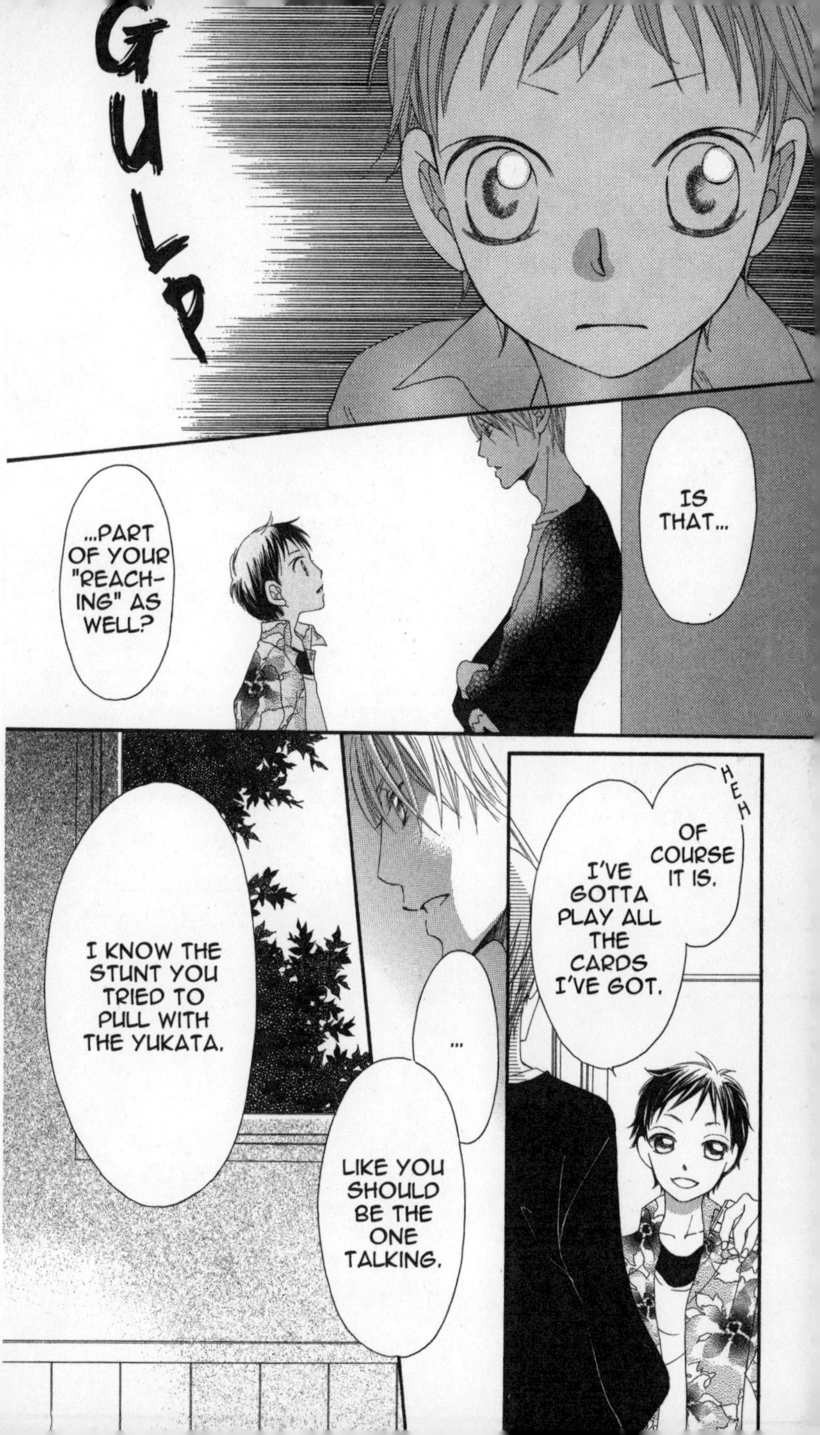
GULP
IS THAT...
...PART OF YOUR "REACHING" AS WELL?
HEH
OF COURSE IT IS.
I'VE GOTTA PLAY ALL THE CARDS I'VE GOT.
...
LIKE YOU SHOULD BE THE ONE TALKING.
I KNOW THE STUNT YOU TRIED TO PULL WITH THE YUKATA.

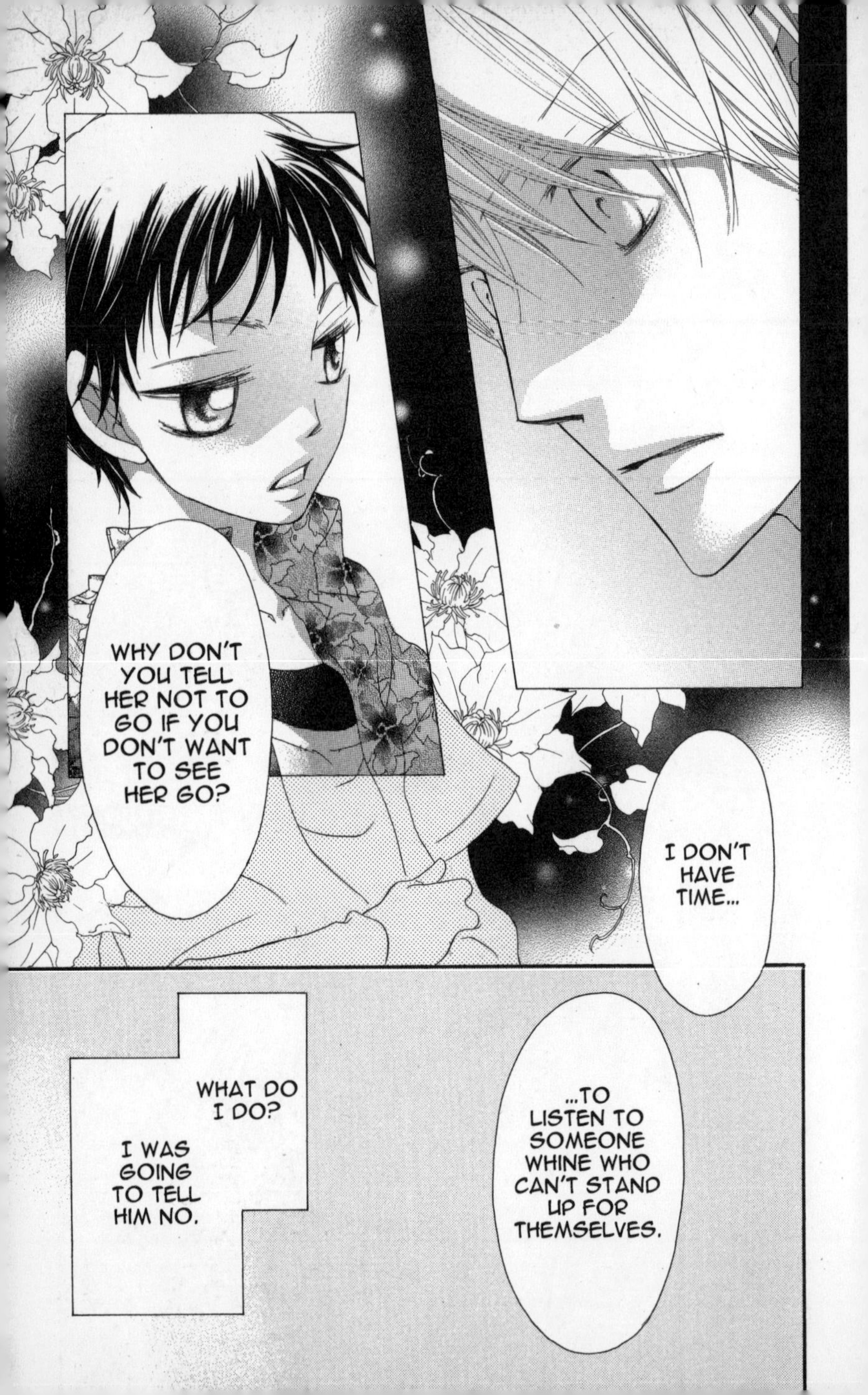
WHY DON'T YOU TELL HER NOT TO GO IF YOU DON'T WANT TO SEE HER GO?
I DON'T HAVE TIME...
...TO LISTEN TO SOMEONE WHINE WHO CAN'T STAND UP FOR THEMSELVES.
WHAT DO I DO?
I WAS GOING TO TELL HIM NO.

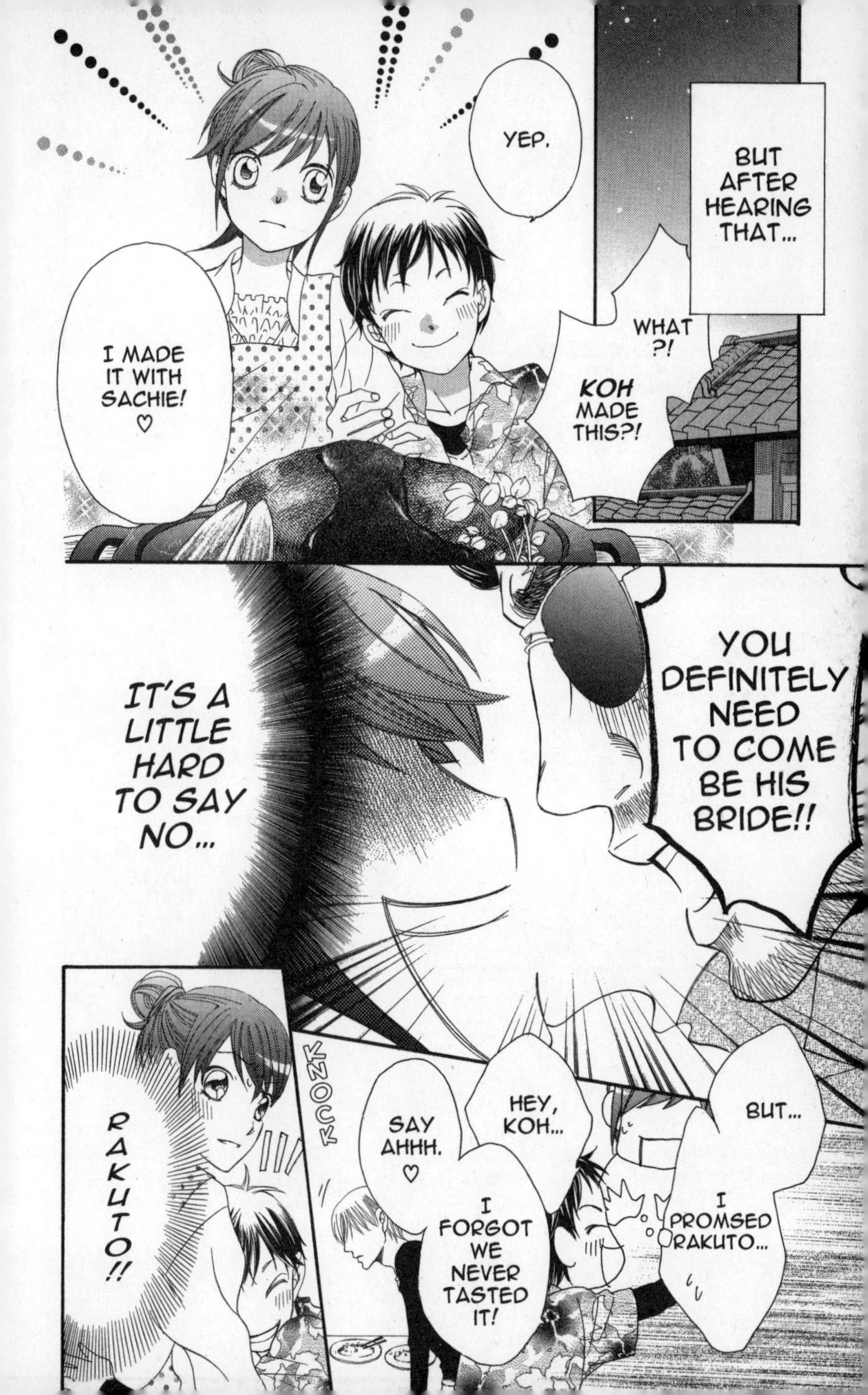
BUT AFTER HEARING THAT...
WHAT?!
KOH MADE THIS?!
YEP.
I MADE IT WITH SACHIE! ♡
YOU DEFINITELY NEED TO COME BE HIS BRIDE!!
IT'S A LITTLE HARD TO SAY NO...
BUT...
I PROMSED RAKUTO...
HEY, KOH...
I FORGOT WE NEVER TASTED IT!
SAY AHHH. ♡
KNOCK
RAKUTO!!

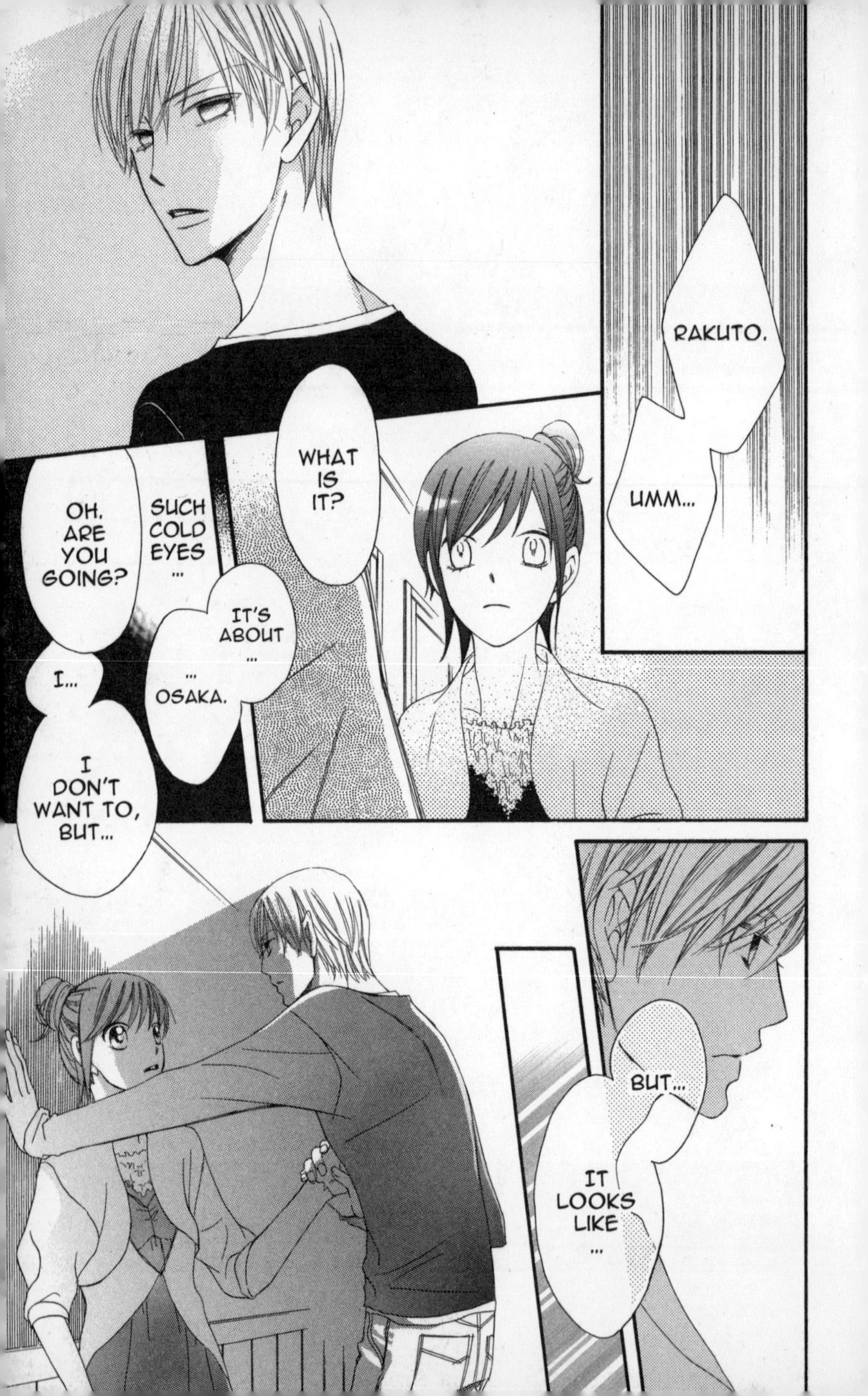
RAKUTO.
UMM...
WHAT IS IT?
SUCH COLD EYES...
IT'S ABOUT...
...OSAKA.
OH. ARE YOU GOING?
I...
I DON'T WANT TO, BUT...
BUT...
IT LOOKS LIKE...

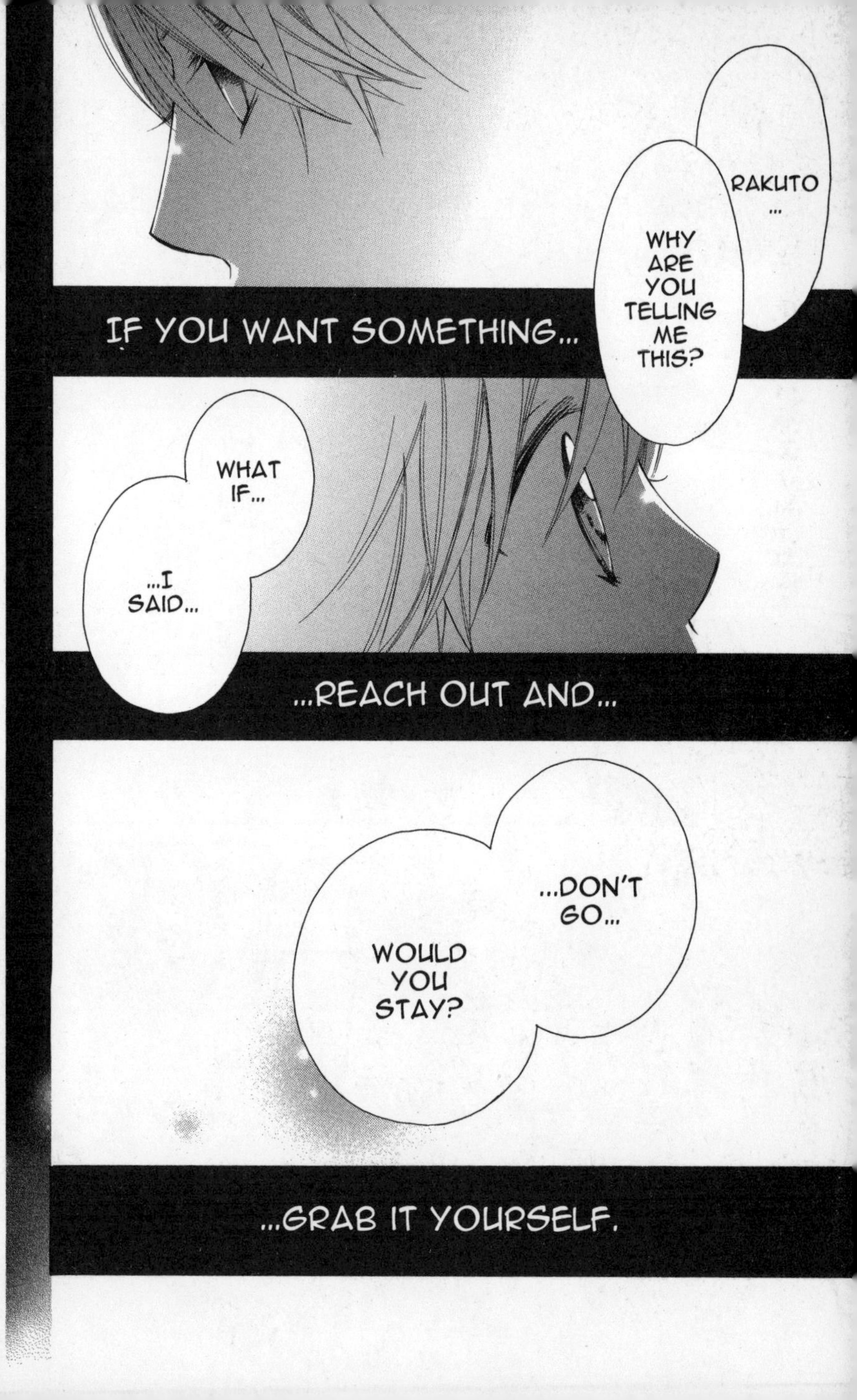
RAKUTO ...
WHY ARE YOU TELLING ME THIS?
IF YOU WANT SOMETHING...
WHAT IF... ...I SAID...
...REACH OUT AND...
...DON'T GO... WOULD YOU STAY?
...GRAB IT YOURSELF.

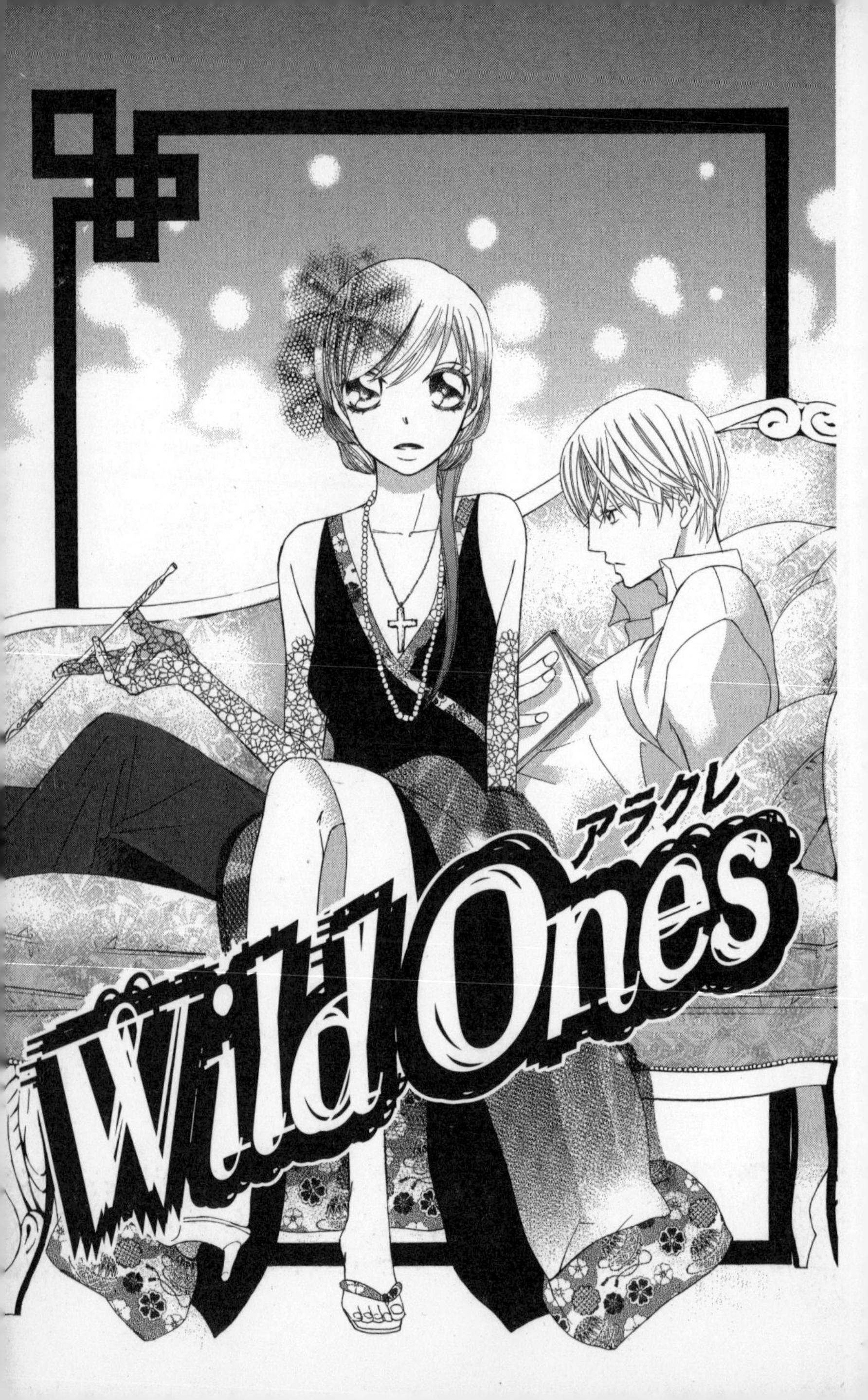
アラクレ
Wild Ones

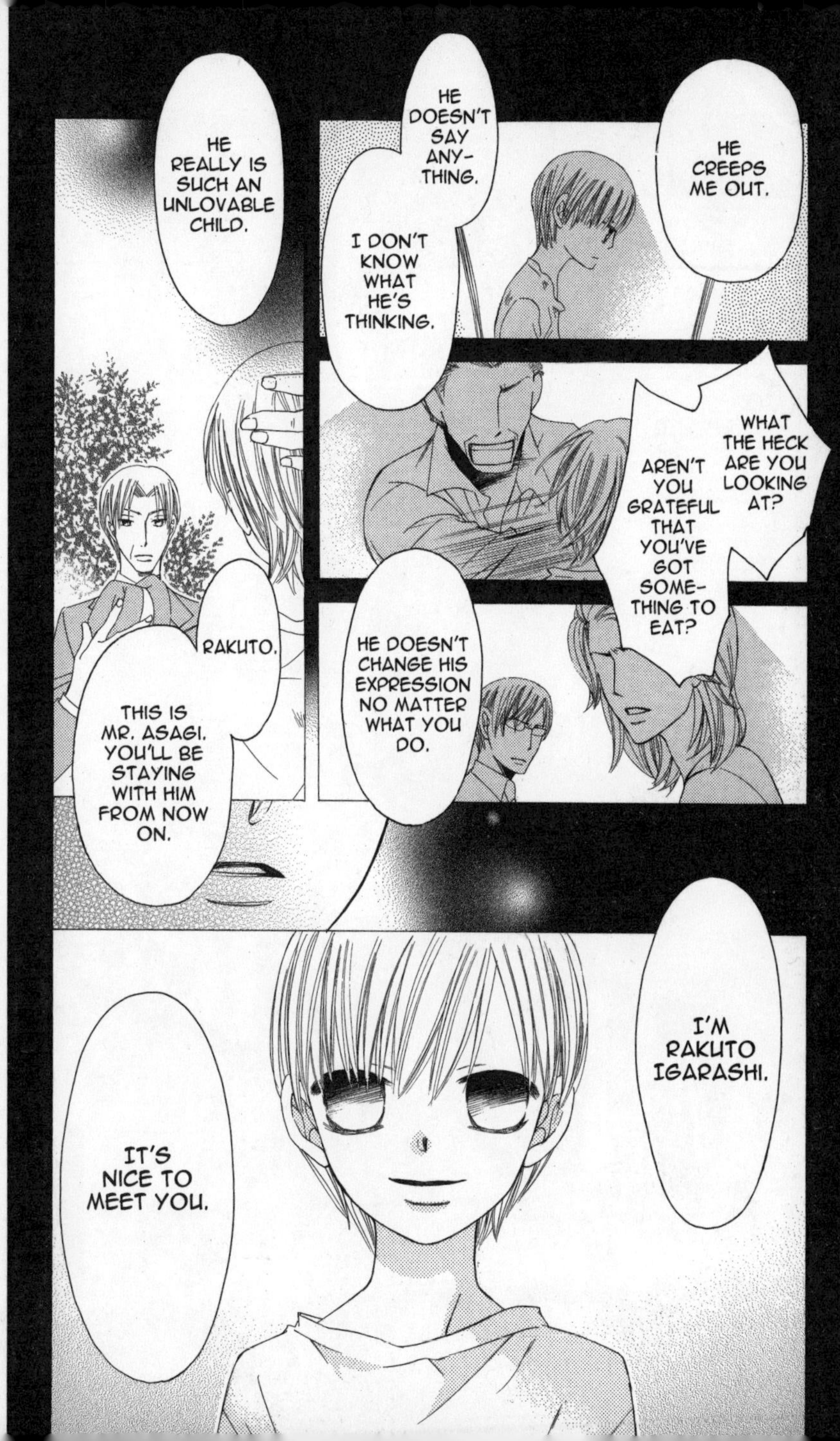
HE CREEPS ME OUT.
HE DOESN'T SAY ANY-THING.
I DON'T KNOW WHAT HE'S THINKING.
WHAT THE HECK ARE YOU LOOKING AT?
AREN'T YOU GRATEFUL THAT YOU'VE GOT SOME-THING TO EAT?
HE DOESN'T CHANGE HIS EXPRESSION NO MATTER WHAT YOU DO.
HE REALLY IS SUCH AN UNLOVABLE CHILD.
RAKUTO.
THIS IS MR. ASAGI. YOU'LL BE STAYING WITH HIM FROM NOW ON.
I'M RAKUTO IGARASHI.
IT'S NICE TO MEET YOU.

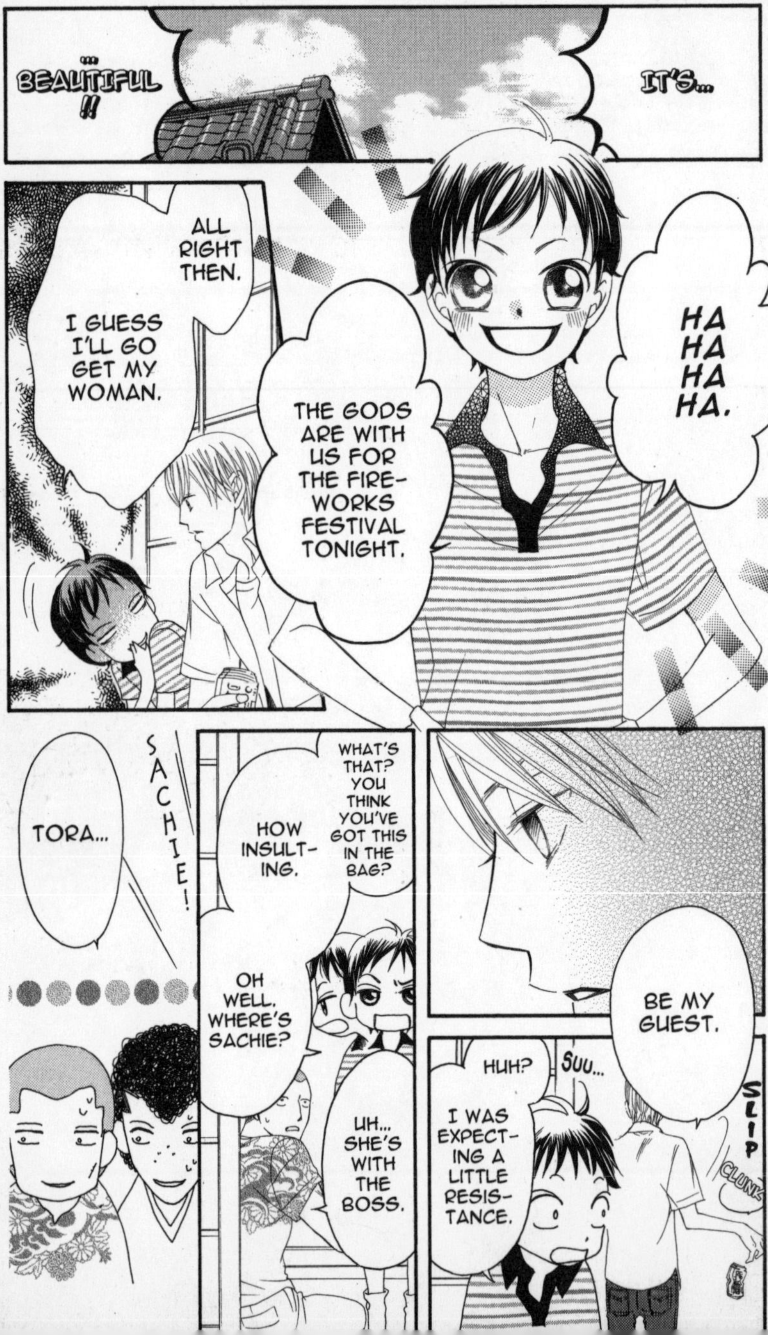
IT'S...
...BEAUTIFUL!!
HAHAHAHA.
THE GODS ARE WITH US FOR THE FIRE-WORKS FESTIVAL TONIGHT.
ALL RIGHT THEN.
I GUESS I'LL GO GET MY WOMAN.
BE MY GUEST.
SLIP
CLUNK
SUU...
HUH?
I WAS EXPECT-ING A LITTLE RESIS-TANCE.
WHAT'S THAT? YOU THINK YOU'VE GOT THIS IN THE BAG?
HOW INSULT-ING.
OH WELL. WHERE'S SACHIE?
UH... SHE'S WITH THE BOSS.
SACHIE!
TORA...

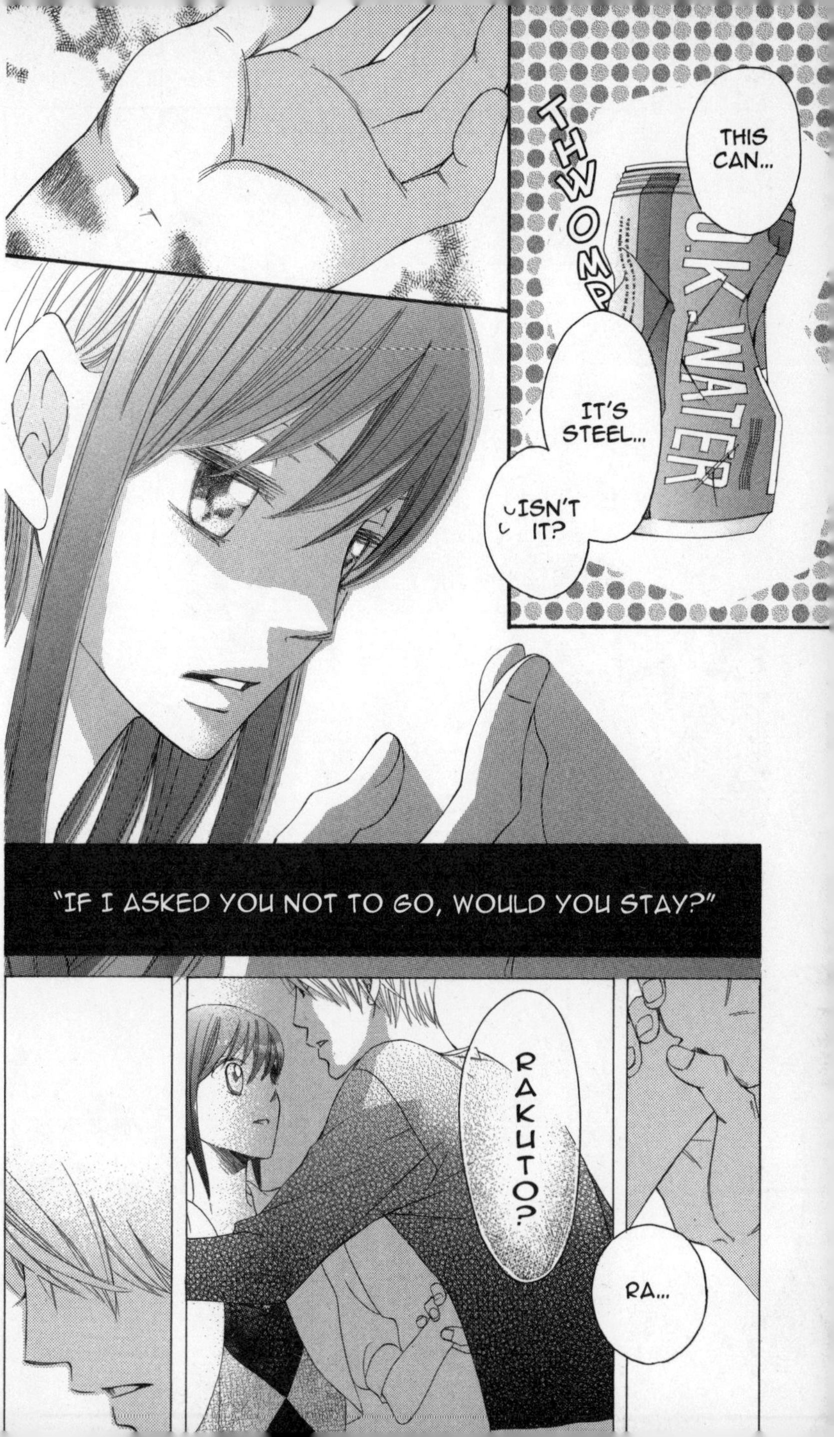
THIS CAN...
THWOMP
O.K. WATER
IT'S STEEL...
ISN'T IT?
"IF I ASKED YOU NOT TO GO, WOULD YOU STAY?"
RA...
RAKUTO?

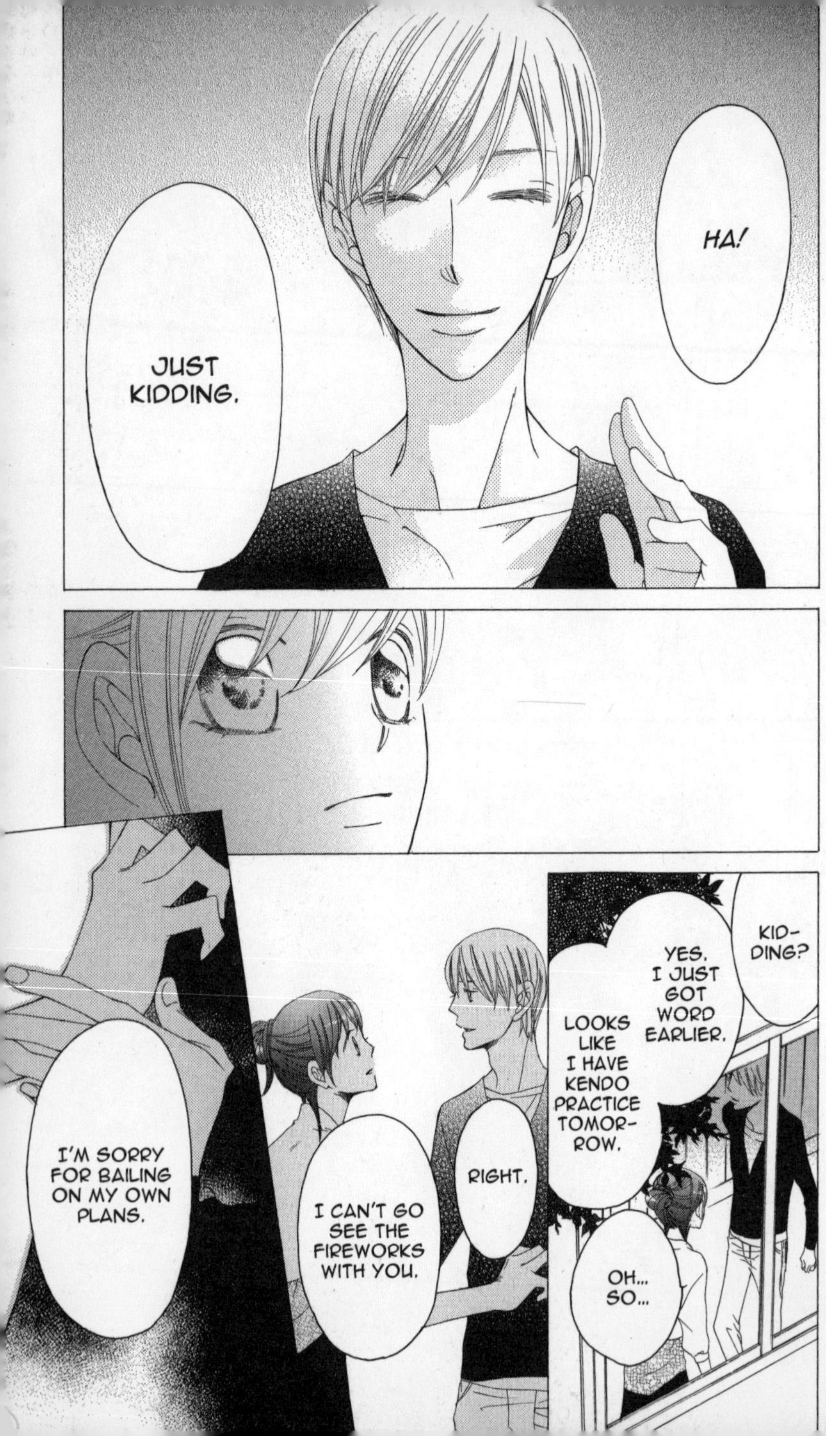
HA!
JUST KIDDING.
KID-DING?
YES. I JUST GOT WORD EARLIER.
LOOKS LIKE I HAVE KENDO PRACTICE TOMOR-ROW.
OH... SO...
RIGHT.
I CAN'T GO SEE THE FIREWORKS WITH YOU.
I'M SORRY FOR BAILING ON MY OWN PLANS.

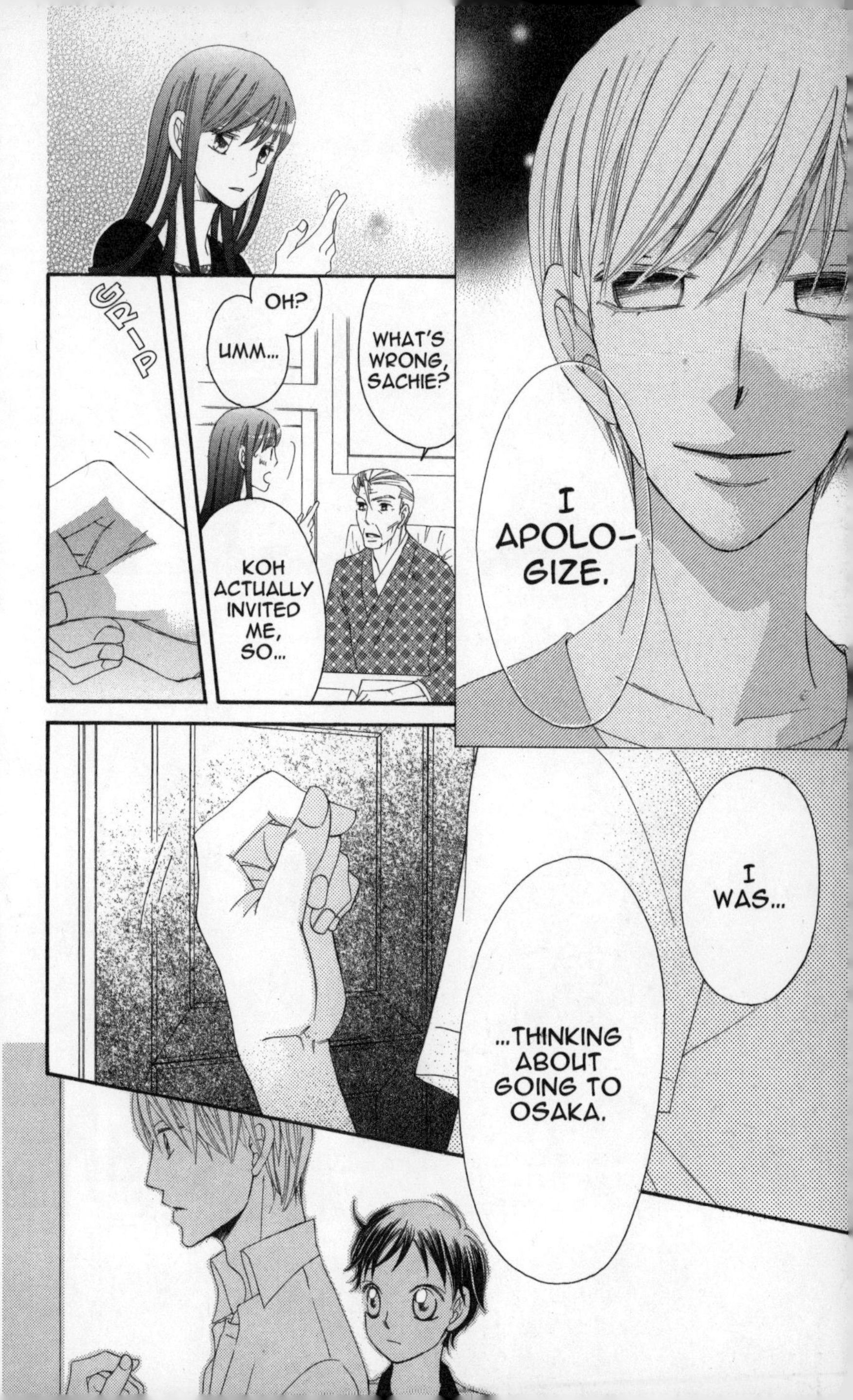
I APOLO-GIZE.
WHAT'S WRONG, SACHIE?
OH?
UMM...
KOH ACTUALLY INVITED ME, SO...
I WAS...
...THINKING ABOUT GOING TO OSAKA.

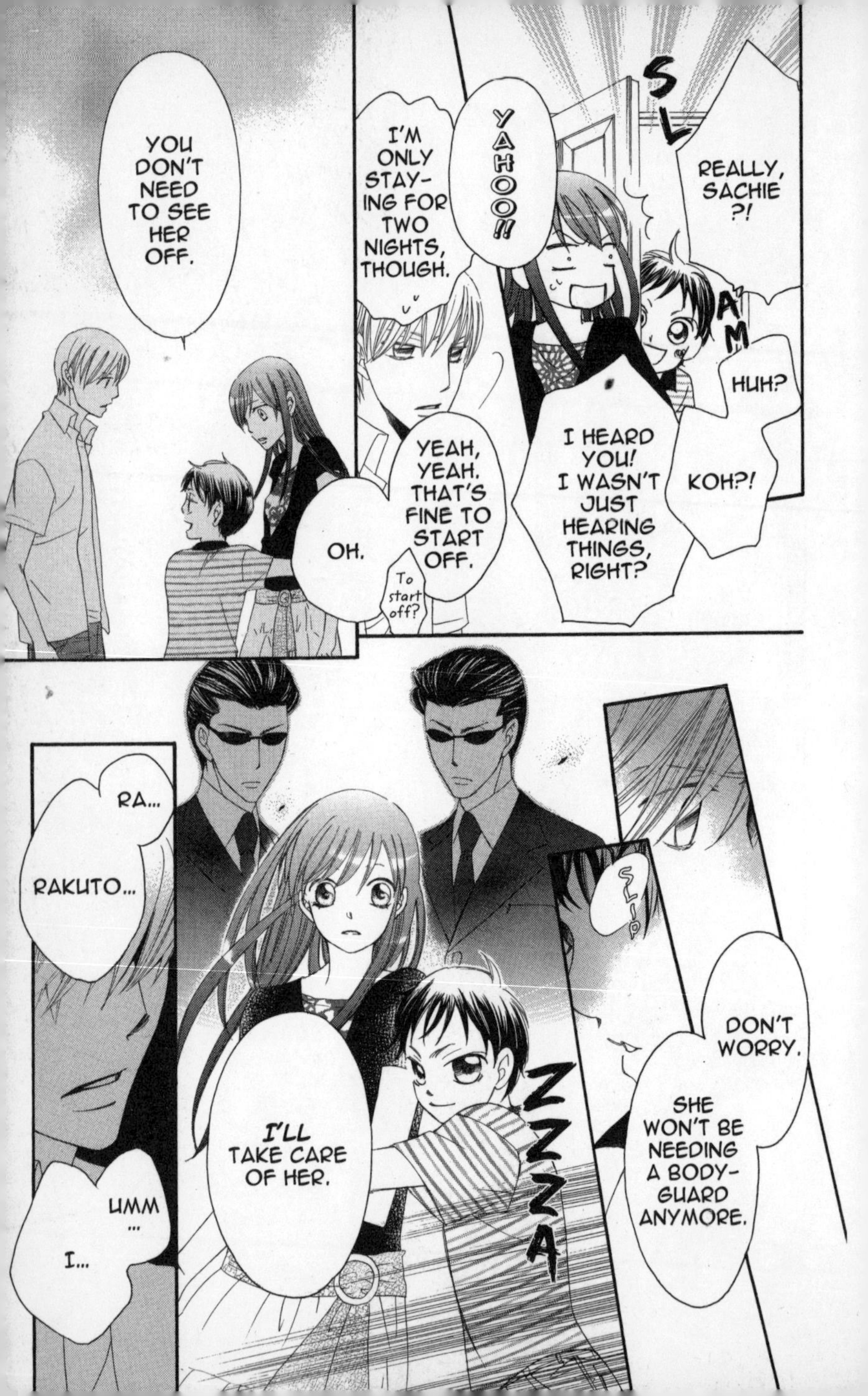

SL
REALLY, SACHIE?!
YAHOO!!
I'M ONLY STAYING FOR TWO NIGHTS, THOUGH.
AM
HUH?
KOH?!
I HEARD YOU! I WASN'T JUST HEARING THINGS, RIGHT?
YEAH, YEAH. THAT'S FINE TO START OFF.
To start off?
OH.
YOU DON'T NEED TO SEE HER OFF.
SLIP
DON'T WORRY.
SHE WON'T BE NEEDING A BODY-GUARD ANYMORE.
ZZZA
I'LL TAKE CARE OF HER.
RA...
RAKUTO...
UMM ...
I...

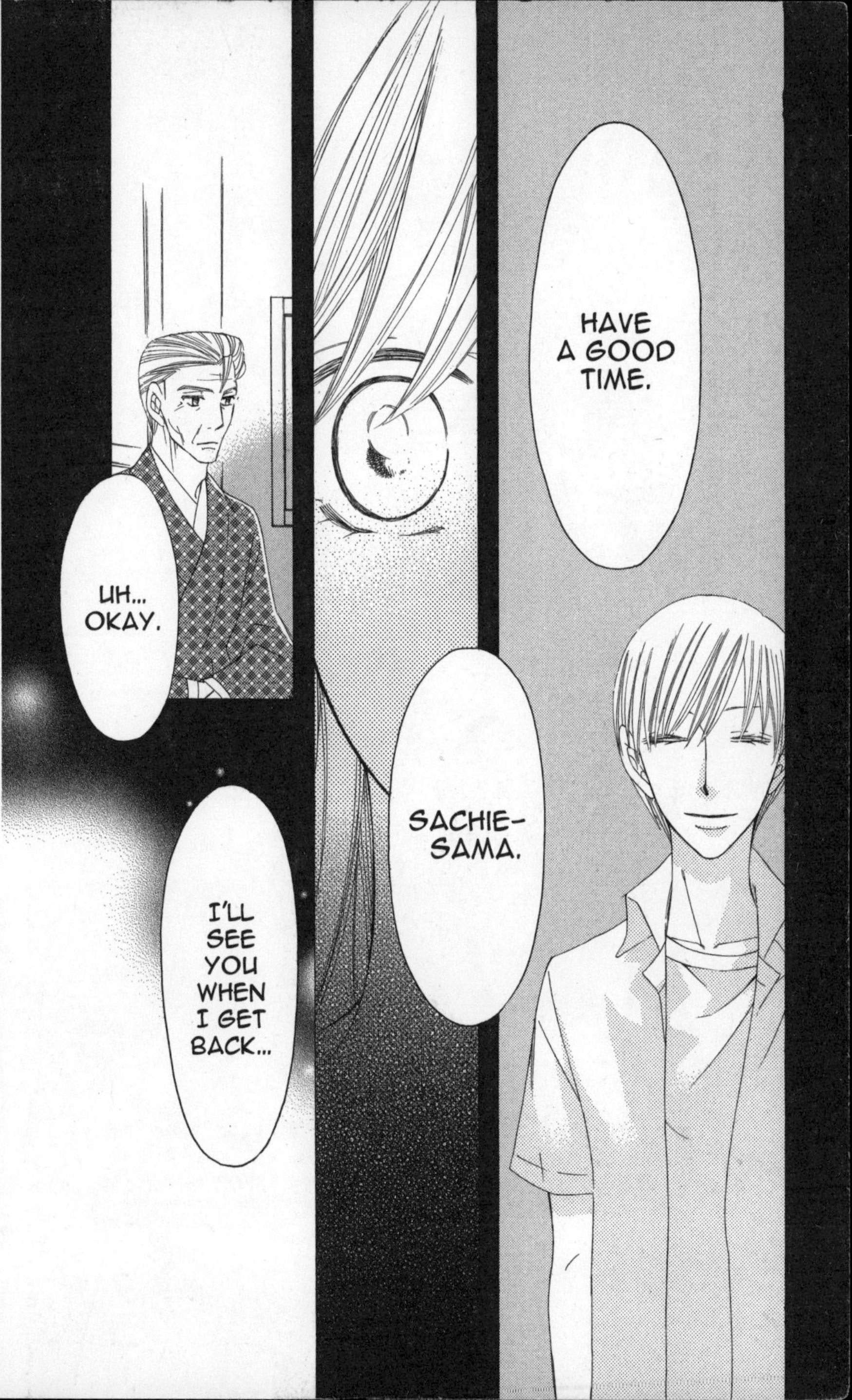
HAVE A GOOD TIME.
SACHIE-SAMA.
UH... OKAY.
I'LL SEE YOU WHEN I GET BACK...

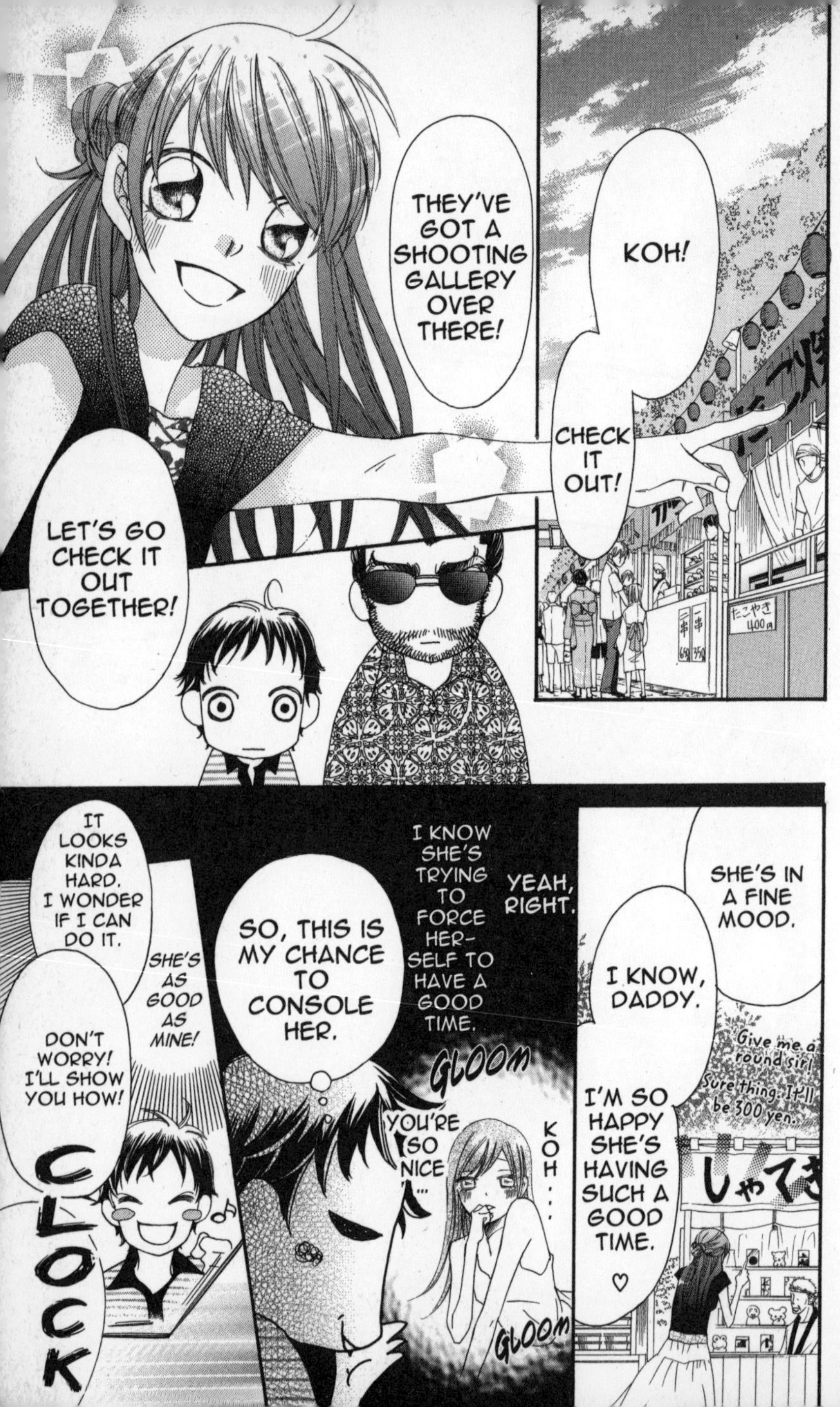
KOH!
CHECK IT OUT!
たこやき 400円
THEY'VE GOT A SHOOTING GALLERY OVER THERE!
LET'S GO CHECK IT OUT TOGETHER!
SHE'S IN A FINE MOOD.
I KNOW, DADDY.
Give me a round sir!
Sure thing. It'll be 300 yen.
しゃてき
I'M SO HAPPY SHE'S HAVING SUCH A GOOD TIME. ♡
YEAH, RIGHT.
I KNOW SHE'S TRYING TO FORCE HER-SELF TO HAVE A GOOD TIME.
SO, THIS IS MY CHANCE TO CONSOLE HER.
GLOOM
KOH...
YOU'RE SO NICE...
GLOOM
IT LOOKS KINDA HARD. I WONDER IF I CAN DO IT.
DON'T WORRY! I'LL SHOW YOU HOW!
SHE'S AS GOOD AS MINE!
CLOCK

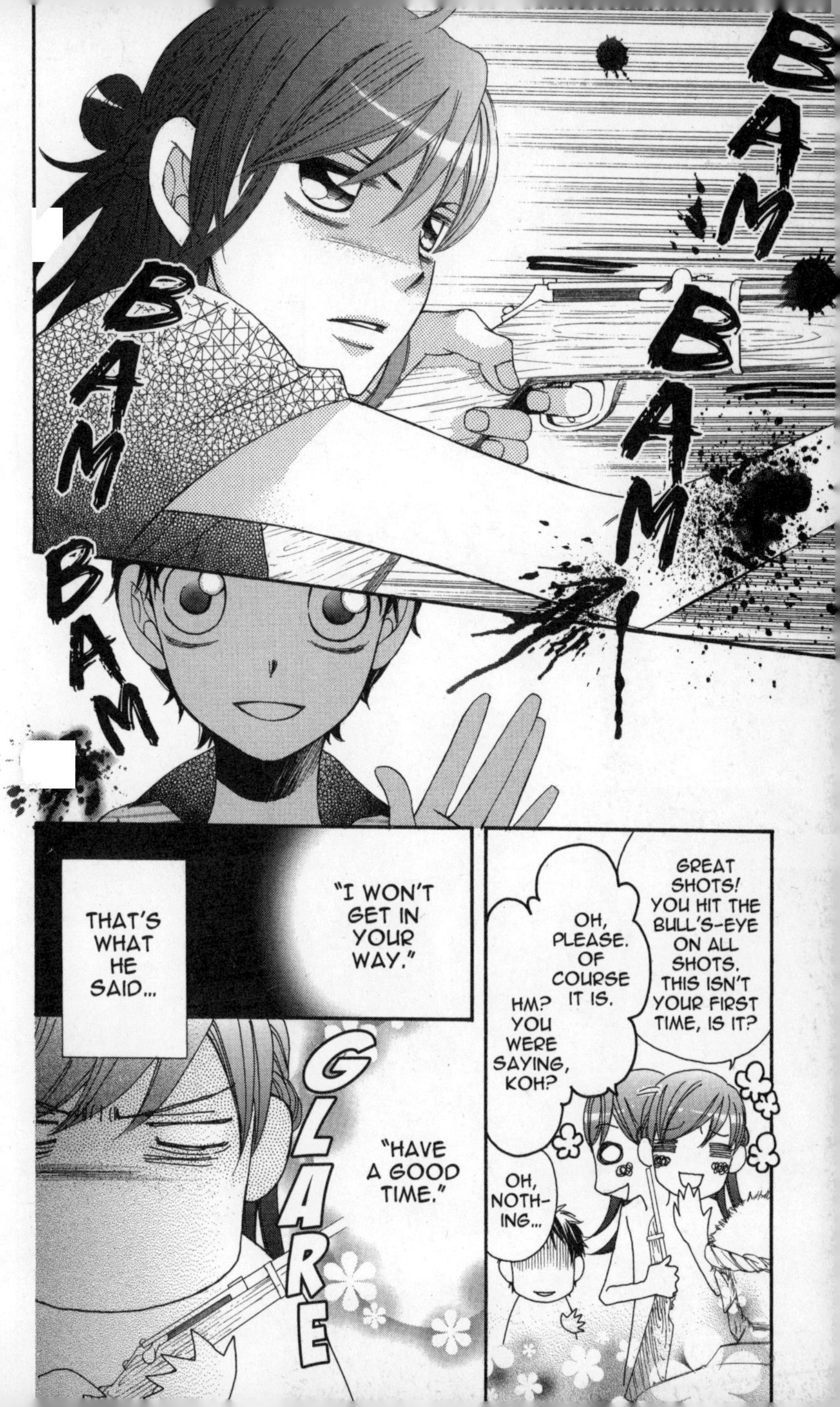
BAM
BAM
BAM
BAM
GREAT SHOTS! YOU HIT THE BULL'S-EYE ON ALL SHOTS. THIS ISN'T YOUR FIRST TIME, IS IT?
OH, PLEASE. OF COURSE IT IS.
HM? YOU WERE SAYING, KOH?
OH, NOTHING...
"I WON'T GET IN YOUR WAY."
THAT'S WHAT HE SAID...
GLARE
"HAVE A GOOD TIME."

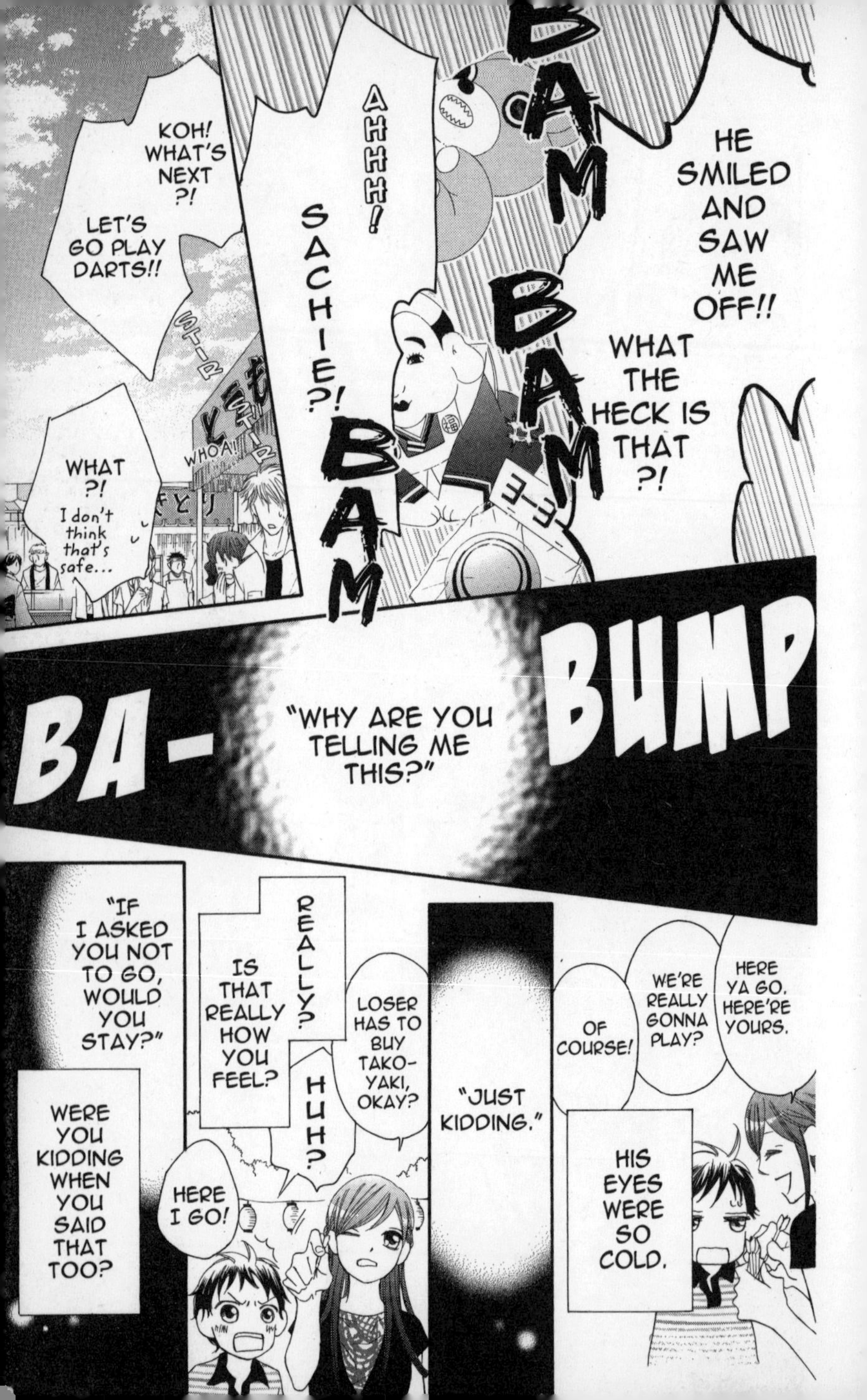
HE SMILED AND SAW ME OFF!!
WHAT THE HECK IS THAT?!
BAM
BAM
AHHHH!
SACHIE?!
BAM
KOH! WHAT'S NEXT?!
LET'S GO PLAY DARTS!!
STIR
STIR
WHOA!
WHAT?!
I don't think that's safe...
BA-BUMP
"WHY ARE YOU TELLING ME THIS?"
HERE YA GO. HERE'RE YOURS.
WE'RE REALLY GONNA PLAY?
OF COURSE!
HIS EYES WERE SO COLD.
"JUST KIDDING."
LOSER HAS TO BUY TAKO-YAKI, OKAY?
REALLY?
IS THAT REALLY HOW YOU FEEL?
HUH?
HERE I GO!
"IF I ASKED YOU NOT TO GO, WOULD YOU STAY?"
WERE YOU KIDDING WHEN YOU SAID THAT TOO?

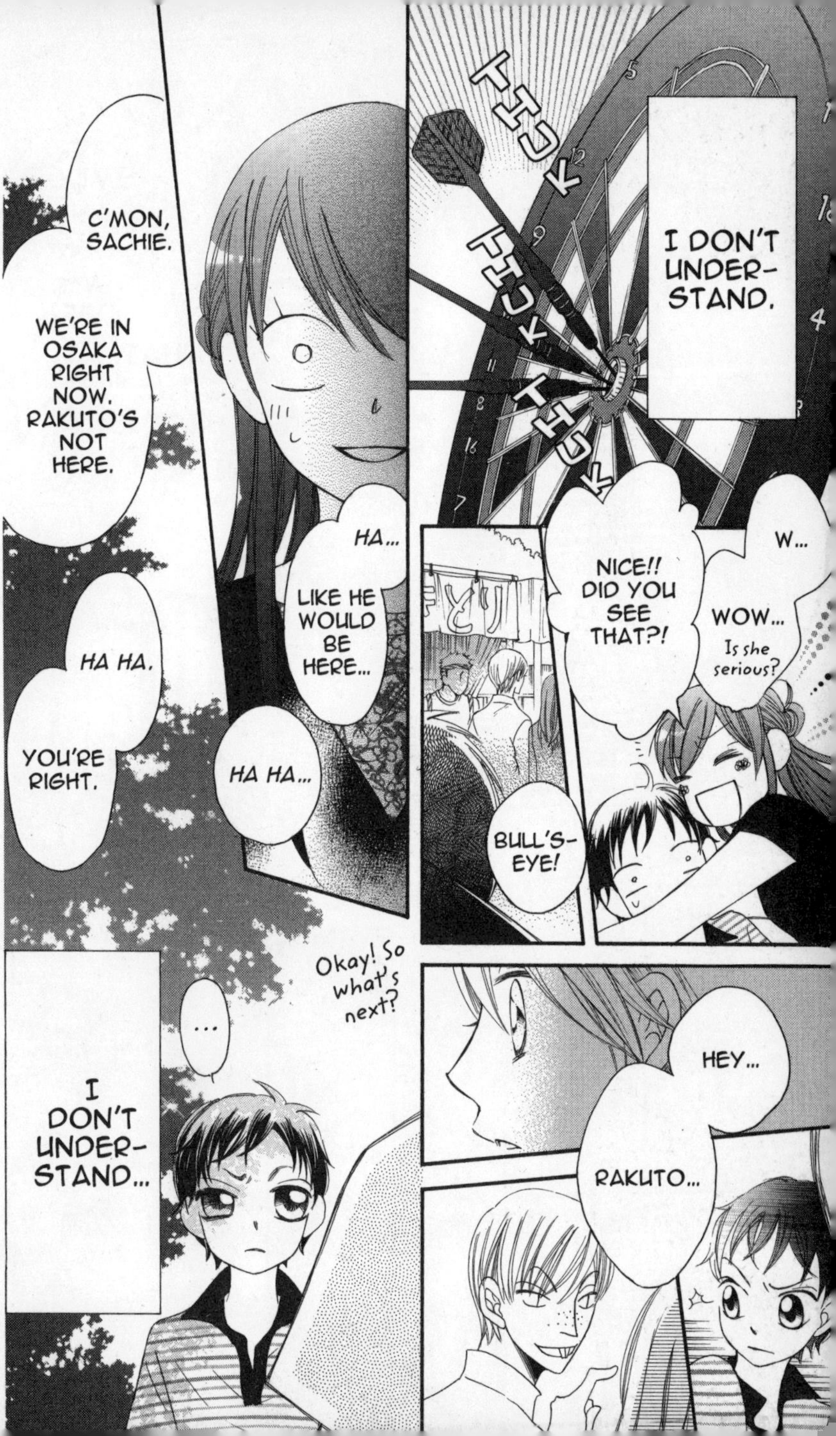
THUK
THUK
THUK
I DON'T UNDERSTAND.
W...
WOW...
Is she serious?
NICE!! DID YOU SEE THAT?!
BULL'S-EYE!
HA...
LIKE HE WOULD BE HERE...
HA HA...
C'MON, SACHIE.
WE'RE IN OSAKA RIGHT NOW. RAKUTO'S NOT HERE.
HA HA.
YOU'RE RIGHT.
HEY...
RAKUTO...
Okay! So what's next?
...
I DON'T UNDERSTAND...

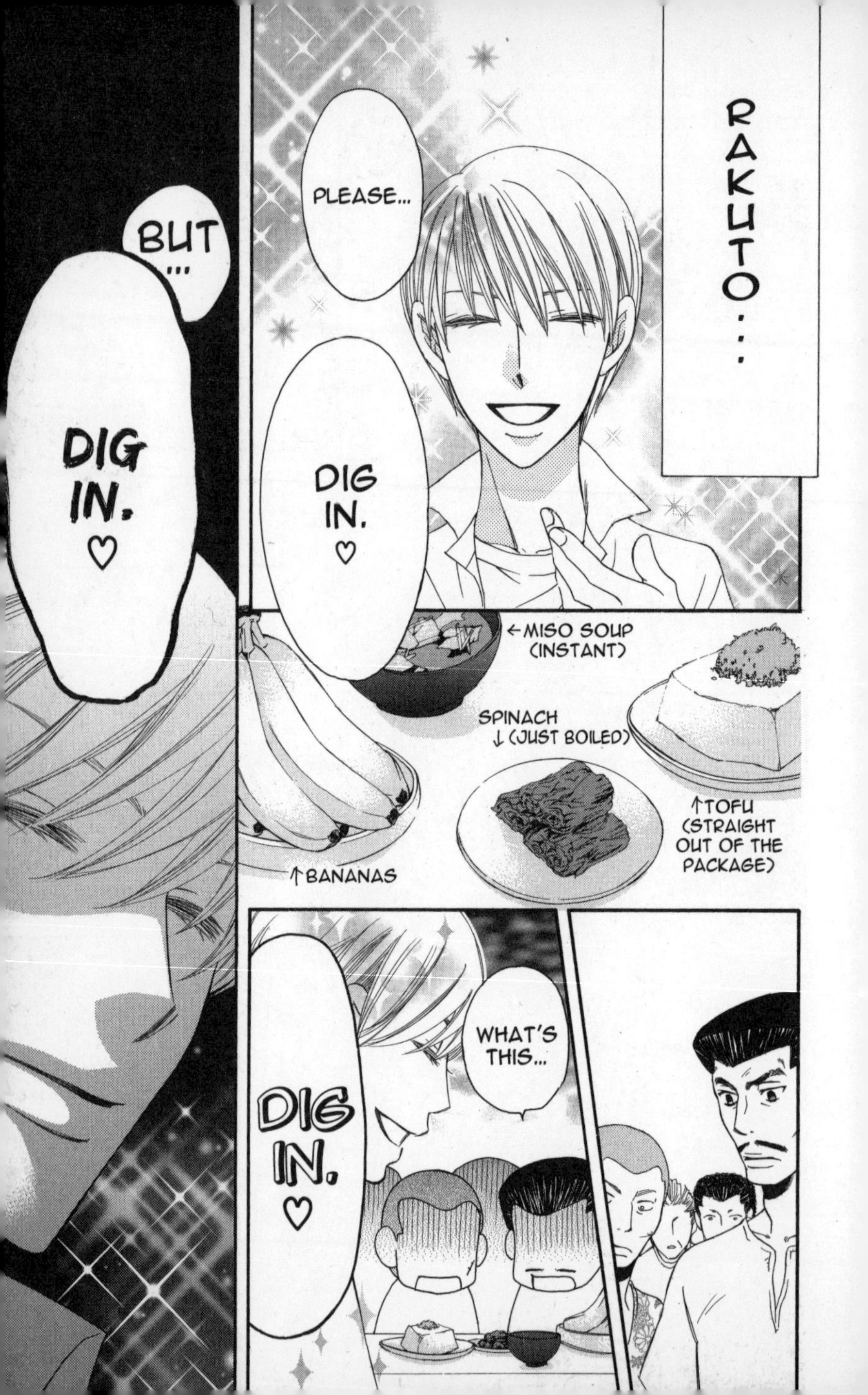
RAKUTO...
PLEASE...
DIG IN. ♡
←MISO SOUP (INSTANT)
↑TOFU (STRAIGHT OUT OF THE PACKAGE)
SPINACH ↓(JUST BOILED)
↑BANANAS
WHAT'S THIS...
DIG IN. ♡
BUT...
DIG IN. ♡

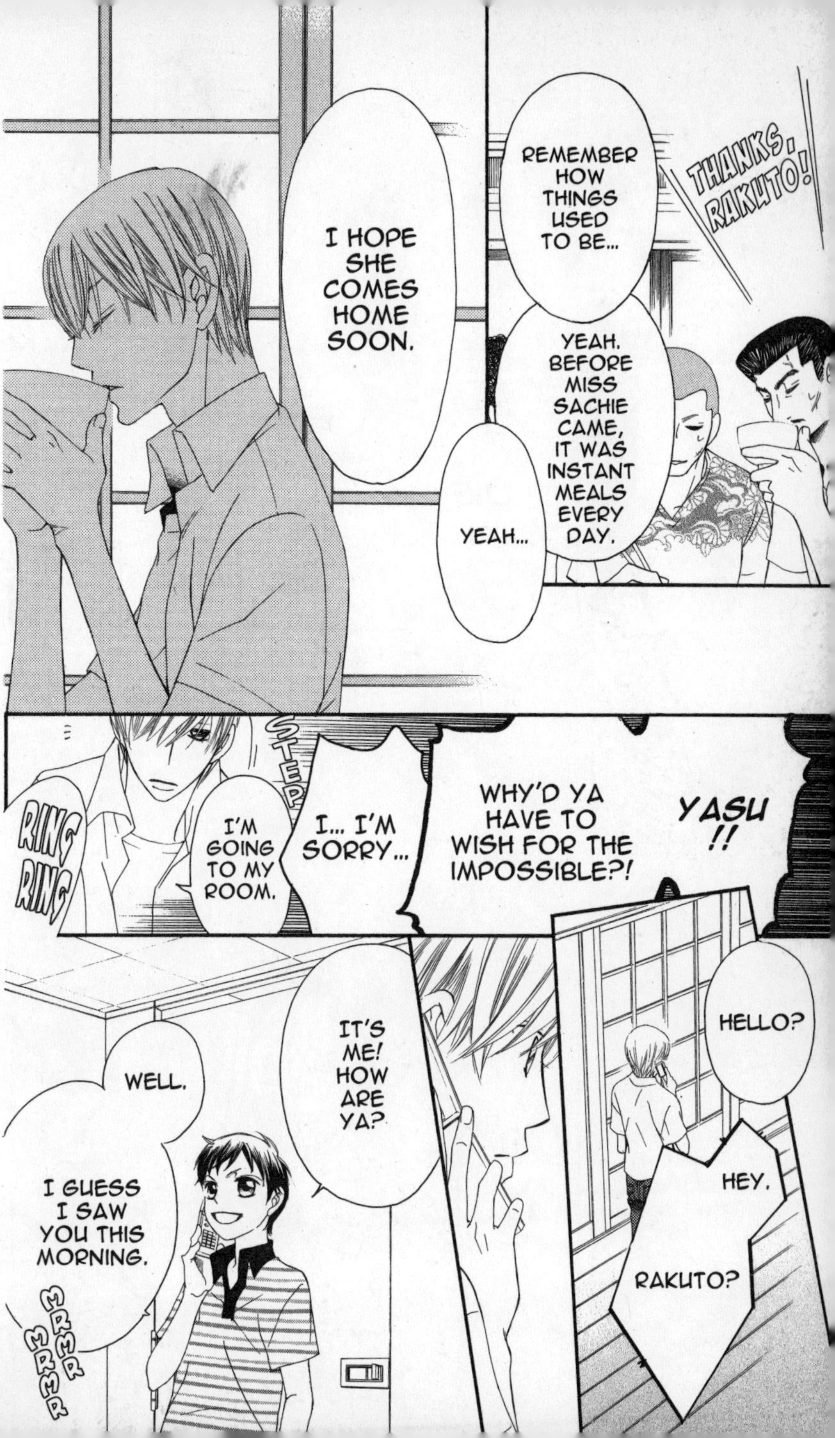
THANKS, RAKUTO!
REMEMBER HOW THINGS USED TO BE...
YEAH. BEFORE MISS SACHIE CAME, IT WAS INSTANT MEALS EVERY DAY.
YEAH...
I HOPE SHE COMES HOME SOON.
YASU!!
WHY'D YA HAVE TO WISH FOR THE IMPOSSIBLE?!
I... I'M SORRY...
STEP
I'M GOING TO MY ROOM.
RING RING
HELLO?
HEY.
RAKUTO?
IT'S ME! HOW ARE YA?
WELL.
I GUESS I SAW YOU THIS MORNING.
MRMR MRMR

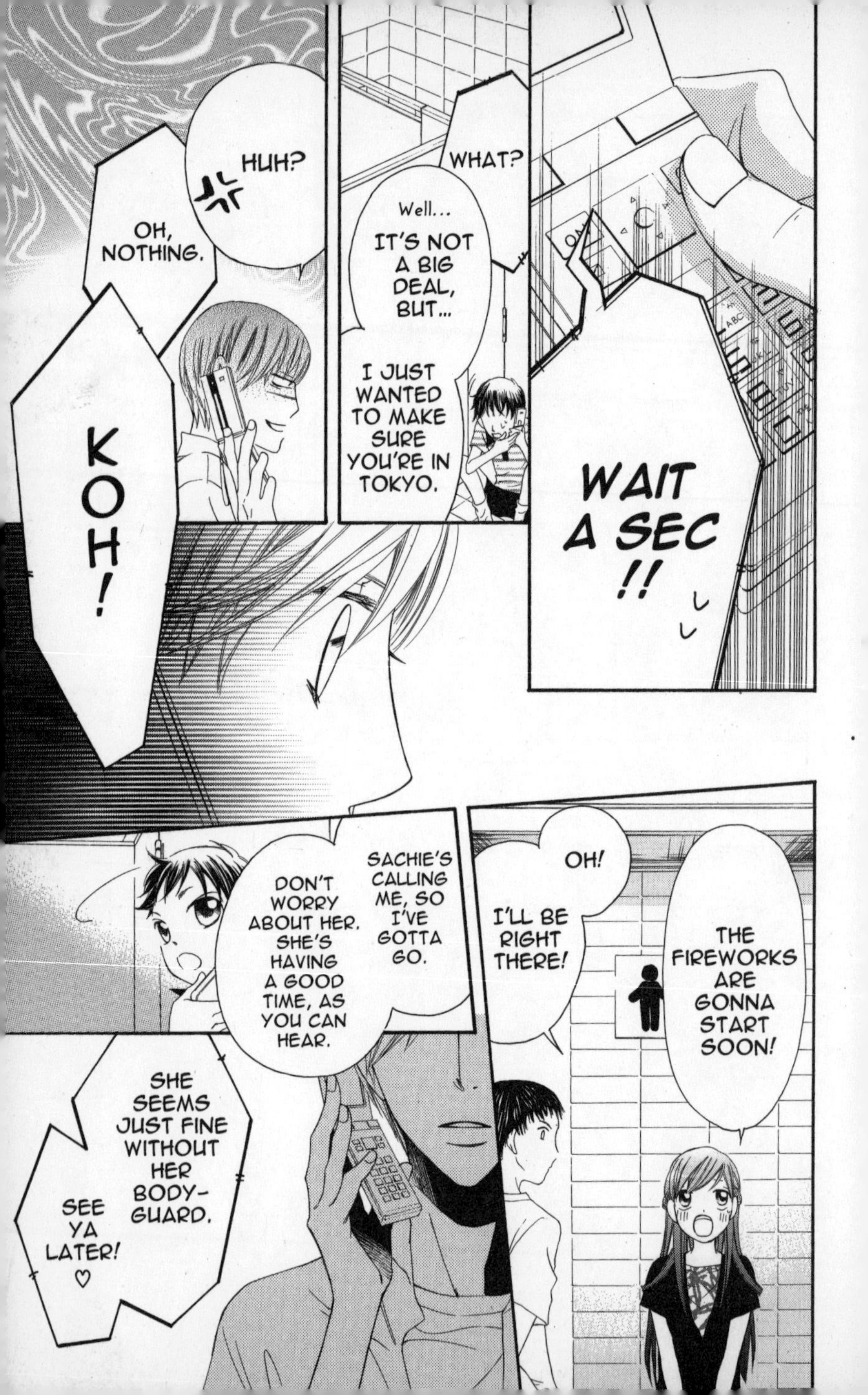
WAIT A SEC!!
WHAT?
Well... IT'S NOT A BIG DEAL, BUT...
I JUST WANTED TO MAKE SURE YOU'RE IN TOKYO.
HUH?
OH, NOTHING.
KOH!
THE FIREWORKS ARE GONNA START SOON!
OH!
I'LL BE RIGHT THERE!
SACHIE'S CALLING ME, SO I'VE GOTTA GO.
DON'T WORRY ABOUT HER. SHE'S HAVING A GOOD TIME, AS YOU CAN HEAR.
SHE SEEMS JUST FINE WITHOUT HER BODY-GUARD.
SEE YA LATER! ♡

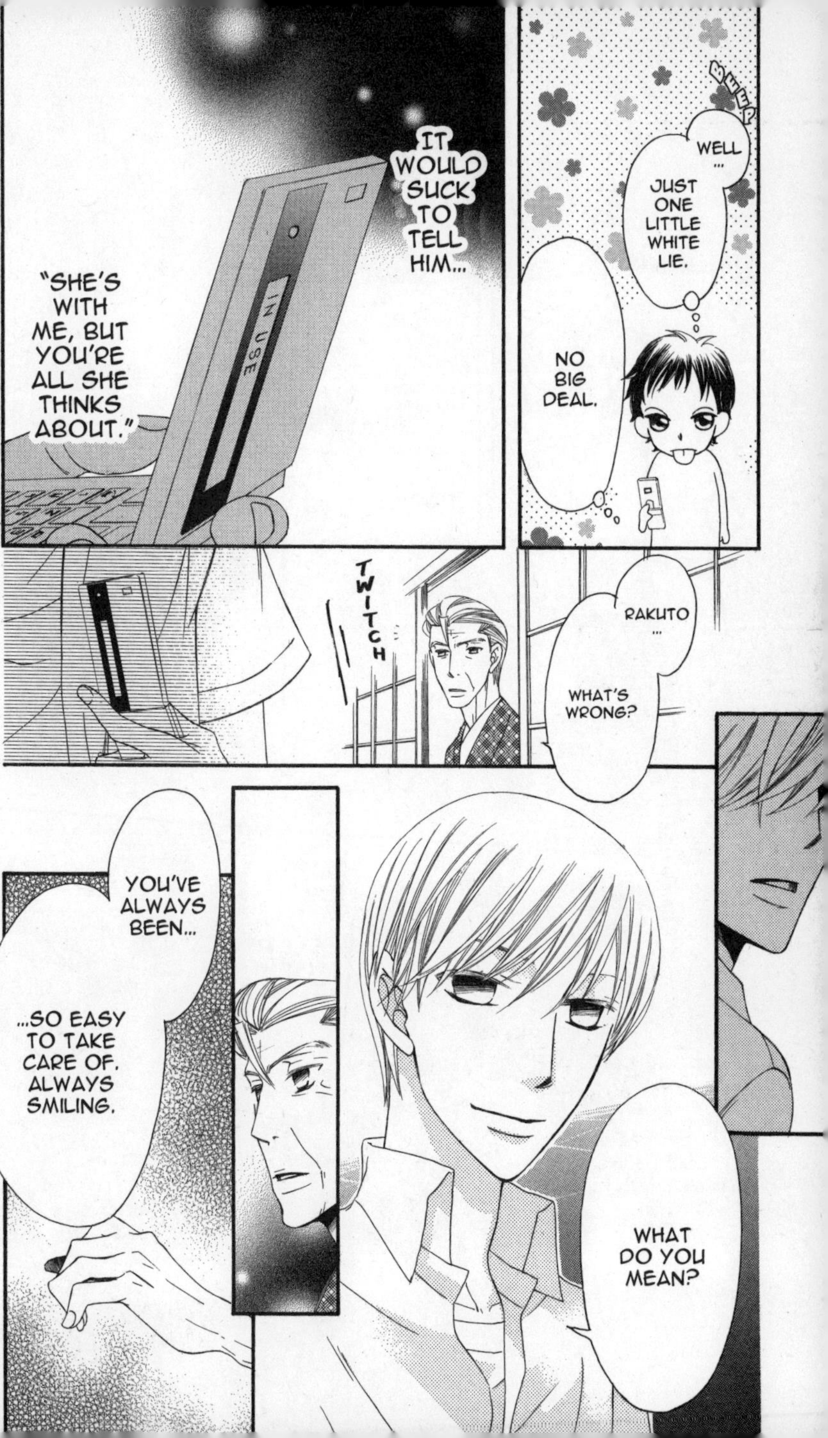
BEEP
WELL ... JUST ONE LITTLE WHITE LIE.
NO BIG DEAL.
IT WOULD SUCK TO TELL HIM...
"SHE'S WITH ME, BUT YOU'RE ALL SHE THINKS ABOUT."
IN USE
RAKUTO ...
WHAT'S WRONG?
TWITCH
YOU'VE ALWAYS BEEN...
...SO EASY TO TAKE CARE OF. ALWAYS SMILING.
WHAT DO YOU MEAN?

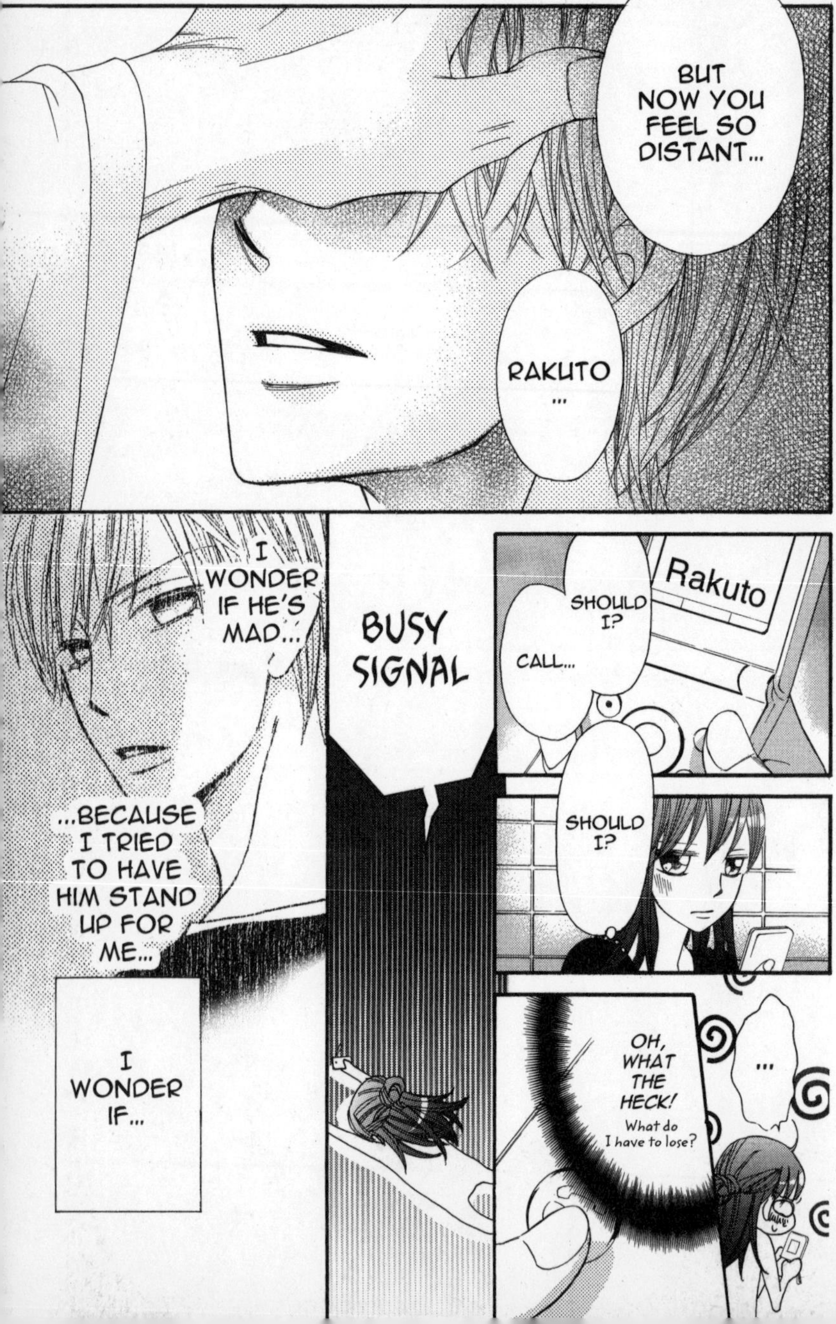
BUT NOW YOU FEEL SO DISTANT...
RAKUTO ...
Rakuto
SHOULD I?
CALL...
SHOULD I?
...
OH, WHAT THE HECK!
What do I have to lose?
BUSY SIGNAL
I WONDER IF HE'S MAD...
...BECAUSE I TRIED TO HAVE HIM STAND UP FOR ME...
I WONDER IF...

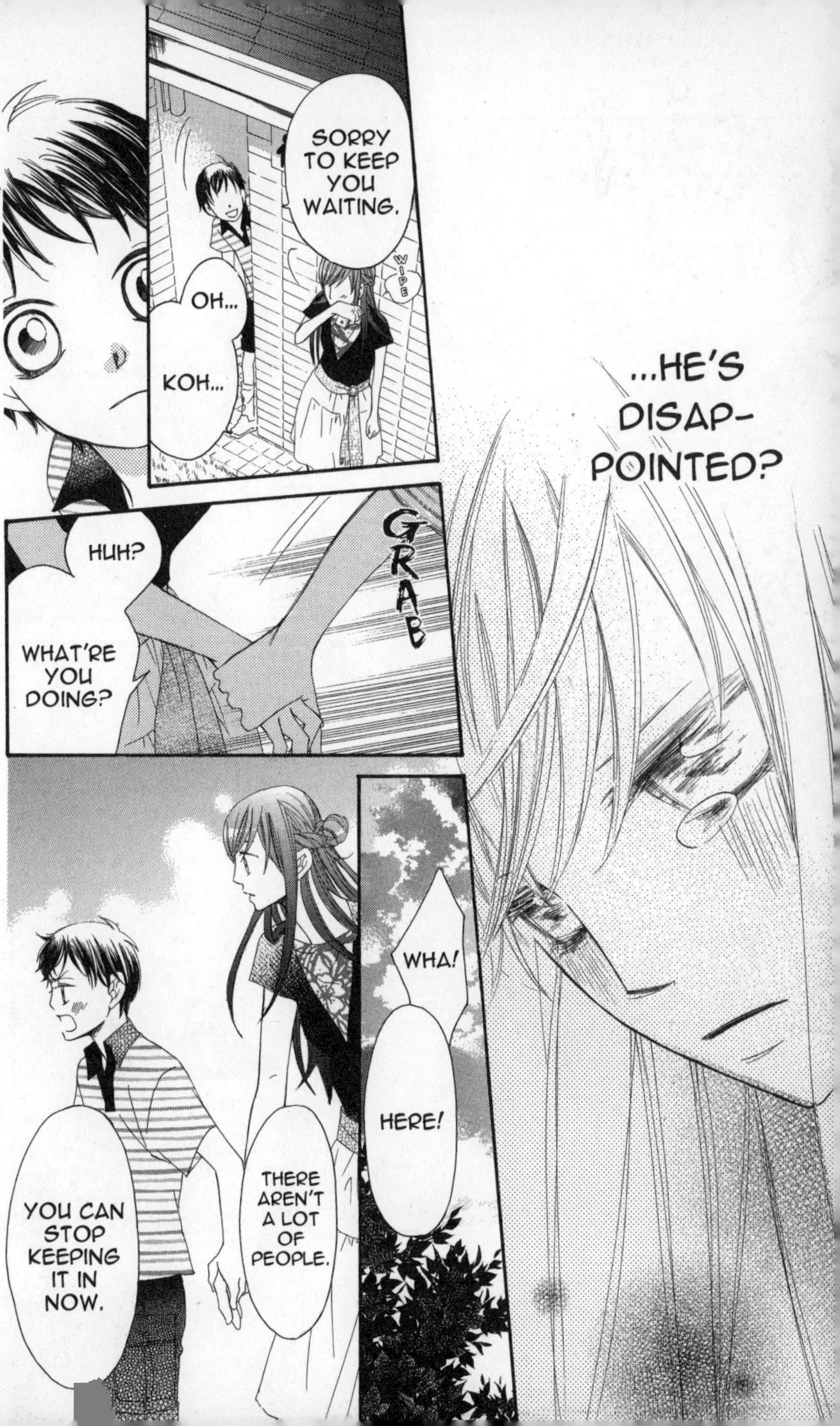
...HE'S DISAPPOINTED?
SORRY TO KEEP YOU WAITING.
WIPE
OH...
KOH...
GRAB
HUH?
WHAT'RE YOU DOING?
WHA!
HERE!
THERE AREN'T A LOT OF PEOPLE.
YOU CAN STOP KEEPING IT IN NOW.

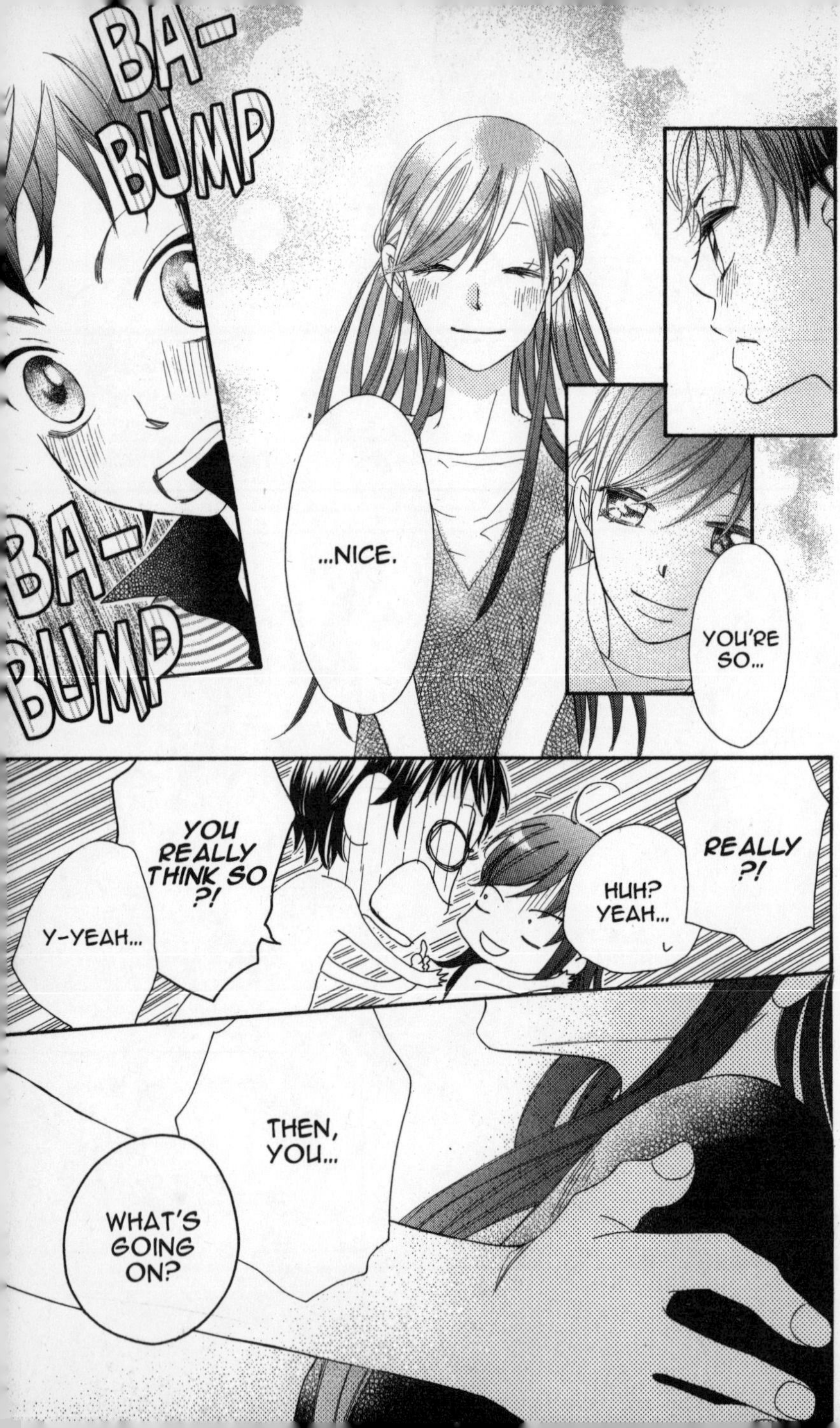
YOU'RE SO...
...NICE.
BA-BUMP
BA-BUMP
REALLY ?!
HUH? YEAH...
YOU REALLY THINK SO ?!
Y-YEAH...
THEN, YOU...
WHAT'S GOING ON?

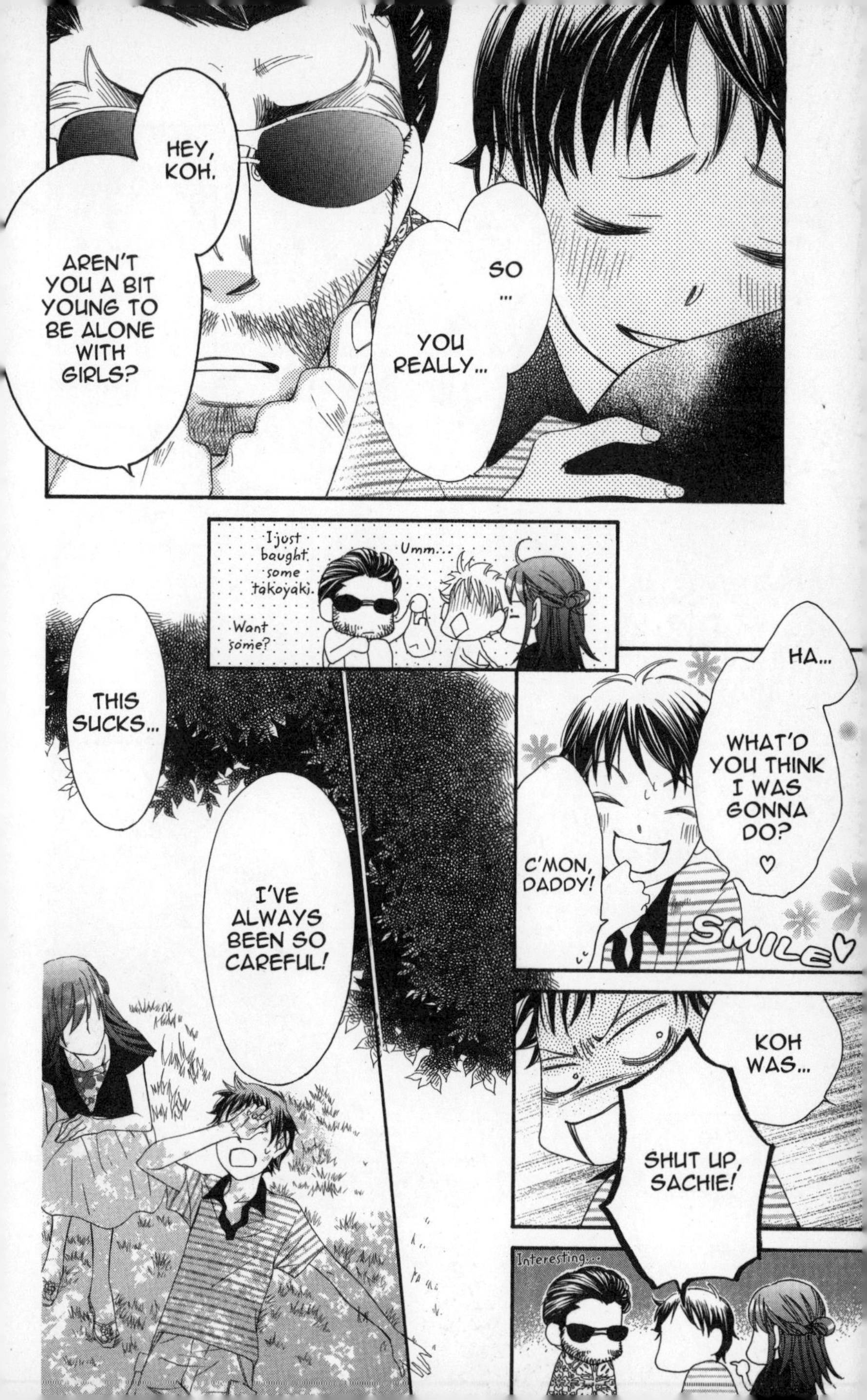
SO ... YOU REALLY...
HEY, KOH.
AREN'T YOU A BIT YOUNG TO BE ALONE WITH GIRLS?
Umm...
I just baught some takoyaki.
Want some?
HA... WHAT'D YOU THINK I WAS GONNA DO? ♡
C'MON, DADDY!
SMILE♡
KOH WAS...
SHUT UP, SACHIE!
Interesting...
THIS SUCKS...
I'VE ALWAYS BEEN SO CAREFUL!

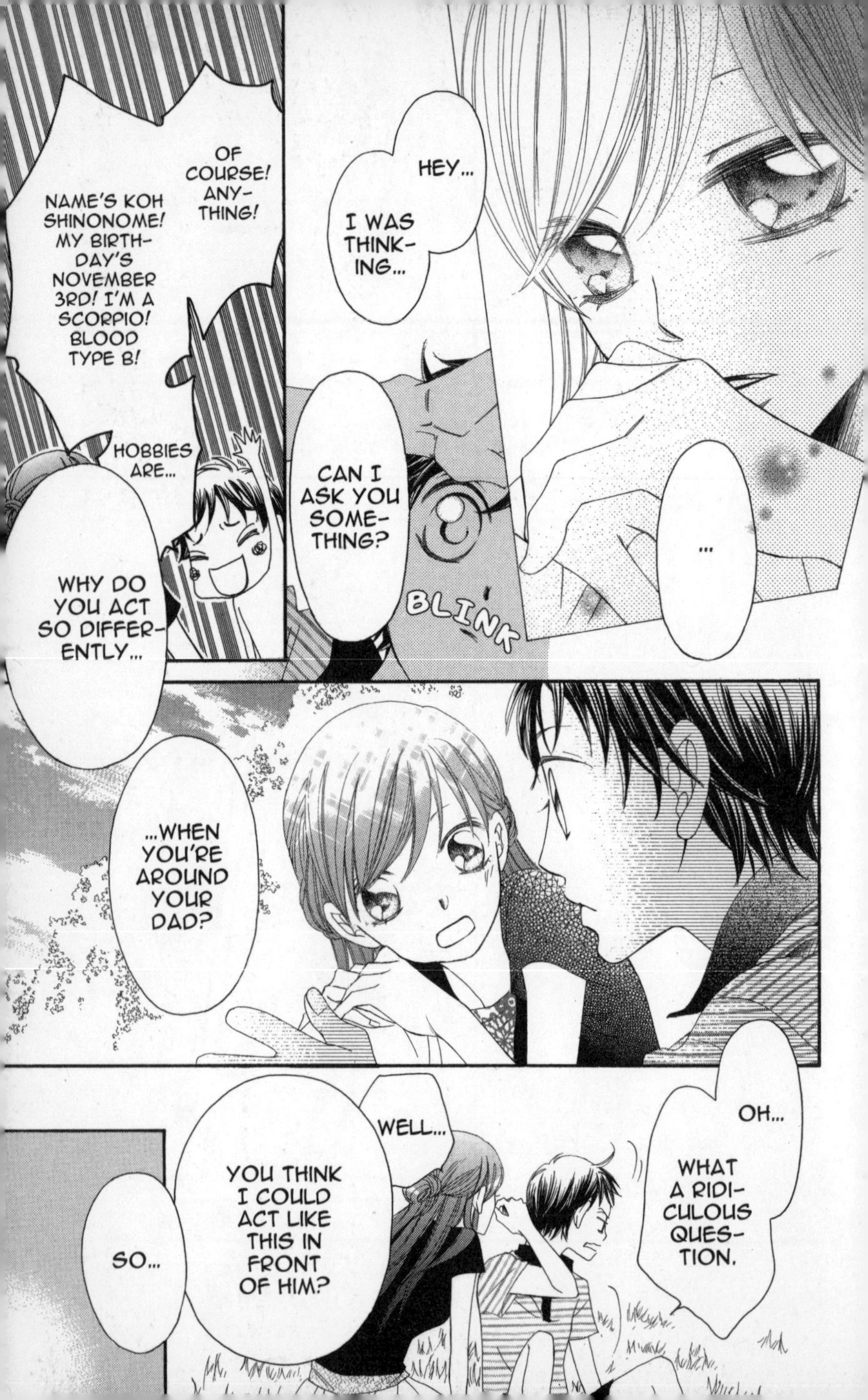
HEY...
I WAS THINKING...
CAN I ASK YOU SOMETHING?
BLINK
...
OF COURSE! ANYTHING!
NAME'S KOH SHINONOME! MY BIRTHDAY'S NOVEMBER 3RD! I'M A SCORPIO! BLOOD TYPE B!
HOBBIES ARE...
WHY DO YOU ACT SO DIFFERENTLY...
...WHEN YOU'RE AROUND YOUR DAD?
OH...
WHAT A RIDICULOUS QUESTION.
WELL...
YOU THINK I COULD ACT LIKE THIS IN FRONT OF HIM?
SO...

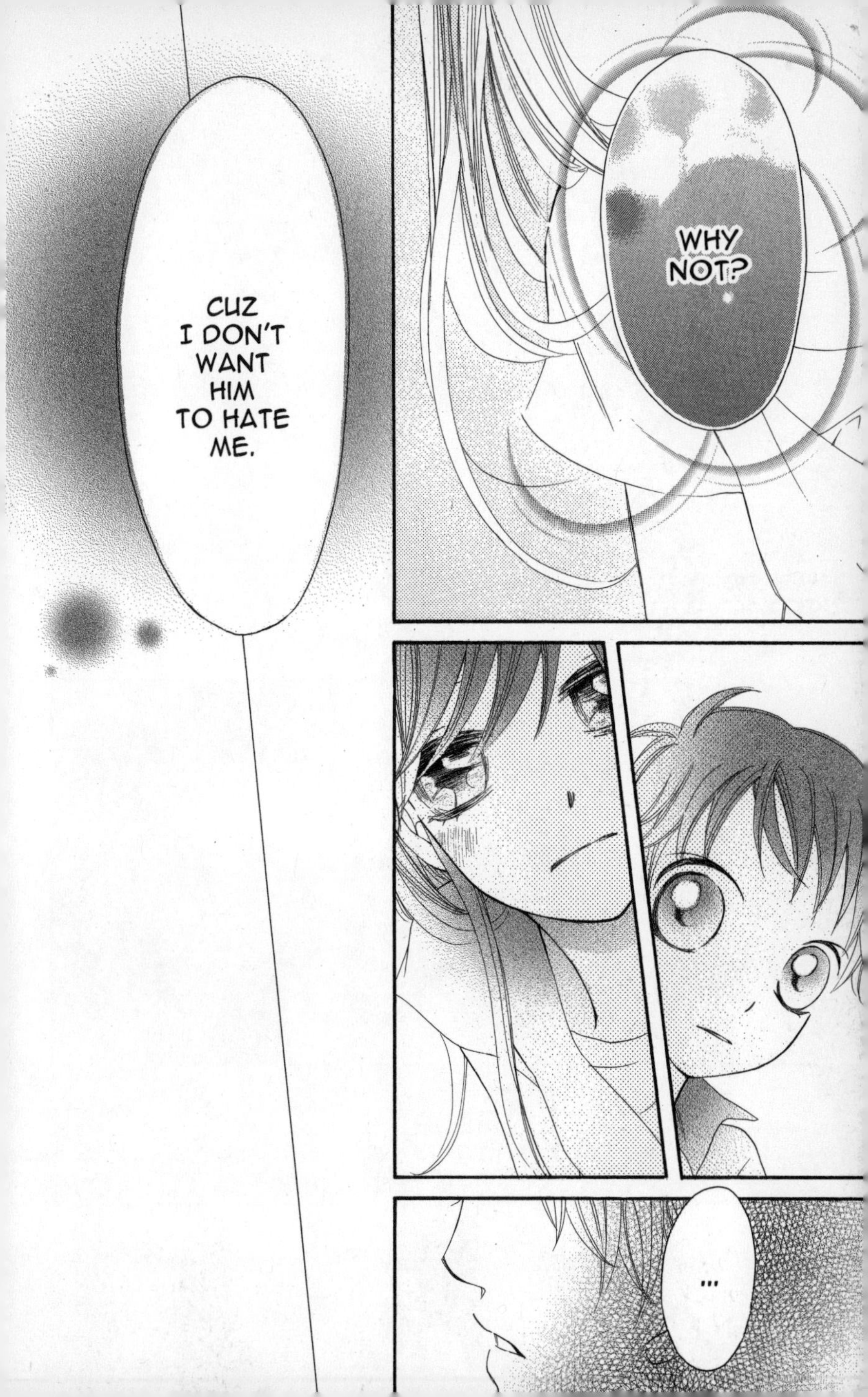
WHY NOT?
...
CUZ I DON'T WANT HIM TO HATE ME.

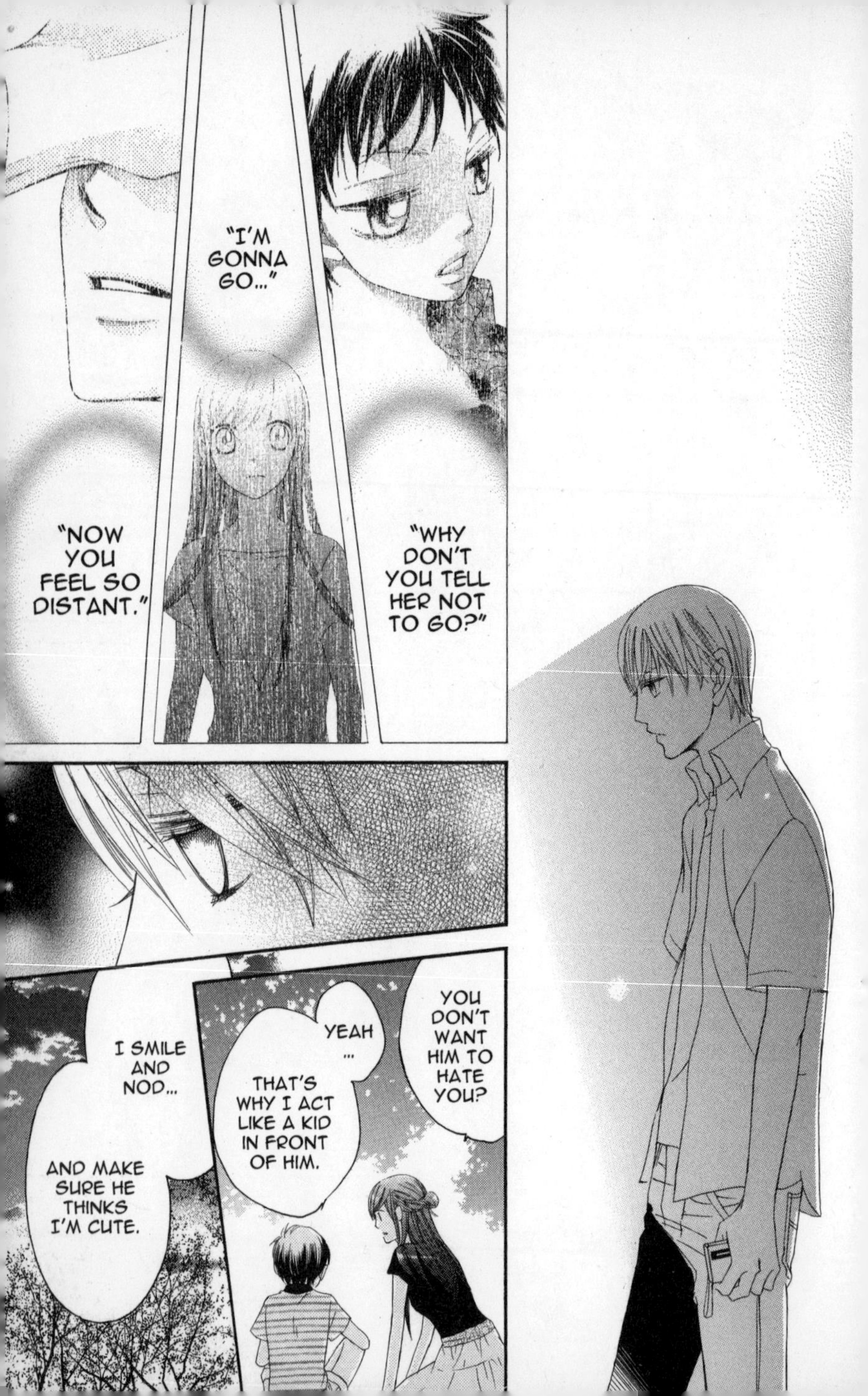
"I'M GONNA GO..."
"WHY DON'T YOU TELL HER NOT TO GO?"
"NOW YOU FEEL SO DISTANT."
YOU DON'T WANT HIM TO HATE YOU?
YEAH...
THAT'S WHY I ACT LIKE A KID IN FRONT OF HIM.
I SMILE AND NOD...
AND MAKE SURE HE THINKS I'M CUTE.

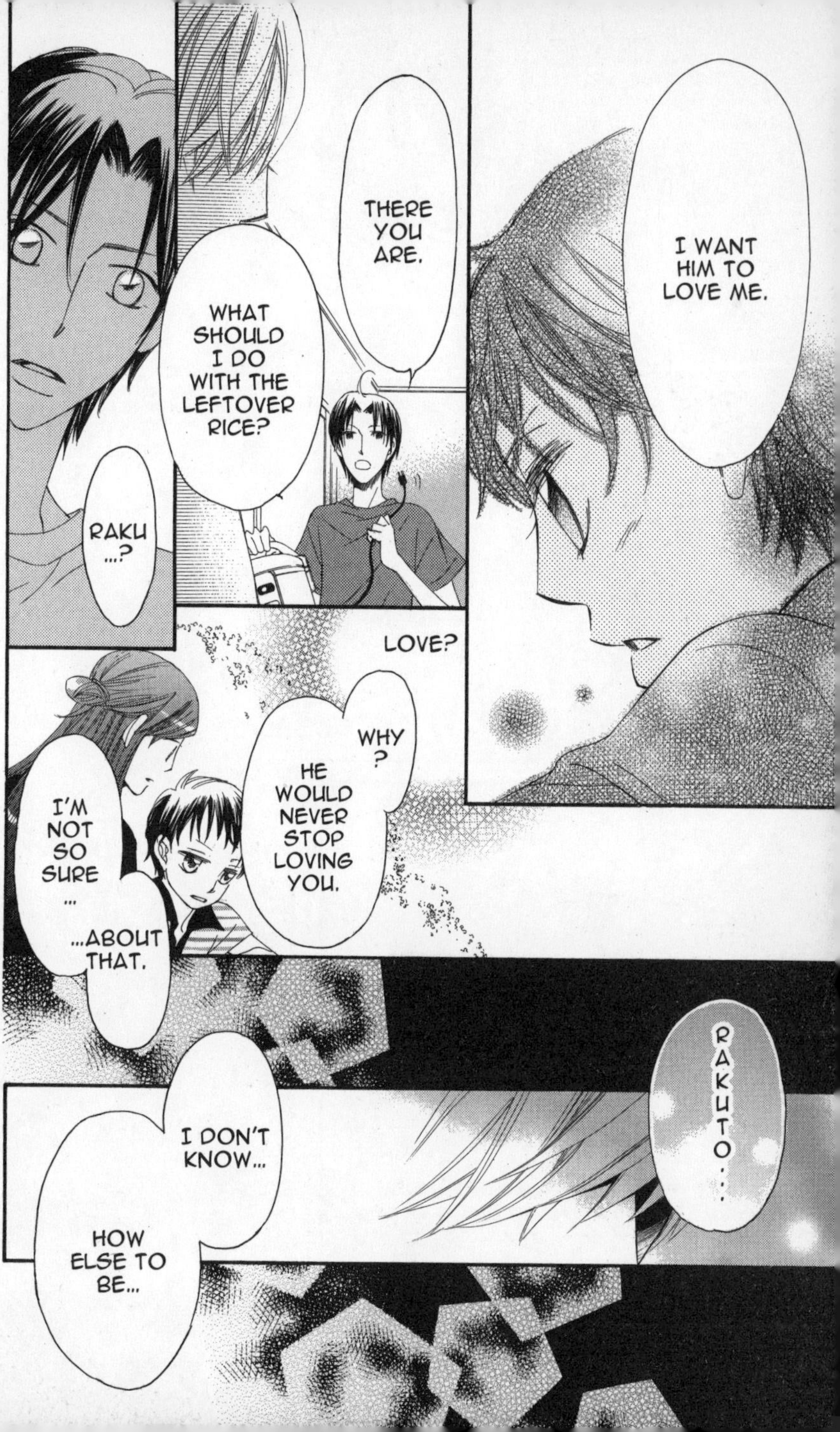
I WANT HIM TO LOVE ME.
THERE YOU ARE.
WHAT SHOULD I DO WITH THE LEFTOVER RICE?
RAKU ...?
LOVE?
WHY? HE WOULD NEVER STOP LOVING YOU.
I'M NOT SO SURE ... ...ABOUT THAT.
RAKUTO...
I DON'T KNOW... HOW ELSE TO BE...

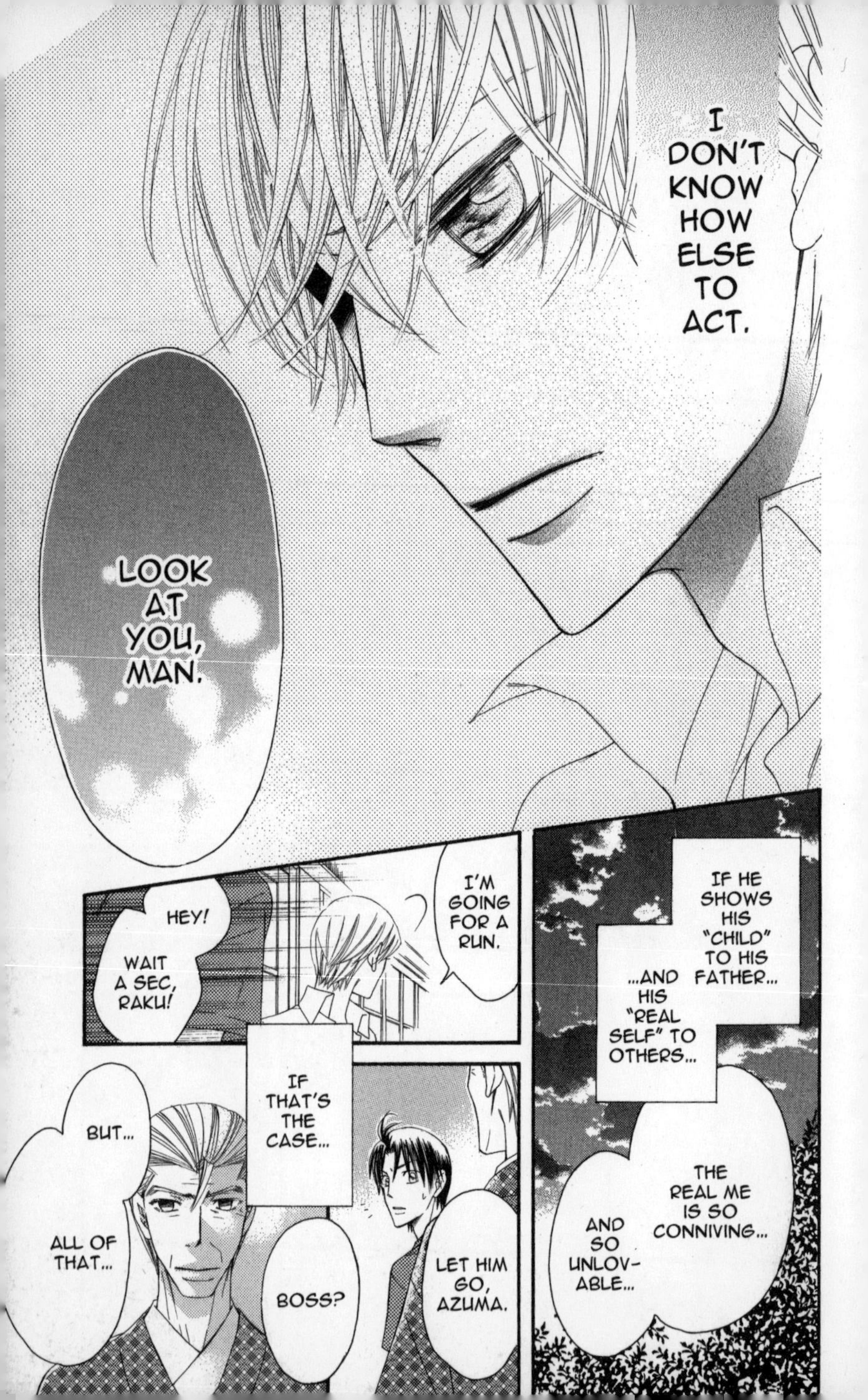

I DON'T KNOW HOW ELSE TO ACT.
LOOK AT YOU, MAN.
IF HE SHOWS HIS "CHILD" TO HIS FATHER...
...AND HIS "REAL SELF" TO OTHERS...
THE REAL ME IS SO CONNIVING...
AND SO UNLOVABLE...
I'M GOING FOR A RUN.
HEY!
WAIT A SEC, RAKU!
IF THAT'S THE CASE...
LET HIM GO, AZUMA.
BOSS?
BUT...
ALL OF THAT...

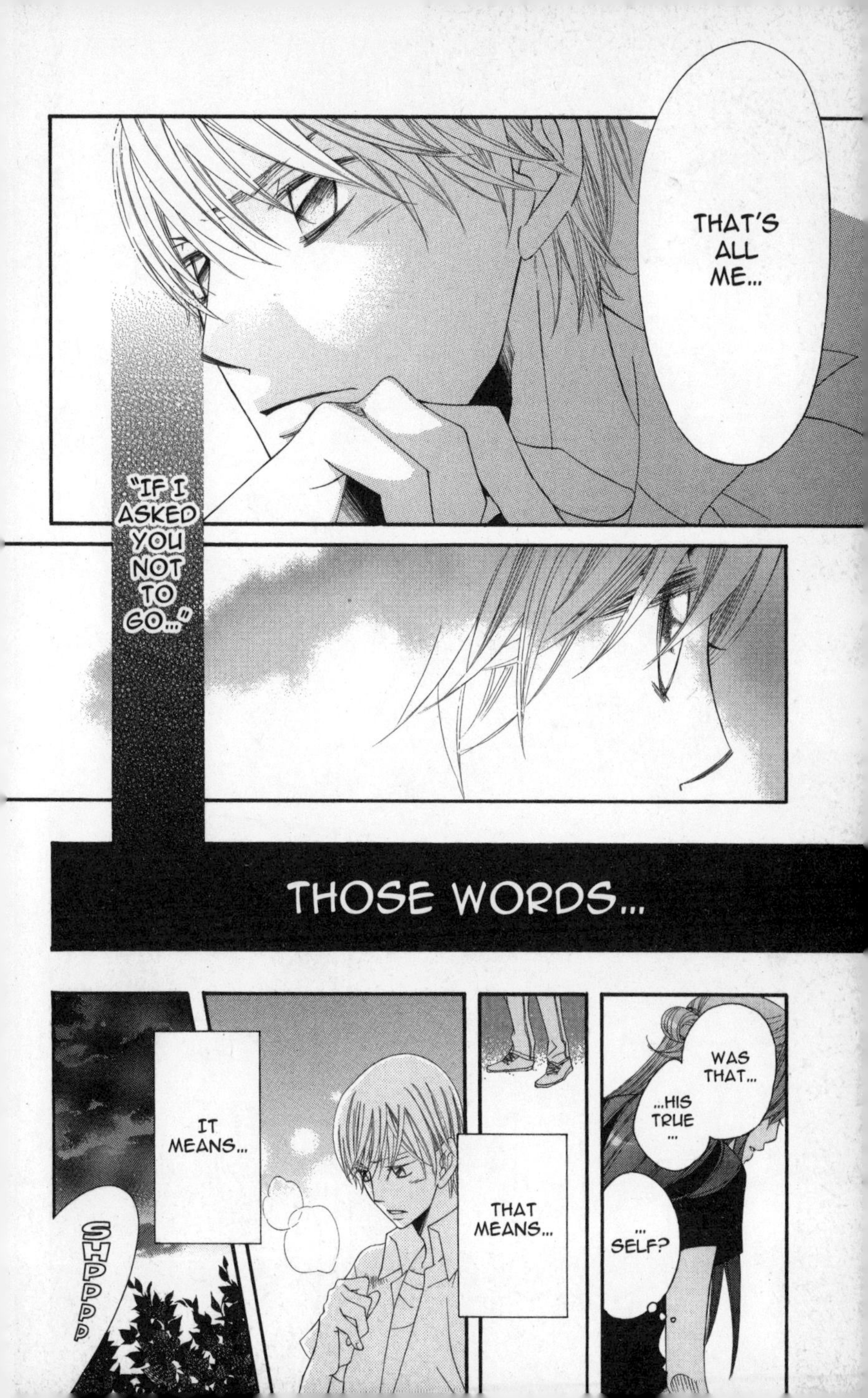
THAT'S ALL ME...
"IF I ASKED YOU NOT TO GO..."
THOSE WORDS...
WAS THAT...
...HIS TRUE ...
... SELF?
IT MEANS...
THAT MEANS...
SHPPPP

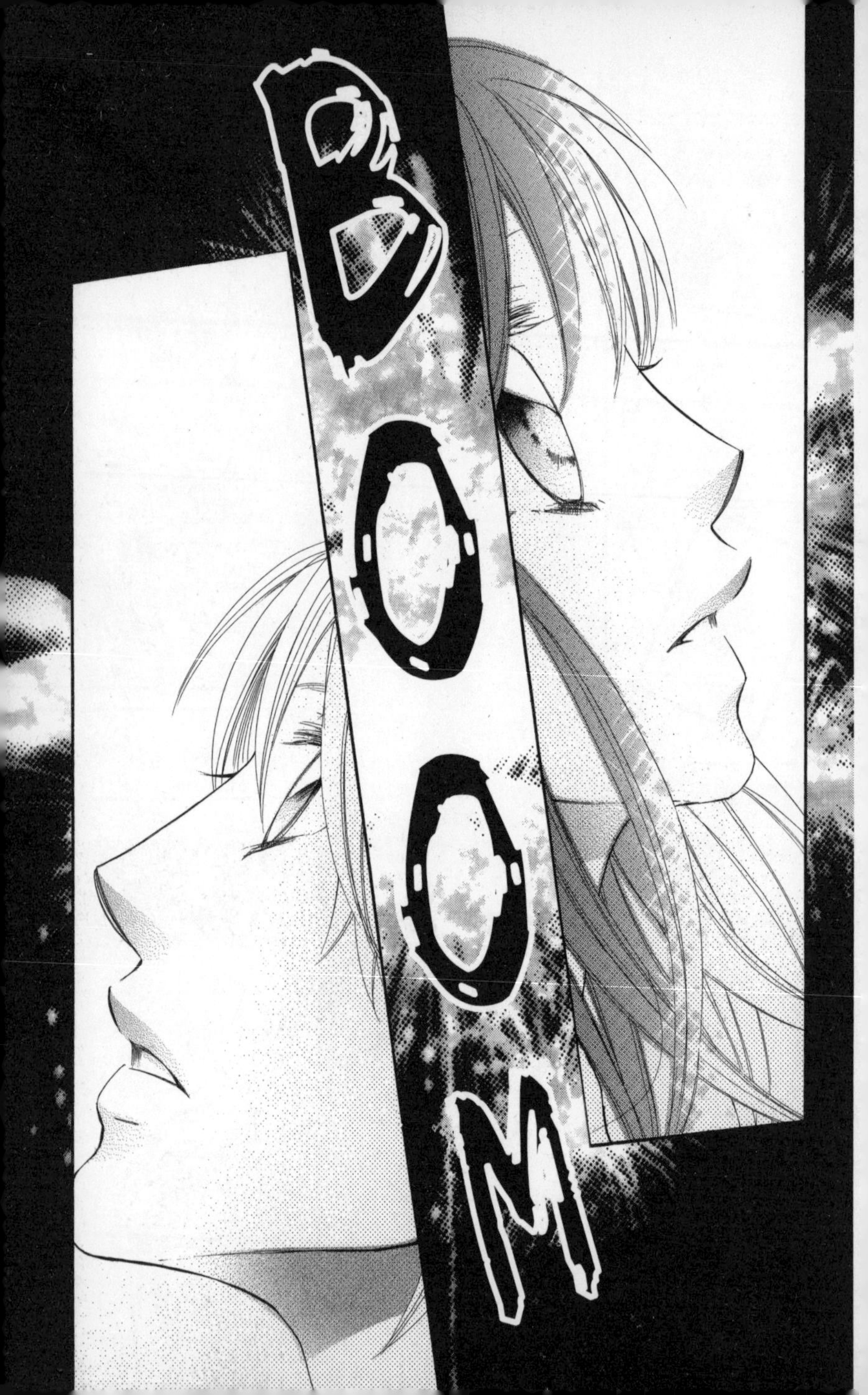
DOOM

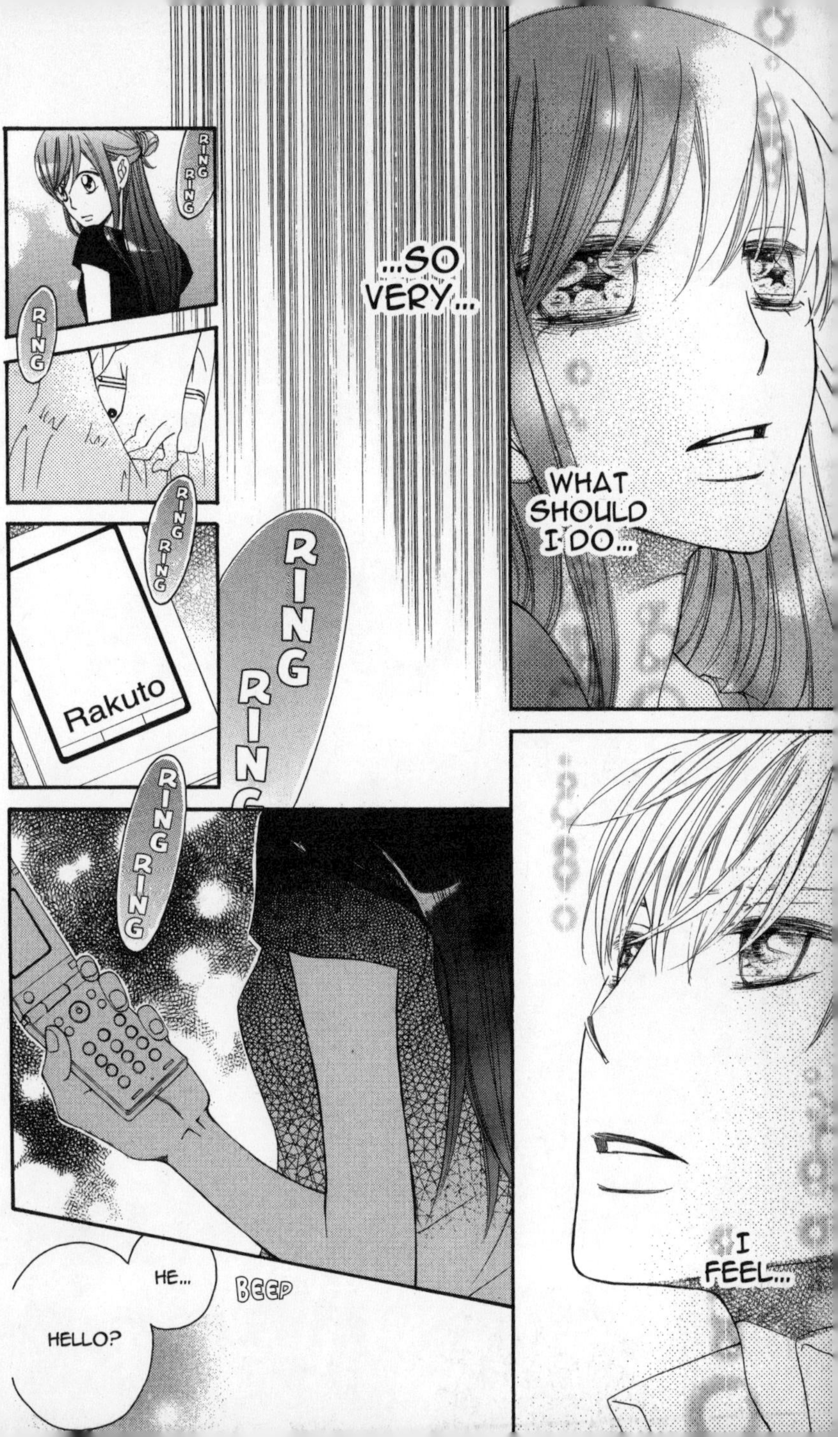
...SO VERY...
WHAT SHOULD I DO...
I FEEL...
RING RING
RING
RING RING
Rakuto
RING RING
RING RING
BEEP
HE...
HELLO?

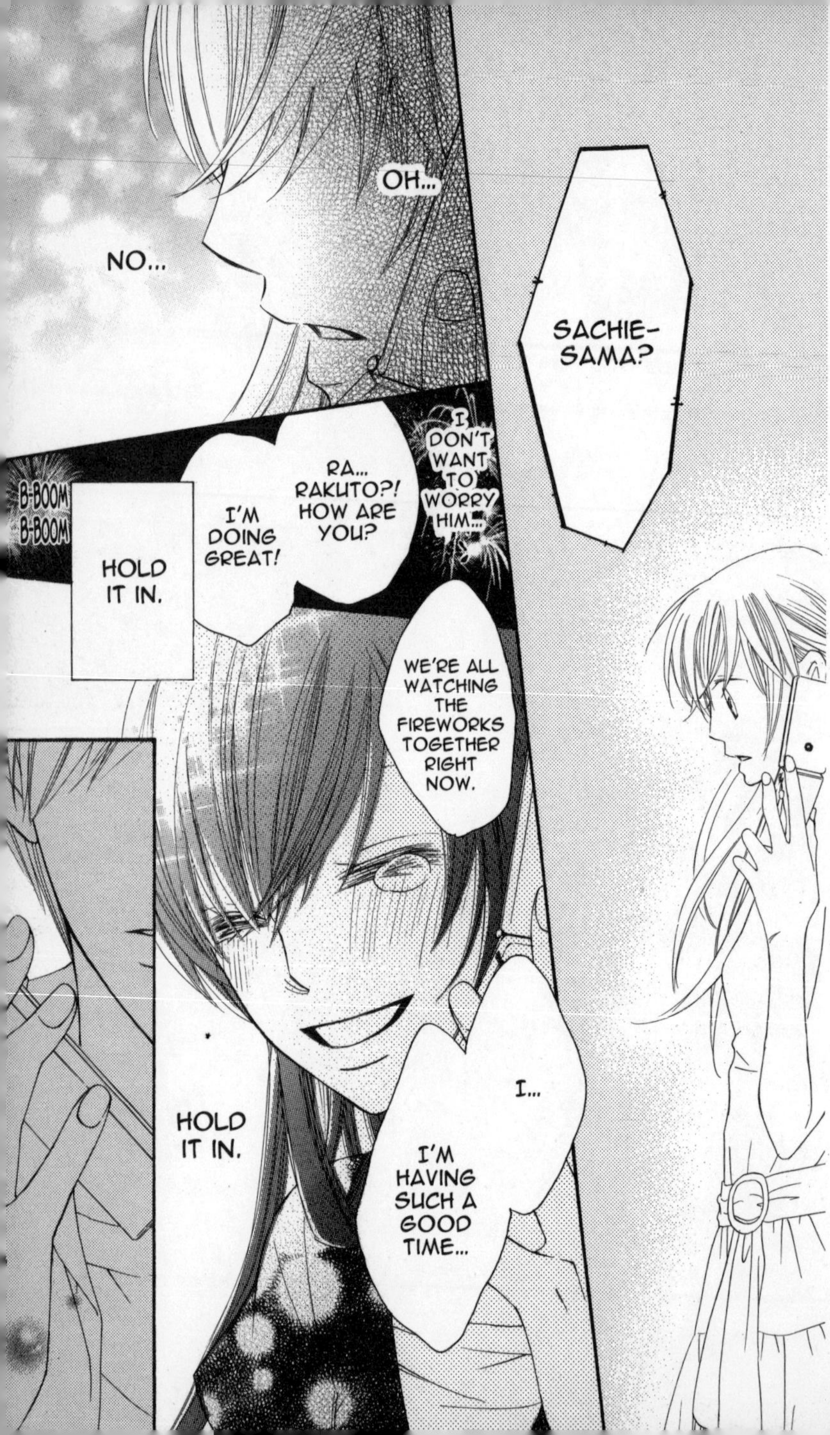
SACHIE-SAMA?
OH...
NO...
I DON'T WANT TO WORRY HIM...
RA... RAKUTO?! HOW ARE YOU?
I'M DOING GREAT!
B-BOOM B-BOOM
HOLD IT IN.
WE'RE ALL WATCHING THE FIREWORKS TOGETHER RIGHT NOW.
I...
I'M HAVING SUCH A GOOD TIME...
HOLD IT IN.

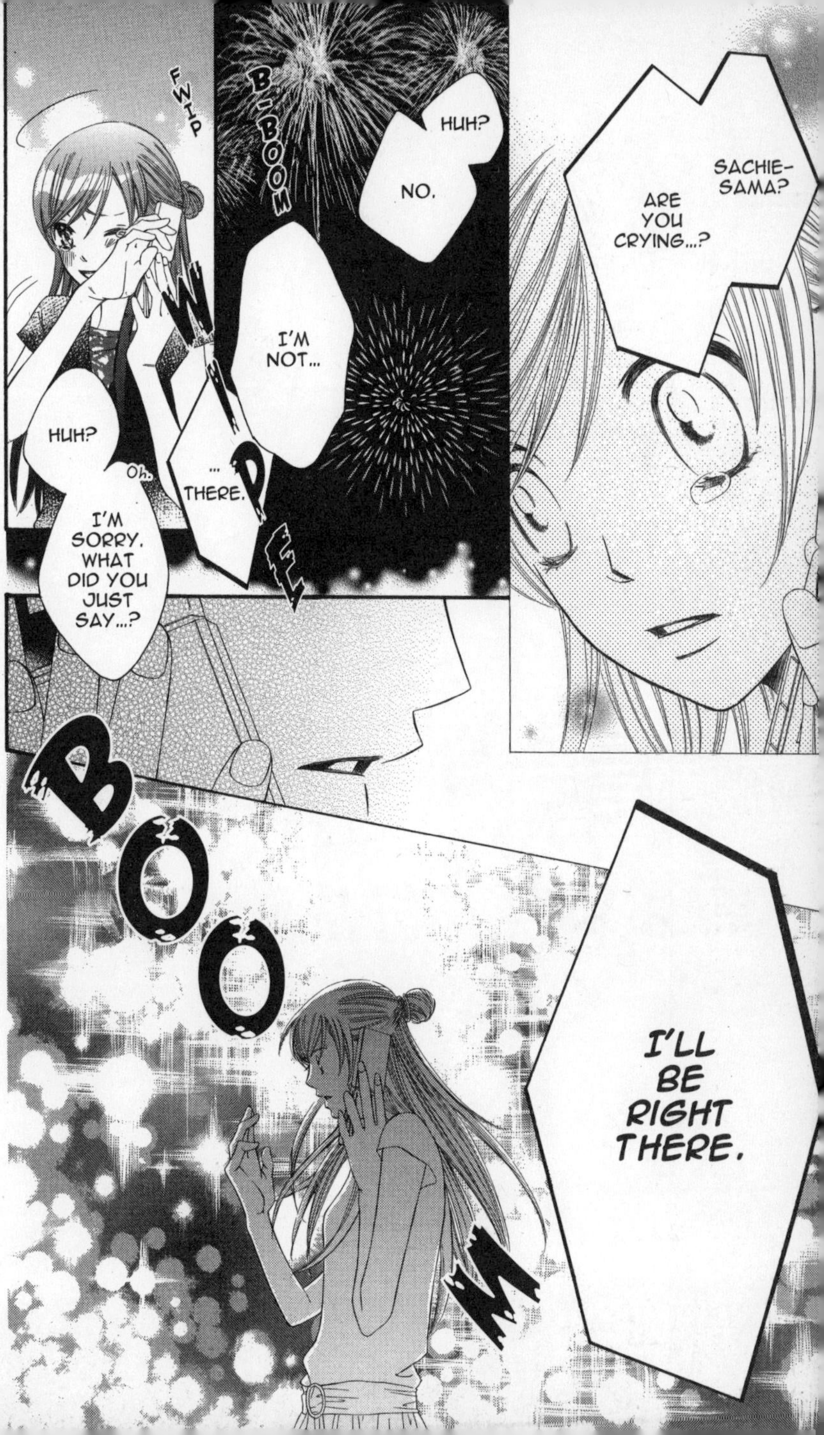
SACHIE-SAMA?
ARE YOU CRYING...?
B-BOOM
HUH?
NO.
I'M NOT...
... THERE.
FWIP
HUH?
Oh.
I'M SORRY. WHAT DID YOU JUST SAY...?
BOOOM
I'LL BE RIGHT THERE.

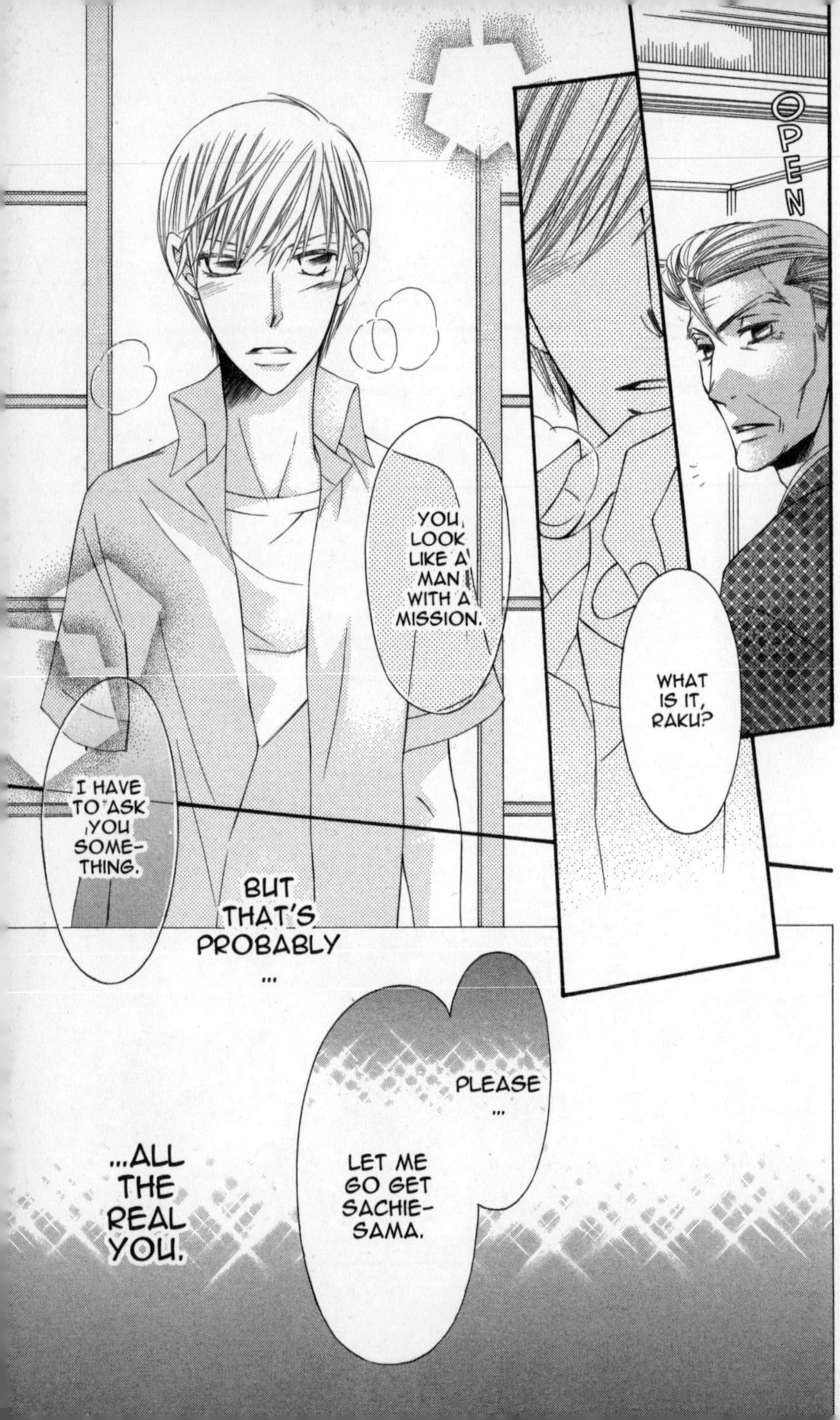
OPEN
WHAT IS IT, RAKU?
YOU LOOK LIKE A MAN WITH A MISSION.
I HAVE TO ASK YOU SOMETHING.
BUT THAT'S PROBABLY ...
PLEASE ...
LET ME GO GET SACHIE-SAMA.
...ALL THE REAL YOU.

RAKUTO AND AZUMA

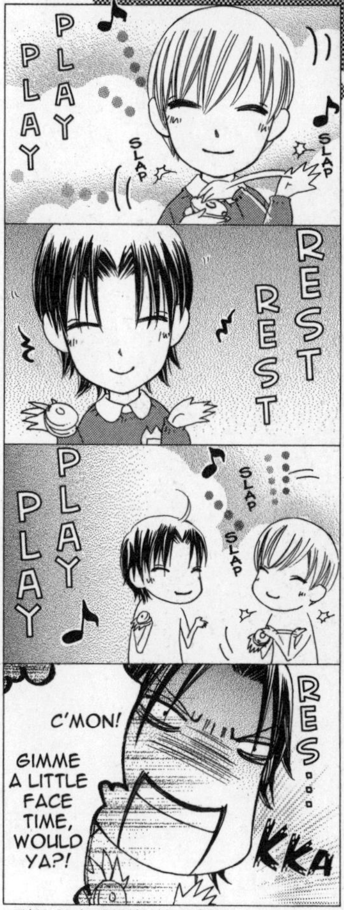
SLAP
SLAP
PLAY
PLAY
REST
REST
REST
SLAP
SLAP
PLAY
PLAY
RES...
KKA
C'MON!
GIMME A LITTLE FACE TIME, WOULD YA?!

THIS IS A FICTIONAL STORY.

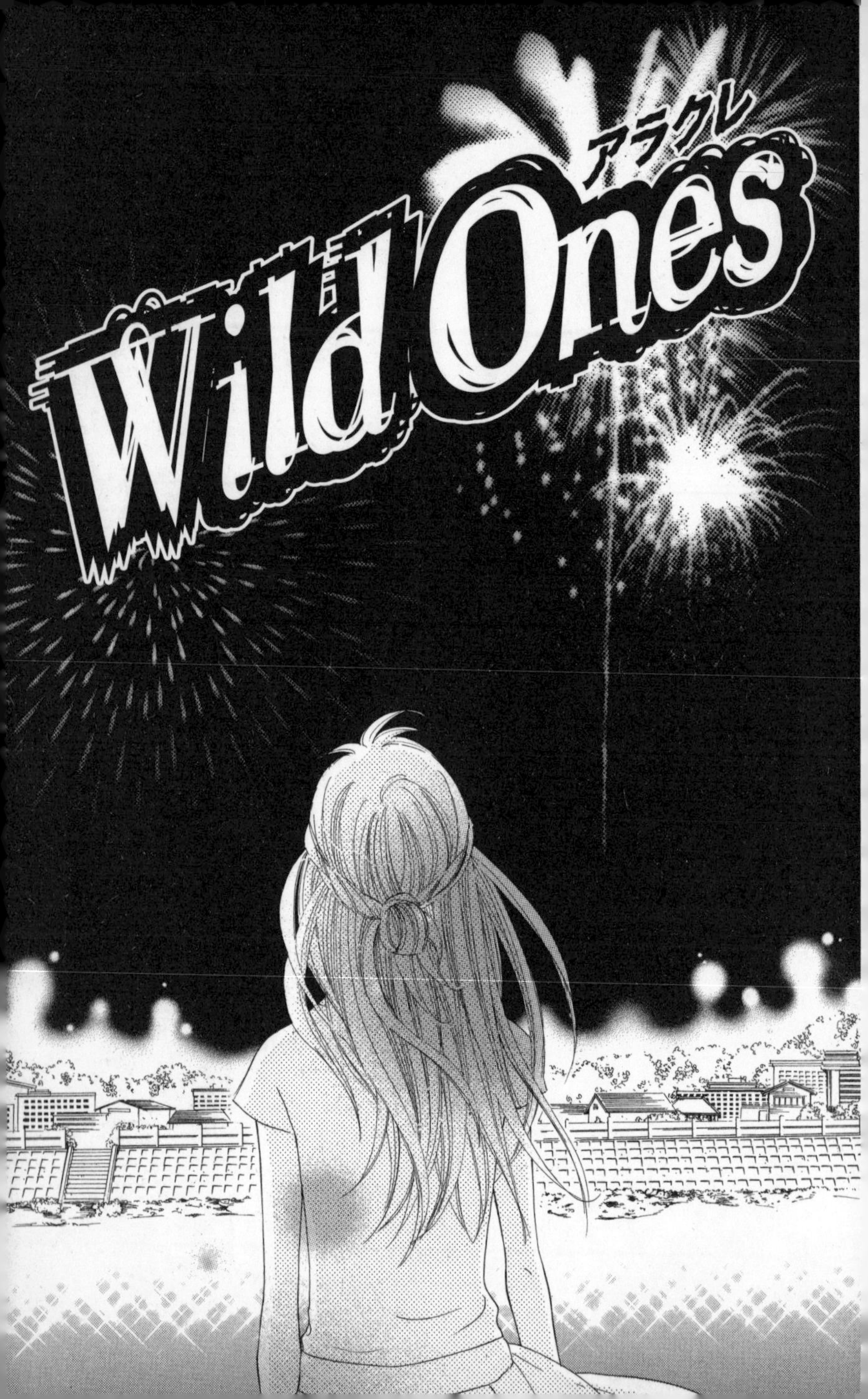
アラクレ
Wild Ones

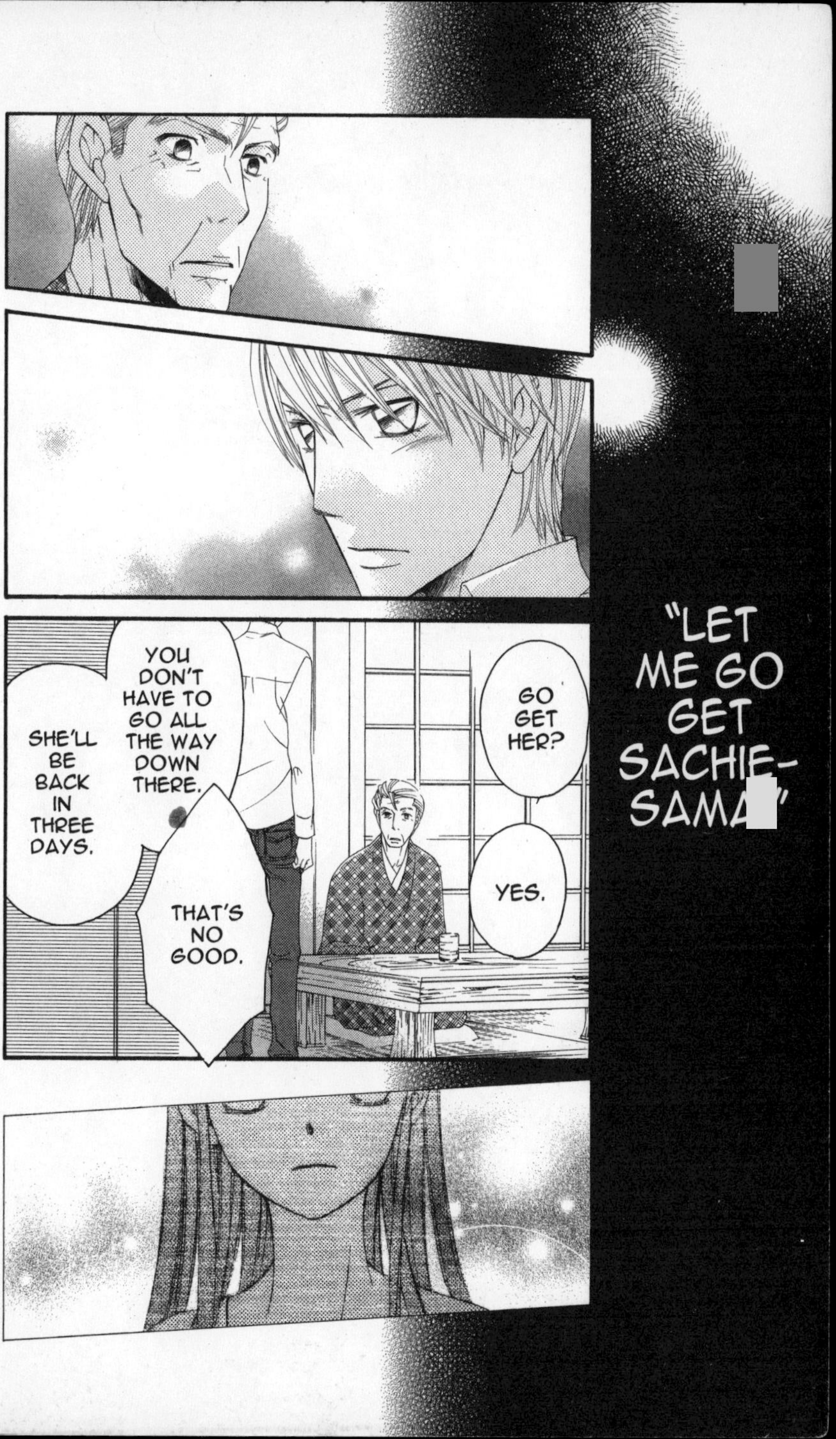
"LET ME GO GET SACHIE-SAMA"
GO GET HER?
YES.
YOU DON'T HAVE TO GO ALL THE WAY DOWN THERE.
SHE'LL BE BACK IN THREE DAYS.
THAT'S NO GOOD.

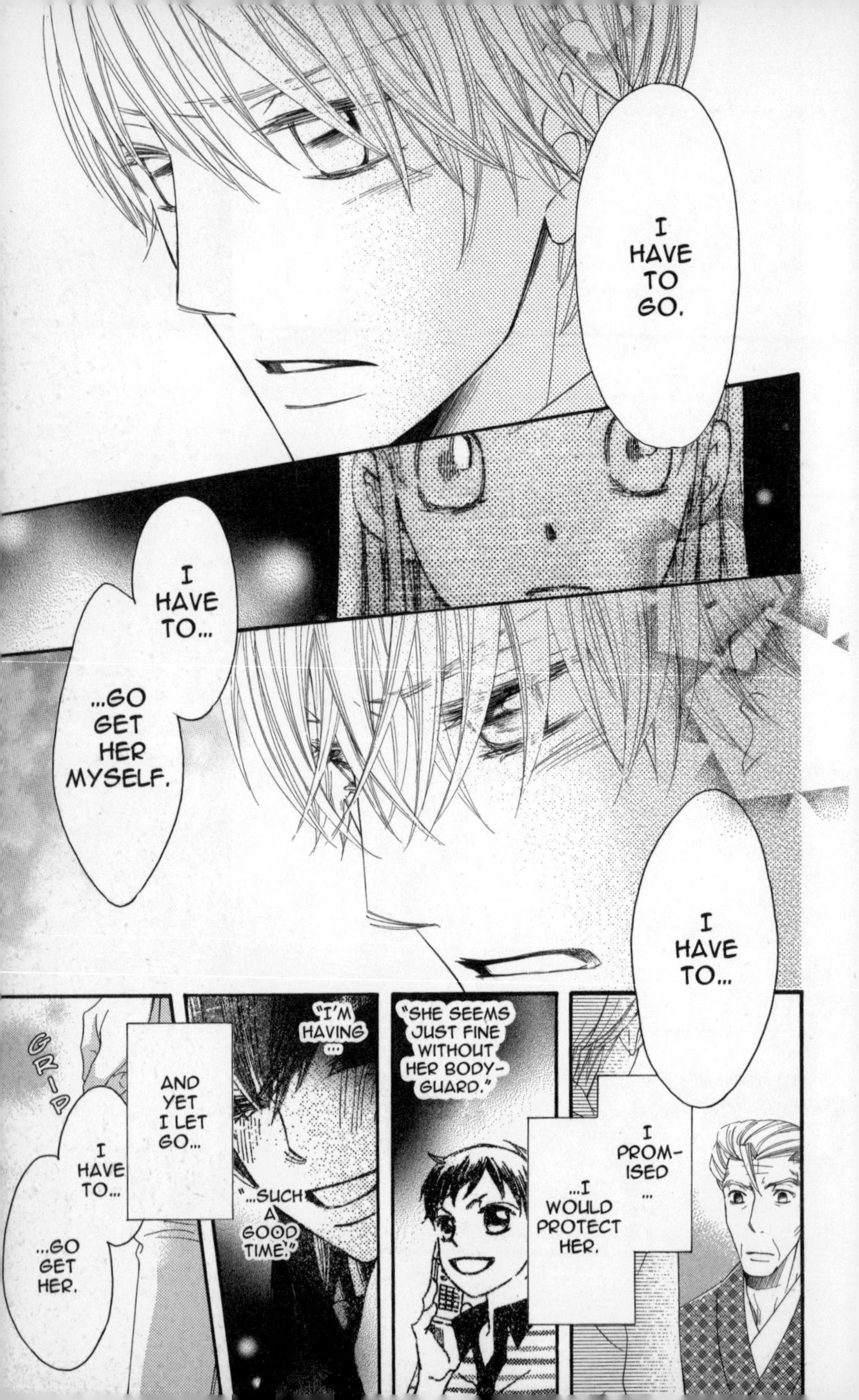

I HAVE TO GO.
I HAVE TO...
...GO GET HER MYSELF.
I HAVE TO...
I PROMISED...
...I WOULD PROTECT HER.
"SHE SEEMS JUST FINE WITHOUT HER BODY-GUARD."
"I'M HAVING...
"...SUCH A GOOD TIME."
AND YET I LET GO...
GRIP
I HAVE TO...
...GO GET HER.

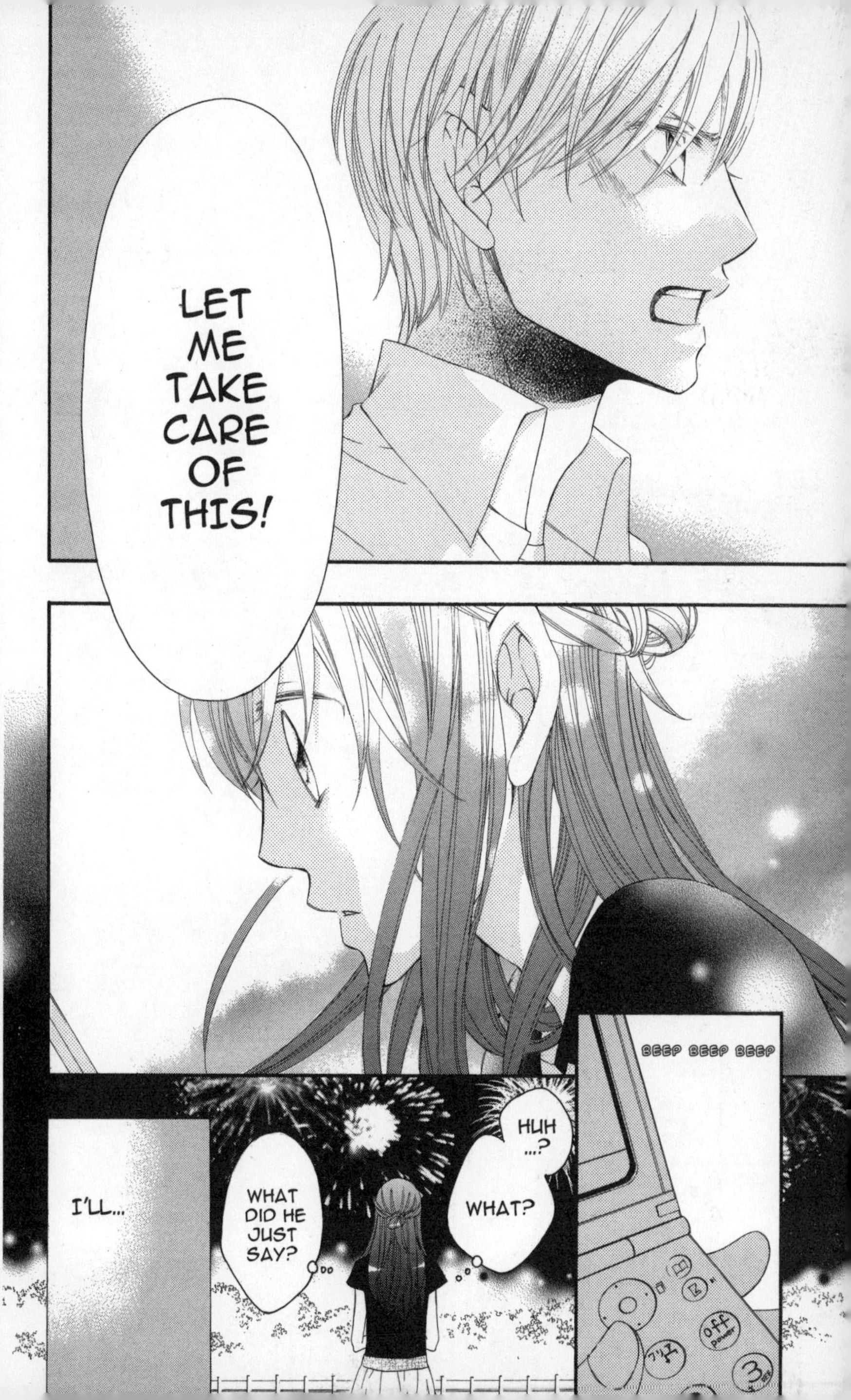
LET ME TAKE CARE OF THIS!
BEEP BEEP BEEP
HUH ...?
WHAT?
WHAT DID HE JUST SAY?
I'LL...

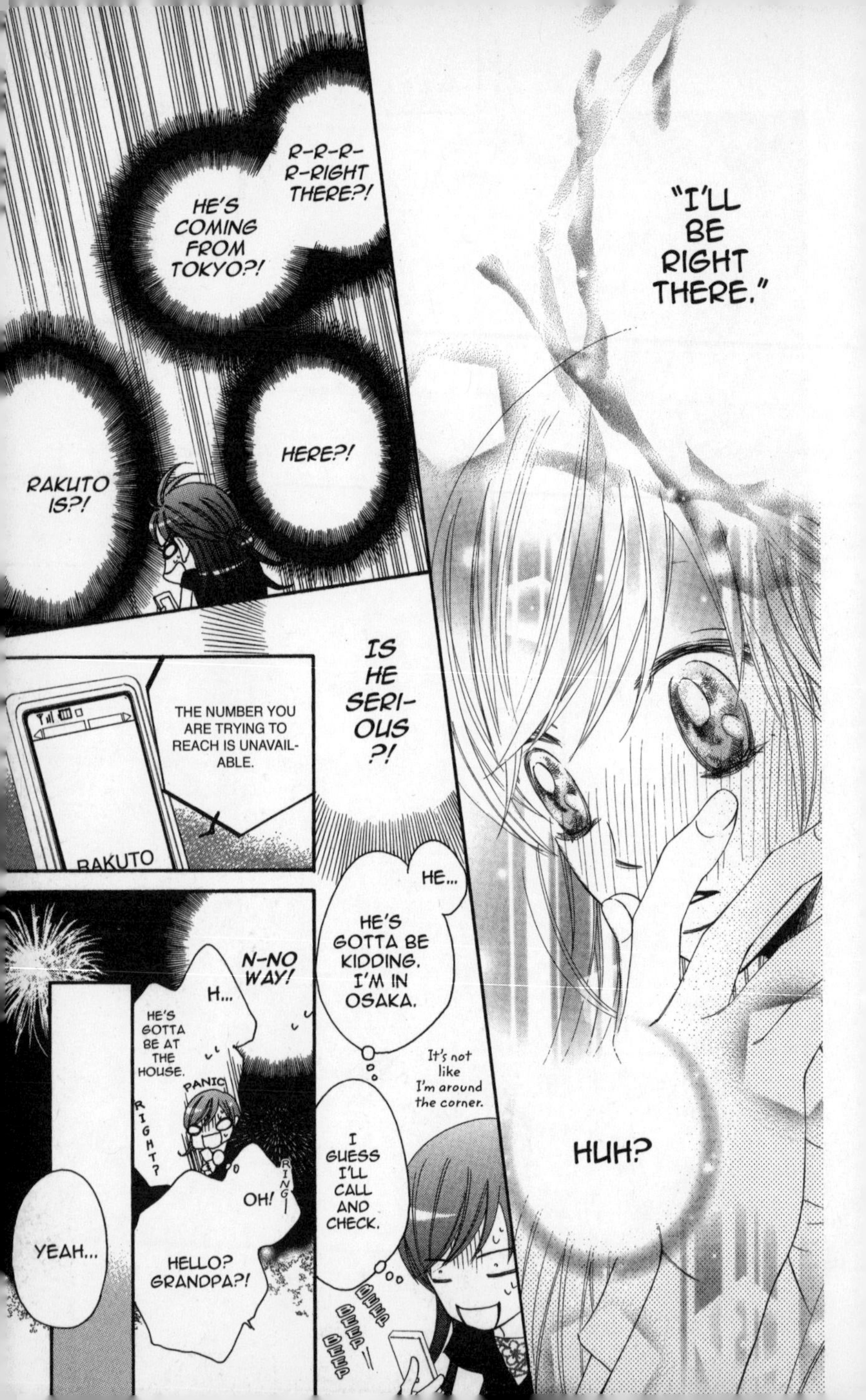
"I'LL BE RIGHT THERE."
HUH?
HE...
HE'S GOTTA BE KIDDING. I'M IN OSAKA.
It's not like I'm around the corner.
I GUESS I'LL CALL AND CHECK.
BEEP BEEP BEEP
R-R-R-R-RIGHT THERE?!
HE'S COMING FROM TOKYO?!
HERE?!
RAKUTO IS?!
IS HE SERI-OUS?!
THE NUMBER YOU ARE TRYING TO REACH IS UNAVAIL-ABLE.
RAKUTO
N-NO WAY!
H...
HE'S GOTTA BE AT THE HOUSE.
PANIC
RIGHT?
RING
OH!
HELLO? GRANDPA?!
YEAH...

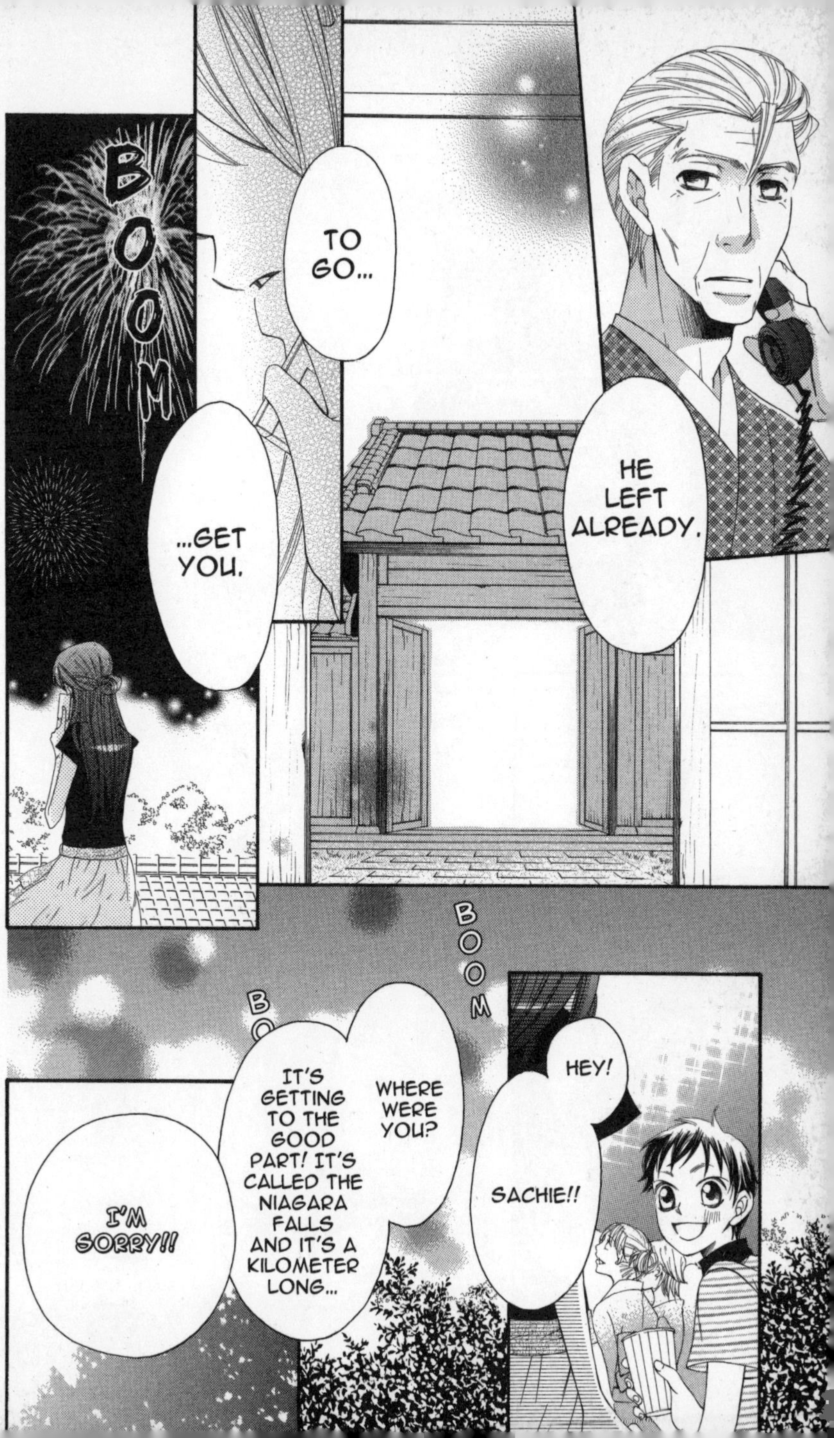
HE LEFT ALREADY.
TO GO...
...GET YOU.
BOOM
BOOM
HEY!
SACHIE!!
WHERE WERE YOU?
IT'S GETTING TO THE GOOD PART! IT'S CALLED THE NIAGARA FALLS AND IT'S A KILOMETER LONG...
I'M SORRY!!

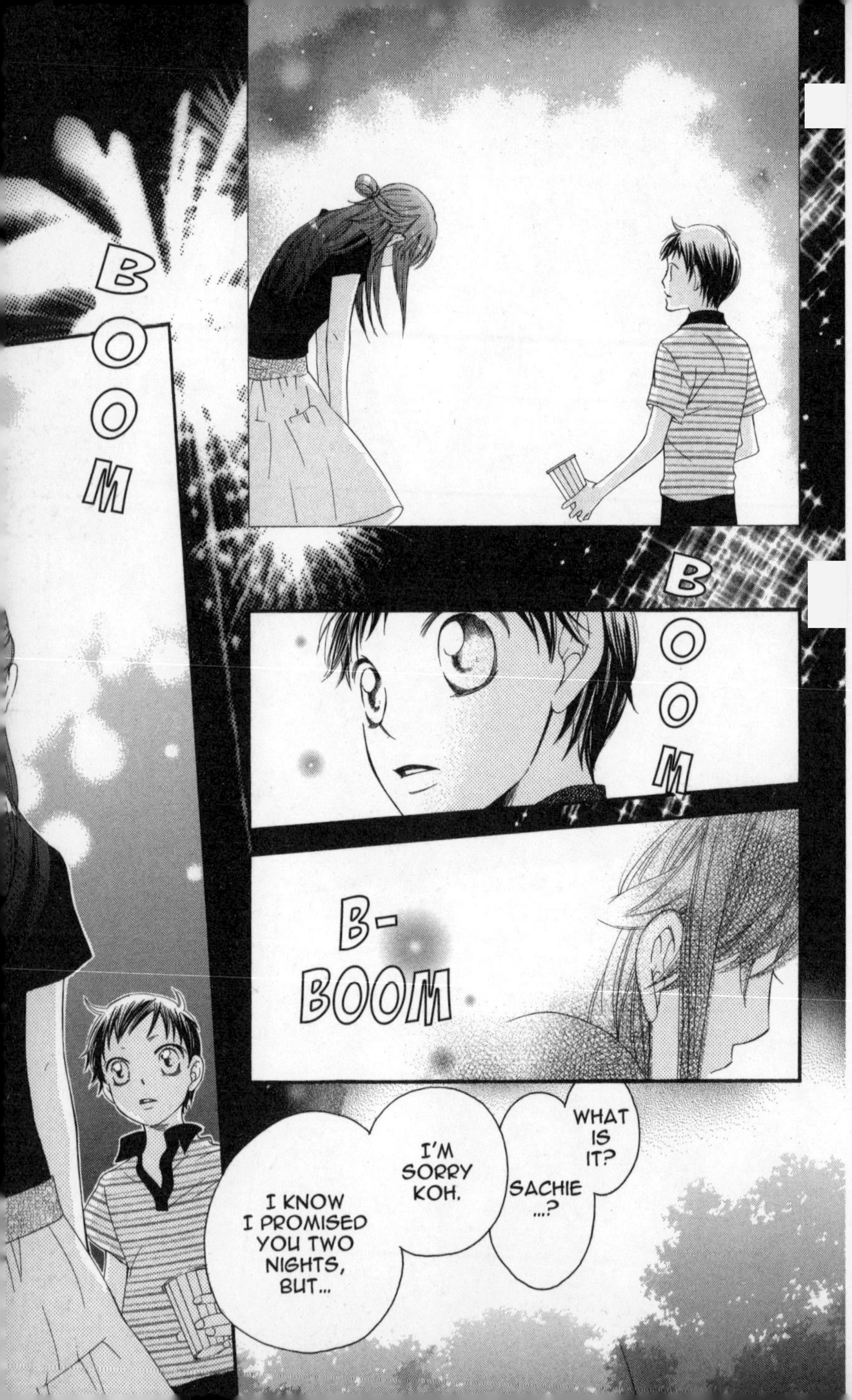
BOOM
B-BOOM
BOOM
WHAT IS IT?
SACHIE ...?
I'M SORRY KOH.
I KNOW I PROMISED YOU TWO NIGHTS, BUT...

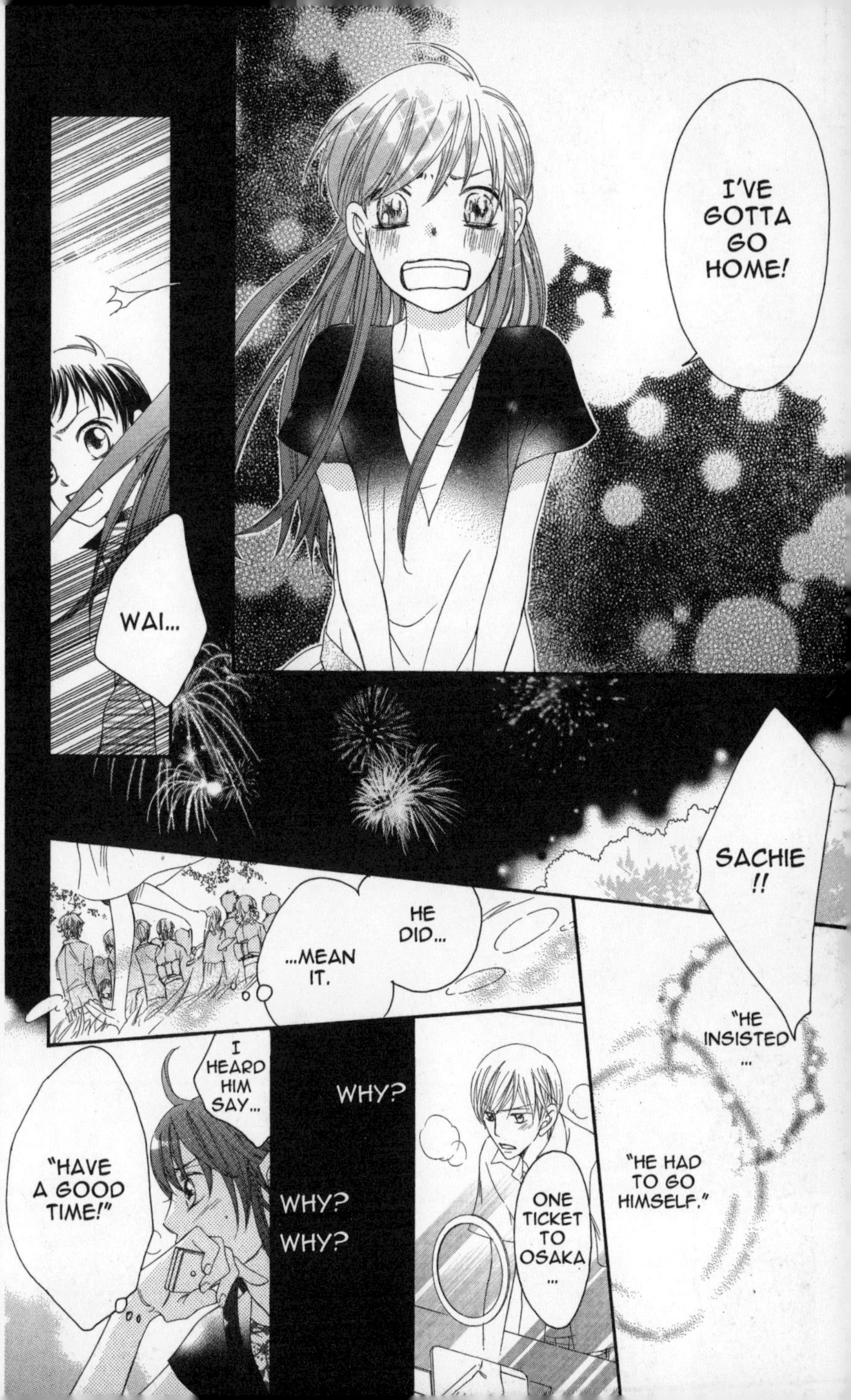
I'VE GOTTA GO HOME!
WAI...
SACHIE!!
HE DID... ...MEAN IT.
"HE INSISTED...
"HE HAD TO GO HIMSELF."
ONE TICKET TO OSAKA...
WHY?
WHY? WHY?
I HEARD HIM SAY...
"HAVE A GOOD TIME!"

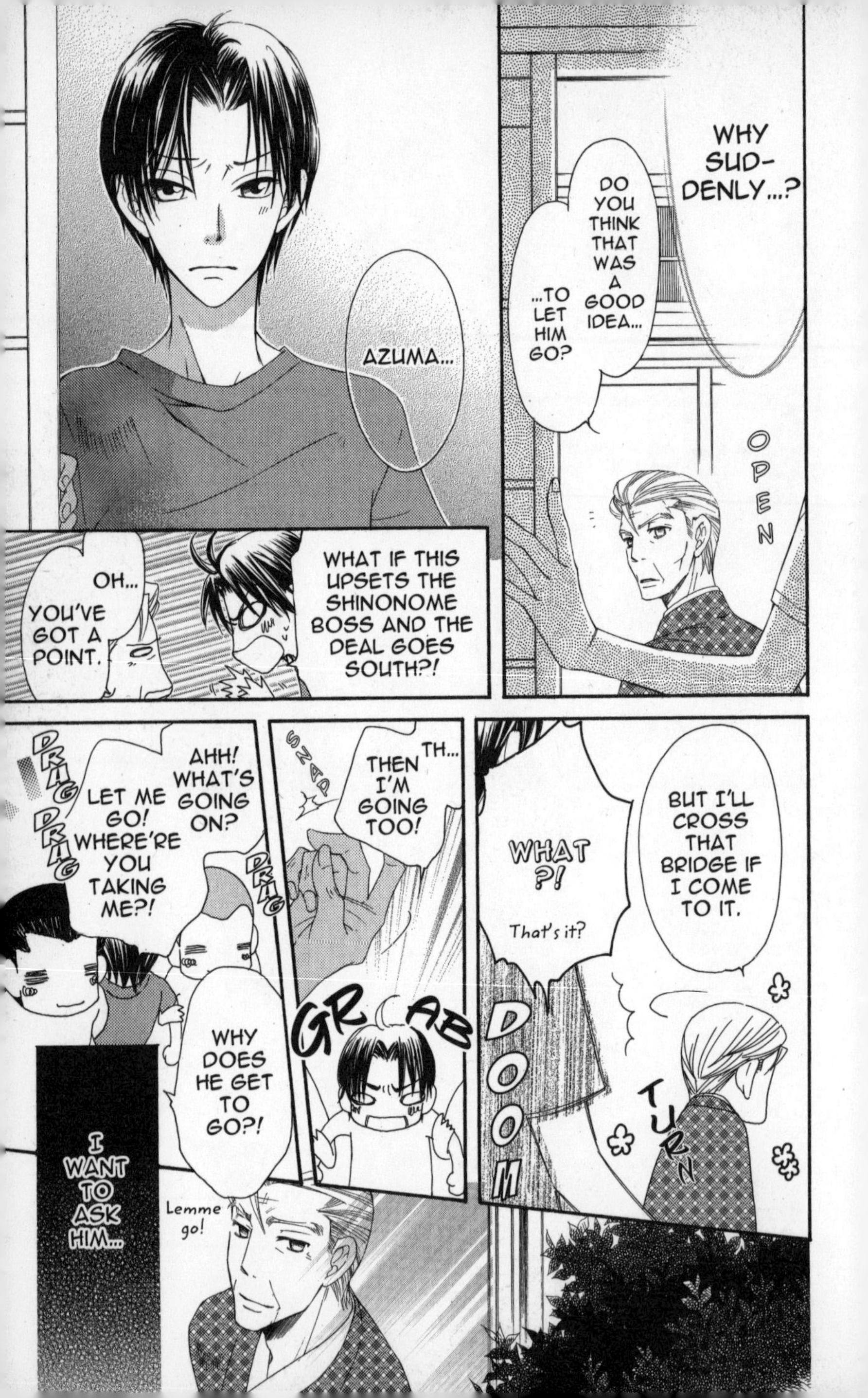

WHY SUDDENLY...?
DO YOU THINK THAT WAS A GOOD IDEA...
...TO LET HIM GO?
OPEN
AZUMA...
WHAT IF THIS UPSETS THE SHINONOME BOSS AND THE DEAL GOES SOUTH?!
OH... YOU'VE GOT A POINT.
BUT I'LL CROSS THAT BRIDGE IF I COME TO IT.
WHAT?!
That's it?
TURN
DOOM
TH...
THEN I'M GOING TOO!
SNAP
GRAB
WHY DOES HE GET TO GO?!
AHH! WHAT'S GOING ON?
LET ME GO! WHERE'RE YOU TAKING ME?!
DRAG DRAG
DRAG
I WANT TO ASK HIM...
Lemme go!

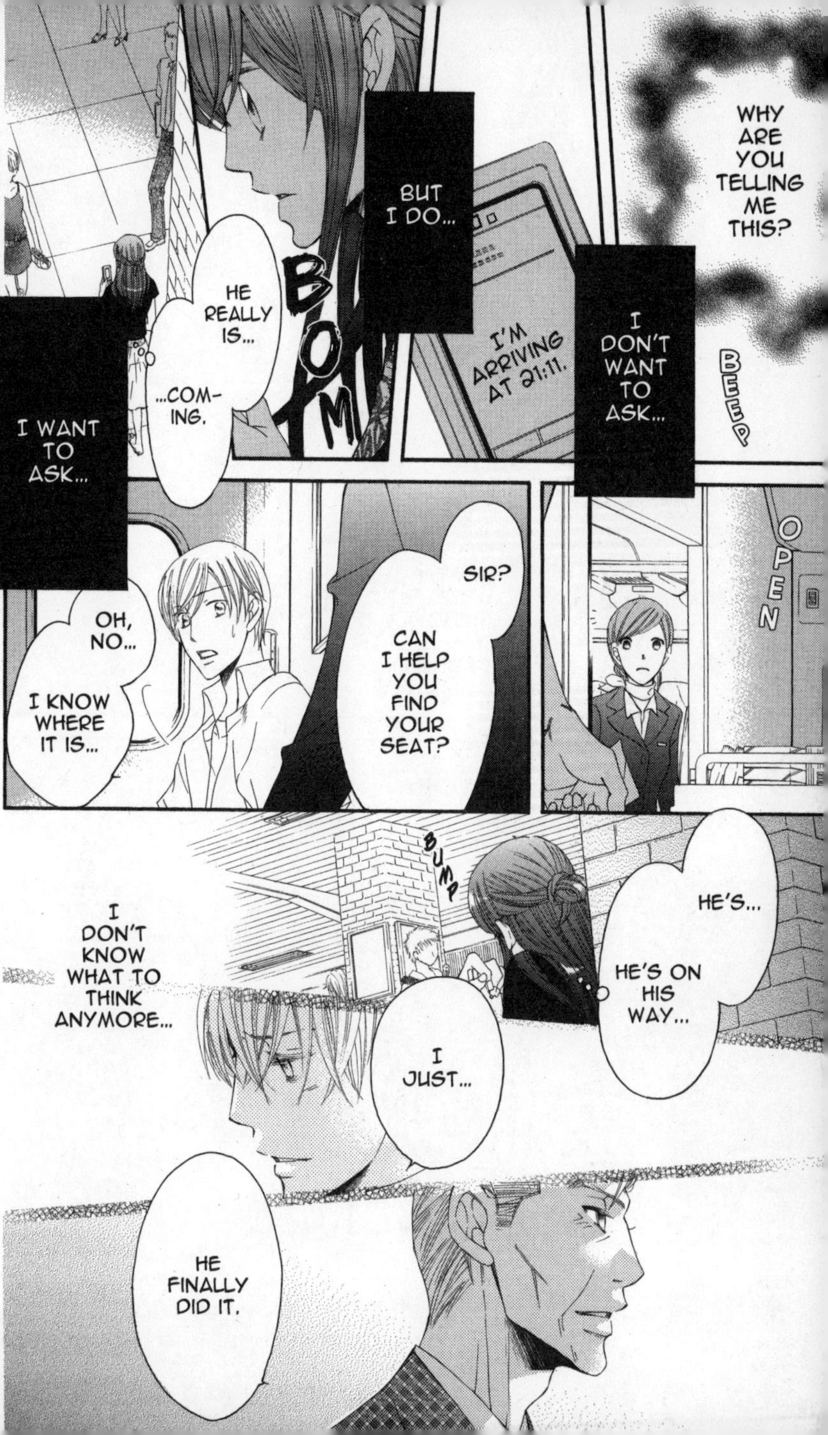
WHY ARE YOU TELLING ME THIS?
BEEP
I DON'T WANT TO ASK...
I'M ARRIVING AT 21:11.
BUT I DO...
BOOM
HE REALLY IS...
...COMING.
I WANT TO ASK...
OPEN
SIR?
CAN I HELP YOU FIND YOUR SEAT?
OH, NO...
I KNOW WHERE IT IS...
BUMP
HE'S...
HE'S ON HIS WAY...
I DON'T KNOW WHAT TO THINK ANYMORE...
I JUST...
HE FINALLY DID IT.

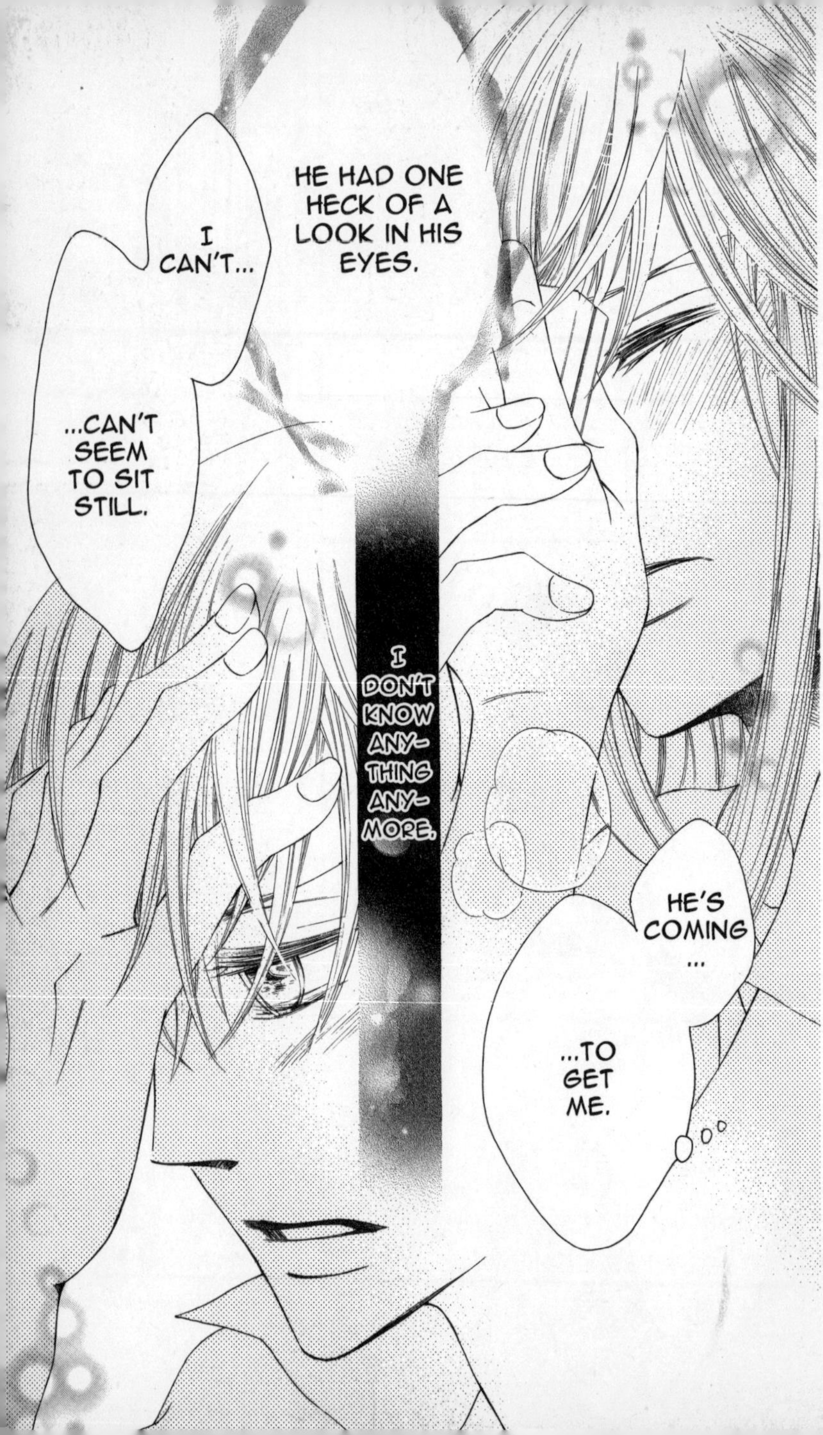
HE HAD ONE HECK OF A LOOK IN HIS EYES.
I CAN'T...
...CAN'T SEEM TO SIT STILL.
I DON'T KNOW ANY-THING ANY-MORE.
HE'S COMING...
...TO GET ME.

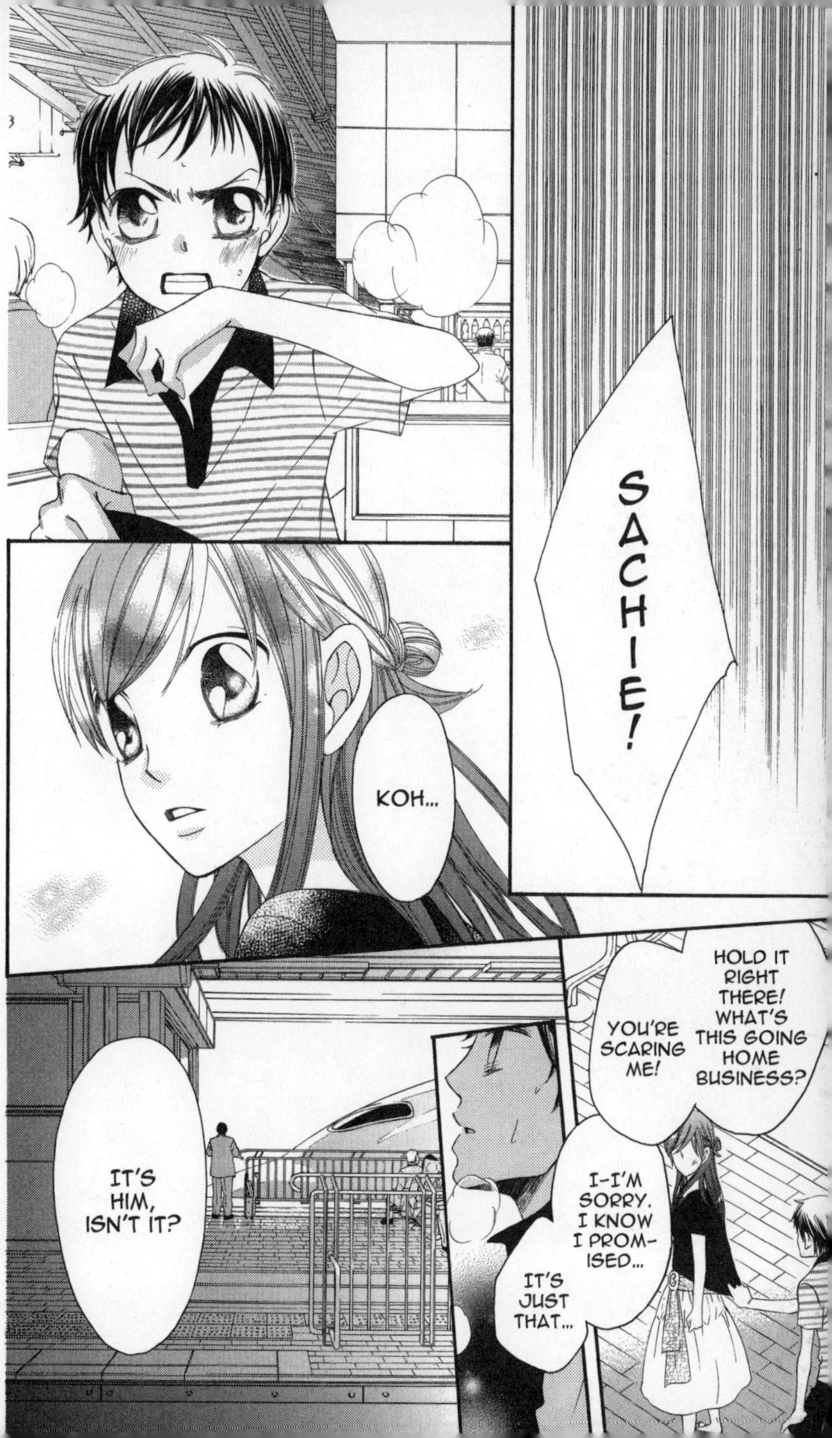
SACHIE!
KOH...
HOLD IT RIGHT THERE! WHAT'S THIS GOING HOME BUSINESS?
YOU'RE SCARING ME!
I-I'M SORRY. I KNOW I PROMISED...
IT'S JUST THAT...
IT'S HIM, ISN'T IT?

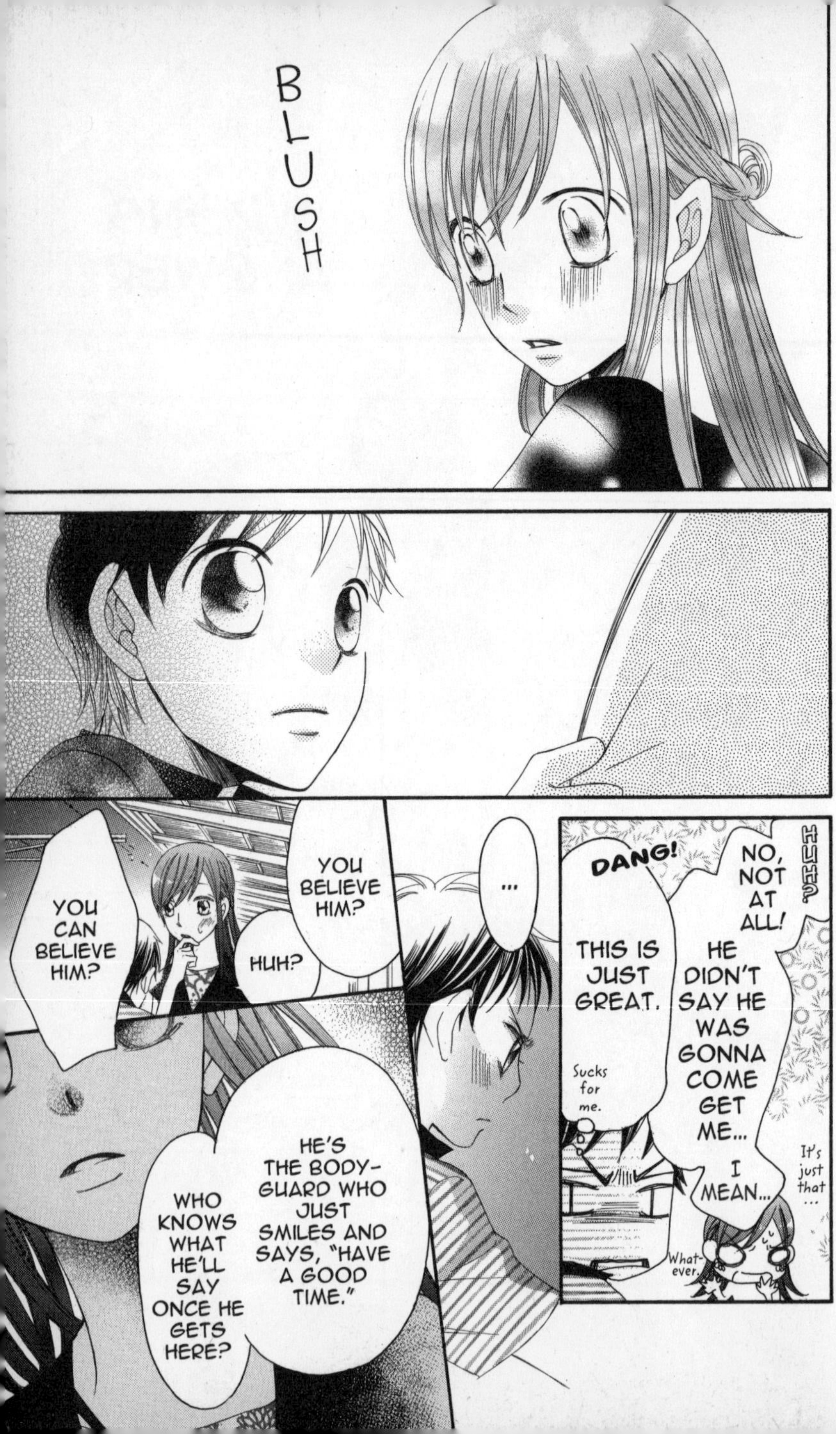
BLUSH
HUH,
NO, NOT AT ALL!
HE DIDN'T SAY HE WAS GONNA COME GET ME... I MEAN...
It's just that...
DANG!
THIS IS JUST GREAT.
Sucks for me.
Whatever.
...
YOU BELIEVE HIM?
HUH?
YOU CAN BELIEVE HIM?
HE'S THE BODY-GUARD WHO JUST SMILES AND SAYS, "HAVE A GOOD TIME."
WHO KNOWS WHAT HE'LL SAY ONCE HE GETS HERE?

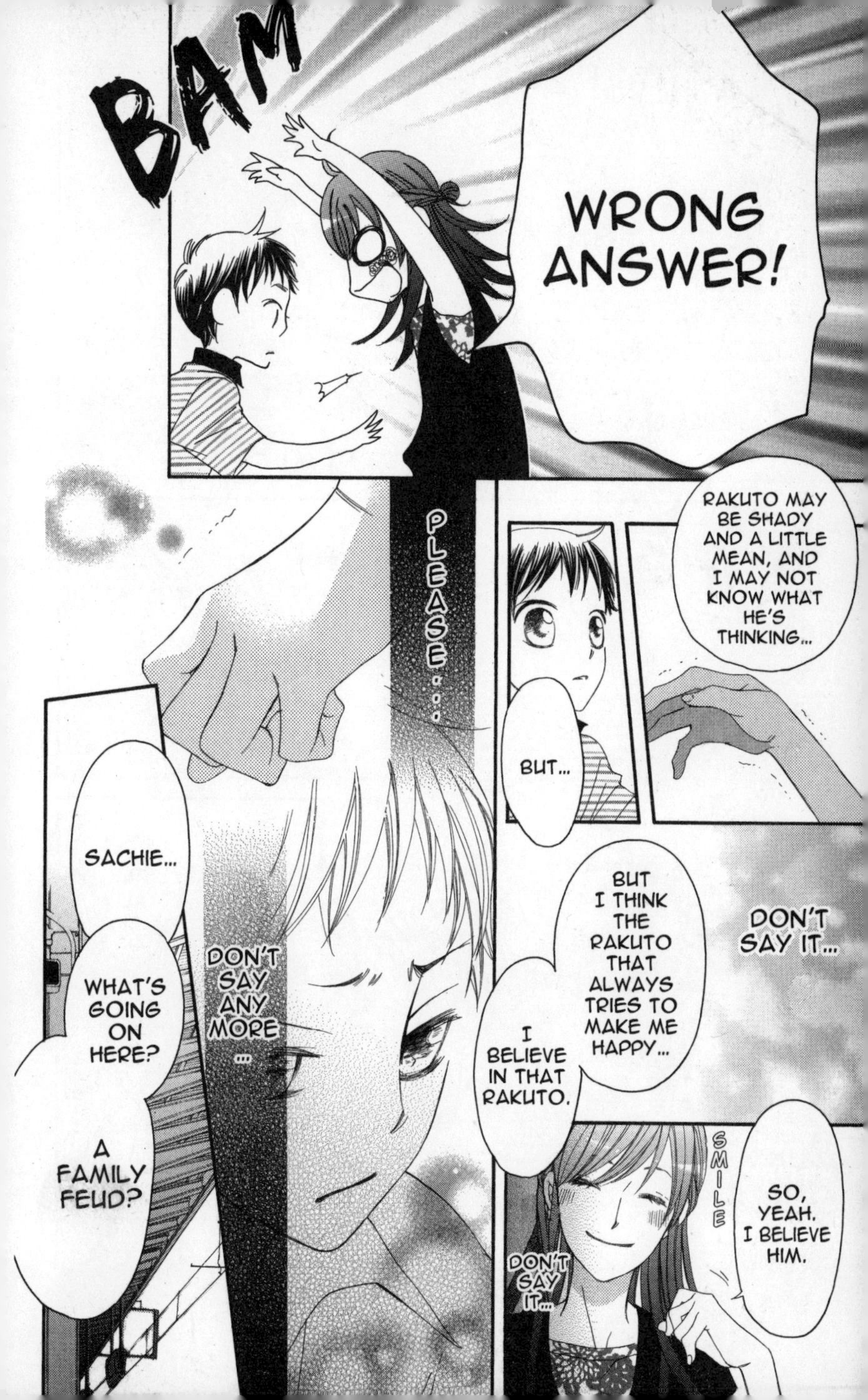
BAM
WRONG ANSWER!
RAKUTO MAY BE SHADY AND A LITTLE MEAN, AND I MAY NOT KNOW WHAT HE'S THINKING...
BUT...
PLEASE...
DON'T SAY IT...
BUT I THINK THE RAKUTO THAT ALWAYS TRIES TO MAKE ME HAPPY...
I BELIEVE IN THAT RAKUTO.
SMILE
SO, YEAH. I BELIEVE HIM.
DON'T SAY IT...
DON'T SAY ANY MORE...
SACHIE...
WHAT'S GOING ON HERE?
A FAMILY FEUD?

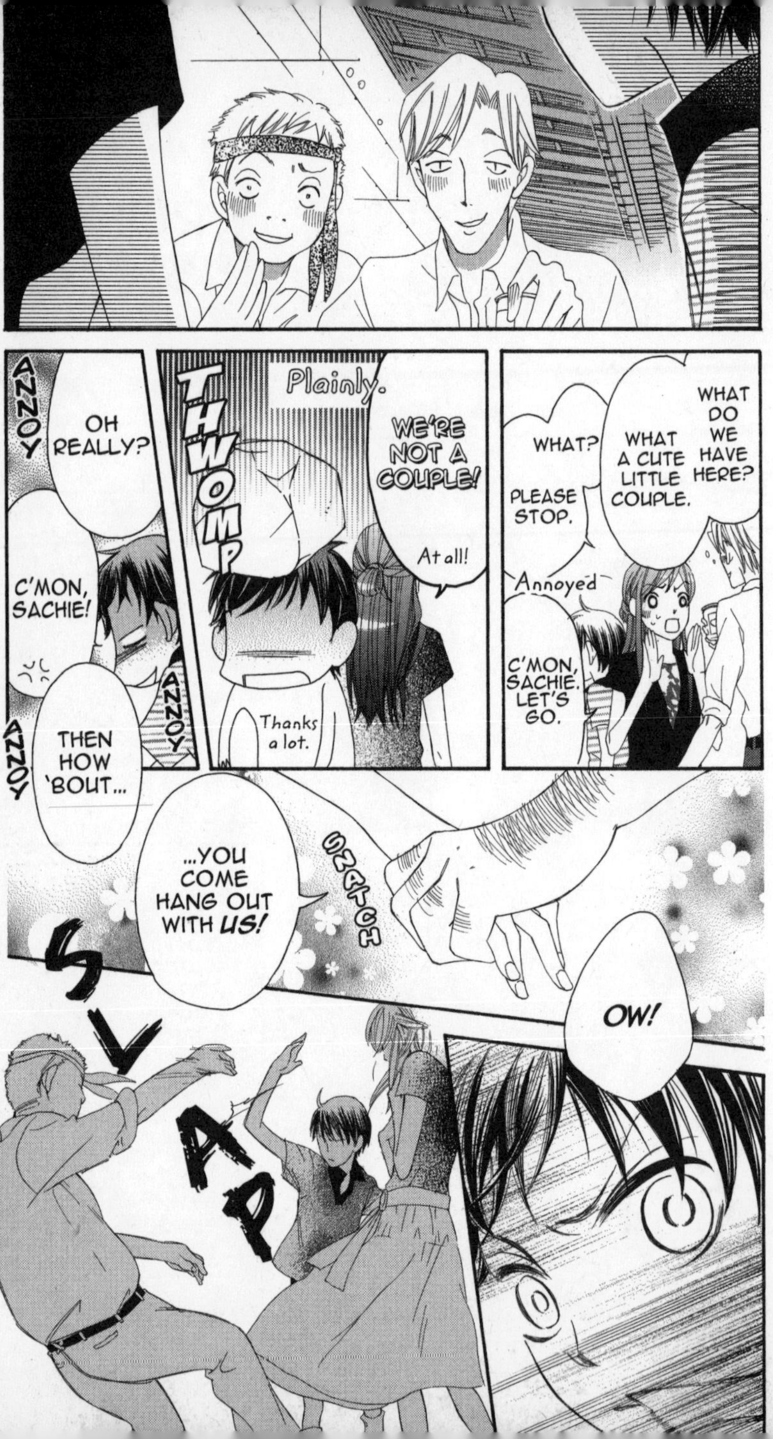
WHAT DO WE HAVE HERE?
WHAT A CUTE LITTLE COUPLE.
WHAT? PLEASE STOP.
Annoyed
C'MON, SACHIE. LET'S GO.
Plainly.
WE'RE NOT A COUPLE!
At all!
THWOMP
Thanks a lot.
ANNOY
OH REALLY?
C'MON, SACHIE!
ANNOY
THEN HOW 'BOUT...
ANNOY
...YOU COME HANG OUT WITH US!
SNATCH
OW!
SVAP

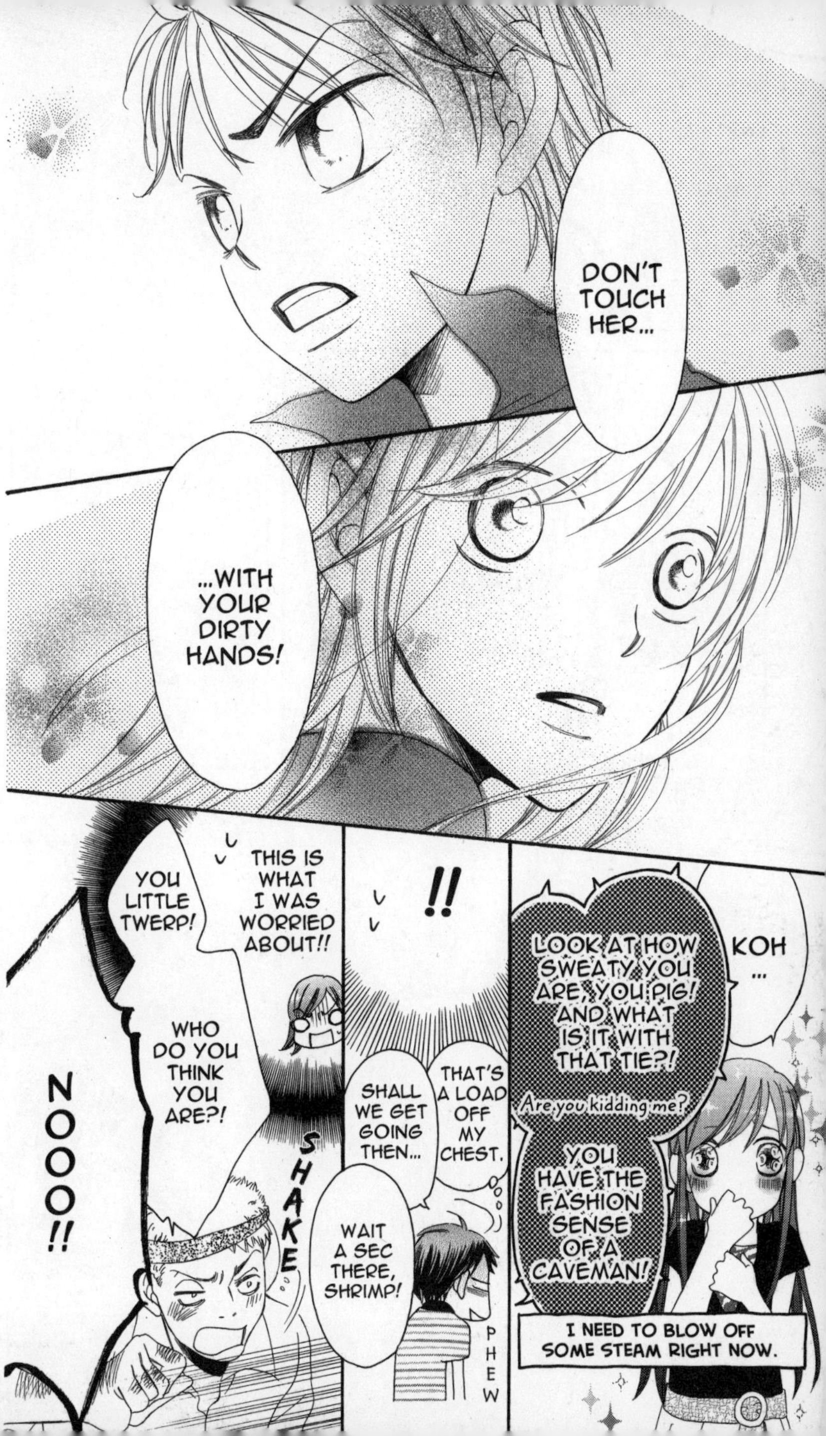
DON'T TOUCH HER...
...WITH YOUR DIRTY HANDS!
KOH...
LOOK AT HOW SWEATY YOU ARE, YOU PIG! AND WHAT IS IT WITH THAT TIE?!
Are you kidding me?
YOU HAVE THE FASHION SENSE OF A CAVEMAN!
I NEED TO BLOW OFF SOME STEAM RIGHT NOW.
!!
THAT'S A LOAD OFF MY CHEST.
SHALL WE GET GOING THEN...
WAIT A SEC THERE, SHRIMP!
PHEW
THIS IS WHAT I WAS WORRIED ABOUT!!
YOU LITTLE TWERP!
WHO DO YOU THINK YOU ARE?!
SHAKE
NOOOO!!

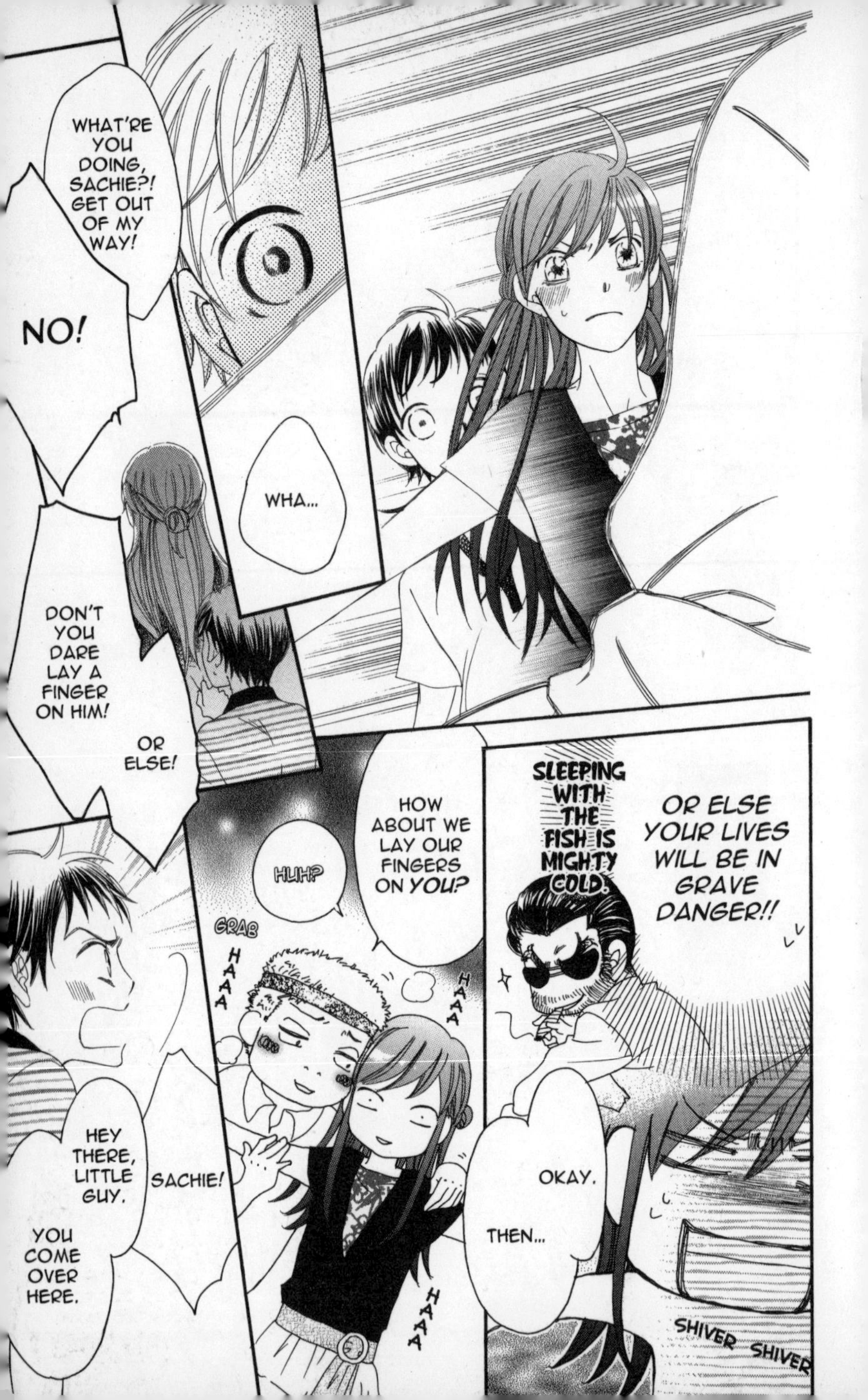
WHA...
WHAT'RE YOU DOING, SACHIE?! GET OUT OF MY WAY!
NO!
DON'T YOU DARE LAY A FINGER ON HIM!
OR ELSE!
OR ELSE YOUR LIVES WILL BE IN GRAVE DANGER!!
SLEEPING WITH THE FISH IS MIGHTY COLD.
OKAY.
THEN...
SHIVER SHIVER
HOW ABOUT WE LAY OUR FINGERS ON YOU?
HUH?
GRAB
HAAA
HAAA
HAAA
SACHIE!
HEY THERE, LITTLE GUY.
YOU COME OVER HERE.

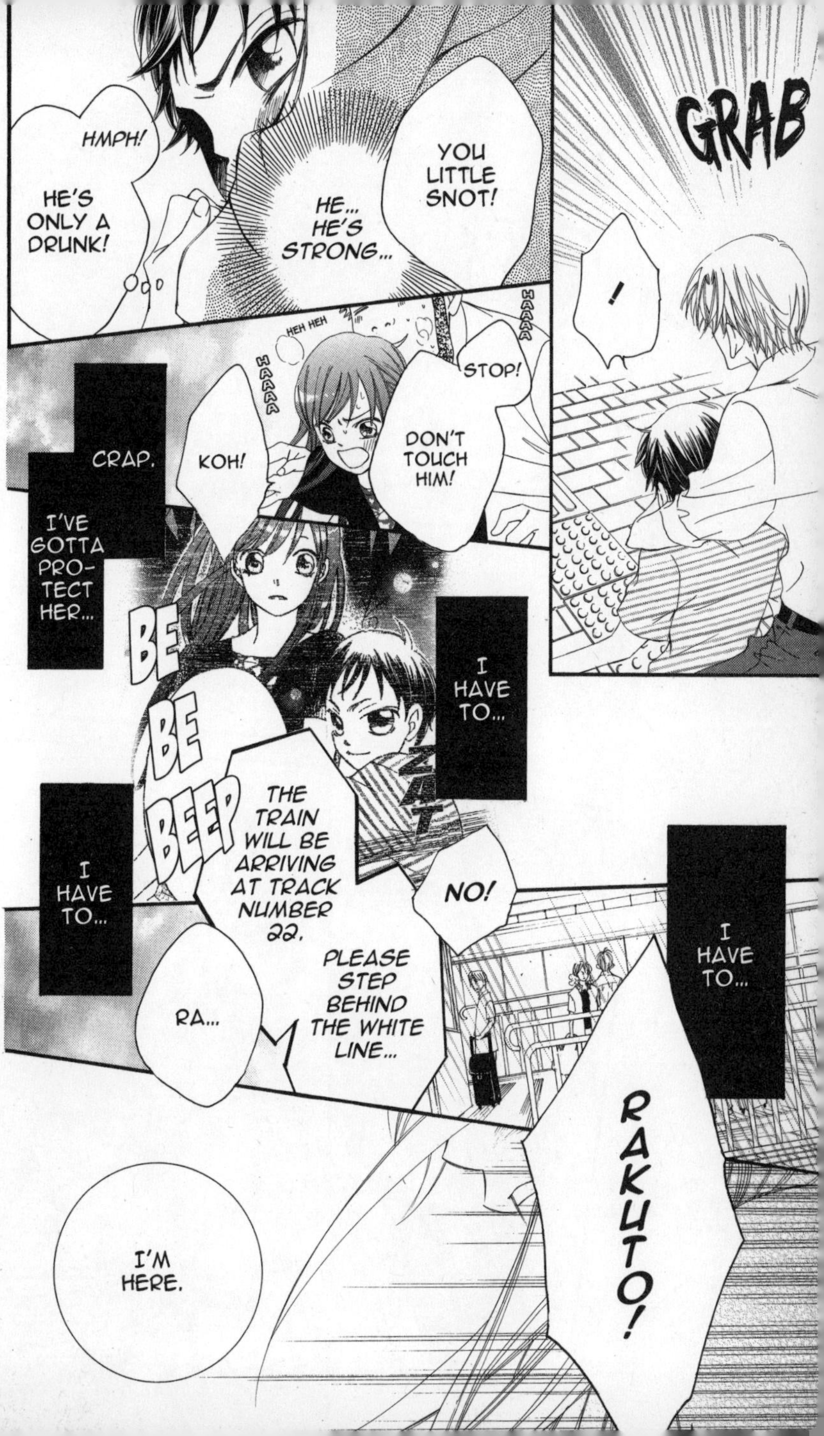
GRAB
!
YOU LITTLE SNOT!
HE... HE'S STRONG...
HMPH!
HE'S ONLY A DRUNK!
HAAAA
HEH HEH
STOP!
DON'T TOUCH HIM!
HAAAA
KOH!
CRAP.
I'VE GOTTA PROTECT HER...
I HAVE TO...
ZAT
THE TRAIN WILL BE ARRIVING AT TRACK NUMBER 22.
BE BE BEEP
NO!
I HAVE TO...
I HAVE TO...
PLEASE STEP BEHIND THE WHITE LINE...
RA...
RAKUTO!
I'M HERE.

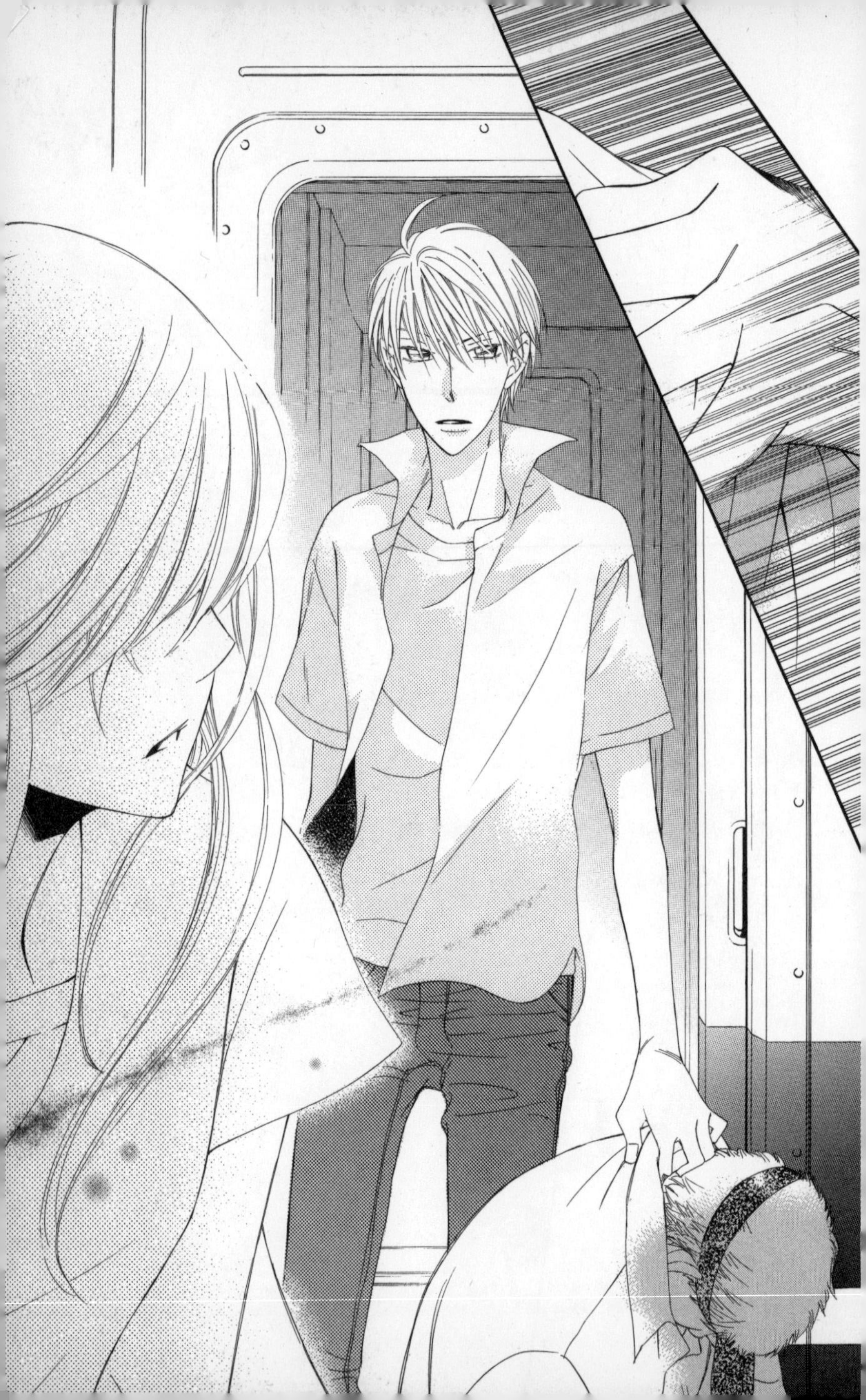

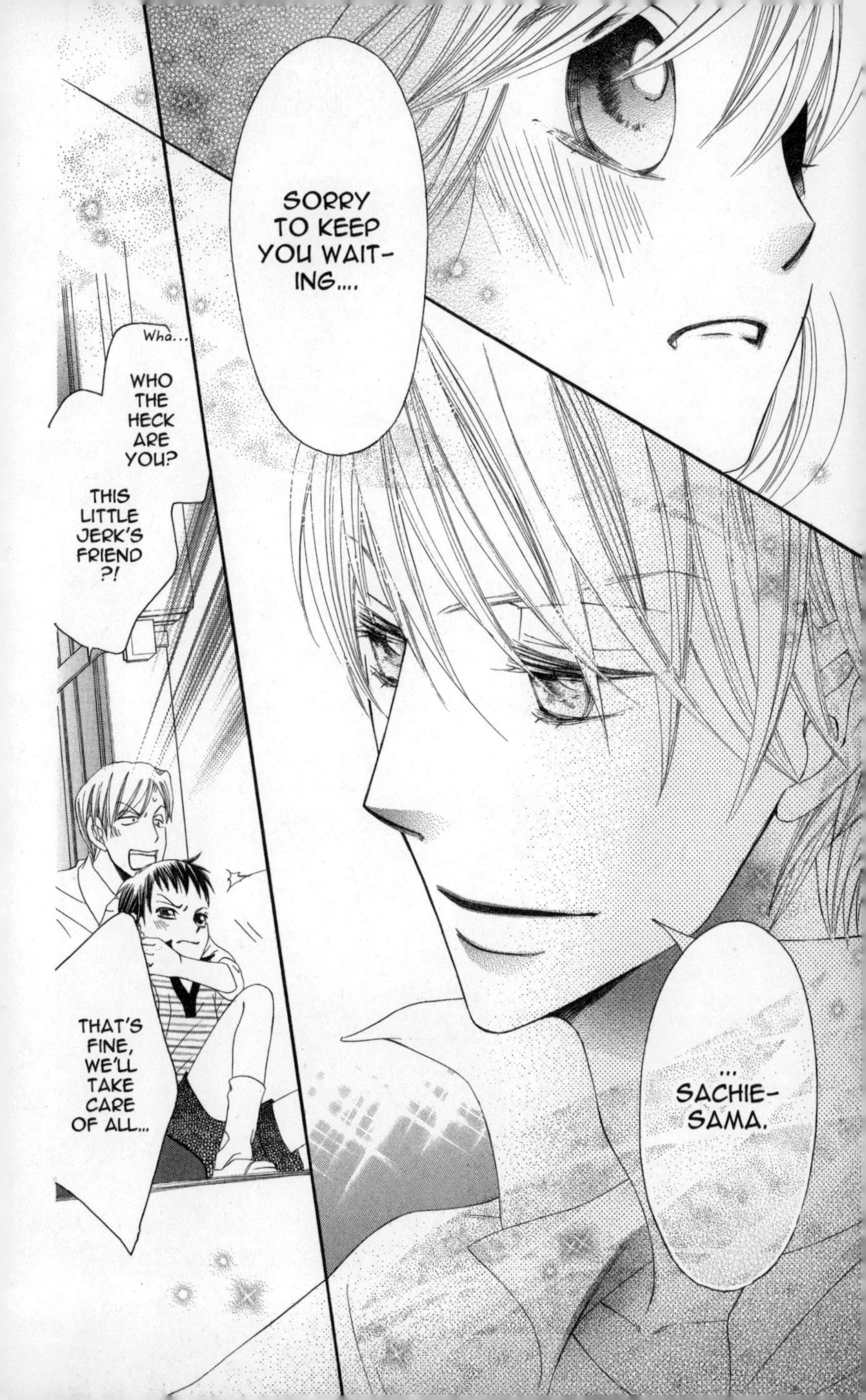
SORRY TO KEEP YOU WAIT-ING....
... SACHIE-SAMA.
Wha...
WHO THE HECK ARE YOU?
THIS LITTLE JERK'S FRIEND ?!
THAT'S FINE, WE'LL TAKE CARE OF ALL...

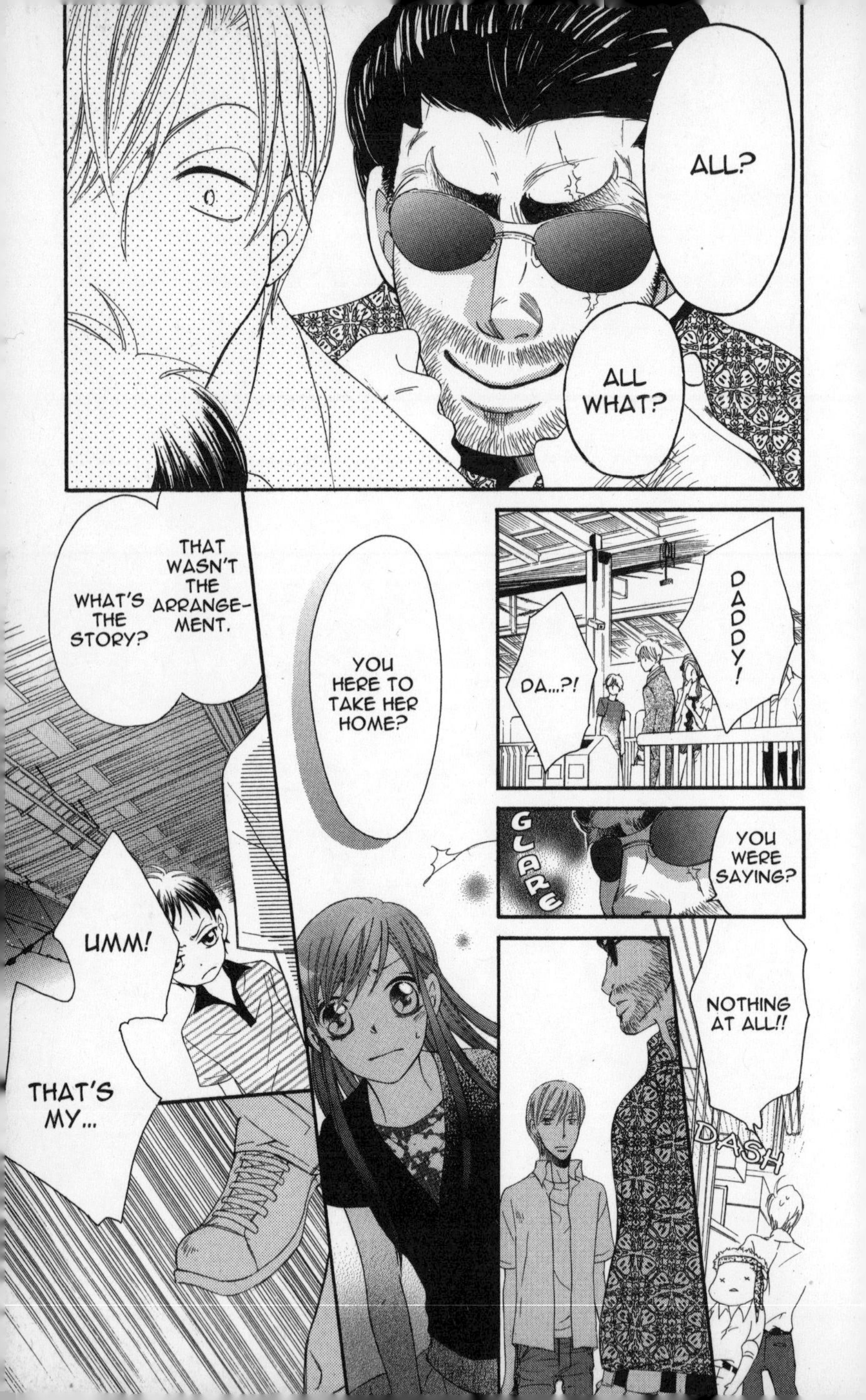
ALL?
ALL WHAT?
DADDY!
DA...?!
GLARE
YOU WERE SAYING?
NOTHING AT ALL!!
DASH
YOU HERE TO TAKE HER HOME?
THAT WASN'T THE ARRANGE-MENT.
WHAT'S THE STORY?
UMM!
THAT'S MY...

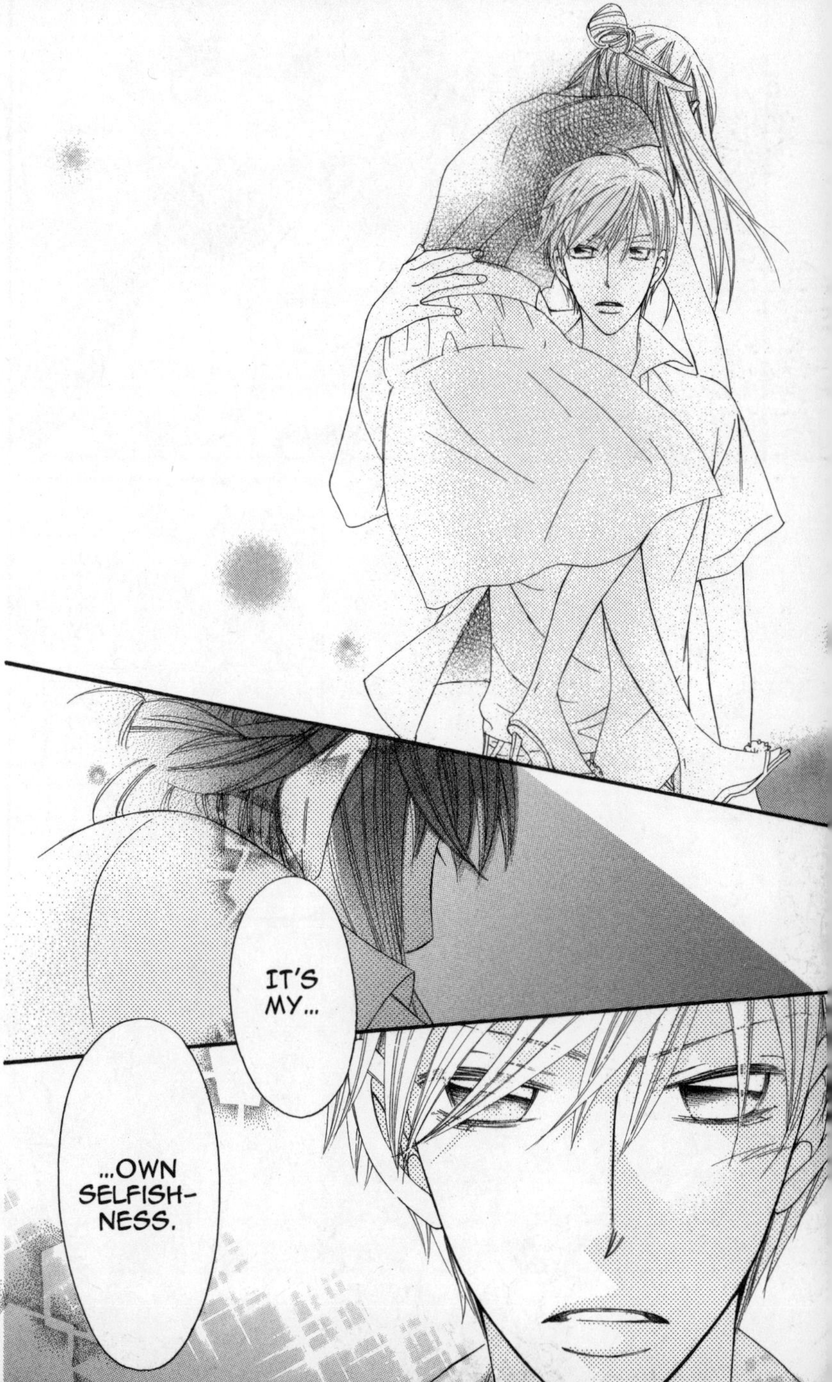
IT'S MY...
...OWN SELFISH-NESS.

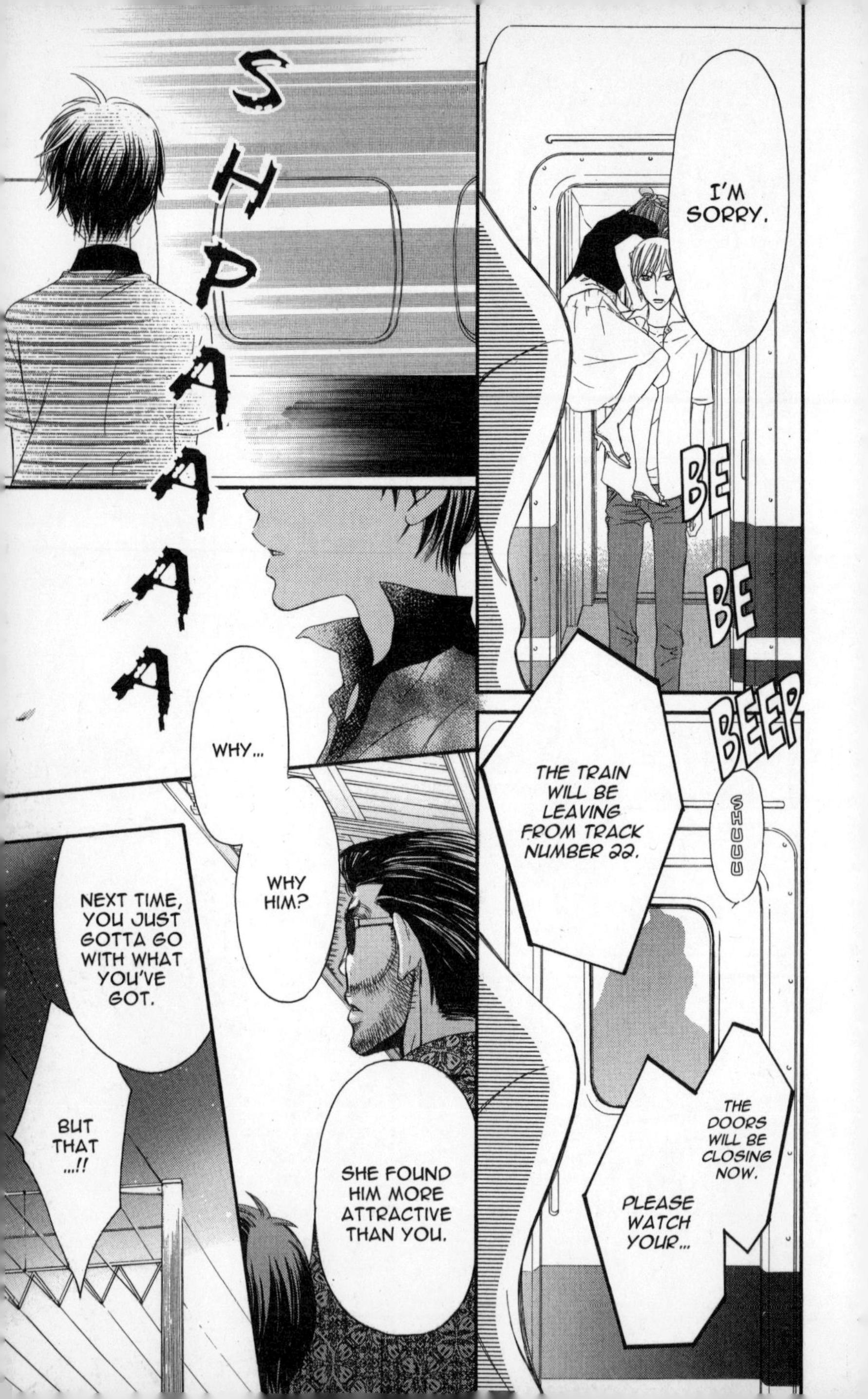
I'M SORRY.
BE
BE
BEEP
THE TRAIN WILL BE LEAVING FROM TRACK NUMBER 22.
SHUUUU
THE DOORS WILL BE CLOSING NOW.
PLEASE WATCH YOUR...
SHPAAAAA
WHY...
WHY HIM?
SHE FOUND HIM MORE ATTRACTIVE THAN YOU.
NEXT TIME, YOU JUST GOTTA GO WITH WHAT YOU'VE GOT.
BUT THAT ...!!

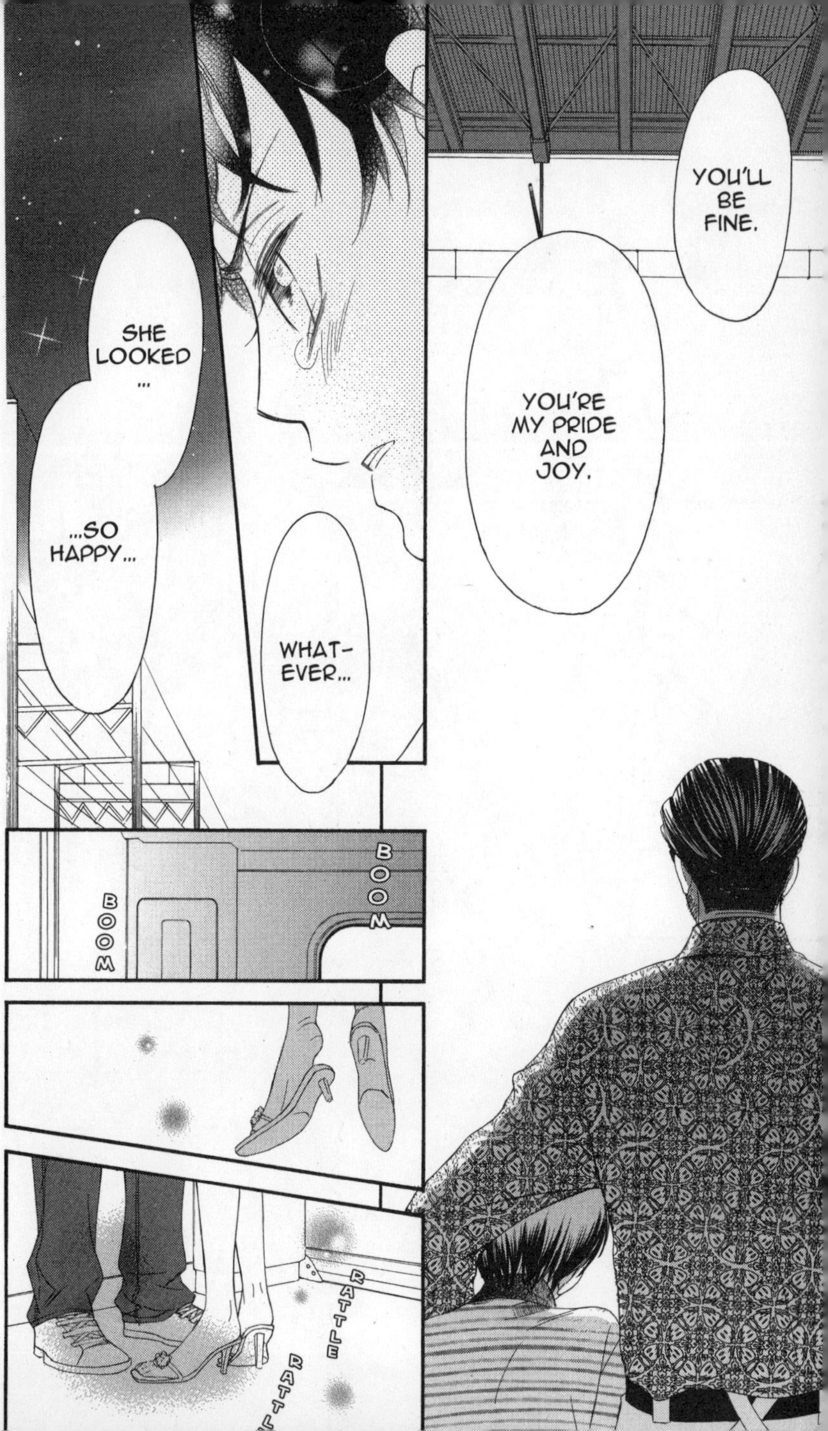
YOU'LL BE FINE.
YOU'RE MY PRIDE AND JOY.
SHE LOOKED ...
...SO HAPPY...
WHAT-EVER...
BOOM
BOOM
RATTLE
RATTLE

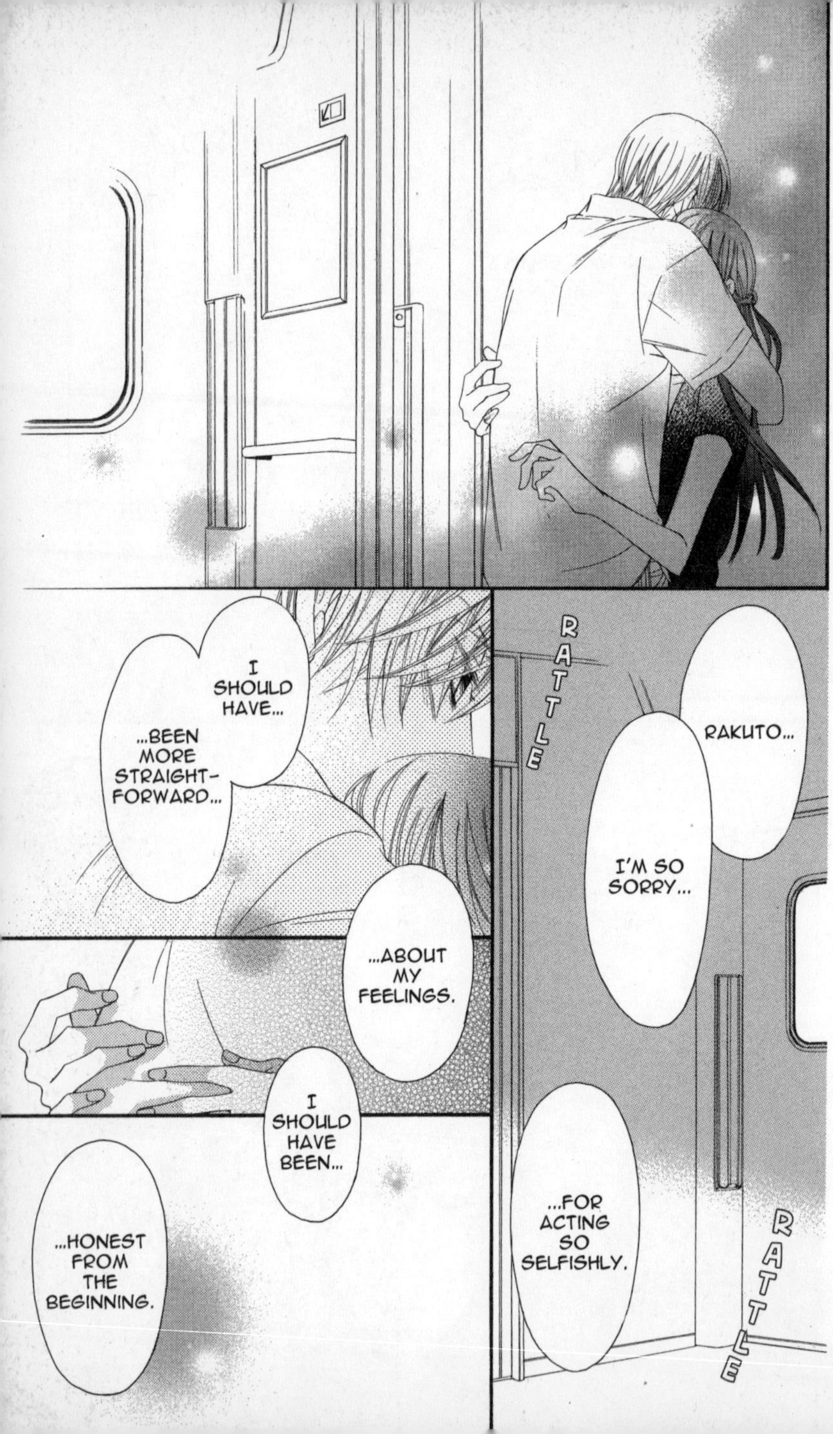
RAKUTO...
RATTLE
I'M SO SORRY...
...FOR ACTING SO SELFISHLY.
RATTLE
I SHOULD HAVE...
...BEEN MORE STRAIGHT-FORWARD...
...ABOUT MY FEELINGS.
I SHOULD HAVE BEEN...
...HONEST FROM THE BEGINNING.

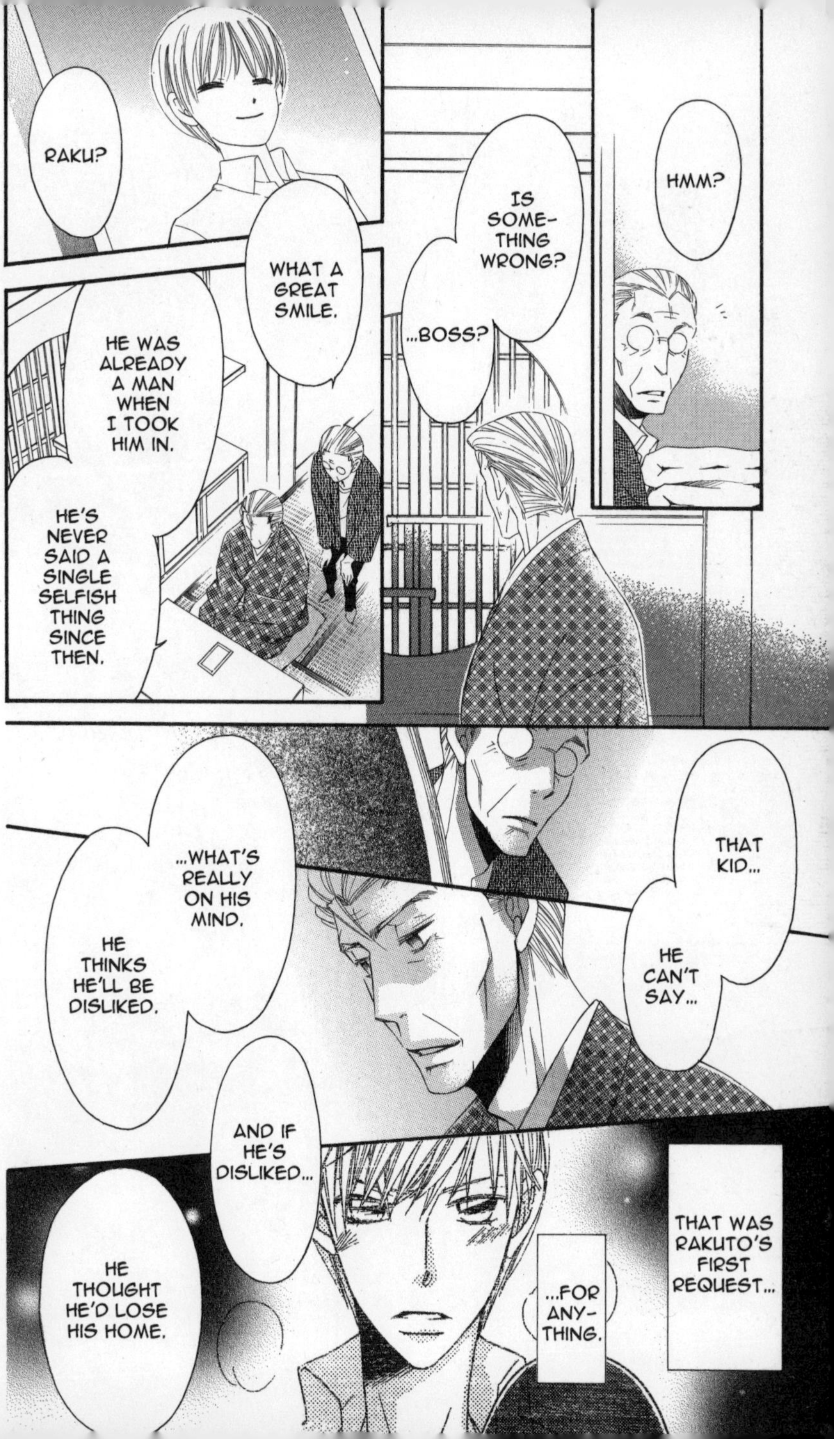
HMM?
IS SOMETHING WRONG?
...BOSS?
RAKU?
WHAT A GREAT SMILE.
HE WAS ALREADY A MAN WHEN I TOOK HIM IN.
HE'S NEVER SAID A SINGLE SELFISH THING SINCE THEN.
THAT KID...
HE CAN'T SAY...
...WHAT'S REALLY ON HIS MIND.
HE THINKS HE'LL BE DISLIKED.
AND IF HE'S DISLIKED...
HE THOUGHT HE'D LOSE HIS HOME.
THAT WAS RAKUTO'S FIRST REQUEST...
...FOR ANYTHING.

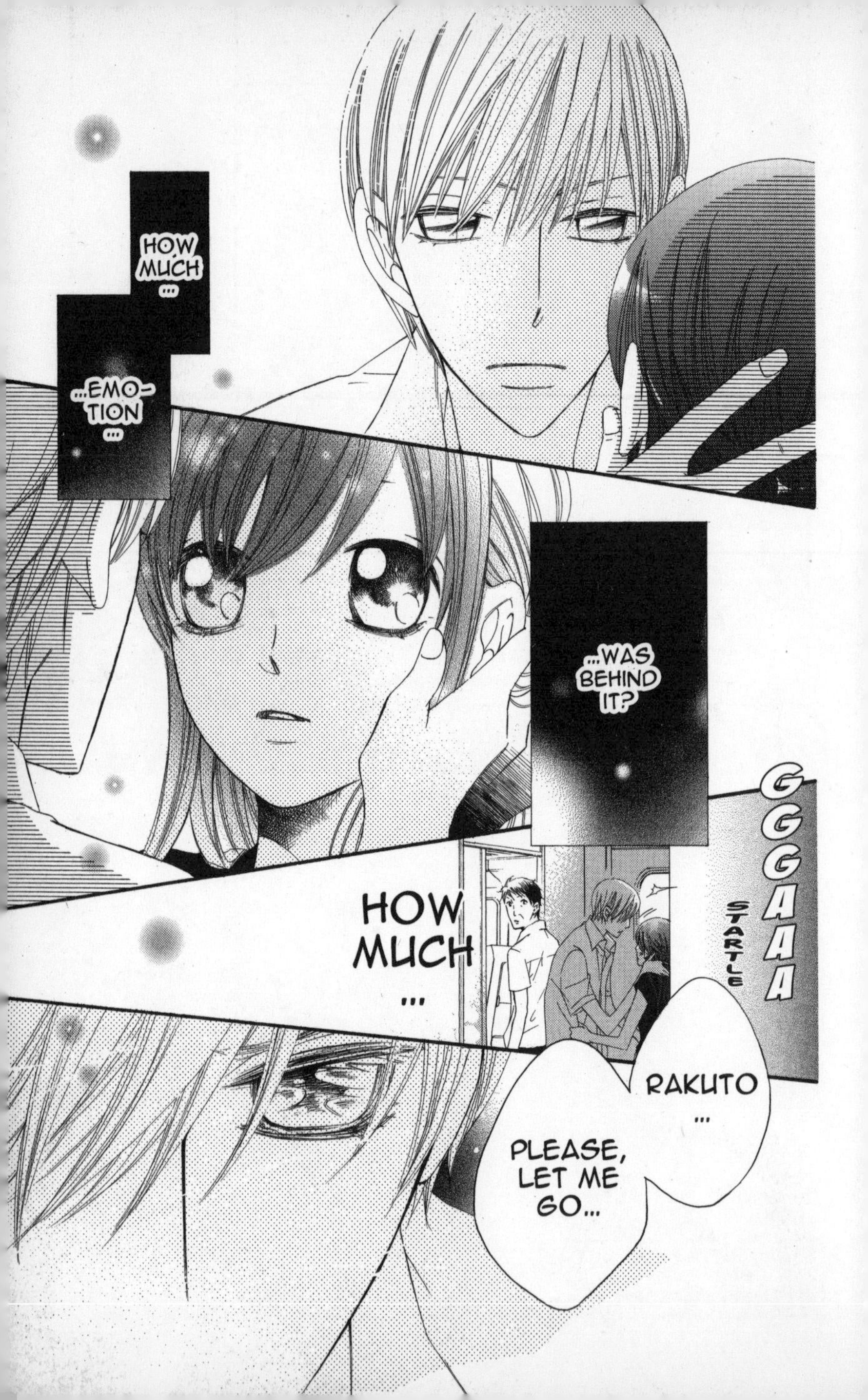
HOW MUCH ...
...EMO-TION ...
...WAS BEHIND IT?
GGGAAA
STARTLE
HOW MUCH ...
RAKUTO ...
PLEASE, LET ME GO...

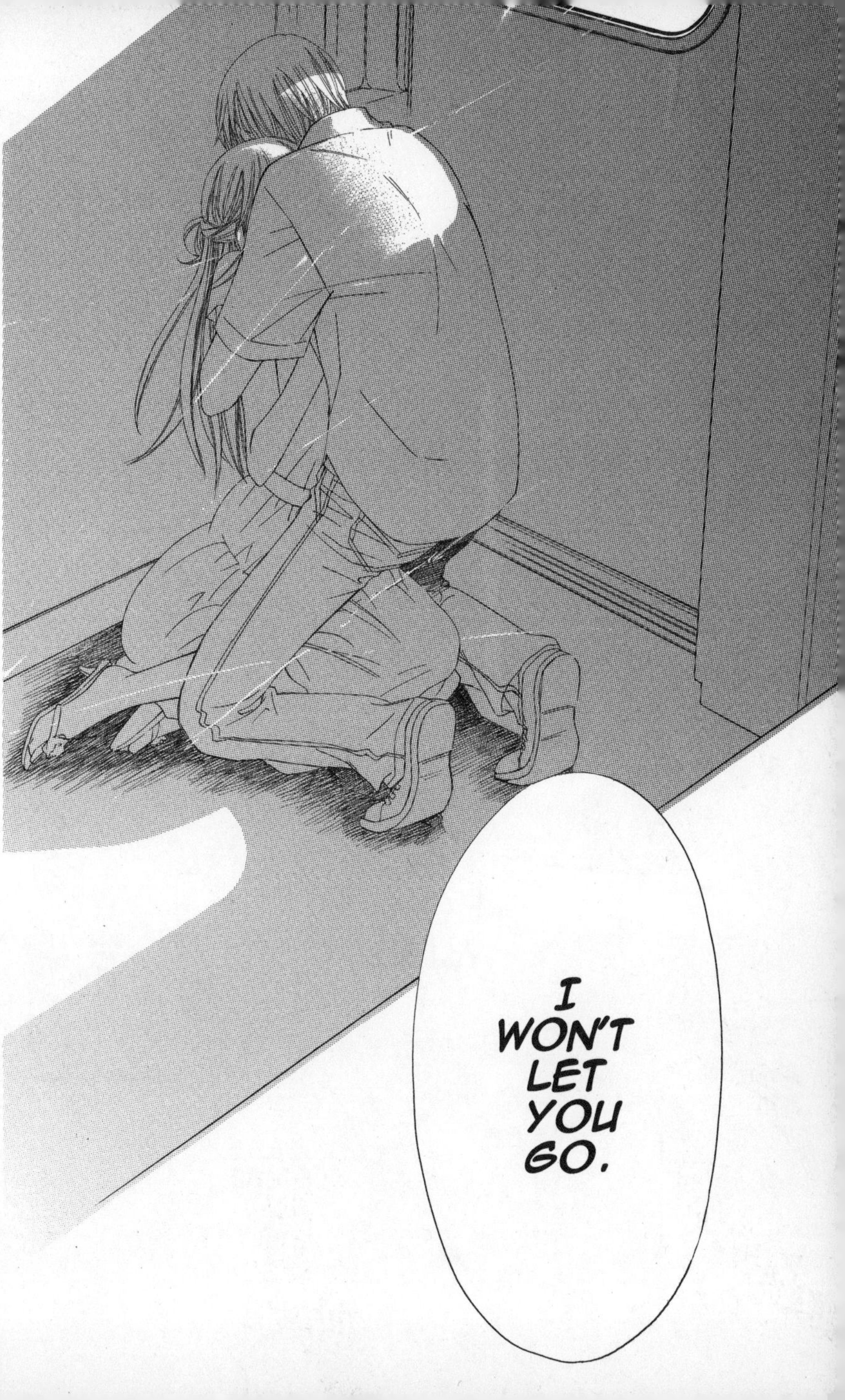
I WON'T LET YOU GO.

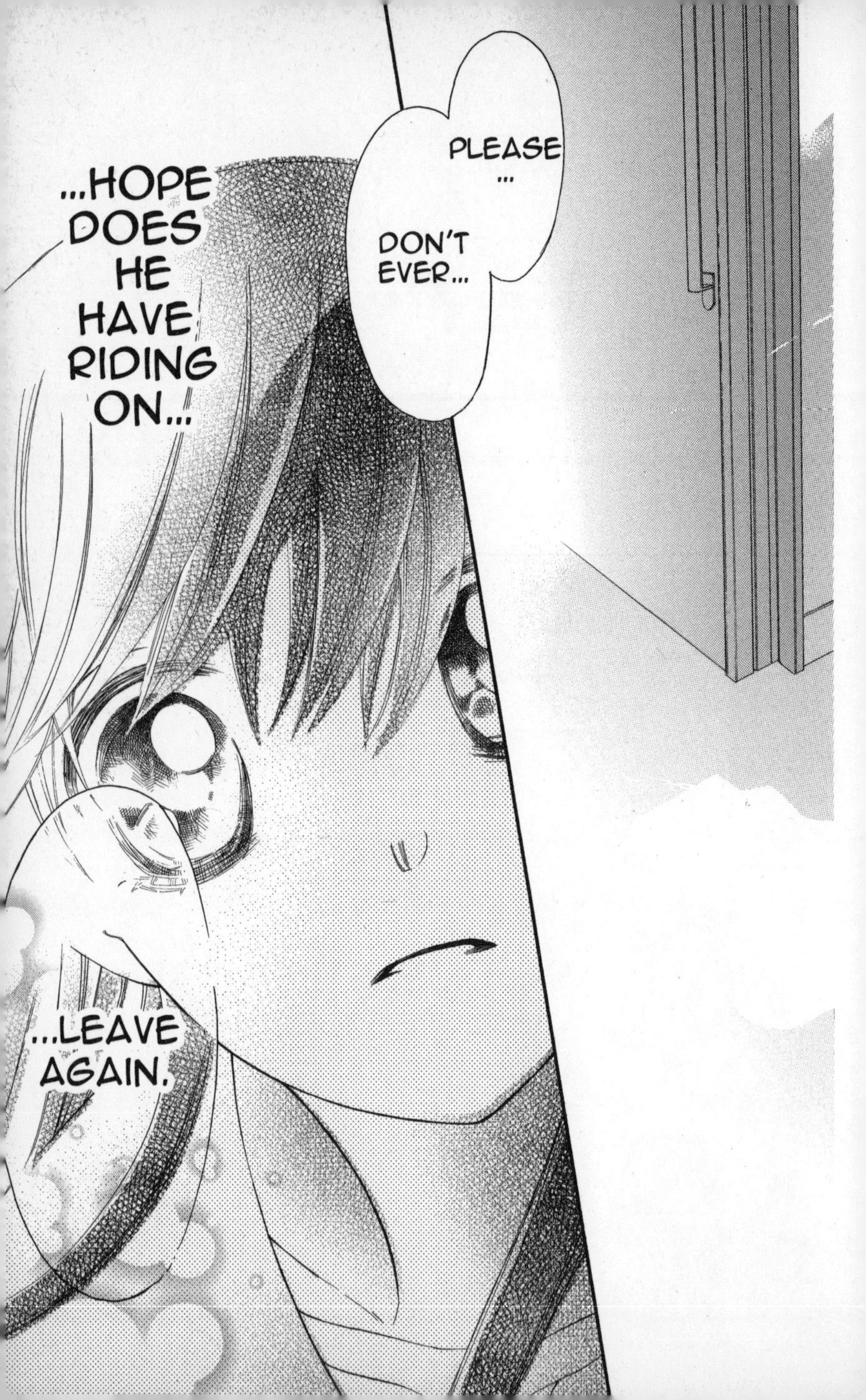
PLEASE ...
DON'T EVER...
...HOPE DOES HE HAVE RIDING ON...
...LEAVE AGAIN.

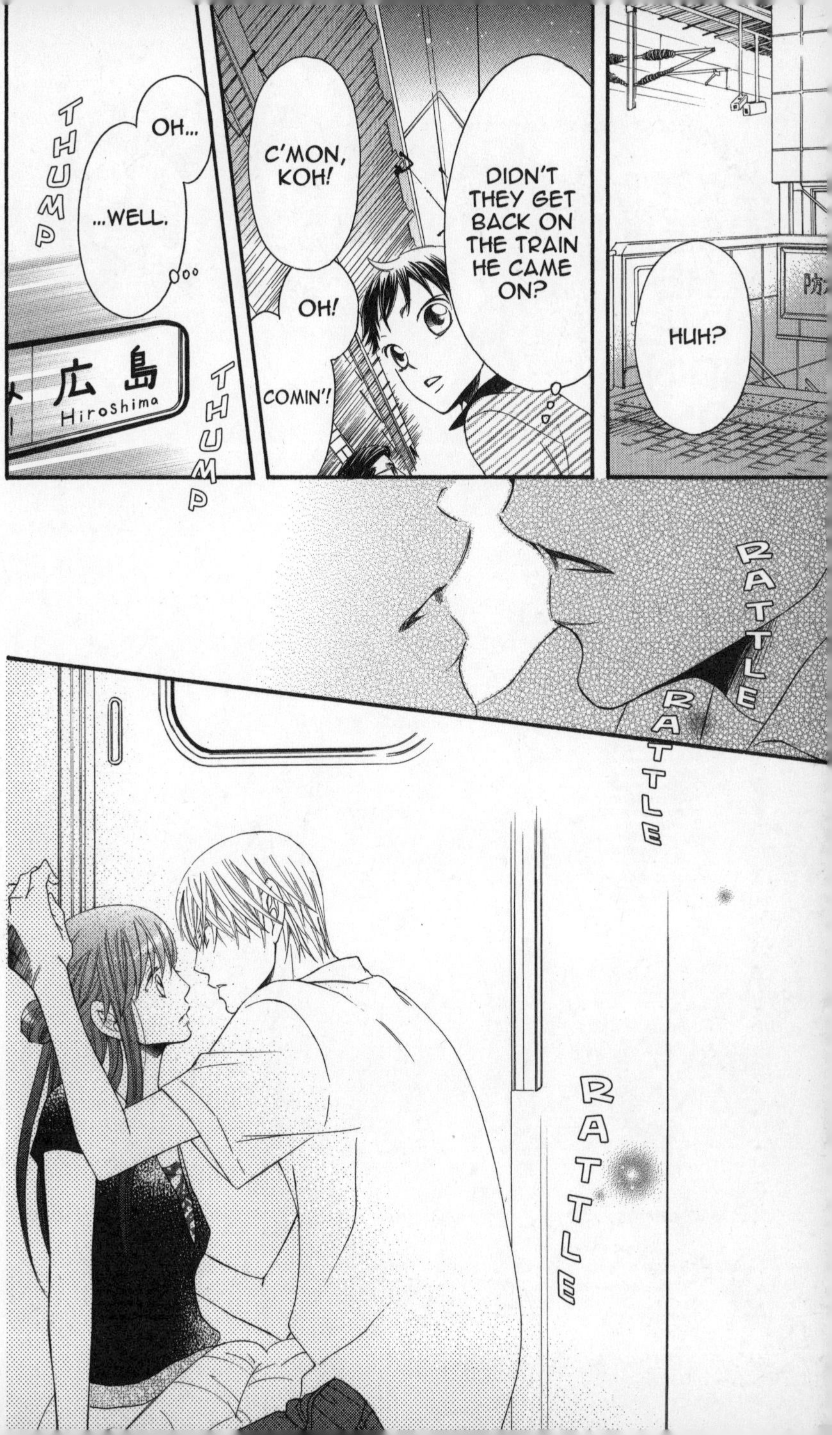
HUH?
DIDN'T THEY GET BACK ON THE TRAIN HE CAME ON?
C'MON, KOH!
OH!
COMIN'!
OH...
...WELL.
THUMP
THUMP
広島
Hiroshima
RATTLE
RATTLE
RATTLE

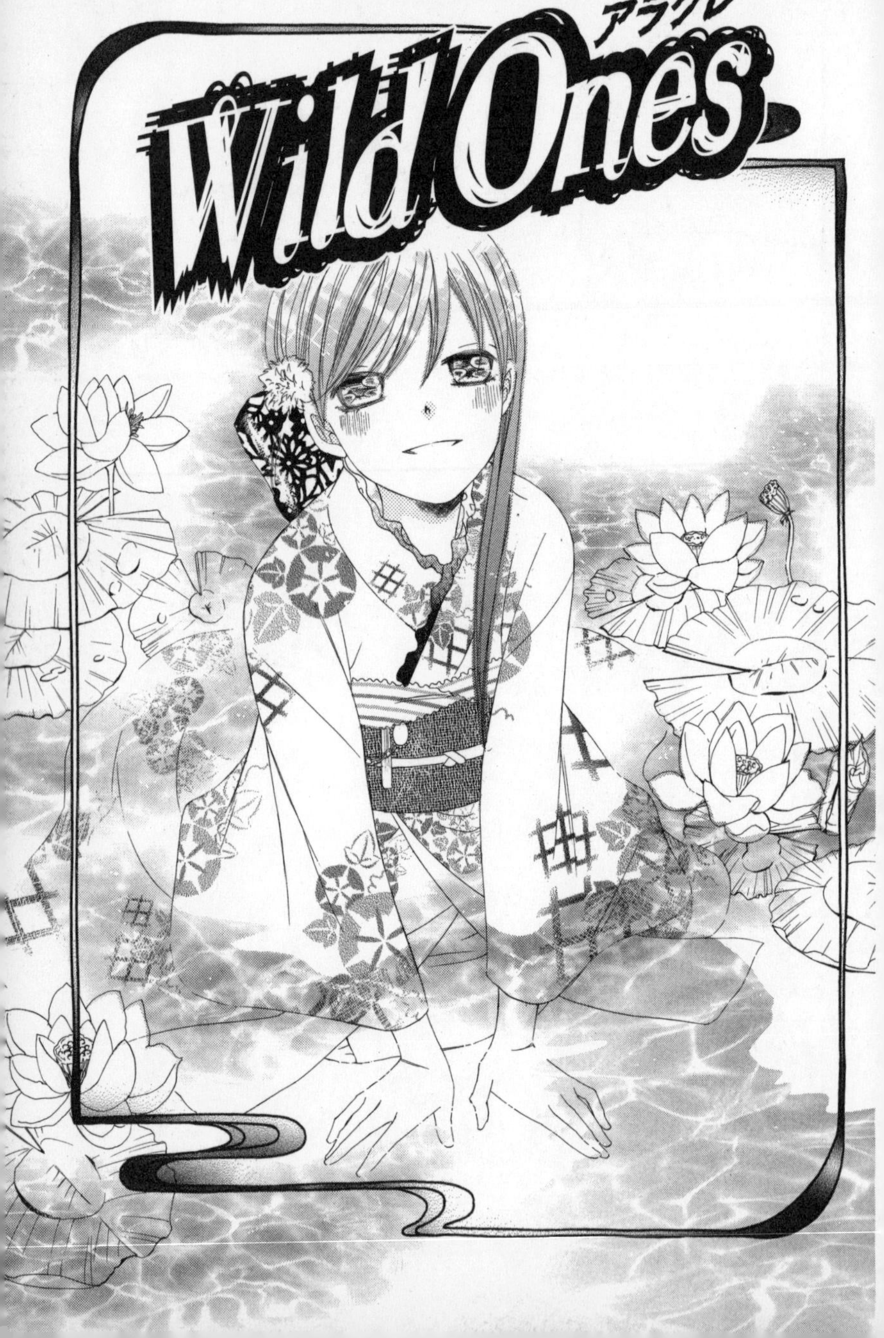
Wild Ones
アラクレ

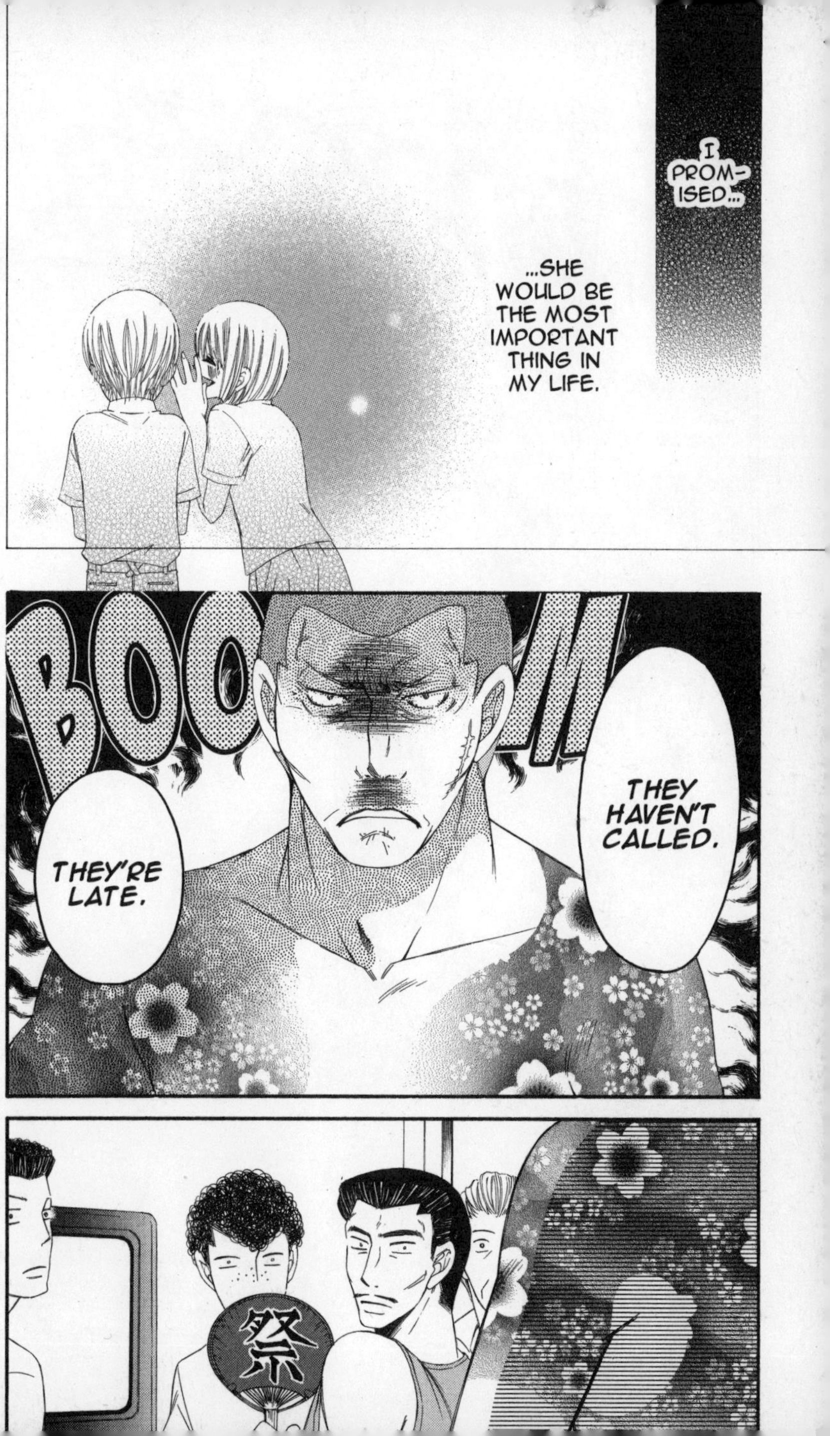
I PROMISED...
...SHE WOULD BE THE MOST IMPORTANT THING IN MY LIFE.
BOOM
THEY HAVEN'T CALLED.
THEY'RE LATE.
祭

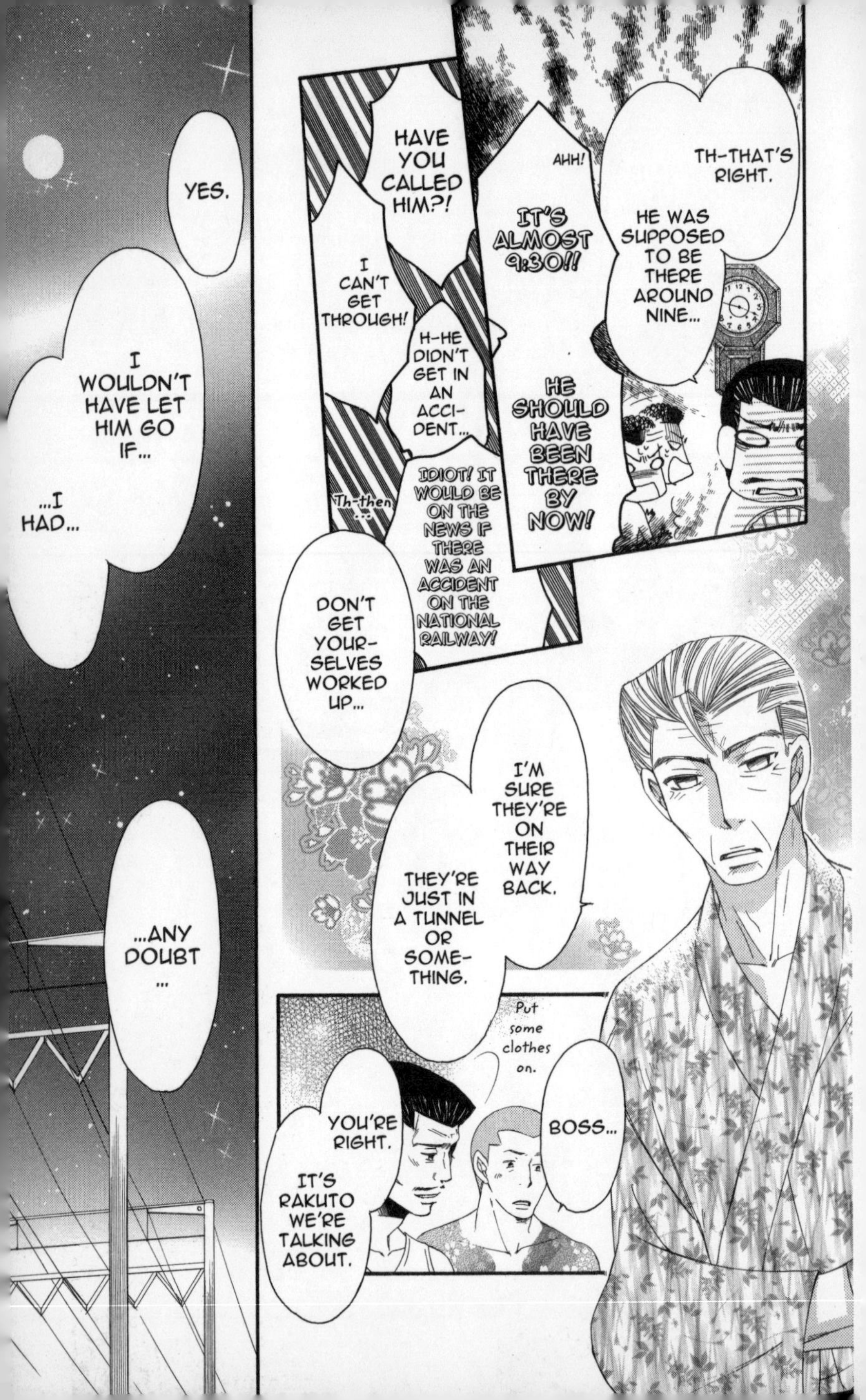
TH-THAT'S RIGHT.
HE WAS SUPPOSED TO BE THERE AROUND NINE...
AHH!
IT'S ALMOST 9:30!!
HE SHOULD HAVE BEEN THERE BY NOW!
HAVE YOU CALLED HIM?!
I CAN'T GET THROUGH!
H-HE DIDN'T GET IN AN ACCI-DENT...
Th-then, ...
IDIOT! IT WOULD BE ON THE NEWS IF THERE WAS AN ACCIDENT ON THE NATIONAL RAILWAY!
DON'T GET YOUR-SELVES WORKED UP...
I'M SURE THEY'RE ON THEIR WAY BACK.
THEY'RE JUST IN A TUNNEL OR SOME-THING.
BOSS...
Put some clothes on.
YOU'RE RIGHT.
IT'S RAKUTO WE'RE TALKING ABOUT.
YES.
I WOULDN'T HAVE LET HIM GO IF...
...I HAD...
...ANY DOUBT...

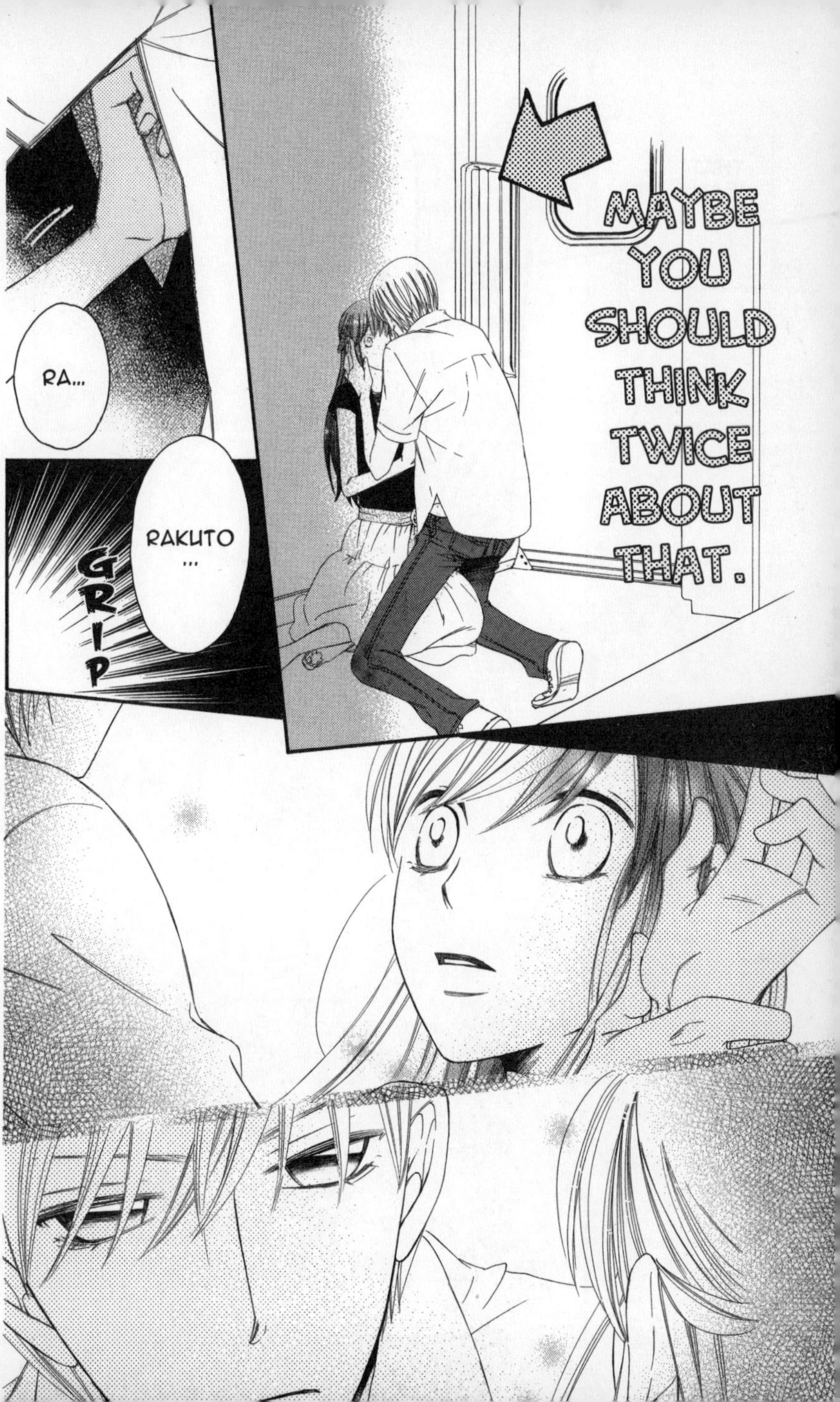
MAYBE YOU SHOULD THINK TWICE ABOUT THAT.
RA...
RAKUTO...
GRIP

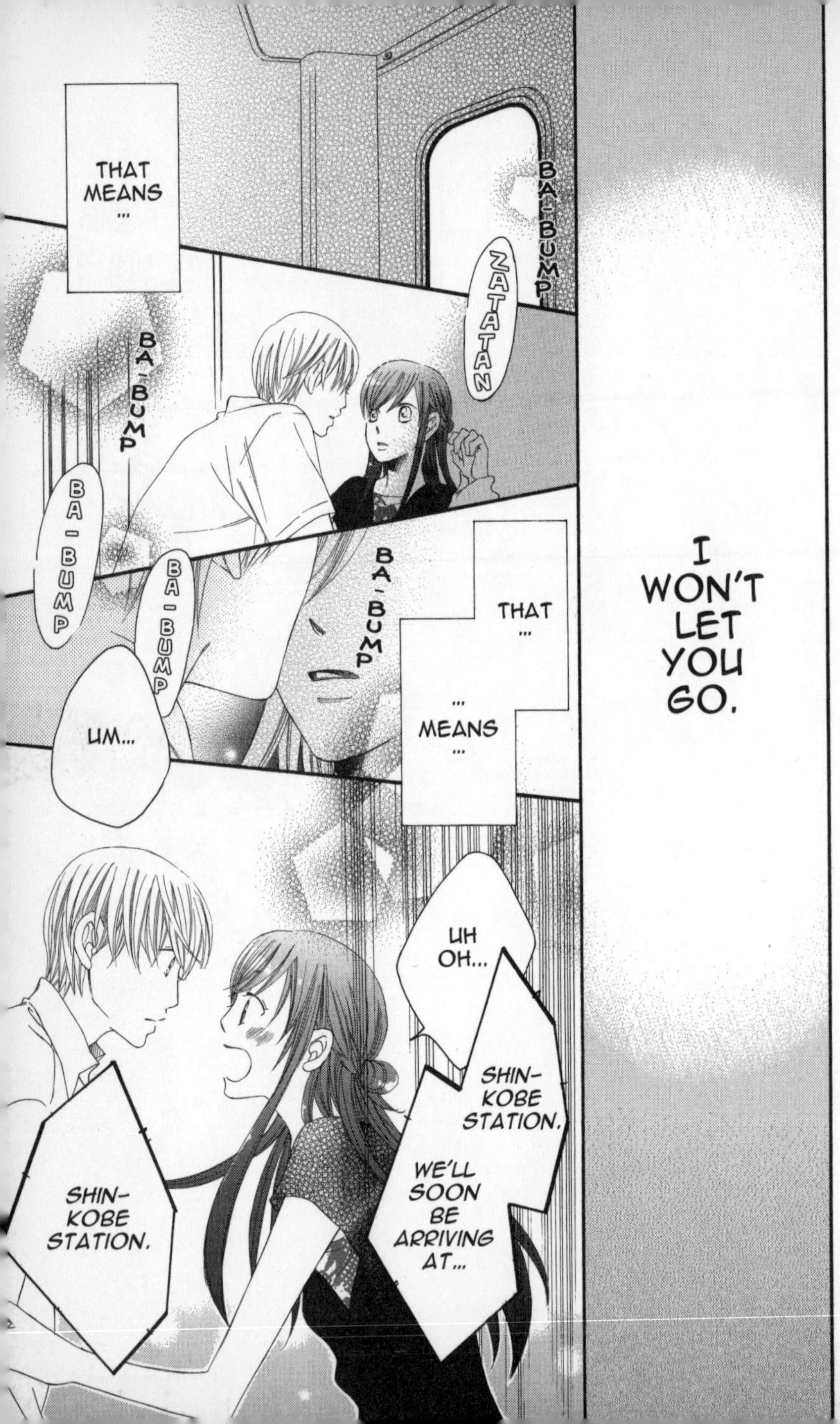
I WON'T LET YOU GO.
BA-BUMP
ZATATAN
THAT MEANS ...
BA-BUMP
BA-BUMP
THAT ... ... MEANS ...
BA-BUMP
BA-BUMP
UM...
UH OH...
SHIN-KOBE STATION.
WE'LL SOON BE ARRIVING AT...
SHIN-KOBE STATION.

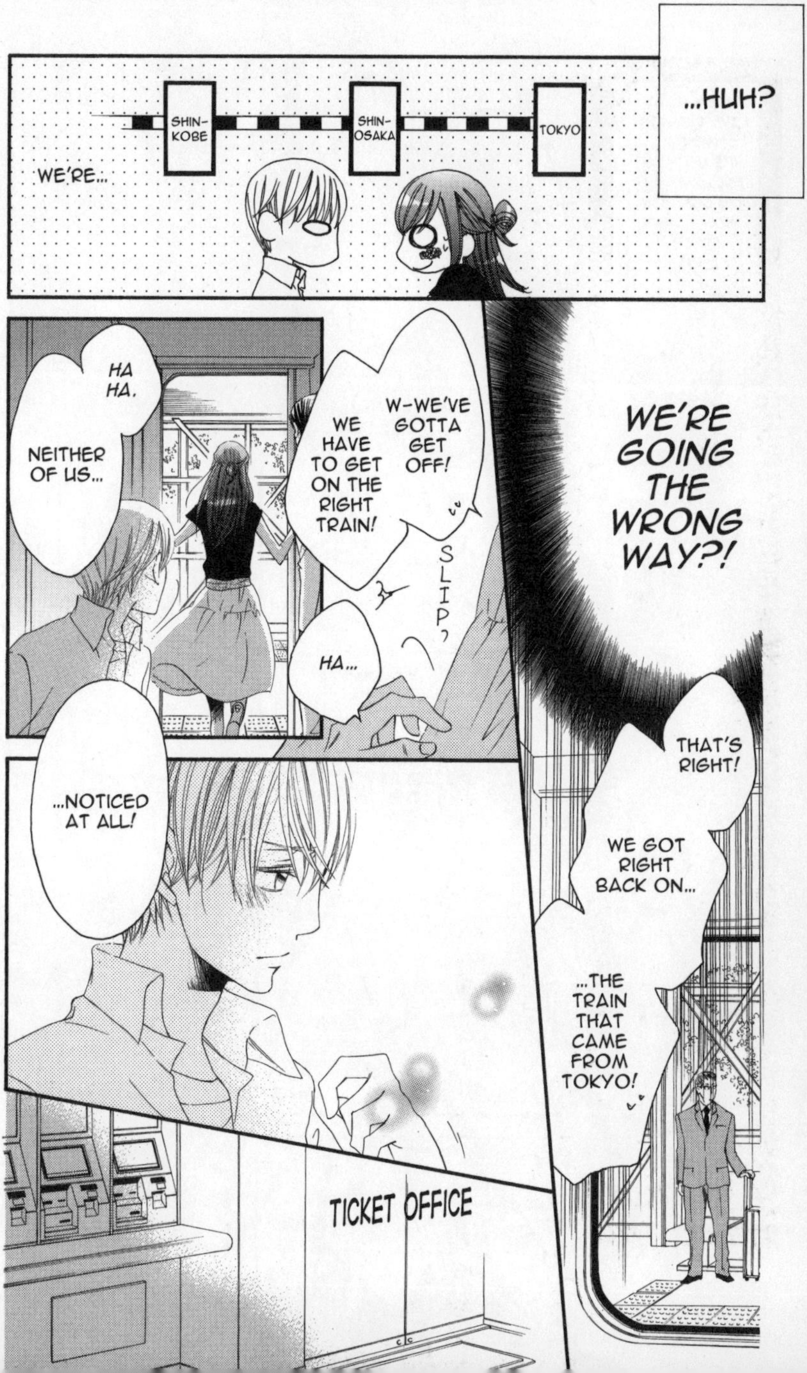
...HUH?
SHIN-KOBE
SHIN-OSAKA
TOKYO
WE'RE...
WE'RE GOING THE WRONG WAY?!
W-WE'VE GOTTA GET OFF!
WE HAVE TO GET ON THE RIGHT TRAIN!
SLIP
HA...
HA HA.
NEITHER OF US...
...NOTICED AT ALL!
THAT'S RIGHT!
WE GOT RIGHT BACK ON...
...THE TRAIN THAT CAME FROM TOKYO!
TICKET OFFICE

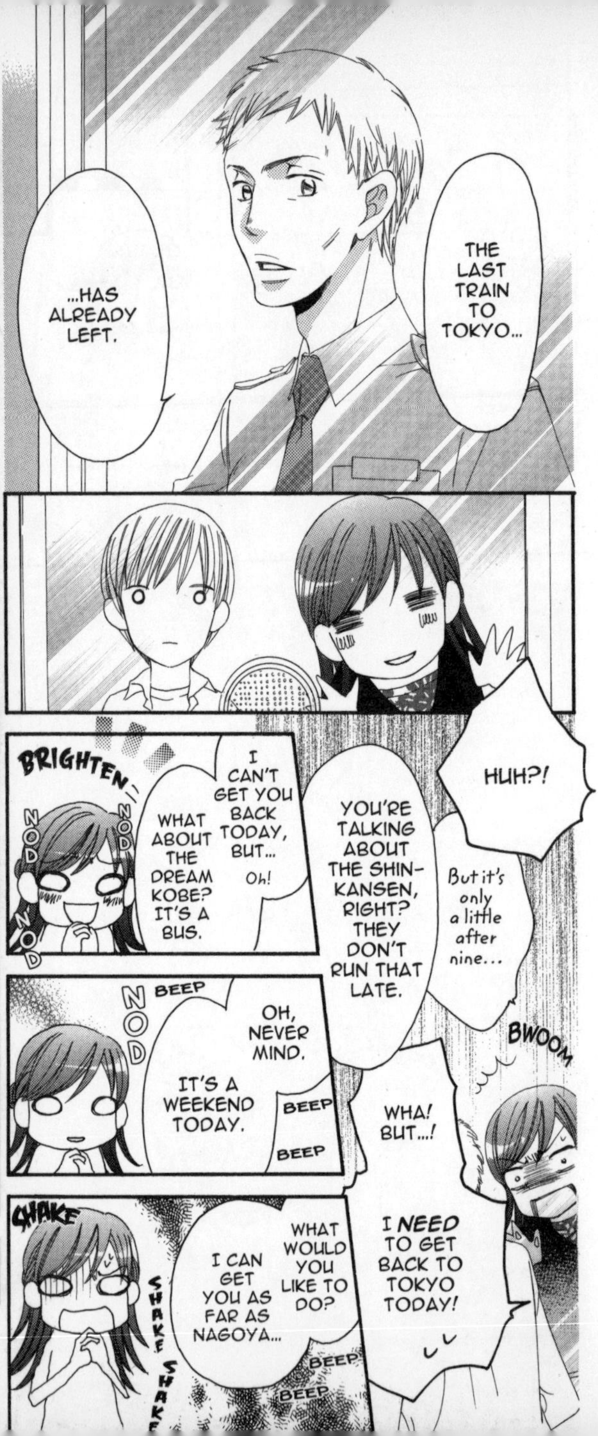
THE LAST TRAIN TO TOKYO...
...HAS ALREADY LEFT.
HUH?!
But it's only a little after nine...
YOU'RE TALKING ABOUT THE SHINKANSEN, RIGHT? THEY DON'T RUN THAT LATE.
I CAN'T GET YOU BACK TODAY, BUT...
Oh!
WHAT ABOUT THE DREAM KOBE? IT'S A BUS.
BRIGHTEN
NOD NOD NOD
BWOOM
WHA! BUT...!
OH, NEVER MIND.
IT'S A WEEKEND TODAY.
NOD
BEEP BEEP BEEP
I NEED TO GET BACK TO TOKYO TODAY!
WHAT WOULD YOU LIKE TO DO?
I CAN GET YOU AS FAR AS NAGOYA...
SHAKE SHAKE SHAKE
BEEP BEEP

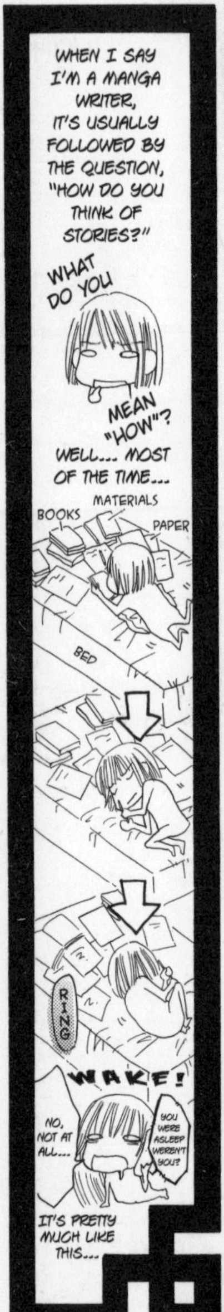
WHEN I SAY I'M A MANGA WRITER, IT'S USUALLY FOLLOWED BY THE QUESTION, "HOW DO YOU THINK OF STORIES?"
WHAT DO YOU MEAN "HOW"?
WELL... MOST OF THE TIME...
MATERIALS
BOOKS
PAPER
BED
RING
WAKE!
YOU WERE ASLEEP WEREN'T YOU?
NO, NOT AT ALL...
IT'S PRETTY MUCH LIKE THIS...

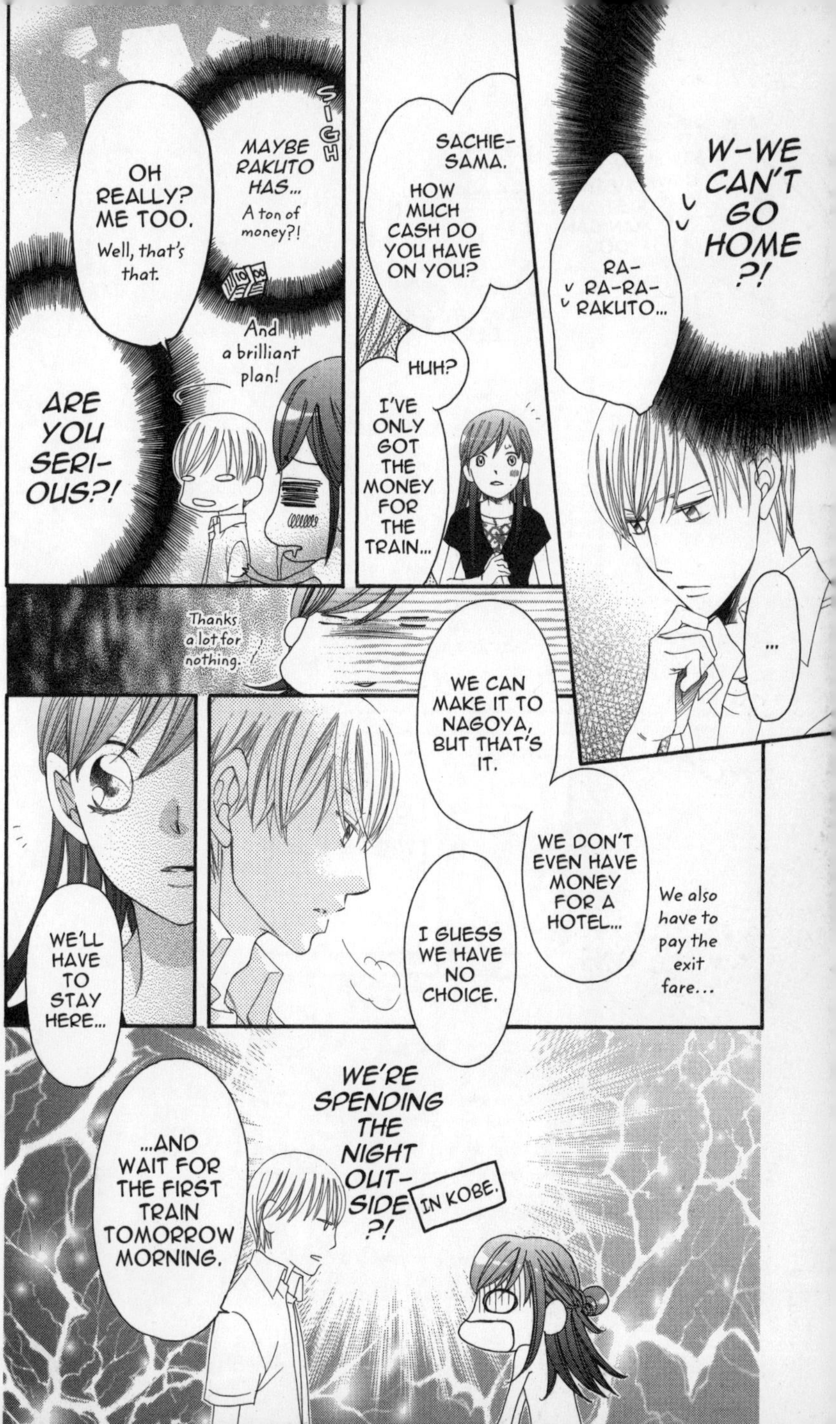
W-WE CAN'T GO HOME?!
RA-RA-RA-RAKUTO...
...
SACHIE-SAMA.
HOW MUCH CASH DO YOU HAVE ON YOU?
HUH?
I'VE ONLY GOT THE MONEY FOR THE TRAIN...
SIGH
MAYBE RAKUTO HAS...
A ton of money?!
And a brilliant plan!
OH REALLY? ME TOO.
Well, that's that.
ARE YOU SERI-OUS?!
Thanks a lot for nothing.
WE CAN MAKE IT TO NAGOYA, BUT THAT'S IT.
WE DON'T EVEN HAVE MONEY FOR A HOTEL...
We also have to pay the exit fare...
I GUESS WE HAVE NO CHOICE.
WE'LL HAVE TO STAY HERE...
...AND WAIT FOR THE FIRST TRAIN TOMORROW MORNING.
WE'RE SPENDING THE NIGHT OUT-SIDE
IN KOBE.
?!

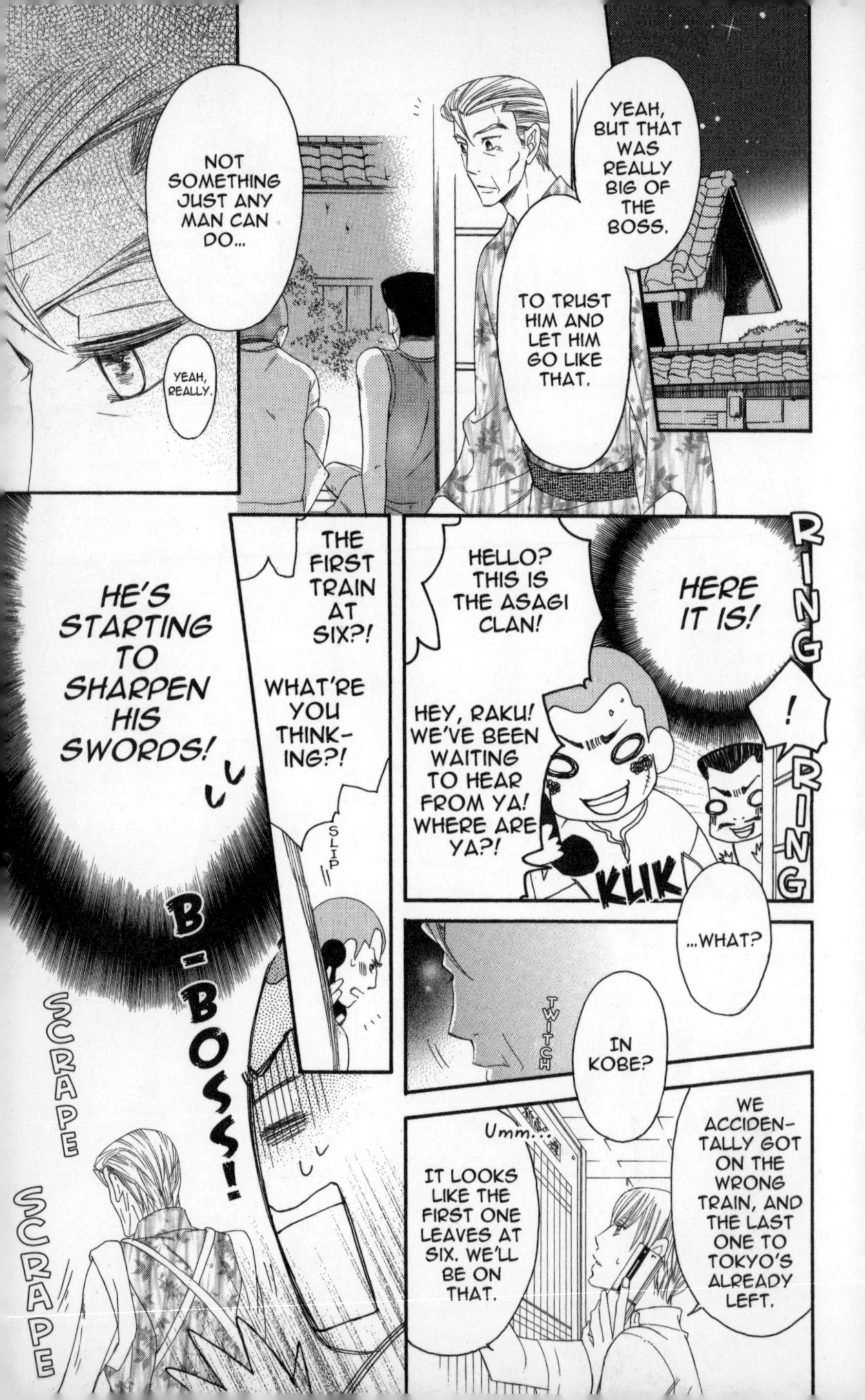
YEAH, BUT THAT WAS REALLY BIG OF THE BOSS.
TO TRUST HIM AND LET HIM GO LIKE THAT.
NOT SOMETHING JUST ANY MAN CAN DO...
YEAH, REALLY.
RING
!
RING
RING
HERE IT IS!
HELLO? THIS IS THE ASAGI CLAN!
HEY, RAKU! WE'VE BEEN WAITING TO HEAR FROM YA! WHERE ARE YA?!
KLIK
...WHAT?
TWITCH
IN KOBE?
WE ACCIDENTALLY GOT ON THE WRONG TRAIN, AND THE LAST ONE TO TOKYO'S ALREADY LEFT.
Umm...
IT LOOKS LIKE THE FIRST ONE LEAVES AT SIX. WE'LL BE ON THAT.
THE FIRST TRAIN AT SIX?!
WHAT'RE YOU THINKING?!
SLIP
HE'S STARTING TO SHARPEN HIS SWORDS!
B-BOSS!
SCRAPE
SCRAPE

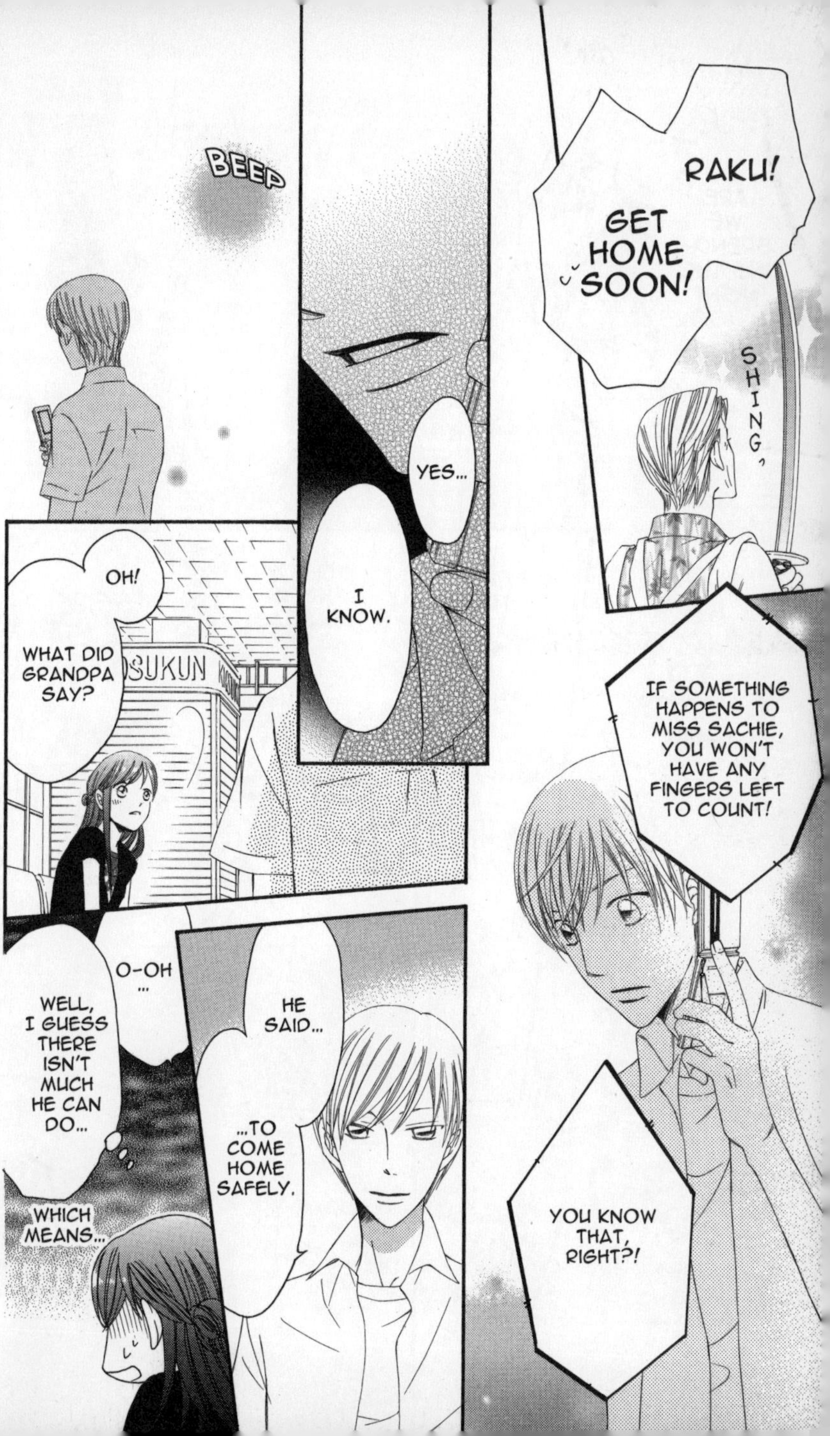
RAKU!
GET HOME SOON!
SHING
IF SOMETHING HAPPENS TO MISS SACHIE, YOU WON'T HAVE ANY FINGERS LEFT TO COUNT!
YOU KNOW THAT, RIGHT?!
YES...
I KNOW.
BEEP
OH!
WHAT DID GRANDPA SAY?
HE SAID...
...TO COME HOME SAFELY.
O-OH...
WELL, I GUESS THERE ISN'T MUCH HE CAN DO...
WHICH MEANS...

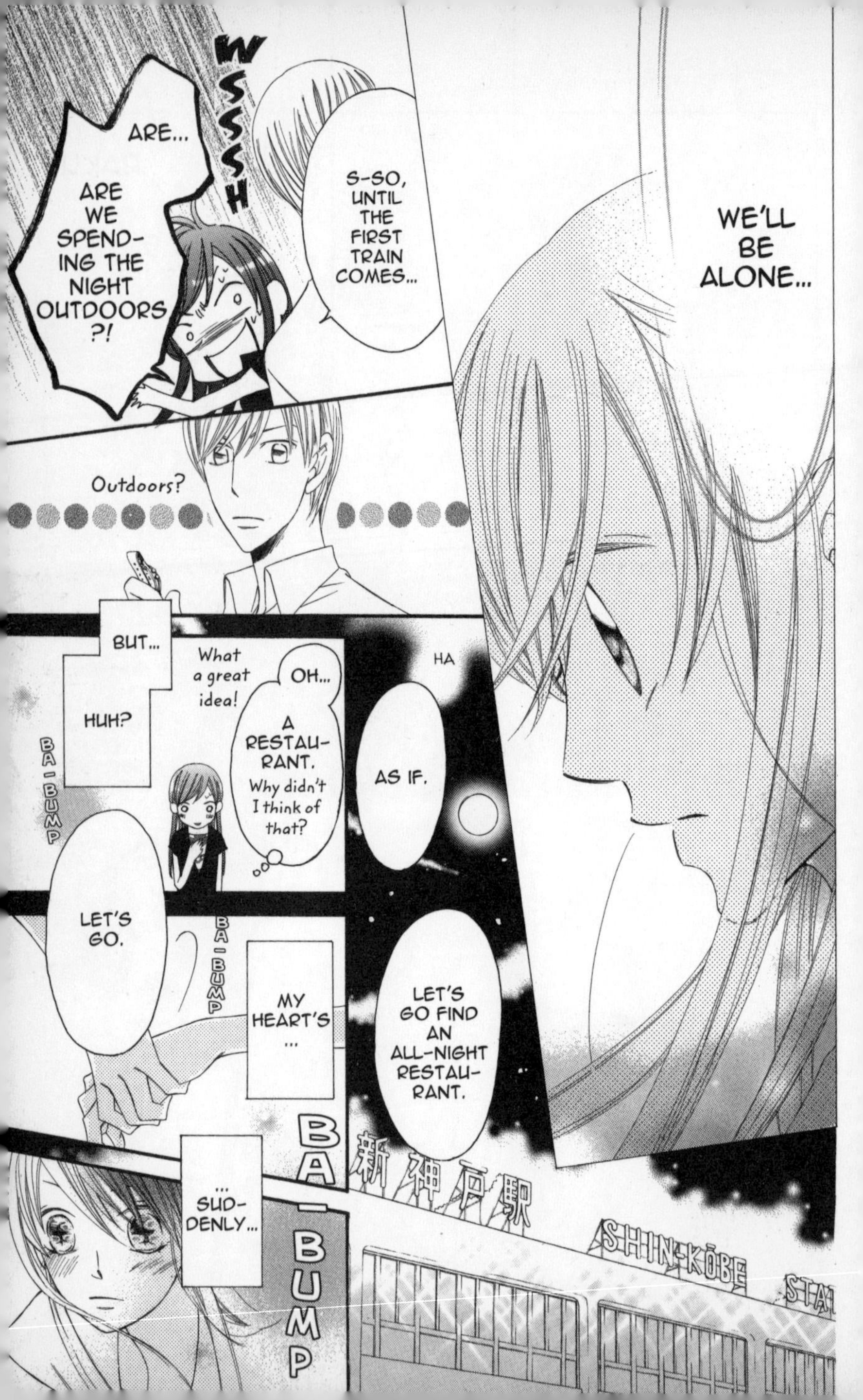

WE'LL BE ALONE...
S-SO, UNTIL THE FIRST TRAIN COMES...
WSSSH
ARE...
ARE WE SPENDING THE NIGHT OUTDOORS?!
Outdoors?
HA
AS IF.
LET'S GO FIND AN ALL-NIGHT RESTAURANT.
OH... A RESTAURANT.
Why didn't I think of that?
What a great idea!
BUT...
HUH?
BA-BUMP
MY HEART'S...
BA-BUMP
LET'S GO.
...SUDDENLY...
BA-BUMP
新神戸駅
SHIN-KŌBE STA

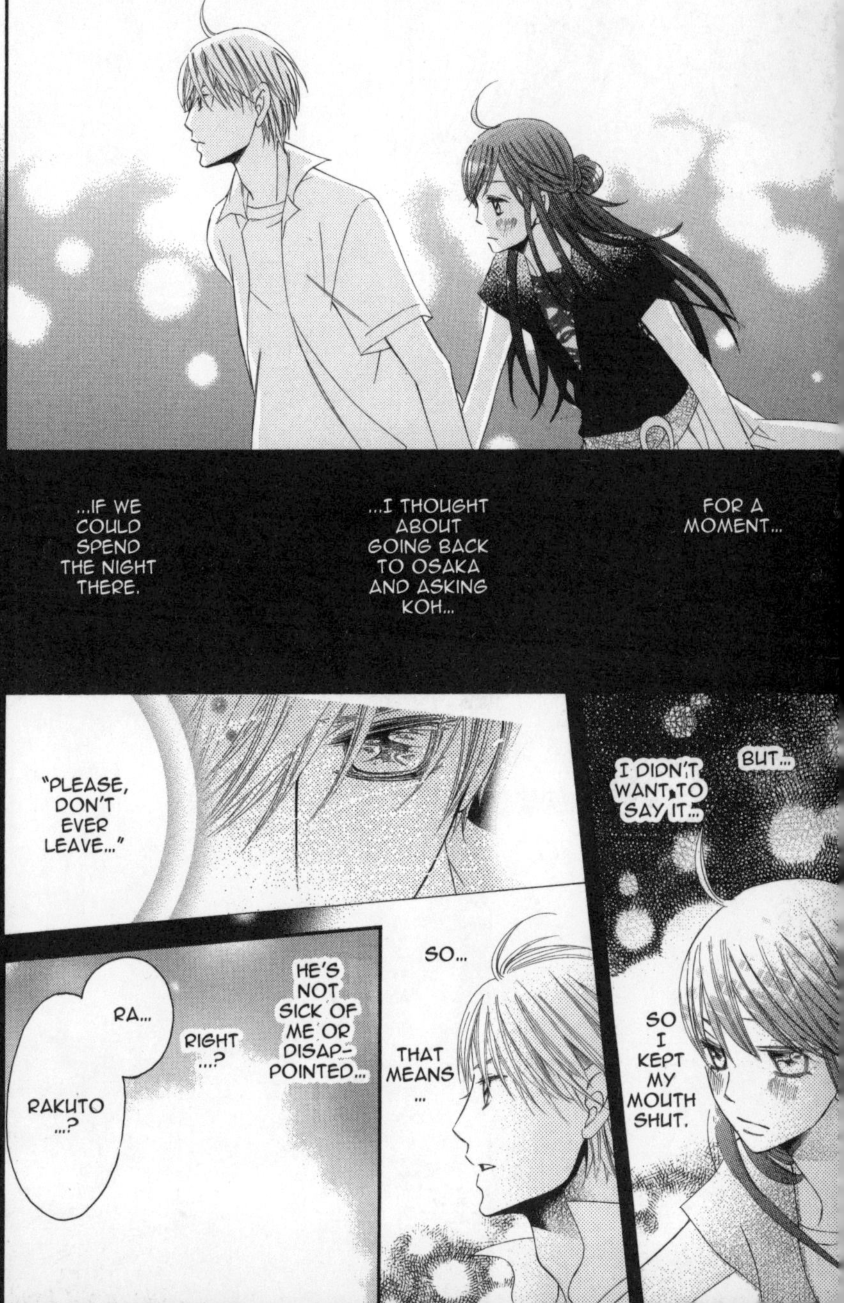
FOR A MOMENT...
...I THOUGHT ABOUT GOING BACK TO OSAKA AND ASKING KOH...
...IF WE COULD SPEND THE NIGHT THERE.
BUT...
I DIDN'T WANT TO SAY IT...
SO I KEPT MY MOUTH SHUT.
"PLEASE, DON'T EVER LEAVE..."
SO...
THAT MEANS...
HE'S NOT SICK OF ME OR DISAP-POINTED...
RIGHT...?
RA...
RAKUTO...?

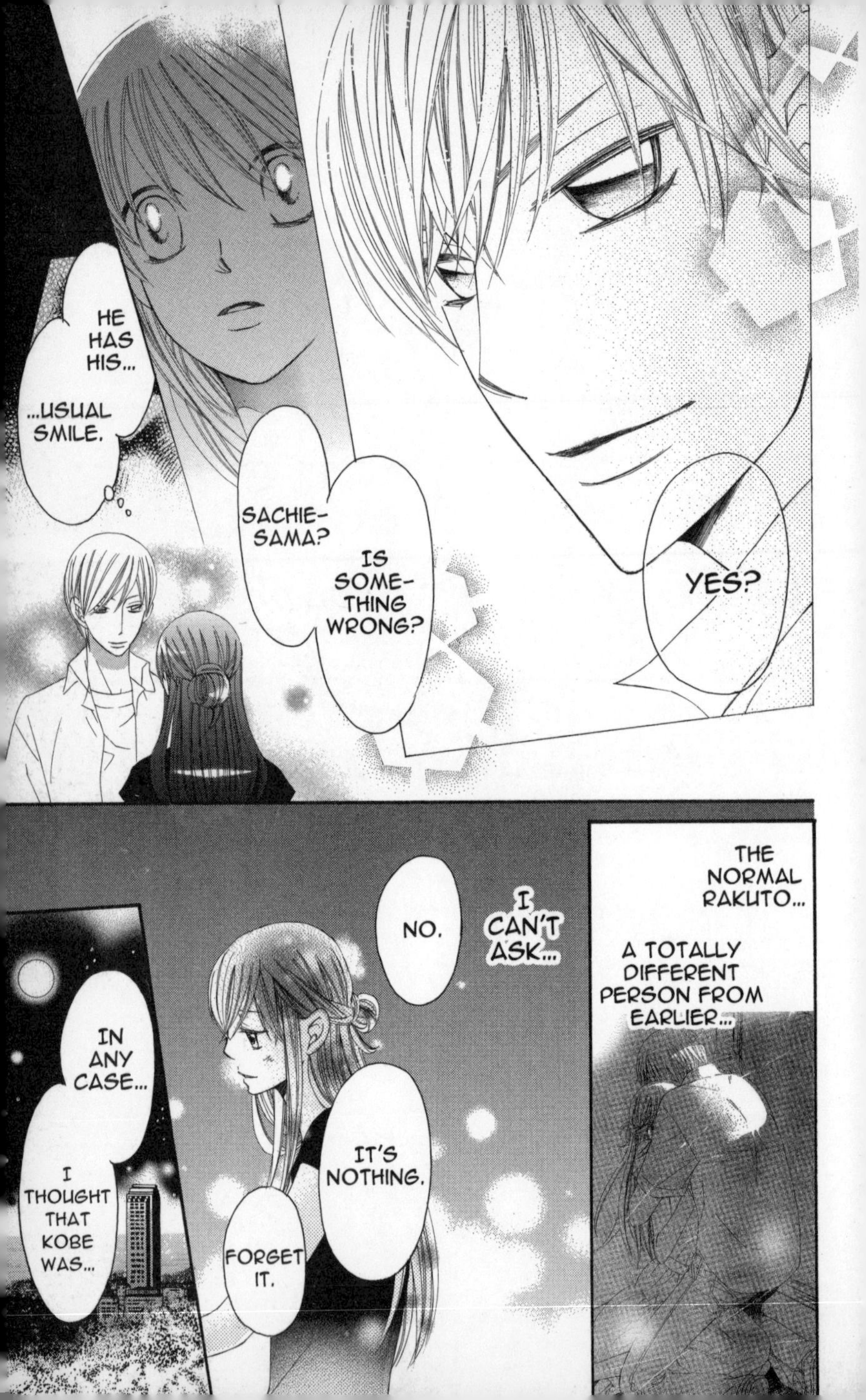
YES?
HE HAS HIS...
...USUAL SMILE.
SACHIE-SAMA?
IS SOMETHING WRONG?
THE NORMAL RAKUTO...
A TOTALLY DIFFERENT PERSON FROM EARLIER...
I CAN'T ASK...
NO.
IT'S NOTHING.
FORGET IT.
IN ANY CASE...
I THOUGHT THAT KOBE WAS...

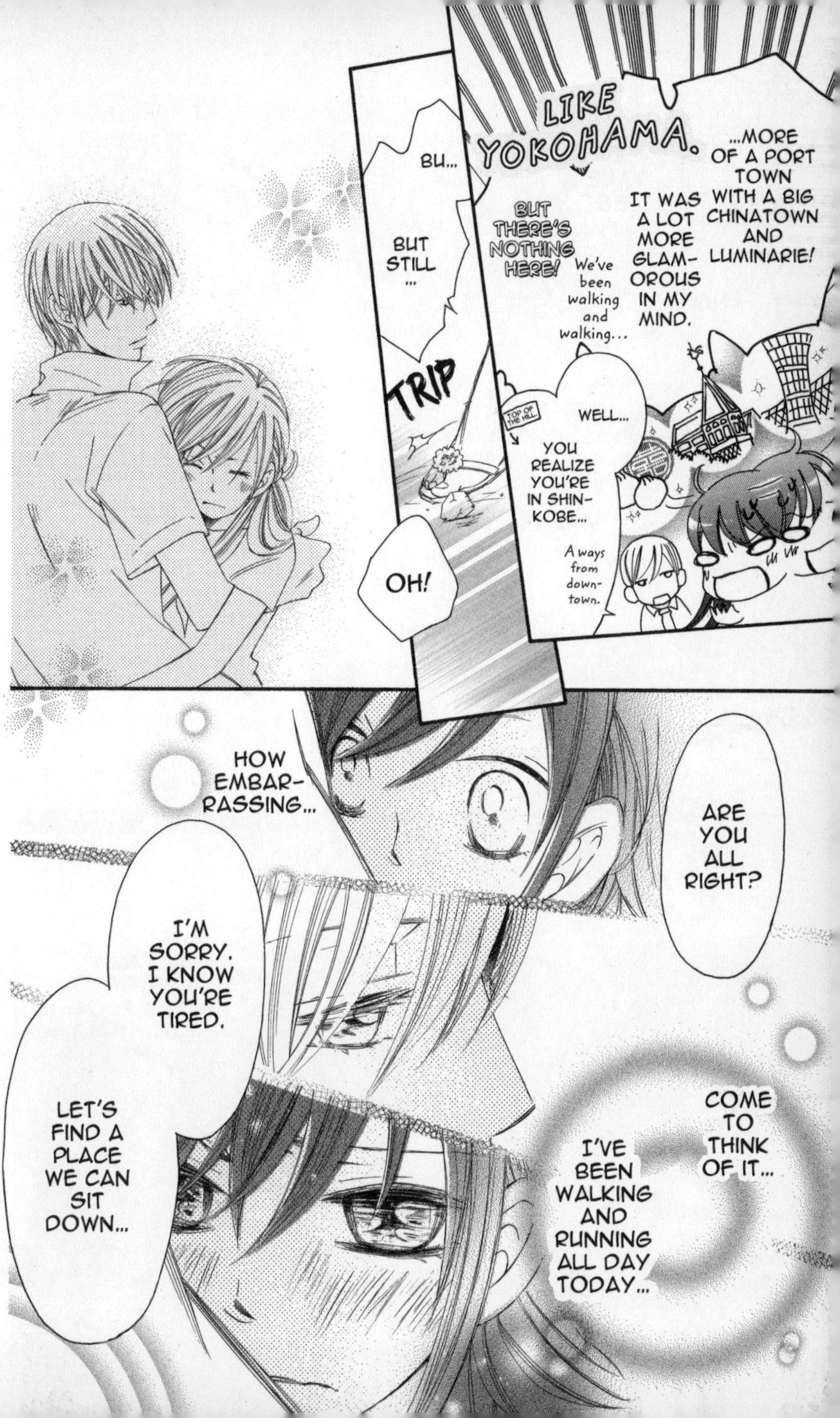
IT WAS A LOT MORE GLAMOROUS IN MY MIND.
...MORE OF A PORT TOWN WITH A BIG CHINATOWN AND LUMINARIE!
LIKE YOKOHAMA.
BUT THERE'S NOTHING HERE!
We've been walking and walking...
TOP OF THE HILL.
WELL...
YOU REALIZE YOU'RE IN SHIN-KOBE...
A ways from downtown.
BU...
BUT STILL...
TRIP
OH!
ARE YOU ALL RIGHT?
HOW EMBARRASSING...
I'M SORRY. I KNOW YOU'RE TIRED.
COME TO THINK OF IT...
I'VE BEEN WALKING AND RUNNING ALL DAY TODAY...
LET'S FIND A PLACE WE CAN SIT DOWN...

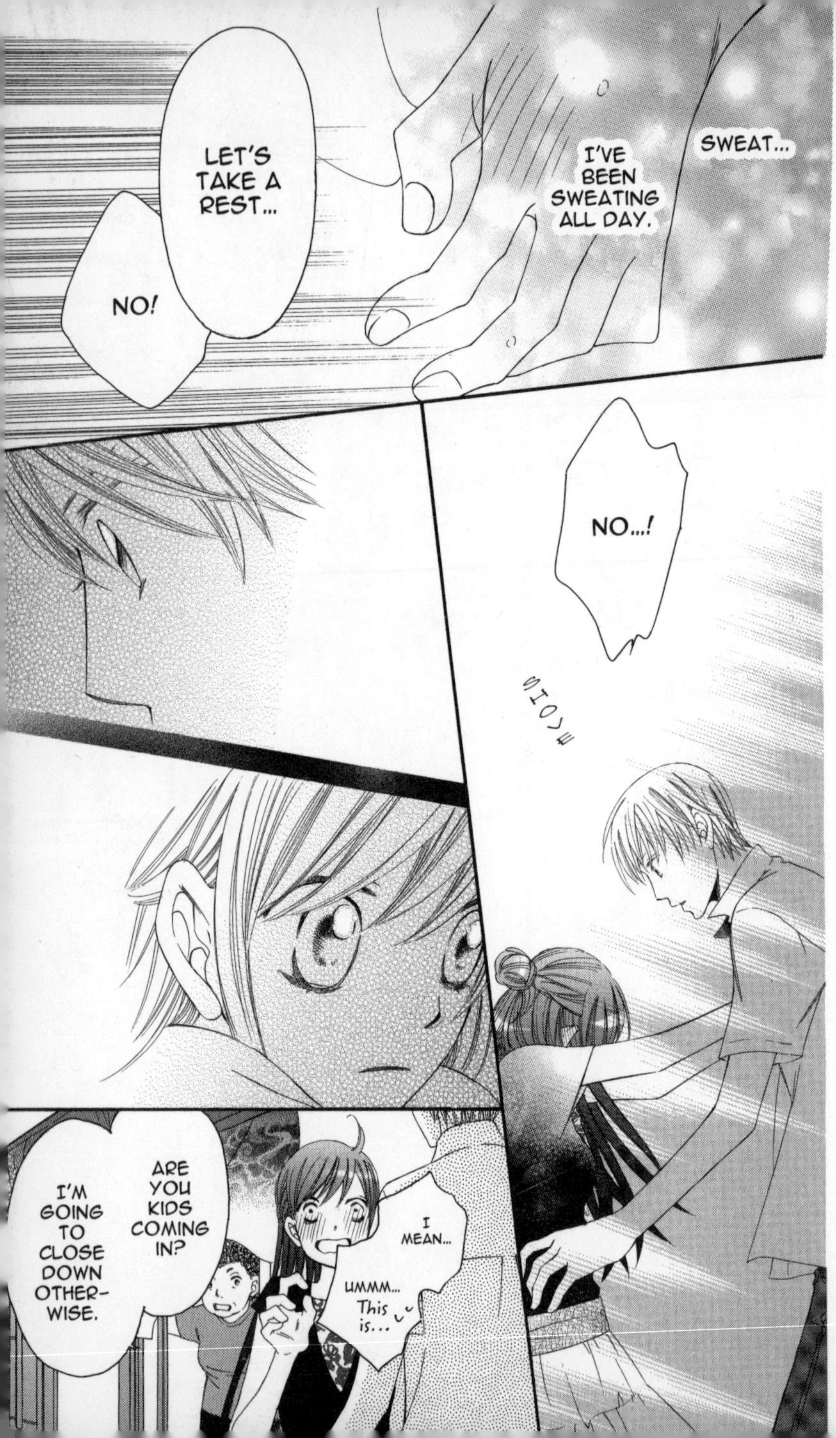
SWEAT...
I'VE BEEN SWEATING ALL DAY.
LET'S TAKE A REST...
NO!
NO...!
I MEAN...
UMMM... This is...
ARE YOU KIDS COMING IN?
I'M GOING TO CLOSE DOWN OTHER-WISE.

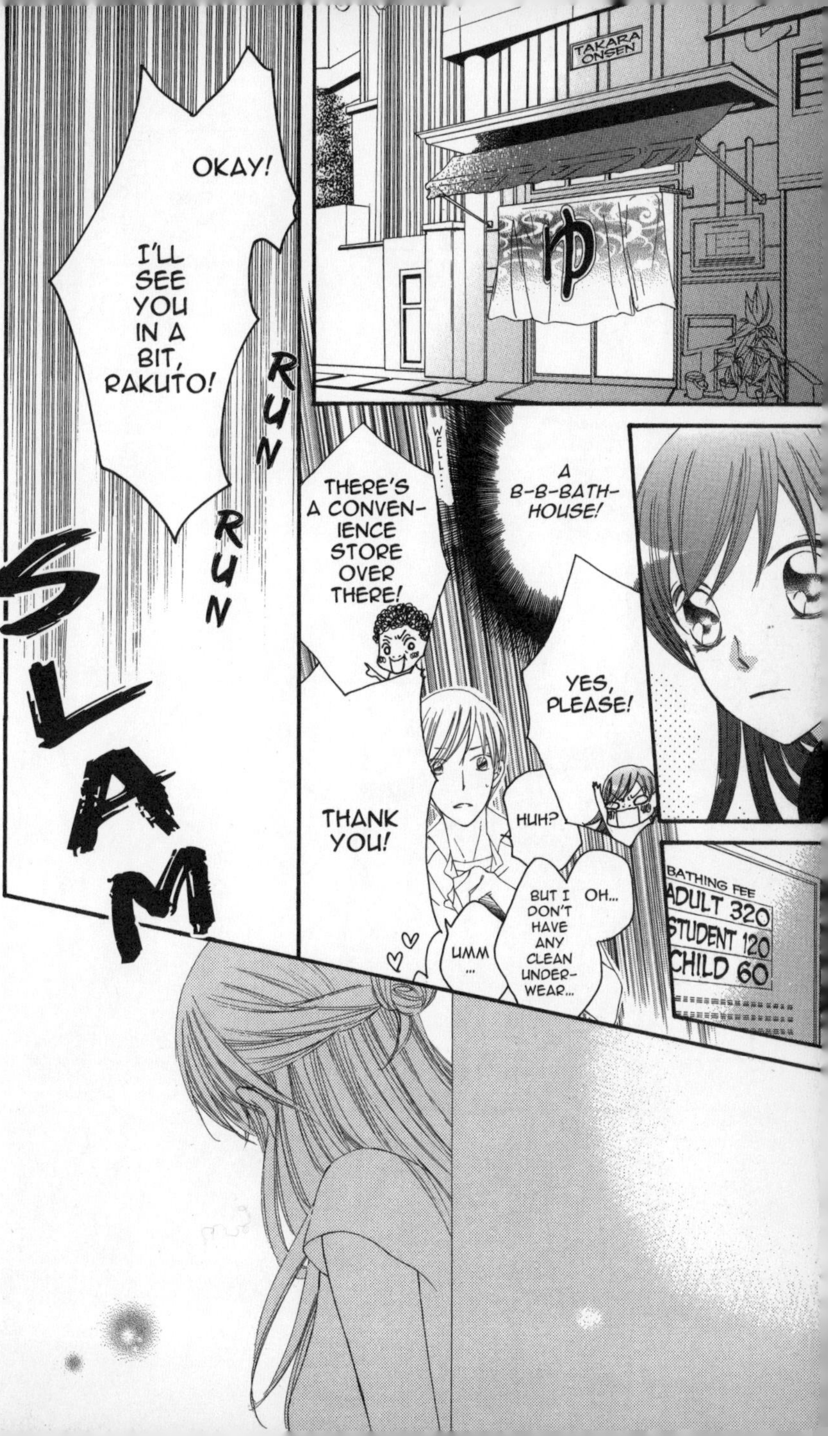
TAKARA ONSEN
ゆ
A B-B-BATH-HOUSE!
WELL...
THERE'S A CONVENIENCE STORE OVER THERE!
YES, PLEASE!
HUH?
OH...
BUT I DON'T HAVE ANY CLEAN UNDERWEAR...
THANK YOU!
UMM...
BATHING FEE
ADULT 320
STUDENT 120
CHILD 60
OKAY!
I'LL SEE YOU IN A BIT, RAKUTO!
RUN
RUN
SLAM

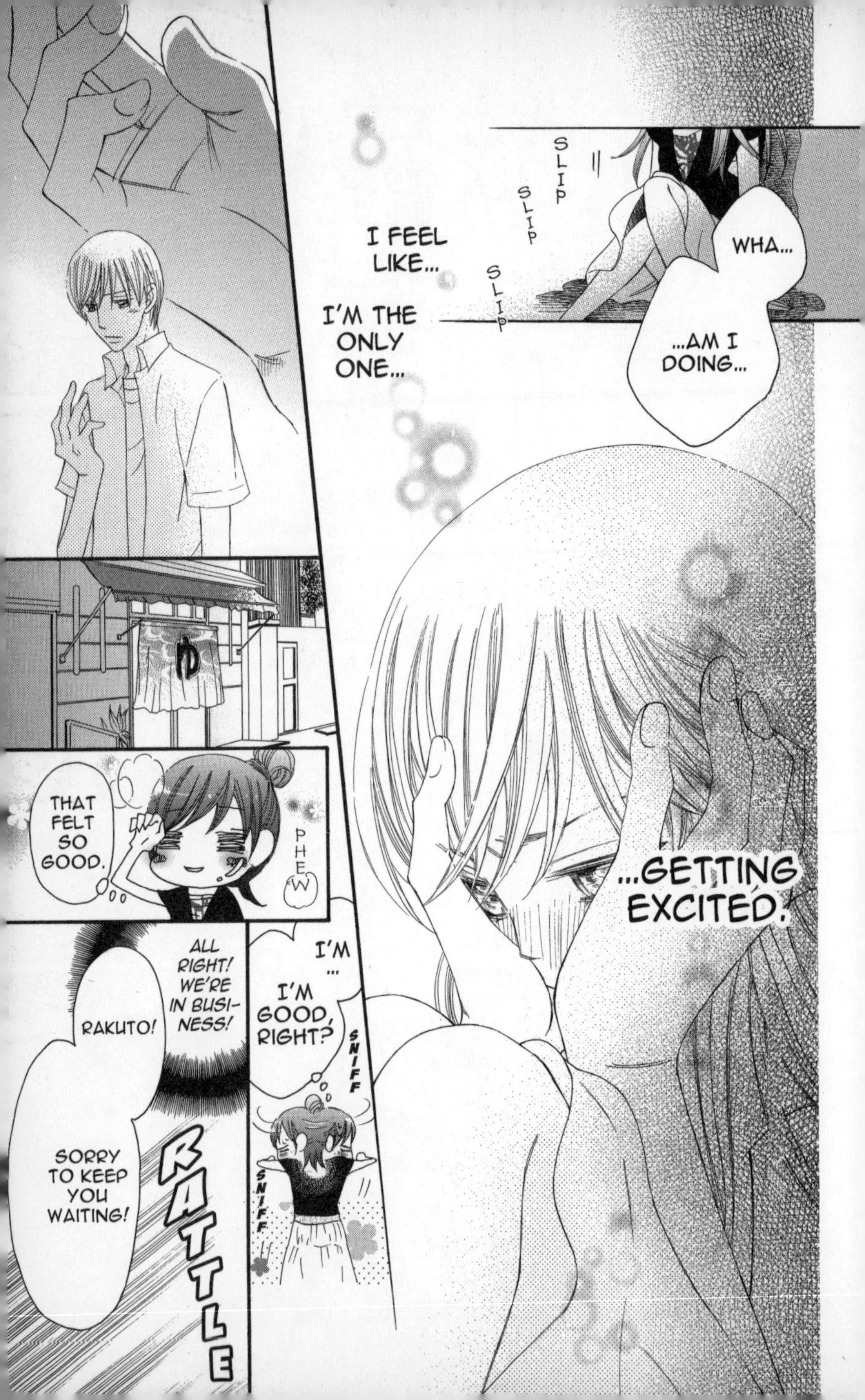

SLIP
SLIP
SLIP
WHA...
...AM I DOING...
I FEEL LIKE...
I'M THE ONLY ONE...
...GETTING EXCITED.
THAT FELT SO GOOD.
PHEW
I'M ...
I'M GOOD, RIGHT?
SNIFF
SNIFF
ALL RIGHT! WE'RE IN BUSINESS!
RAKUTO!
SORRY TO KEEP YOU WAITING!
RATTLE

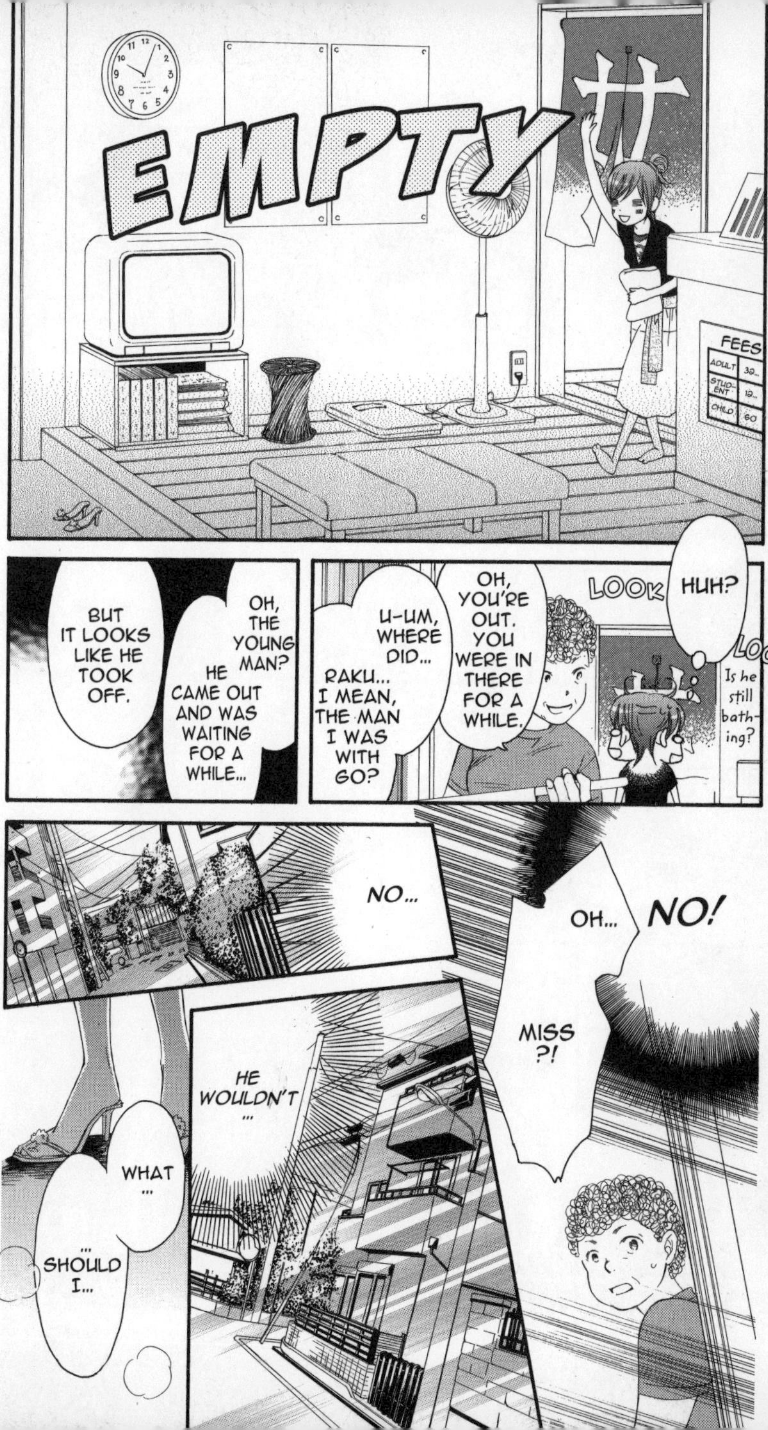
EMPTY
FEES
ADULT
STUDENT
CHILD
60
HUH?
LOOK
LOOK
Is he still bathing?
OH, YOU'RE OUT. YOU WERE IN THERE FOR A WHILE.
U-UM, WHERE DID... RAKU... I MEAN, THE MAN I WAS WITH GO?
OH, THE YOUNG MAN? HE CAME OUT AND WAS WAITING FOR A WHILE...
BUT IT LOOKS LIKE HE TOOK OFF.
NO!
OH...
MISS ?!
NO...
HE WOULDN'T ...
WHAT ...
... SHOULD I...

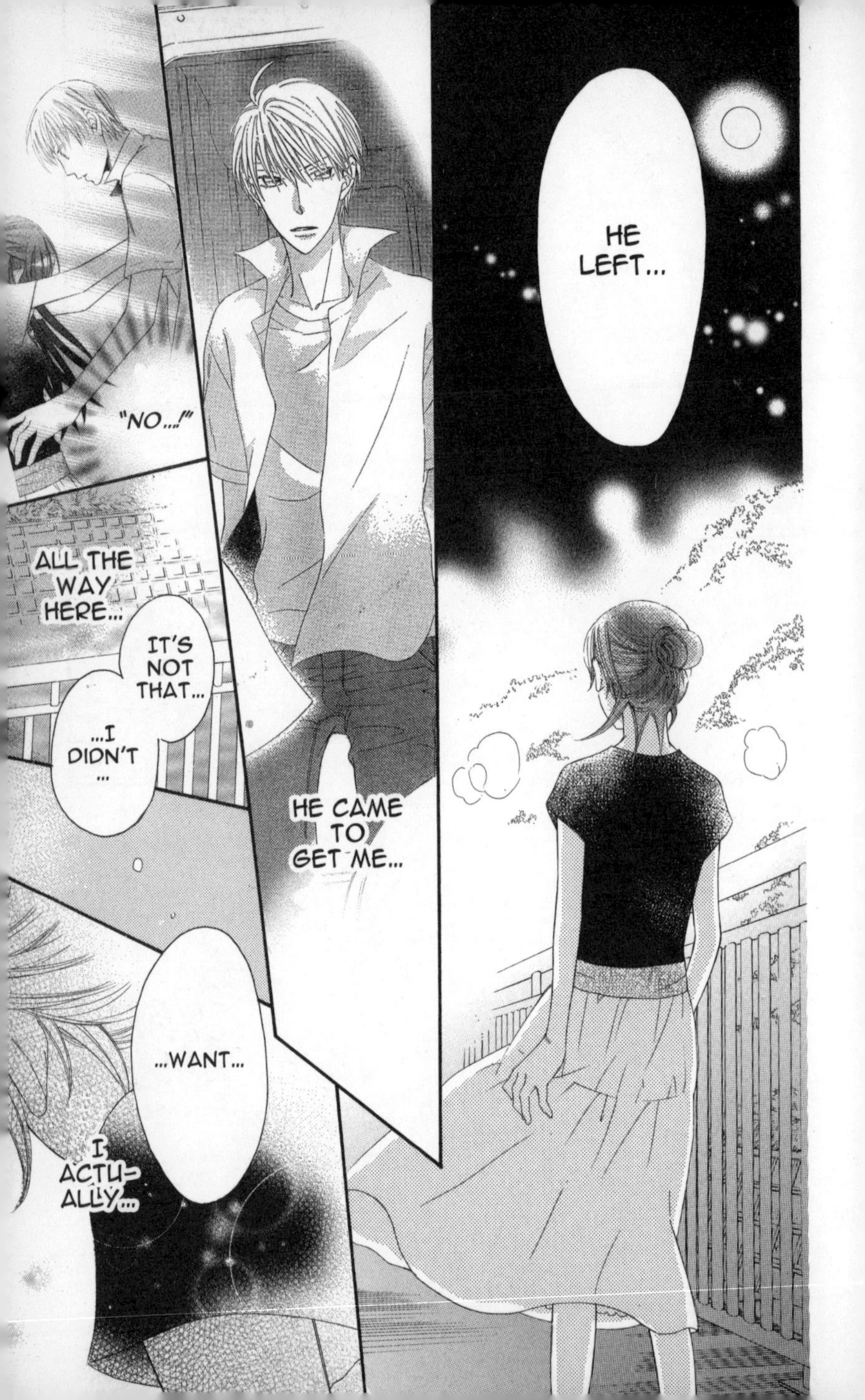
HE LEFT...
HE CAME TO GET ME...
"NO...!"
ALL THE WAY HERE...
IT'S NOT THAT...
...I DIDN'T ...
...WANT...
I ACTU-ALLY...

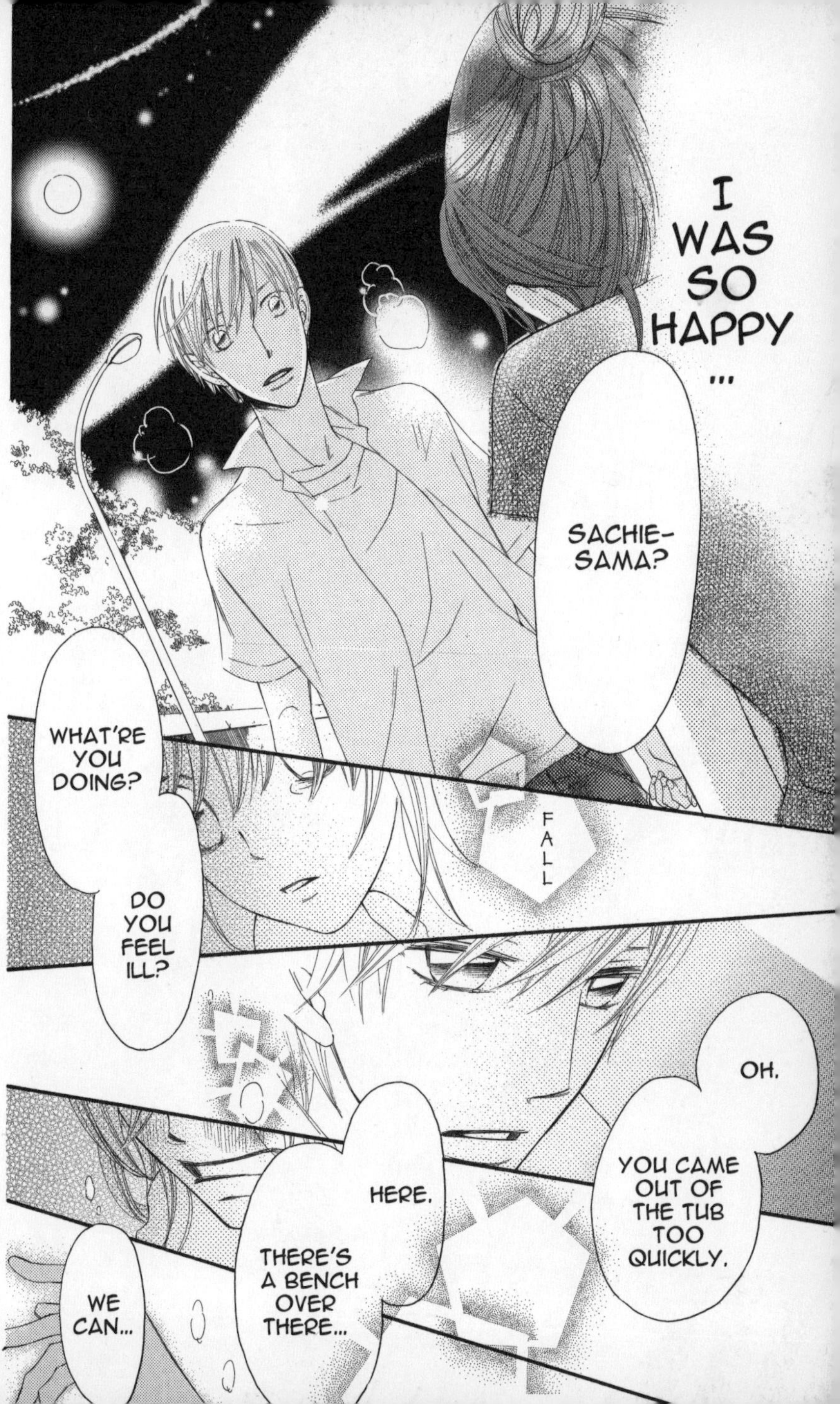
I WAS SO HAPPY ...
SACHIE-SAMA?
WHAT'RE YOU DOING?
FALL
DO YOU FEEL ILL?
OH.
YOU CAME OUT OF THE TUB TOO QUICKLY.
HERE.
THERE'S A BENCH OVER THERE...
WE CAN...

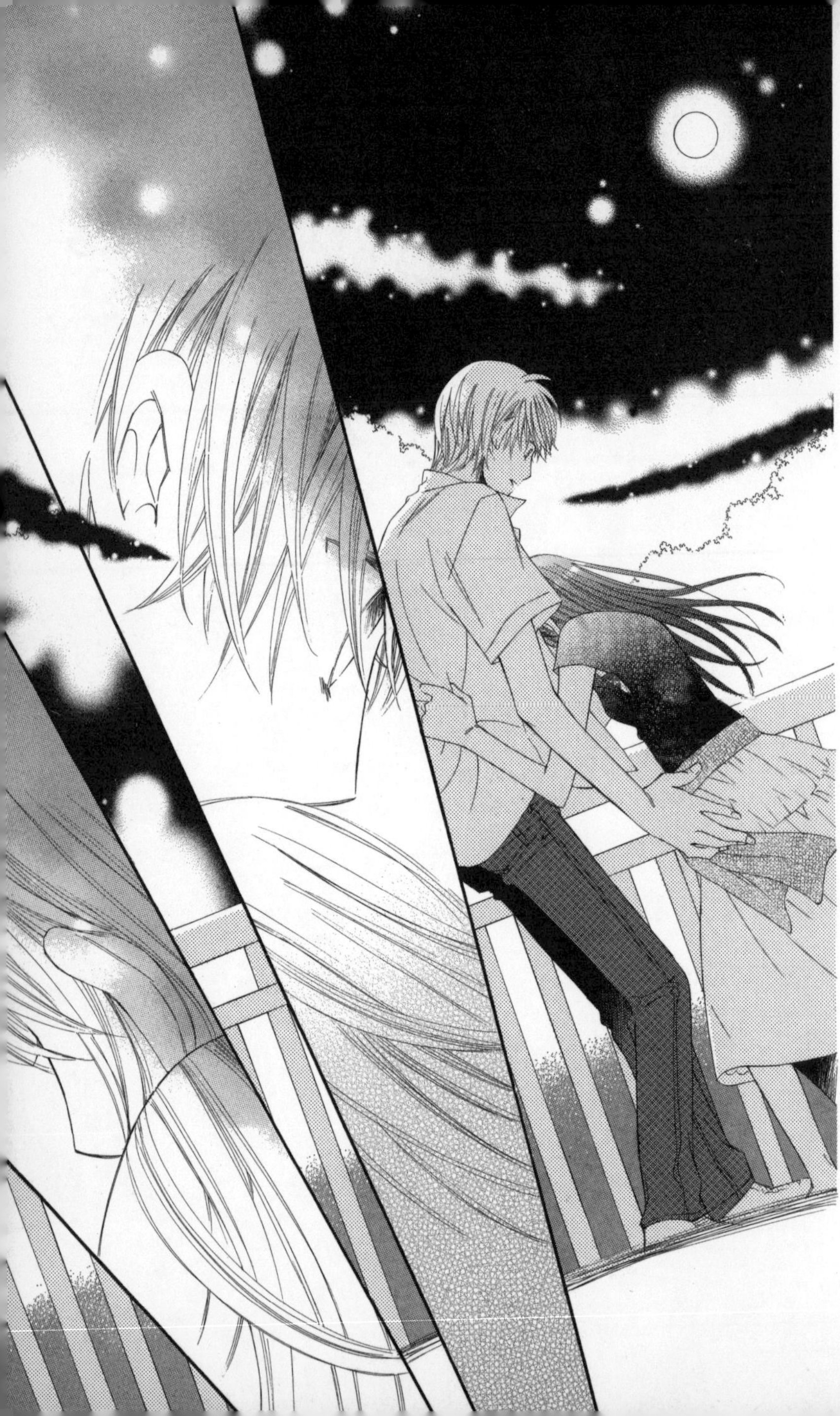

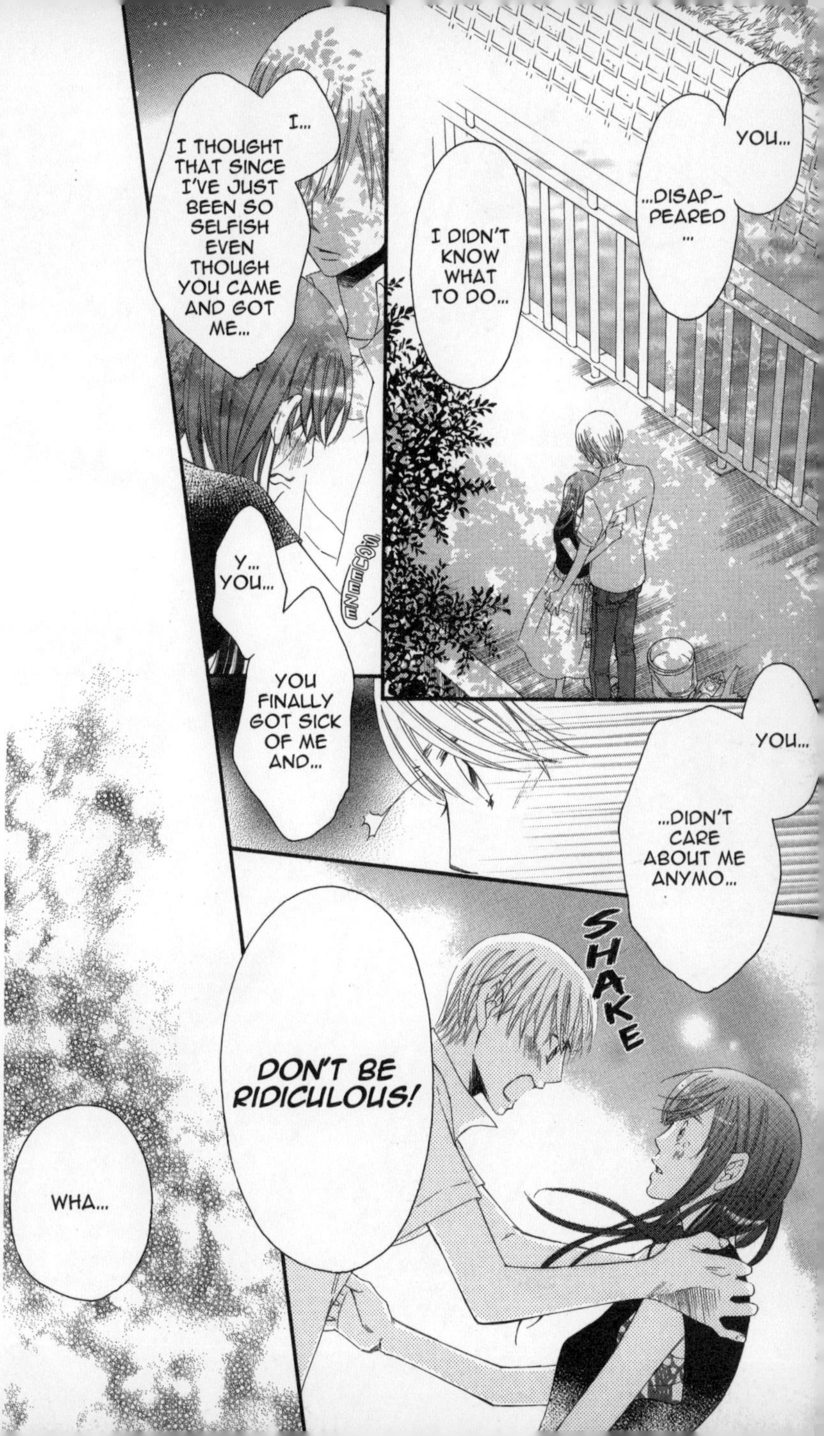
YOU... ...DISAPPEARED...
I DIDN'T KNOW WHAT TO DO...
I... I THOUGHT THAT SINCE I'VE JUST BEEN SO SELFISH EVEN THOUGH YOU CAME AND GOT ME...
SQUEEZE
Y... YOU...
YOU FINALLY GOT SICK OF ME AND...
YOU... ...DIDN'T CARE ABOUT ME ANYMO...
SHAKE
DON'T BE RIDICULOUS!
WHA...

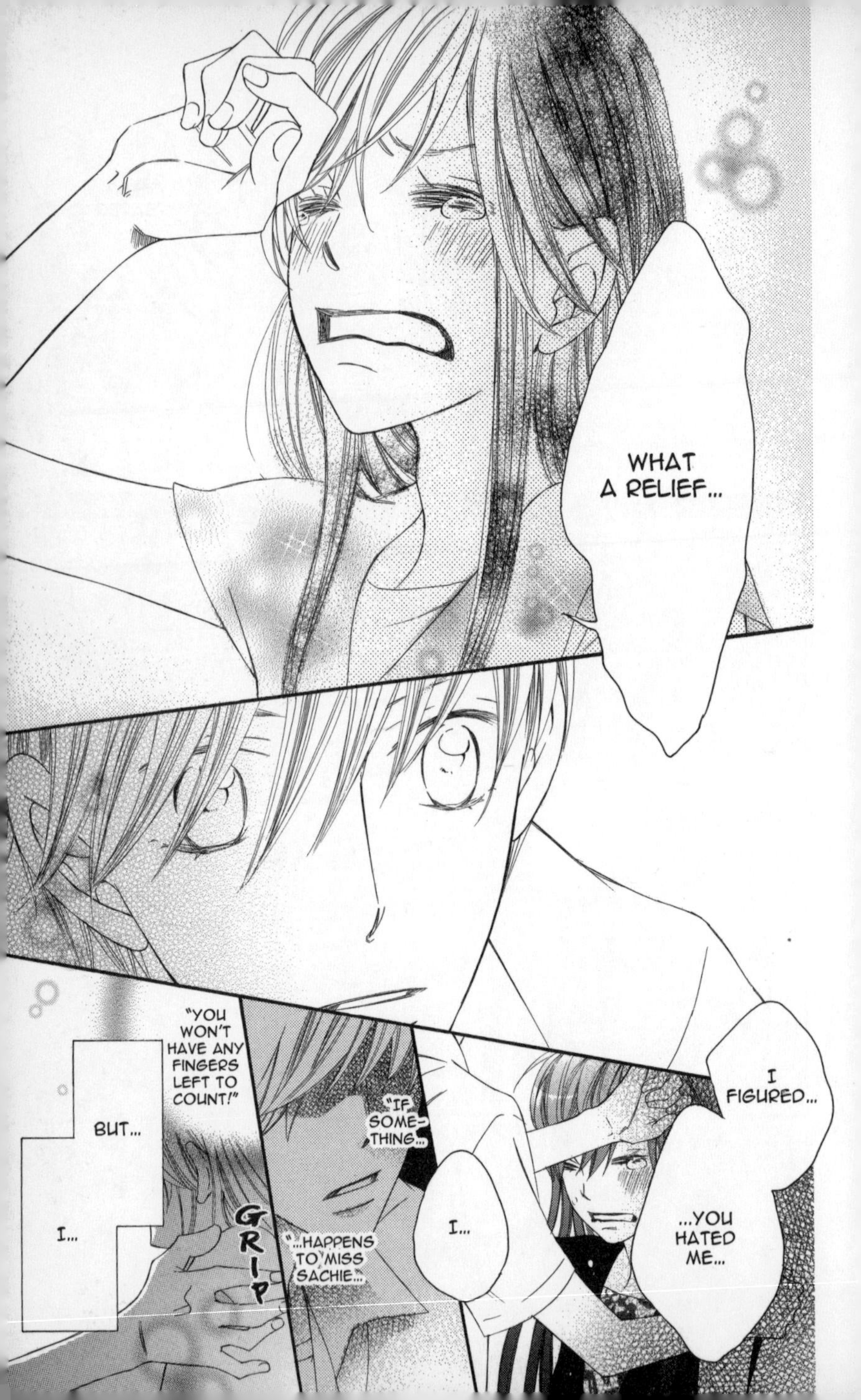
WHAT A RELIEF...
I FIGURED...
...YOU HATED ME...
I...
"IF SOME-THING...
"...HAPPENS TO MISS SACHIE..."
GRIP
"YOU WON'T HAVE ANY FINGERS LEFT TO COUNT!"
BUT...
I...

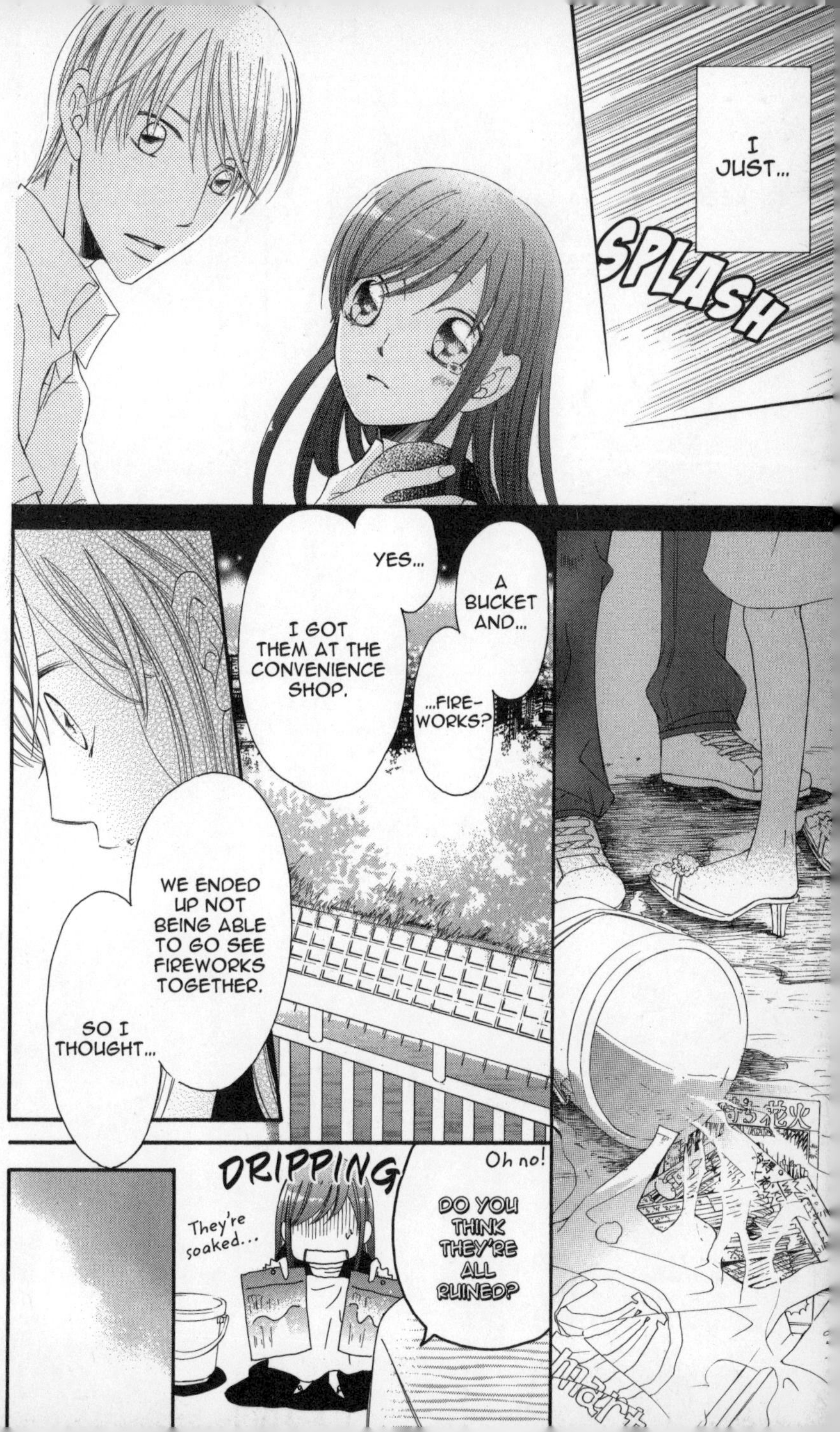
I JUST...
SPLASH
A BUCKET AND... ...FIREWORKS?
YES... I GOT THEM AT THE CONVENIENCE SHOP.
WE ENDED UP NOT BEING ABLE TO GO SEE FIREWORKS TOGETHER.
SO I THOUGHT...
Oh no!
DO YOU THINK THEY'RE ALL RUINED?
DRIPPING
They're soaked...

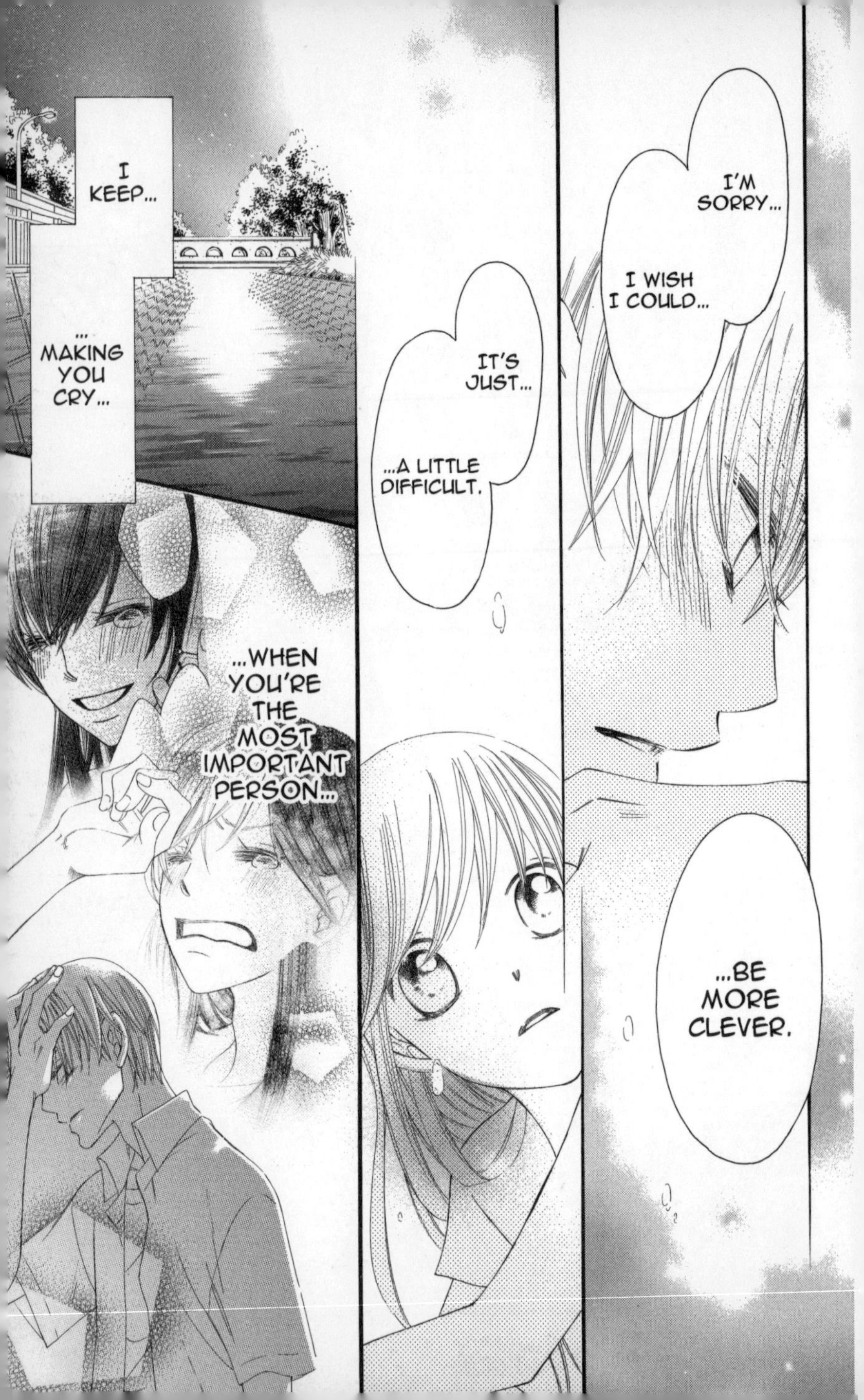
I'M SORRY...
I WISH I COULD...
...BE MORE CLEVER.
IT'S JUST...
...A LITTLE DIFFICULT.
I KEEP...
...MAKING YOU CRY...
...WHEN YOU'RE THE MOST IMPORTANT PERSON...

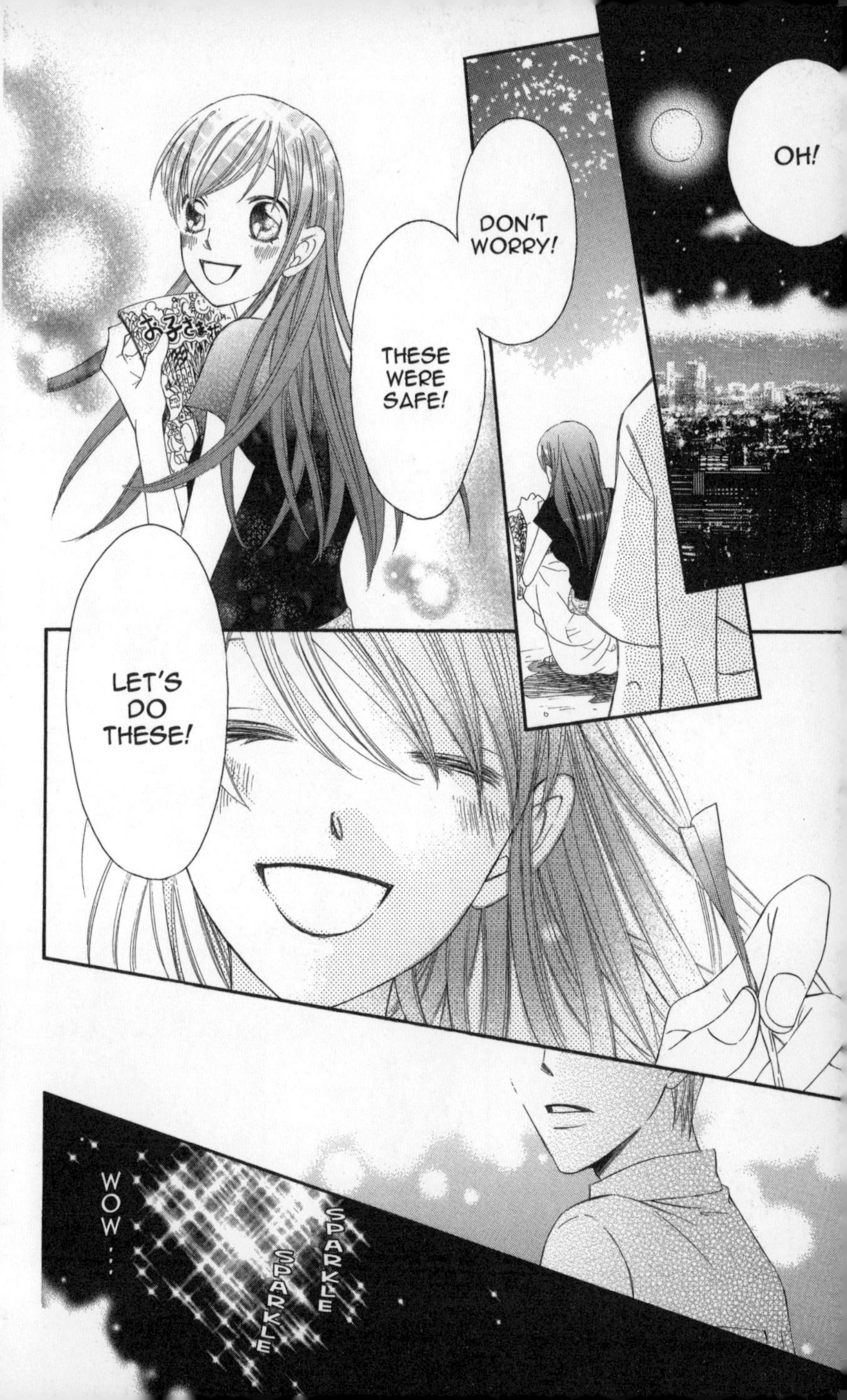
OH!
DON'T WORRY!
THESE WERE SAFE!
LET'S DO THESE!
WOW...
SPARKLE
SPARKLE

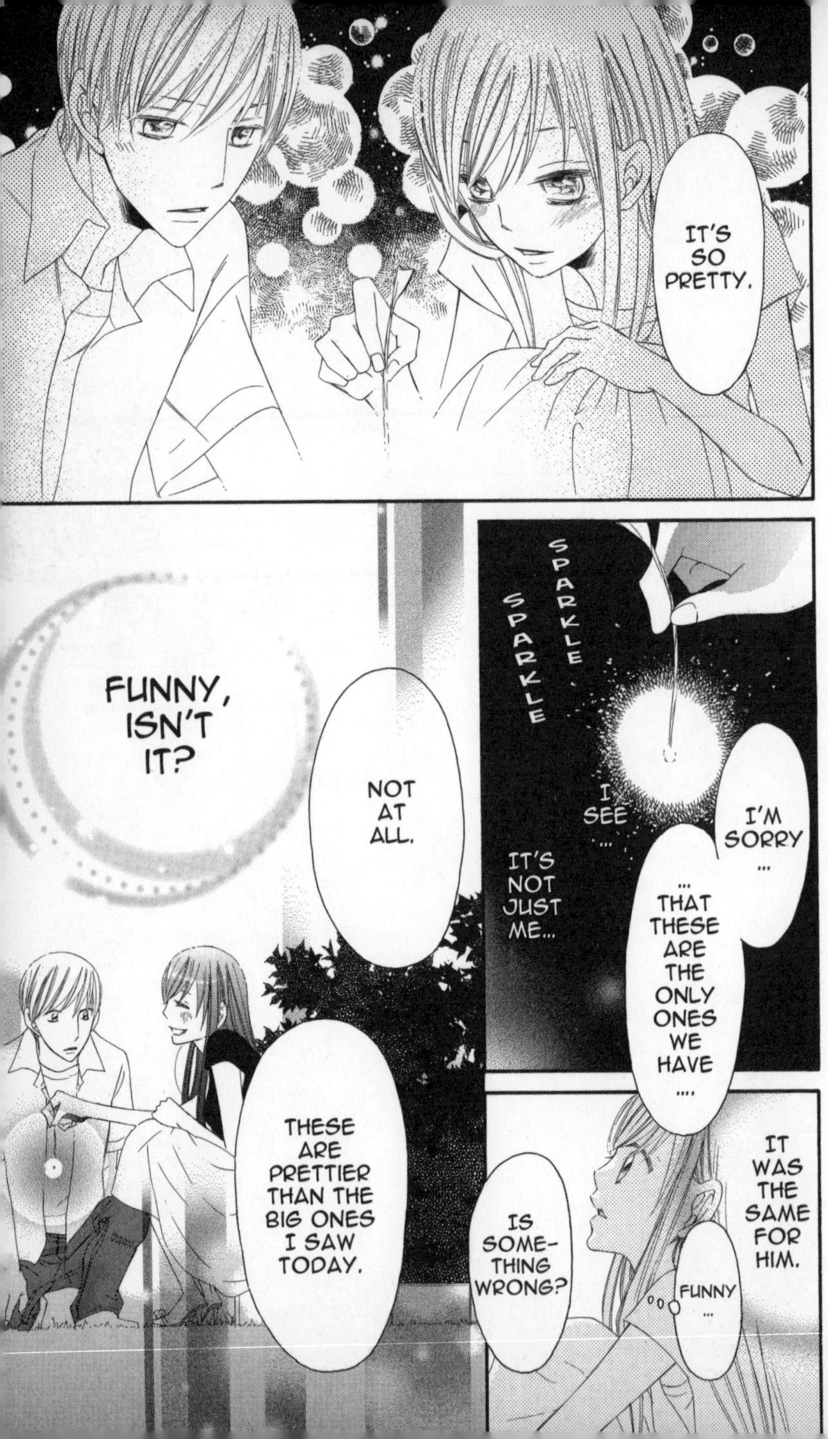
IT'S SO PRETTY.
SPARKLE SPARKLE
I'M SORRY...
...THAT THESE ARE THE ONLY ONES WE HAVE....
I SEE...
IT'S NOT JUST ME...
IT WAS THE SAME FOR HIM.
FUNNY...
IS SOMETHING WRONG?
NOT AT ALL.
FUNNY, ISN'T IT?
THESE ARE PRETTIER THAN THE BIG ONES I SAW TODAY.

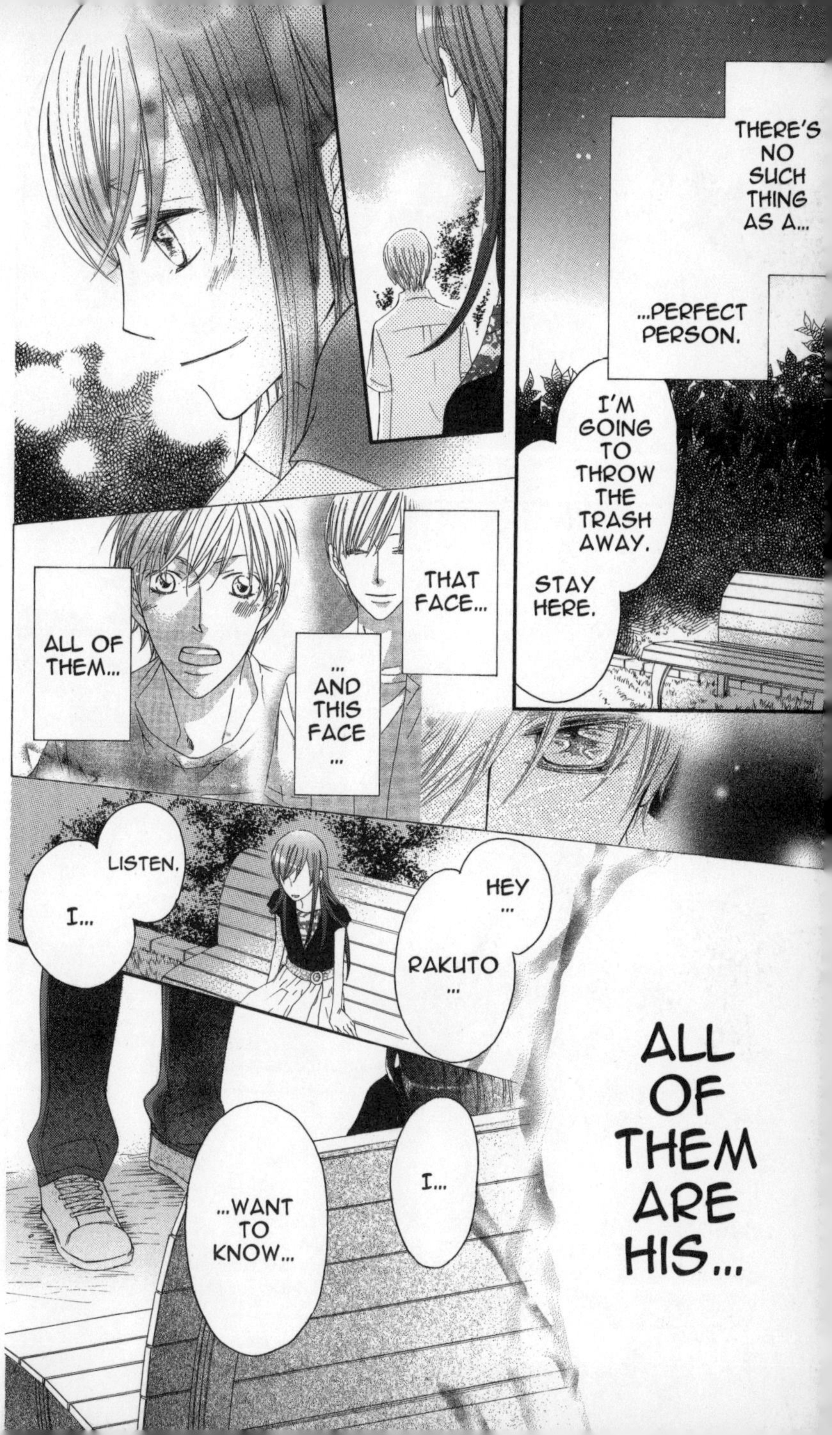
THERE'S NO SUCH THING AS A...
...PERFECT PERSON.
I'M GOING TO THROW THE TRASH AWAY.
STAY HERE.
THAT FACE...
...AND THIS FACE...
ALL OF THEM...
HEY... RAKUTO...
LISTEN. I...
ALL OF THEM ARE HIS...
I...
...WANT TO KNOW...

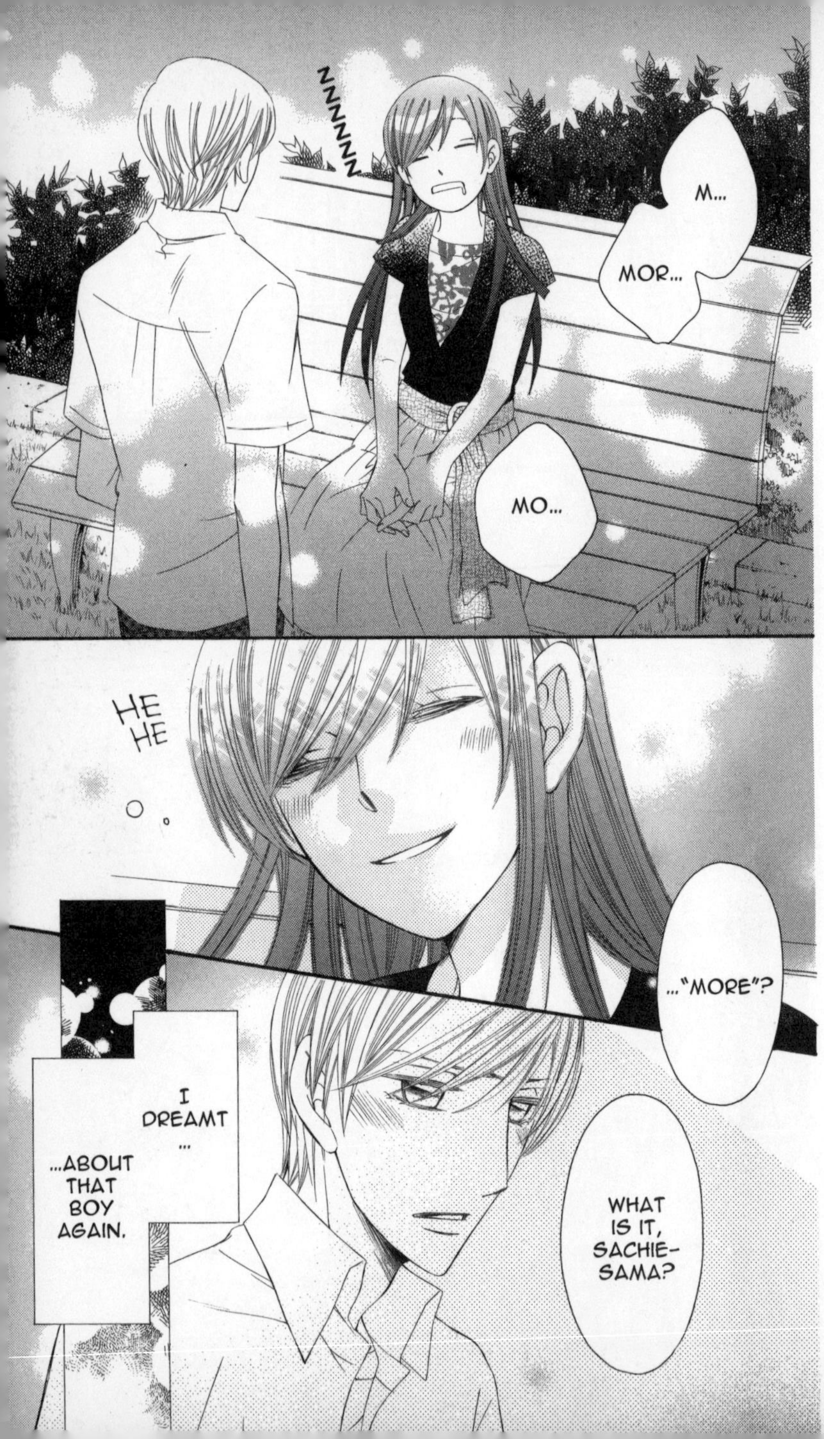
M...
MOR...
ZZZZZZ
MO...
HE HE
..."MORE"?
WHAT IS IT, SACHIE-SAMA?
I DREAMT ...
...ABOUT THAT BOY AGAIN.

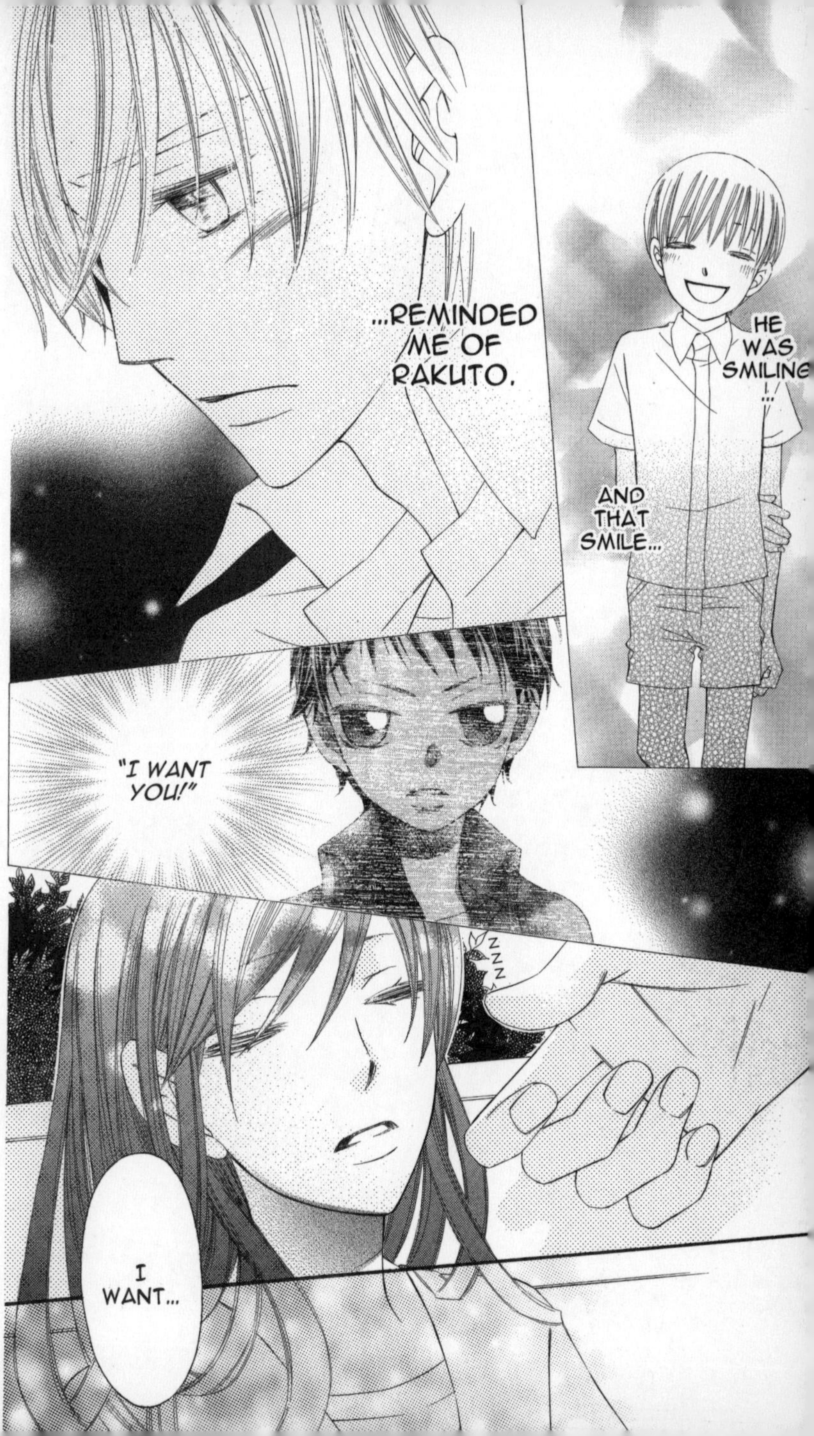
HE WAS SMILING...
AND THAT SMILE...
...REMINDED ME OF RAKUTO.
"I WANT YOU!"
ZZZ
I WANT...

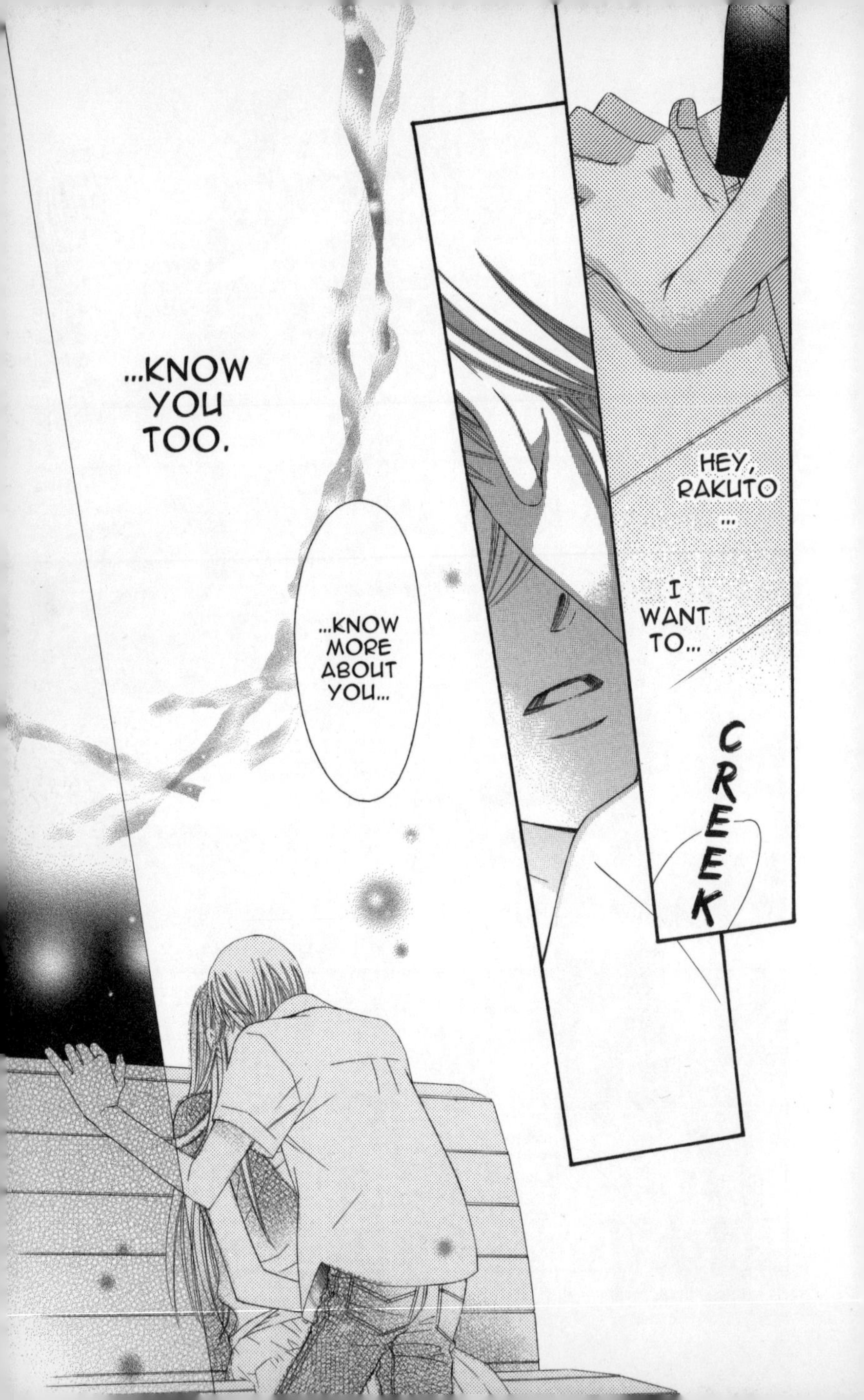
HEY, RAKUTO ...
I WANT TO...
CREEK
...KNOW MORE ABOUT YOU...
...KNOW YOU TOO.

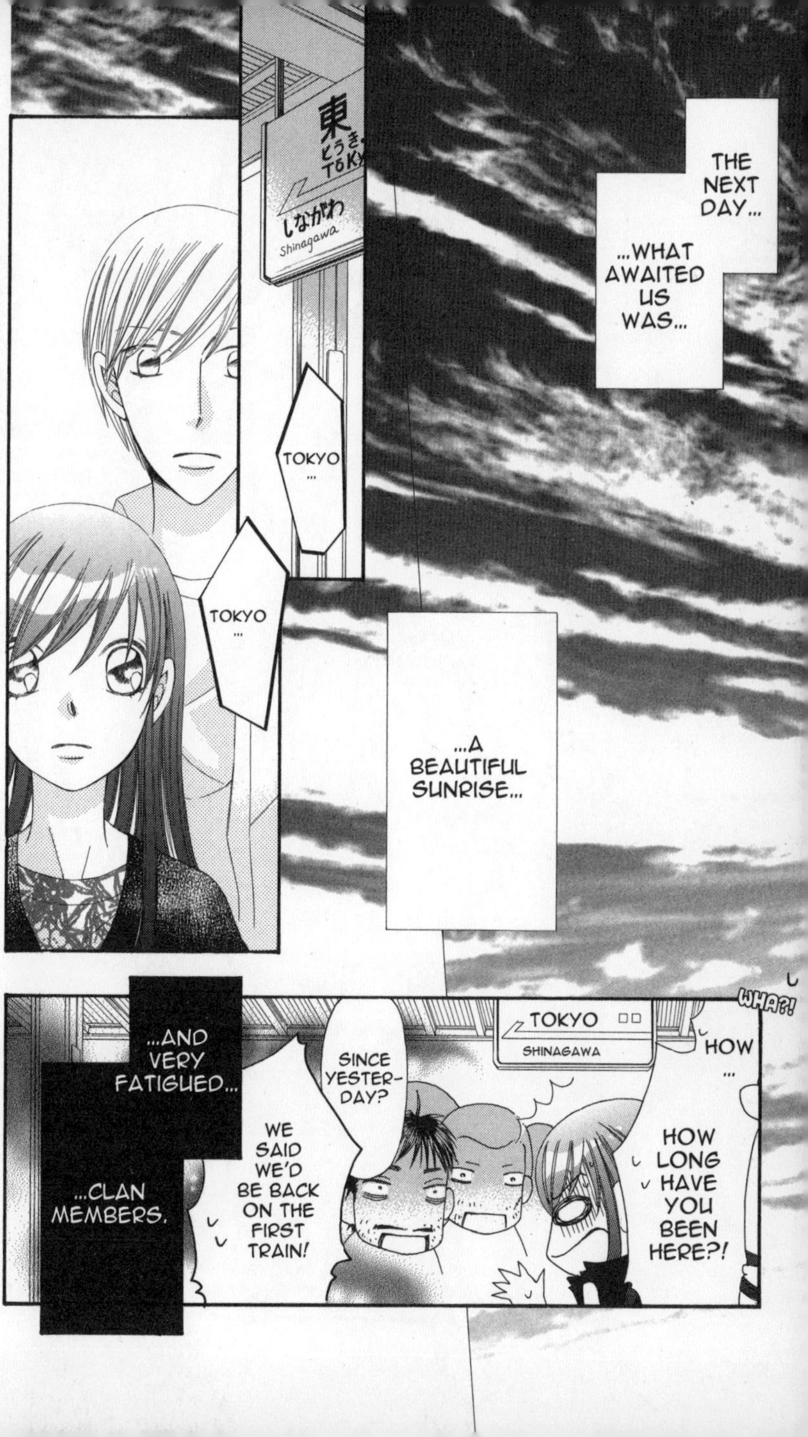
THE NEXT DAY...
...WHAT AWAITED US WAS...
...A BEAUTIFUL SUNRISE...
東
しながわ
Shinagawa
TOKYO ...
TOKYO ...
WHA?!
HOW ...
HOW LONG HAVE YOU BEEN HERE?!
TOKYO
SHINAGAWA
SINCE YESTER-DAY?
WE SAID WE'D BE BACK ON THE FIRST TRAIN!
...AND VERY FATIGUED...
...CLAN MEMBERS.

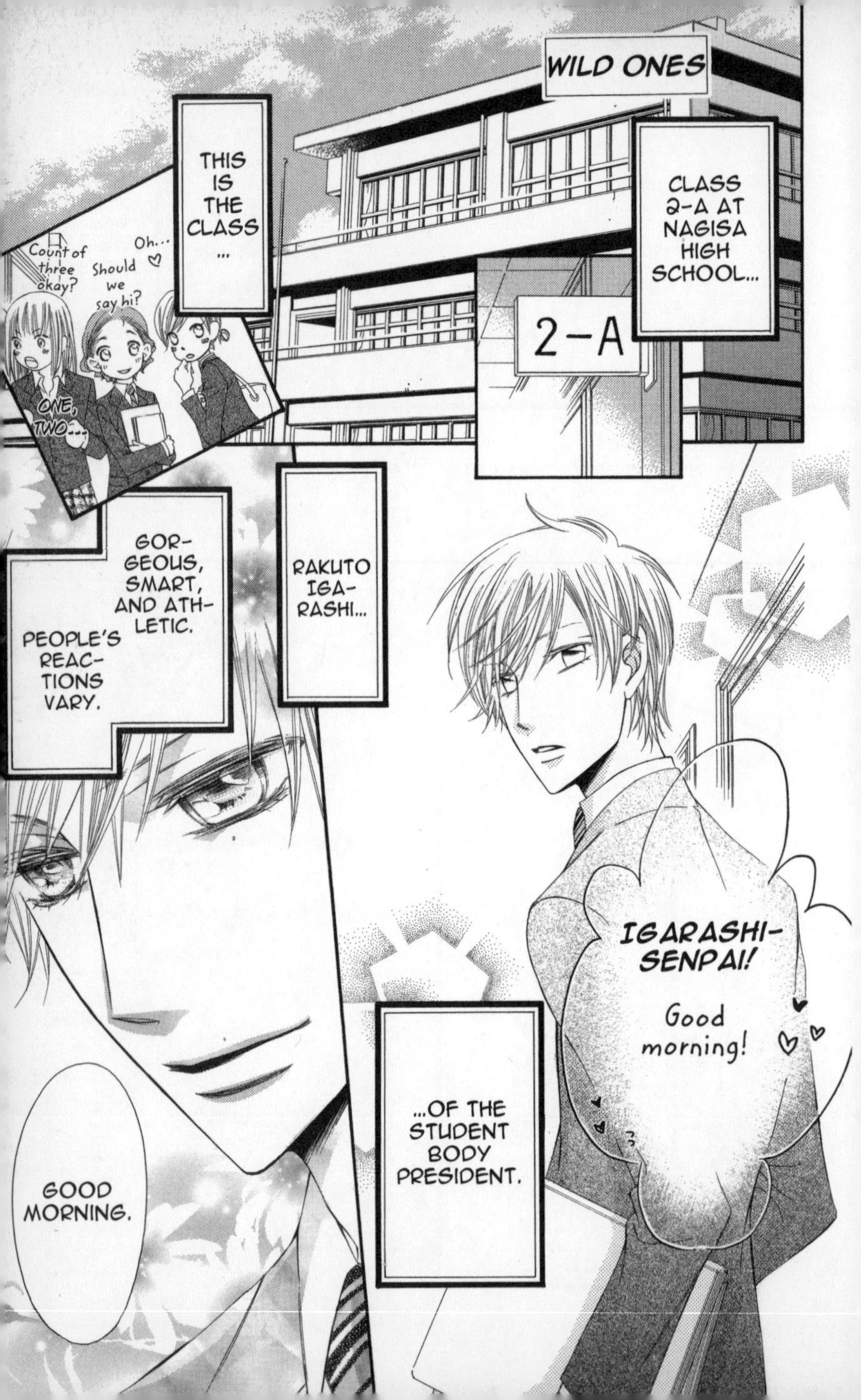
WILD ONES
CLASS 2-A AT NAGISA HIGH SCHOOL...
2-A
THIS IS THE CLASS...
Oh... ♡
Should we say hi?
Count of three okay?
ONE, TWO...
IGARASHI-SENPAI!
Good morning!
RAKUTO IGARASHI...
GORGEOUS, SMART, AND ATHLETIC.
PEOPLE'S REACTIONS VARY.
...OF THE STUDENT BODY PRESIDENT.
GOOD MORNING.

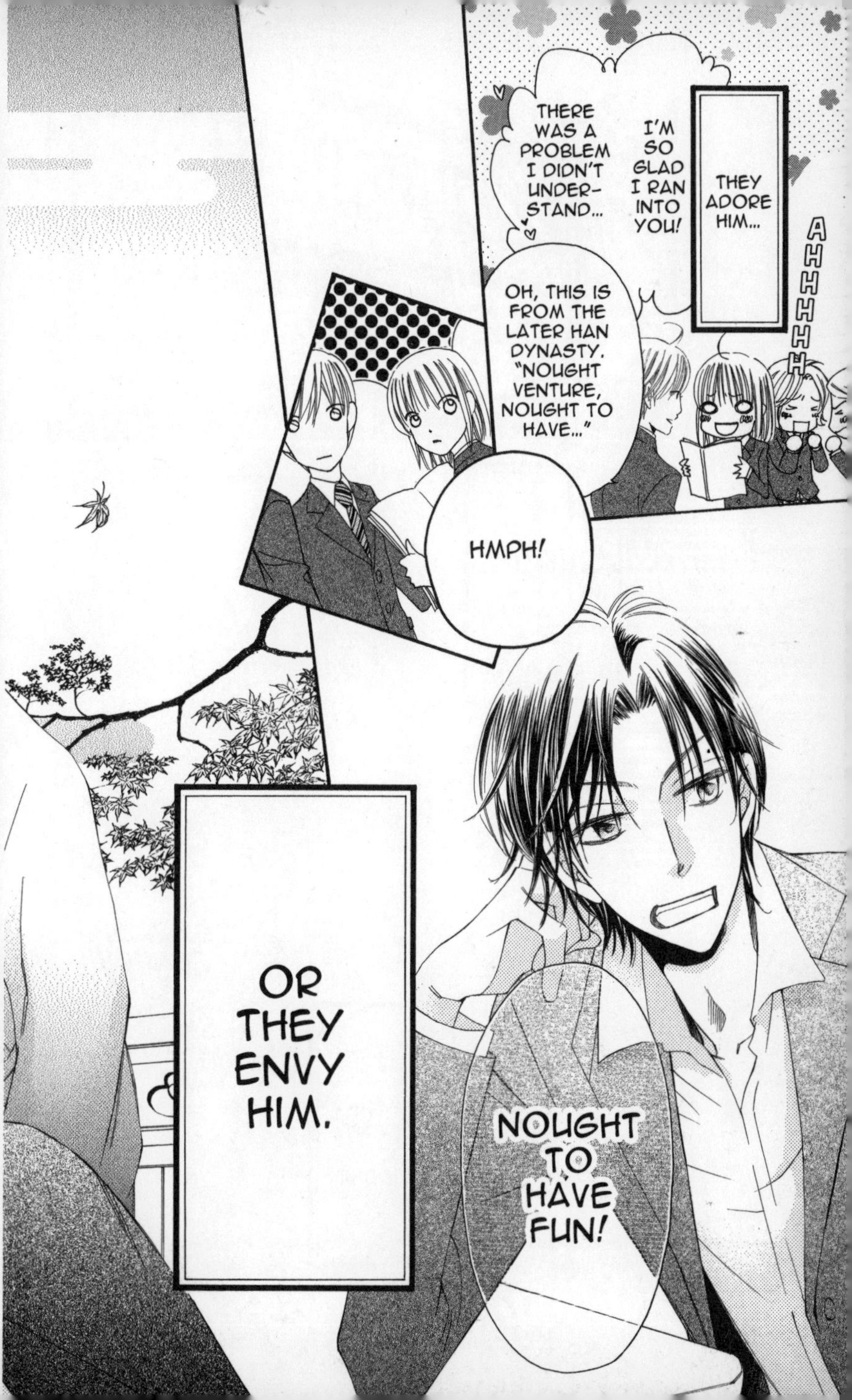
THEY ADORE HIM...
AHHHHHH
I'M SO GLAD I RAN INTO YOU!
THERE WAS A PROBLEM I DIDN'T UNDER-STAND...
OH, THIS IS FROM THE LATER HAN DYNASTY. "NOUGHT VENTURE, NOUGHT TO HAVE..."
HMPH!
OR THEY ENVY HIM.
NOUGHT TO HAVE FUN!

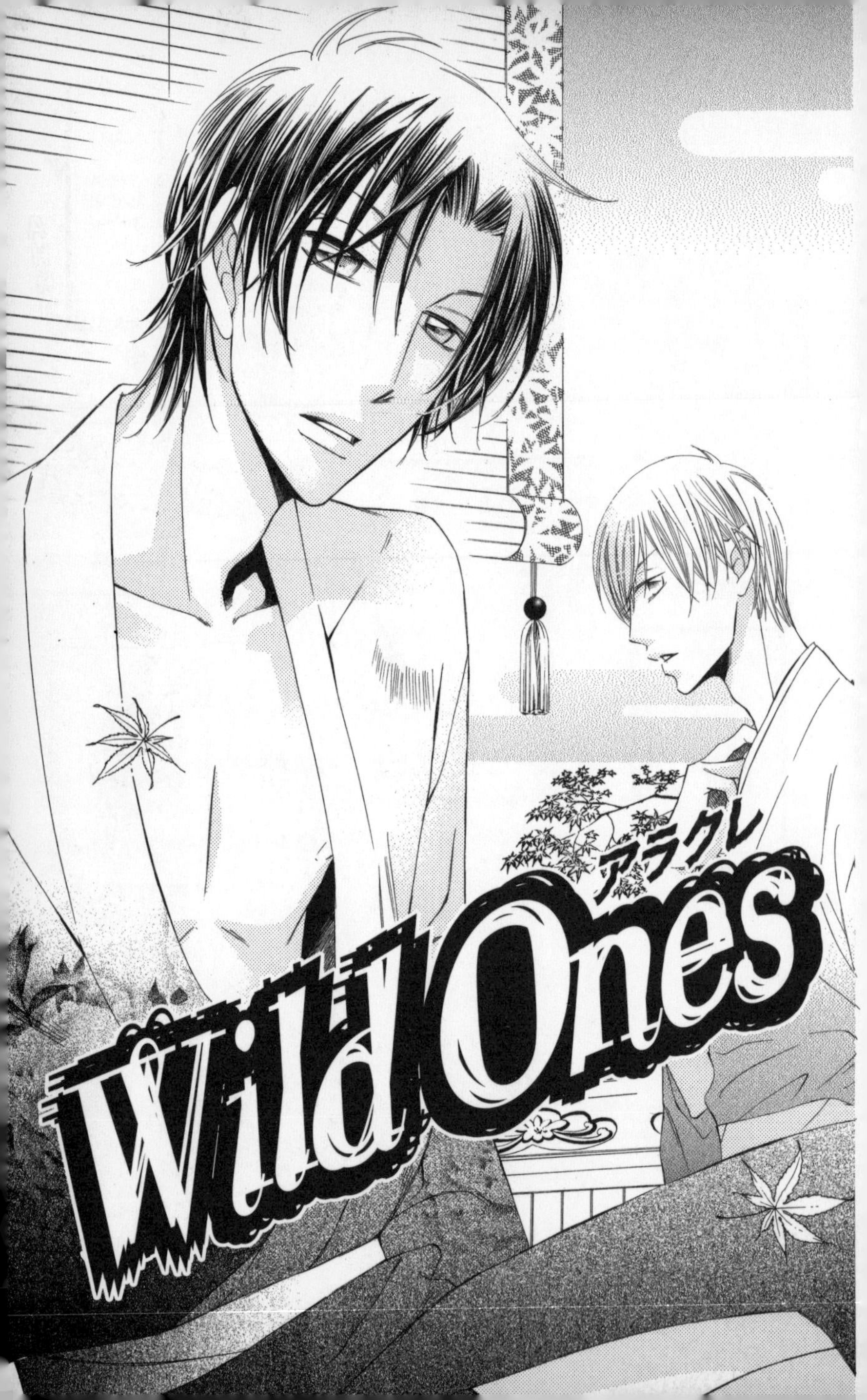

アラクレ
Wild Ones

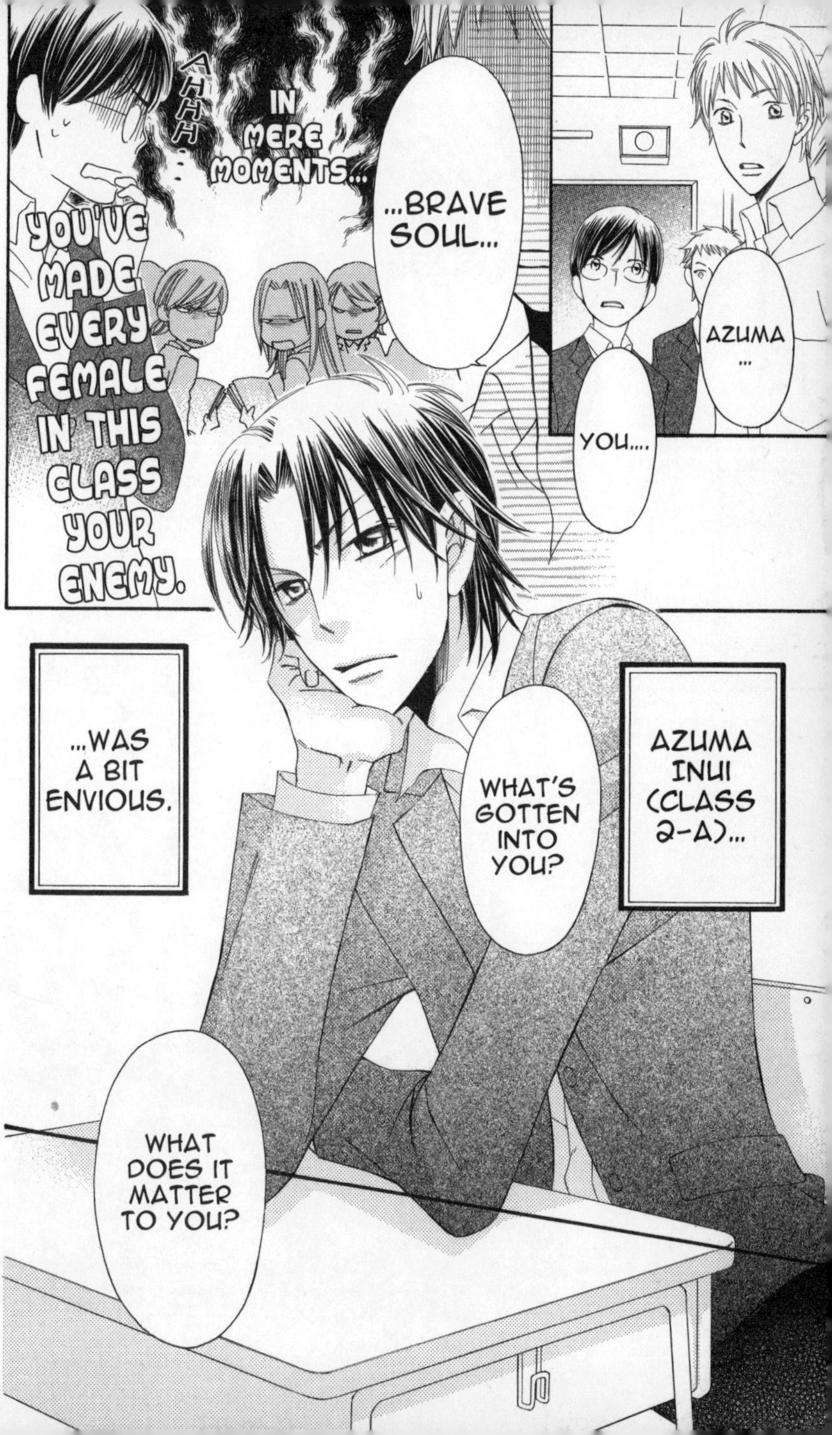
AZUMA ...
YOU....
...BRAVE SOUL...
IN MERE MOMENTS...
AHHH...
YOU'VE MADE EVERY FEMALE IN THIS CLASS YOUR ENEMY.
AZUMA INUI (CLASS 2-A)...
WHAT'S GOTTEN INTO YOU?
...WAS A BIT ENVIOUS.
WHAT DOES IT MATTER TO YOU?

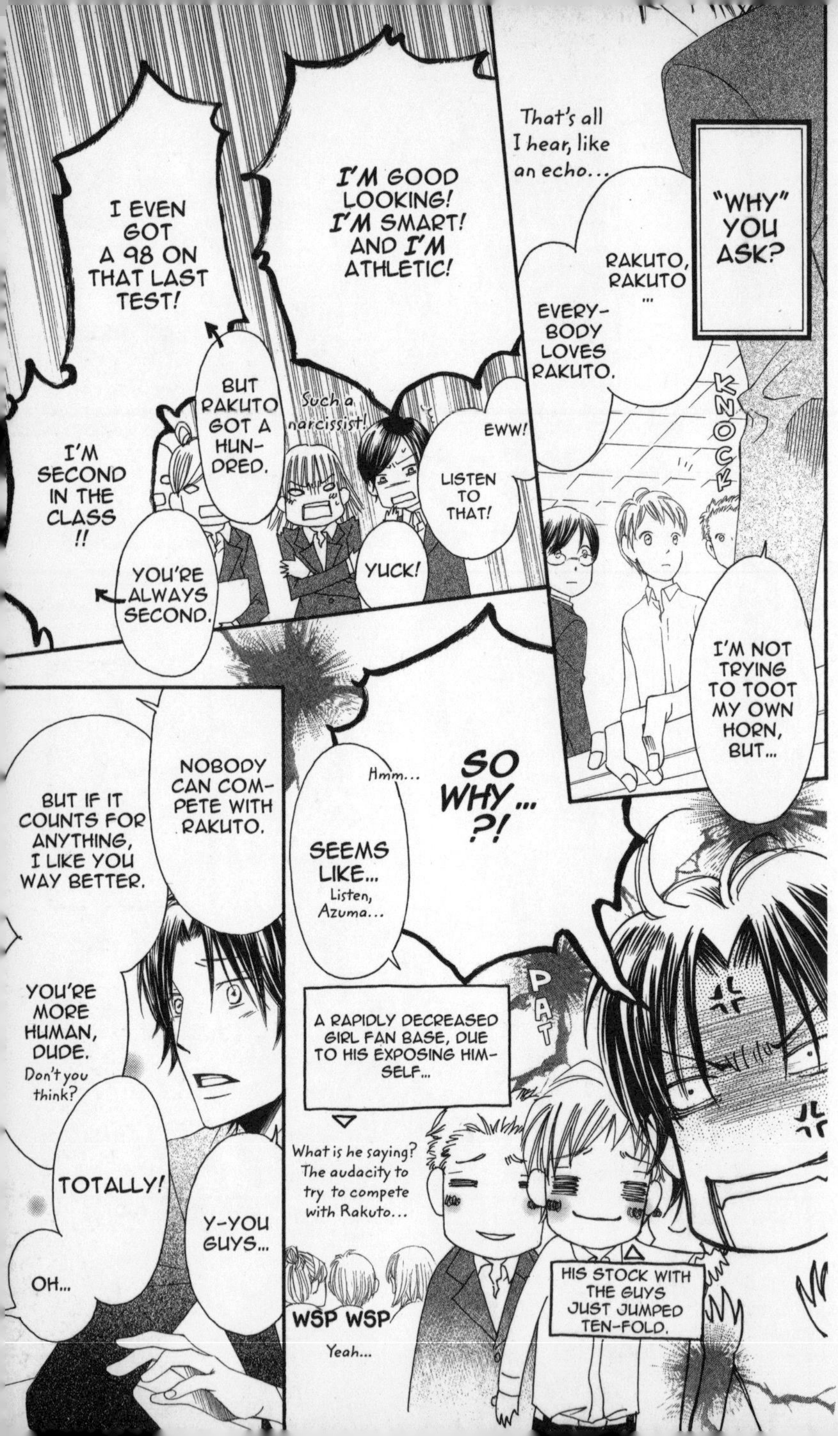

"WHY" YOU ASK?
That's all I hear, like an echo...
RAKUTO, RAKUTO ...
EVERYBODY LOVES RAKUTO.
KNOCK
I'M NOT TRYING TO TOOT MY OWN HORN, BUT...
I'M GOOD LOOKING! I'M SMART! AND I'M ATHLETIC!
I EVEN GOT A 98 ON THAT LAST TEST!
EWW!
LISTEN TO THAT!
Such a narcissist!
BUT RAKUTO GOT A HUNDRED.
YUCK!
I'M SECOND IN THE CLASS !!
YOU'RE ALWAYS SECOND.
SO WHY...?!
Hmm...
SEEMS LIKE...
Listen, Azuma...
PAT
A RAPIDLY DECREASED GIRL FAN BASE, DUE TO HIS EXPOSING HIMSELF...
What is he saying? The audacity to try to compete with Rakuto...
HIS STOCK WITH THE GUYS JUST JUMPED TEN-FOLD.
WSP WSP
Yeah...
NOBODY CAN COMPETE WITH RAKUTO.
BUT IF IT COUNTS FOR ANYTHING, I LIKE YOU WAY BETTER.
YOU'RE MORE HUMAN, DUDE.
Don't you think?
TOTALLY!
Y-YOU GUYS...
OH...

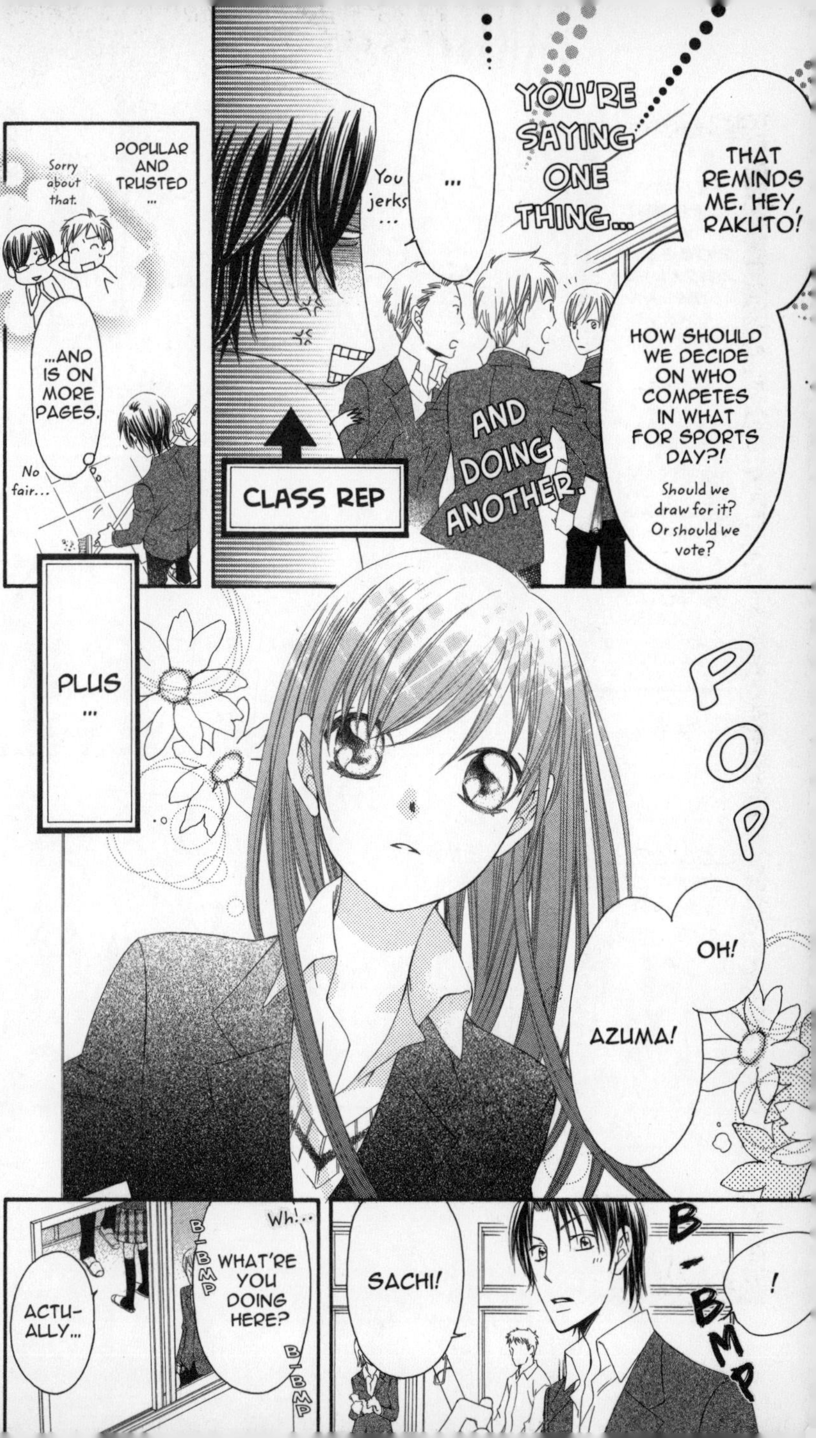
THAT REMINDS ME. HEY, RAKUTO!
HOW SHOULD WE DECIDE ON WHO COMPETES IN WHAT FOR SPORTS DAY?!
Should we draw for it? Or should we vote?
YOU'RE SAYING ONE THING...
AND DOING ANOTHER.
...
You jerks...
CLASS REP
POPULAR AND TRUSTED...
Sorry about that.
Couldn't help it.
...AND IS ON MORE PAGES.
No fair...
PLUS...
POP
OH!
AZUMA!
B-BMP
!
SACHI!
Wh!...
B-BMP
WHAT'RE YOU DOING HERE?
B-BMP
ACTU-ALLY...

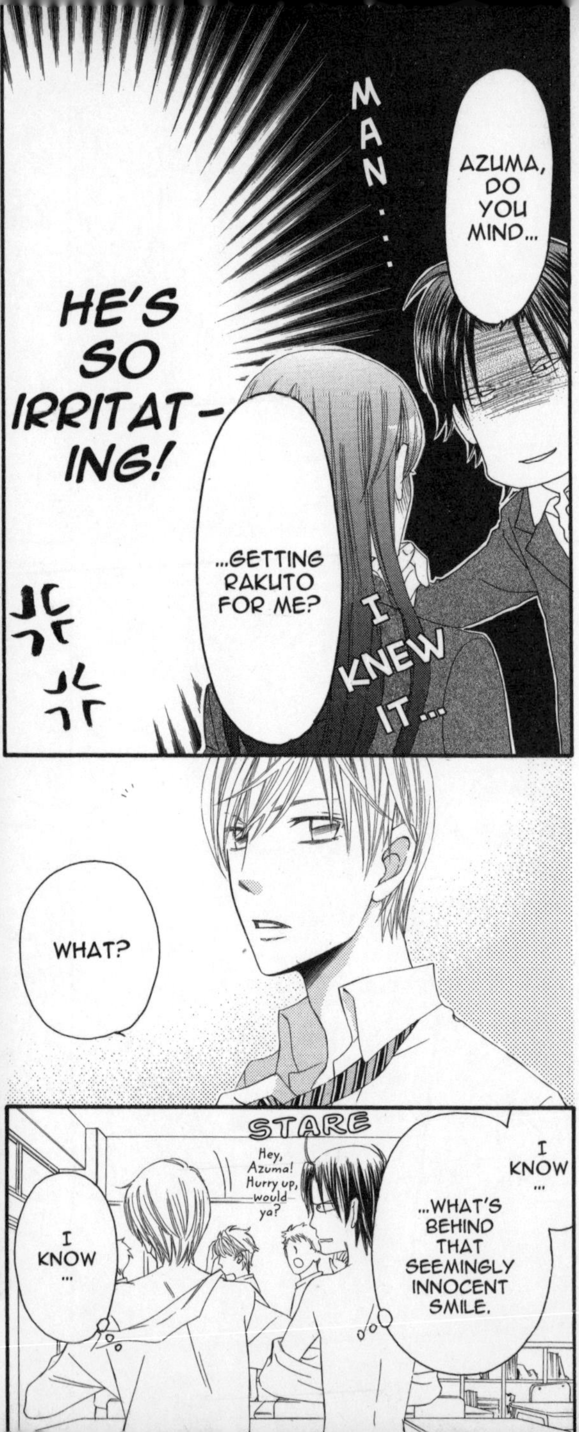
AZUMA, DO YOU MIND...
MAN...
HE'S SO IRRITAT-ING!
...GETTING RAKUTO FOR ME?
I KNEW IT...
WHAT?
I KNOW...
...WHAT'S BEHIND THAT SEEMINGLY INNOCENT SMILE.
STARE
Hey, Azuma! Hurry up, would ya?
I KNOW...

I WROTE SOMEWHERE THAT MY PHONE BILL IS RIDICULOUSLY CHEAP. AND SOMEONE POINTED OUT THAT IT'S A LANDLINE...

WOW. YES, IT'S TRUE. I GUESS YOU DON'T USE LANDLINES IF YOU HAVE A CELL THESE DAYS... NO WONDER IT'S SO CHEAP.

ALTHOUGH MY CELL LOG STILL HAS...

...RECORDS OF CALLS FROM A YEAR AGO.

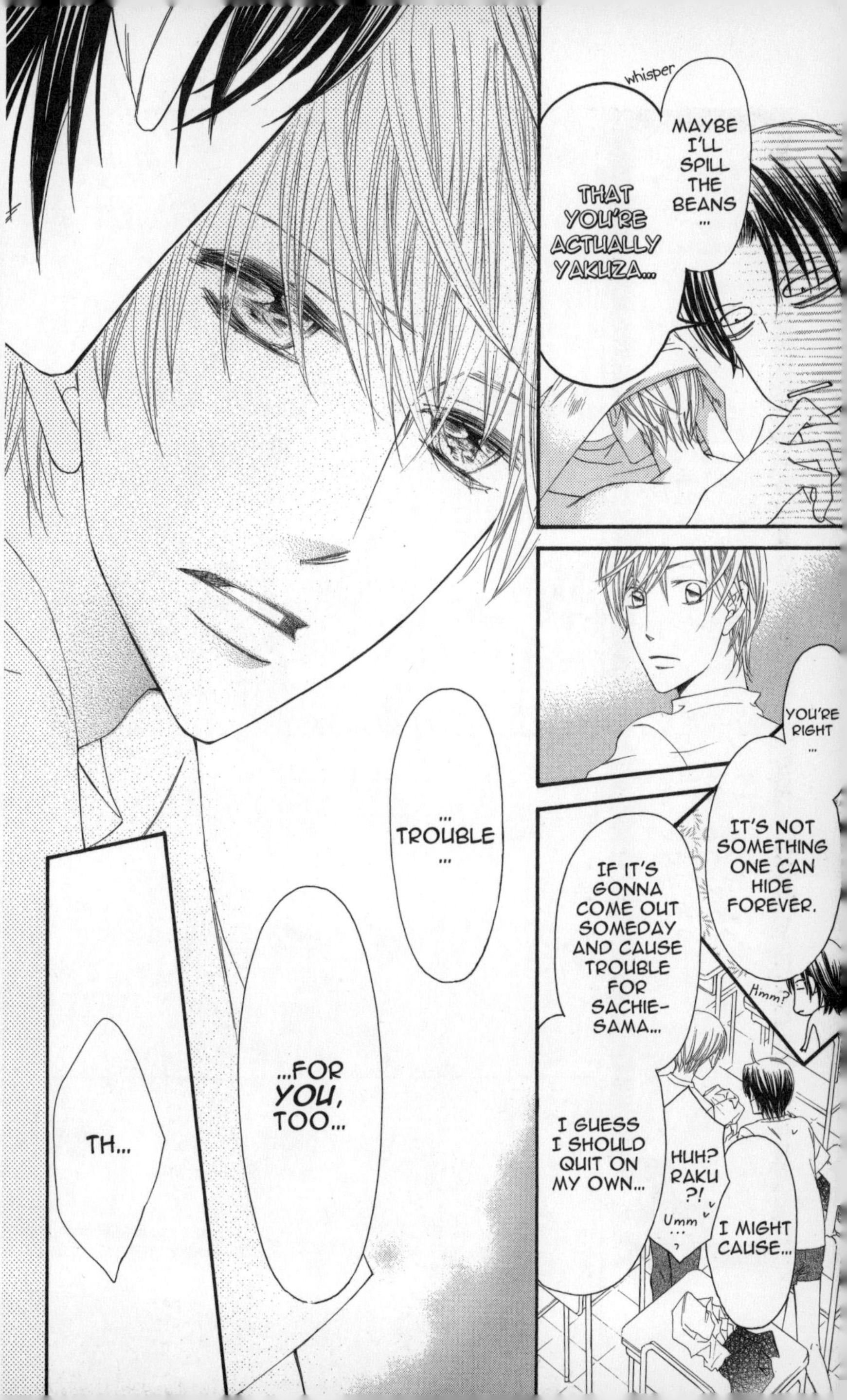
whisper
MAYBE I'LL SPILL THE BEANS...
THAT YOU'RE ACTUALLY YAKUZA...
YOU'RE RIGHT...
IT'S NOT SOMETHING ONE CAN HIDE FOREVER.
IF IT'S GONNA COME OUT SOMEDAY AND CAUSE TROUBLE FOR SACHIE-SAMA...
Hmm?
I MIGHT CAUSE...
HUH? RAKU?!
Umm...
I GUESS I SHOULD QUIT ON MY OWN...
...TROUBLE...
...FOR *YOU*, TOO...
TH...

THESE DAYS I OFTEN SEE A CLASSMATE OF MINE FROM HIGH SCHOOL ON TV.

HIS NAME IS CHAD MULLANE, AND HE WAS AN EXCHANGE STUDENT, BUT HE'S GOT A PROMISING CAREER WITH YOSHIMOTO NOW. HE WRITES ME BACK EMAILS WITH BETTER JAPANESE THAN ME...

IT'S INSPIRING, REALLY...

I ALWAYS GET CHAD UPDATES FROM MY LITTLE SISTER AND MY MOTHER. LIKE WHAT SHOW HE'S ON, OR WHAT DRAMA SERIES HE'S STARRING IN. (LOL) WE'RE ALL HUGE FANS.

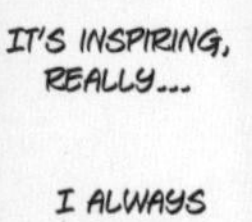

GO CHAD! LET'S GO GRAB A BITE TO EAT SOON!

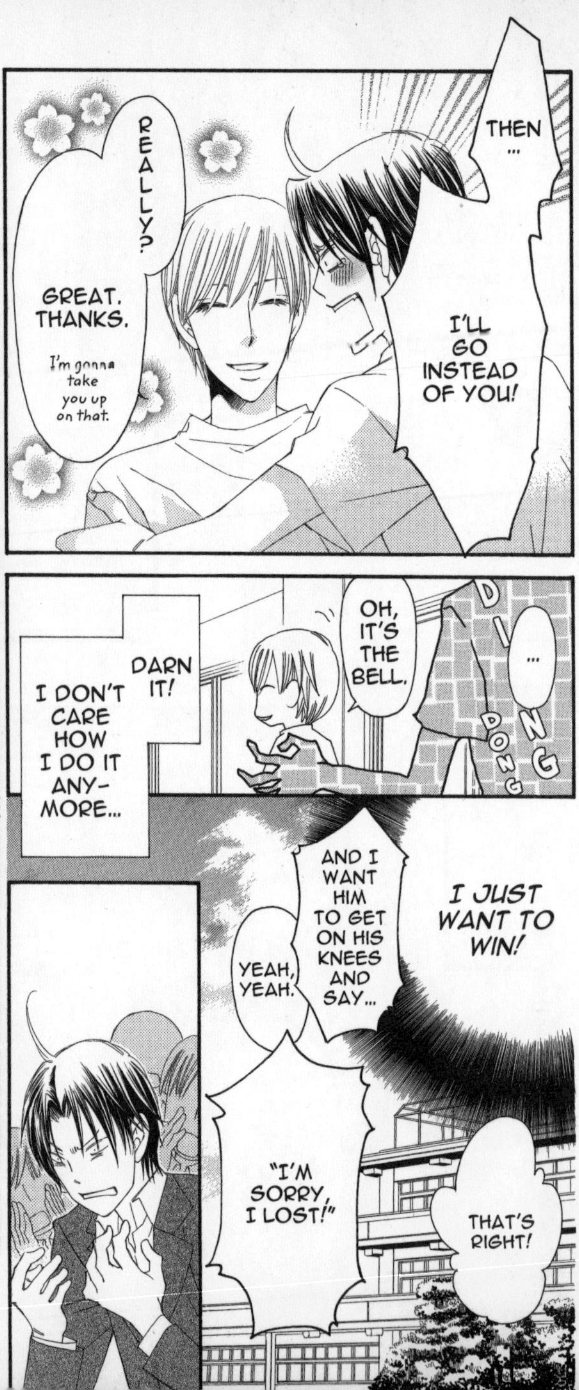
THEN...
I'LL GO INSTEAD OF YOU!
REALLY?
GREAT. THANKS.
I'm gonna take you up on that.
DING DONG
...
OH, IT'S THE BELL.
DARN IT!
I DON'T CARE HOW I DO IT ANYMORE...
I JUST WANT TO WIN!
AND I WANT HIM TO GET ON HIS KNEES AND SAY...
YEAH, YEAH.
THAT'S RIGHT!
"I'M SORRY, I LOST!"

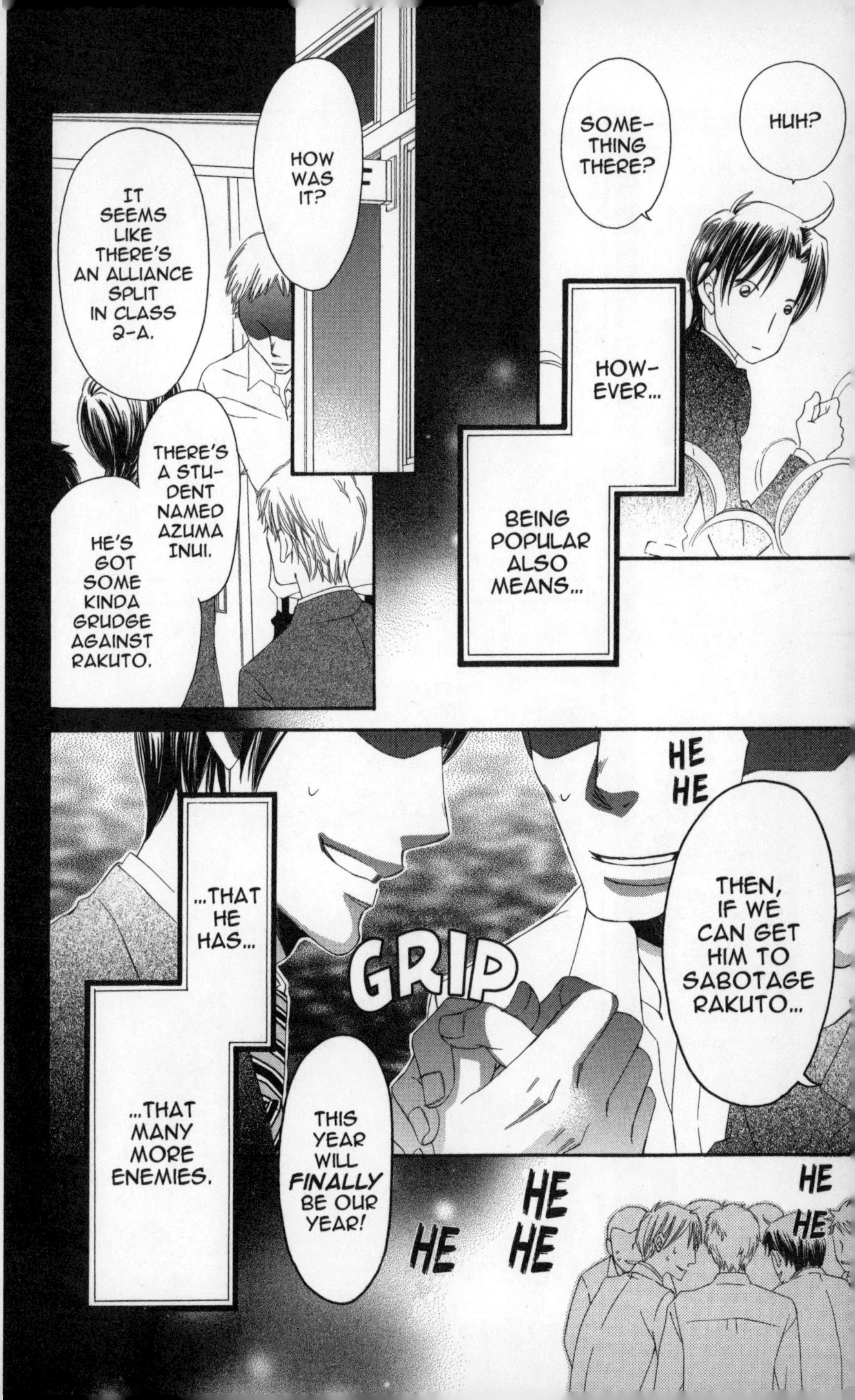
HUH?
SOME-THING THERE?
HOW-EVER...
BEING POPULAR ALSO MEANS...
HOW WAS IT?
IT SEEMS LIKE THERE'S AN ALLIANCE SPLIT IN CLASS 2-A.
THERE'S A STU-DENT NAMED AZUMA INUI.
HE'S GOT SOME KINDA GRUDGE AGAINST RAKUTO.
HE HE
THEN, IF WE CAN GET HIM TO SABOTAGE RAKUTO...
GRIP
...THAT HE HAS...
HE HE
HE HE
HE
THIS YEAR WILL *FINALLY* BE OUR YEAR!
...THAT MANY MORE ENEMIES.

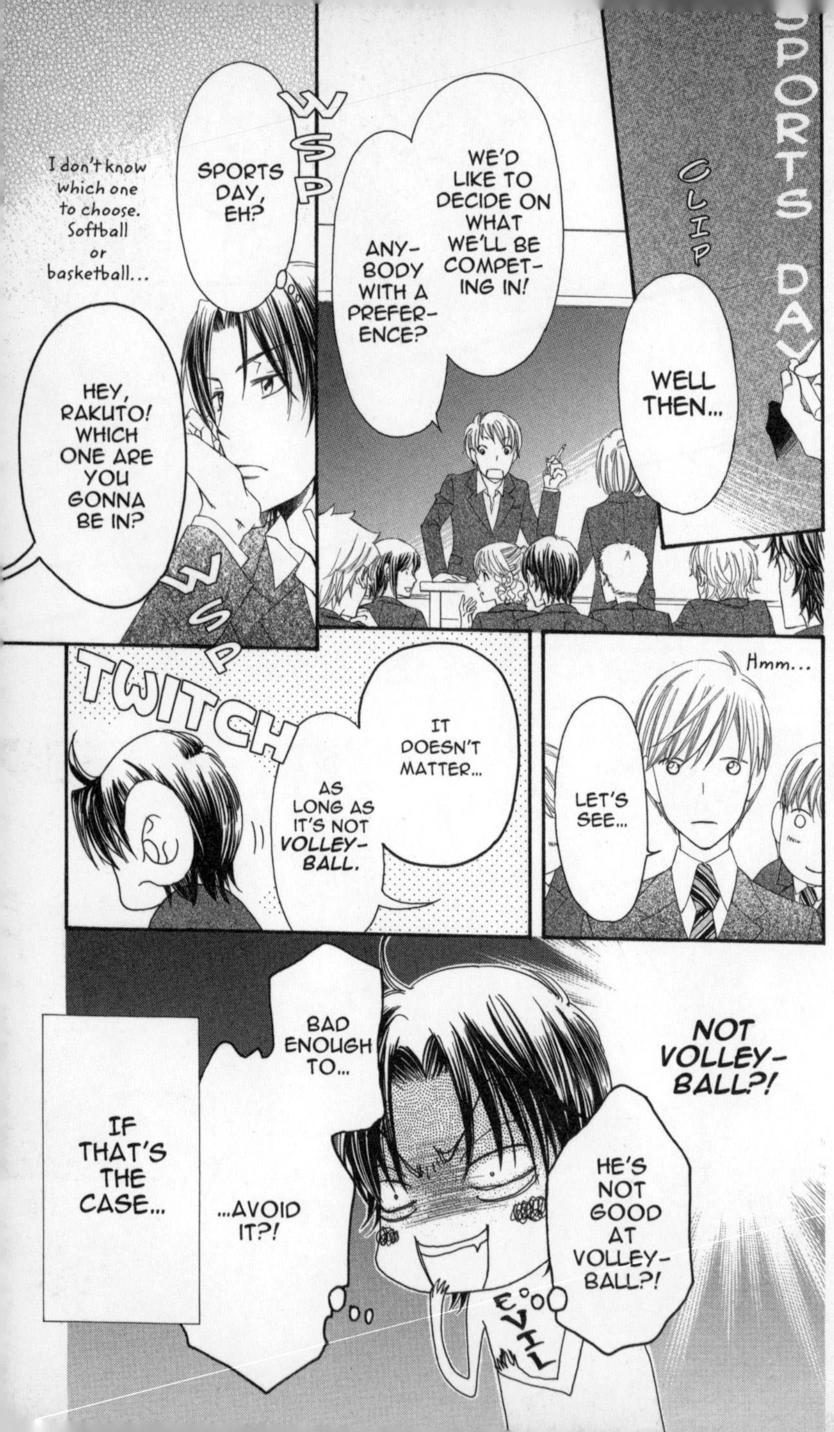

SPORTS DAY
CLIP
WELL THEN...
WE'D LIKE TO DECIDE ON WHAT WE'LL BE COMPETING IN!
ANYBODY WITH A PREFERENCE?
WSP
SPORTS DAY, EH?
I don't know which one to choose. Softball or basketball...
HEY, RAKUTO! WHICH ONE ARE YOU GONNA BE IN?
WSP
Hmm...
LET'S SEE...
TWITCH
IT DOESN'T MATTER...
AS LONG AS IT'S NOT *VOLLEYBALL.*
NOT VOLLEY-BALL?!
HE'S NOT GOOD AT VOLLEY-BALL?!
EVIL
BAD ENOUGH TO...
...AVOID IT?!
IF THAT'S THE CASE...

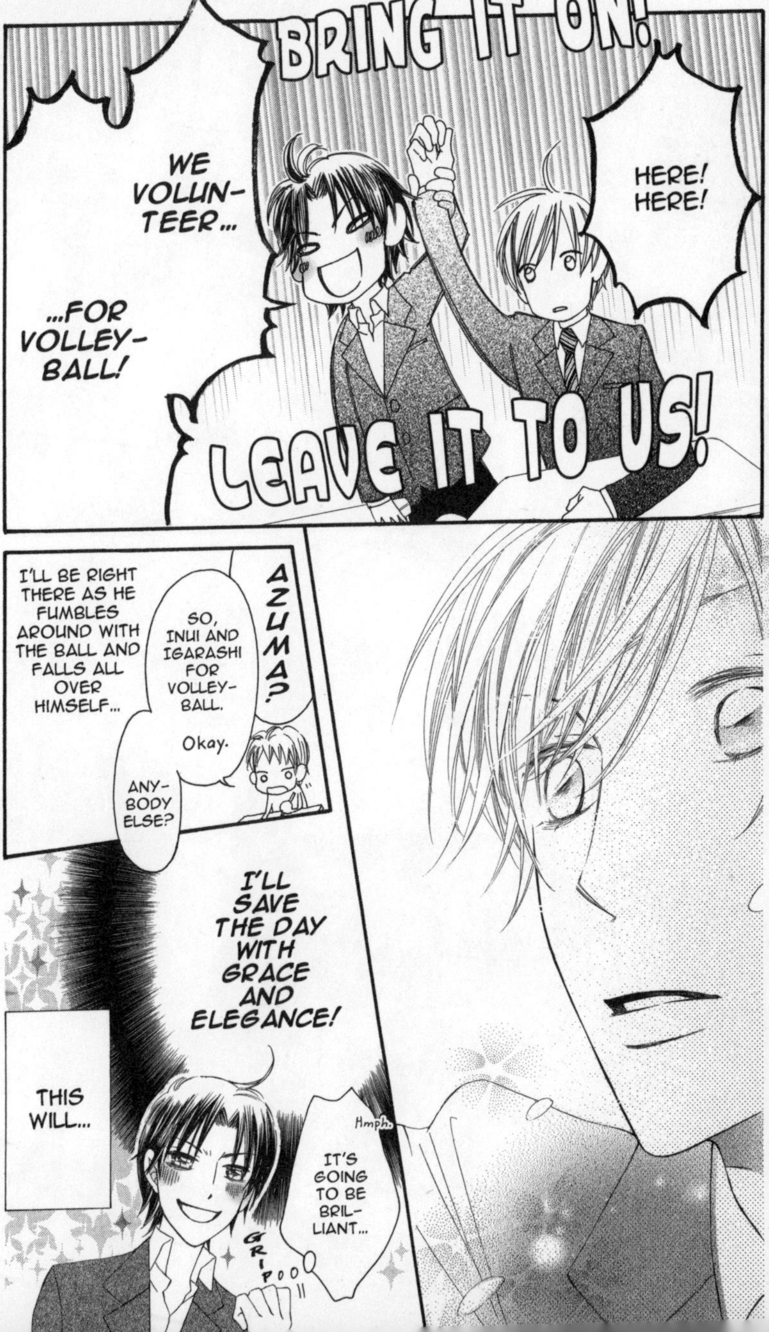
BRING IT ON!
HERE! HERE!
WE VOLUNTEER...
...FOR VOLLEYBALL!
LEAVE IT TO US!
AZUMA?
SO, INUI AND IGARASHI FOR VOLLEYBALL.
Okay.
ANYBODY ELSE?
I'LL BE RIGHT THERE AS HE FUMBLES AROUND WITH THE BALL AND FALLS ALL OVER HIMSELF...
I'LL SAVE THE DAY WITH GRACE AND ELEGANCE!
Hmph.
IT'S GOING TO BE BRILLIANT...
GRIP
THIS WILL...

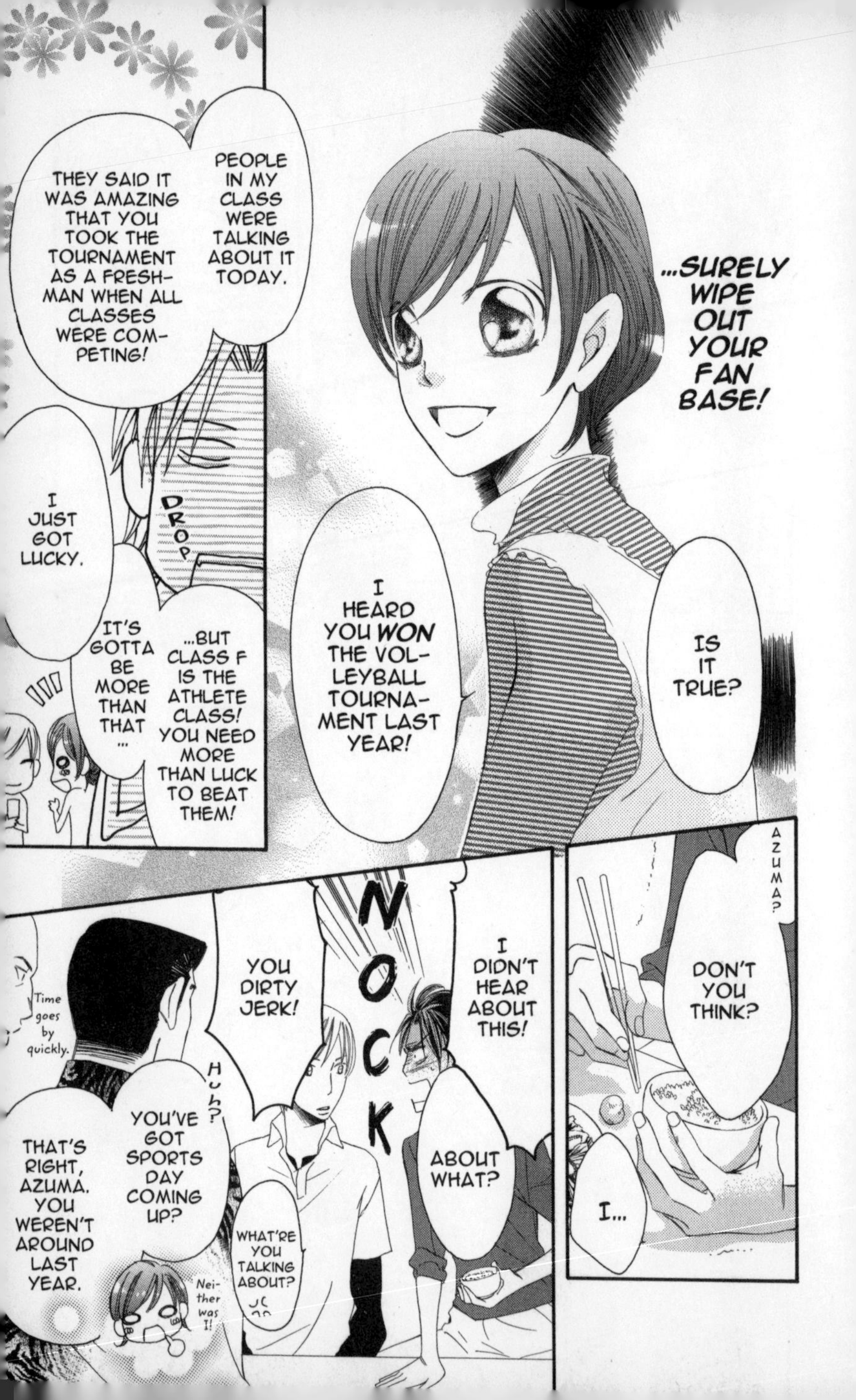
...SURELY WIPE OUT YOUR FAN BASE!
I HEARD YOU WON THE VOL-LEYBALL TOURNA-MENT LAST YEAR!
IS IT TRUE?
PEOPLE IN MY CLASS WERE TALKING ABOUT IT TODAY.
THEY SAID IT WAS AMAZING THAT YOU TOOK THE TOURNAMENT AS A FRESH-MAN WHEN ALL CLASSES WERE COM-PETING!
DROP
I JUST GOT LUCKY.
...BUT CLASS F IS THE ATHLETE CLASS! YOU NEED MORE THAN LUCK TO BEAT THEM!
IT'S GOTTA BE MORE THAN THAT...
AZUMA?
DON'T YOU THINK?
I...
I DIDN'T HEAR ABOUT THIS!
NOCK
YOU DIRTY JERK!
ABOUT WHAT?
Huh?
YOU'VE GOT SPORTS DAY COMING UP?
Time goes by quickly.
THAT'S RIGHT, AZUMA. YOU WEREN'T AROUND LAST YEAR.
WHAT'RE YOU TALKING ABOUT?
Nei-ther was I!

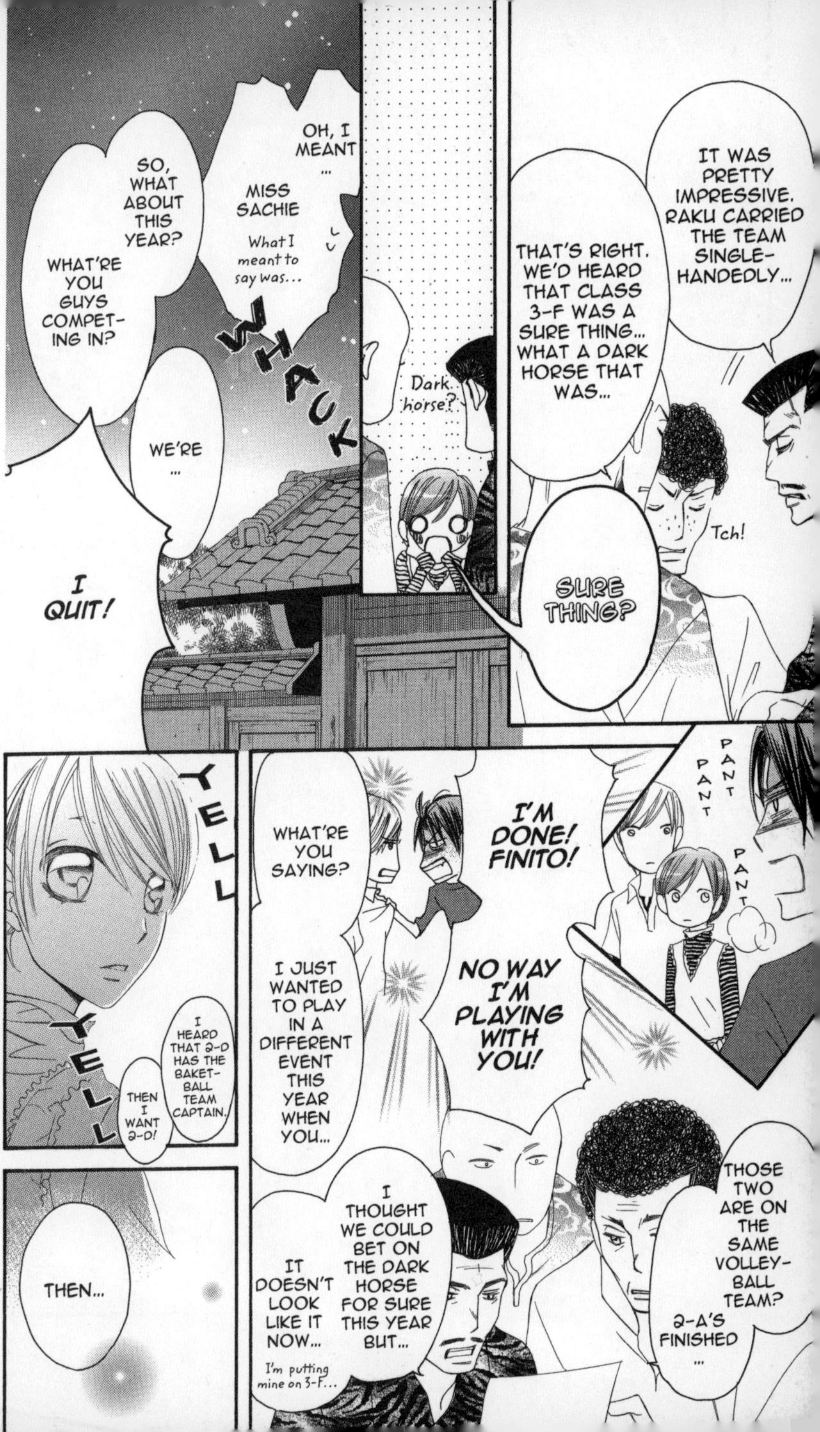
IT WAS PRETTY IMPRESSIVE. RAKU CARRIED THE TEAM SINGLE-HANDEDLY...
THAT'S RIGHT. WE'D HEARD THAT CLASS 3-F WAS A SURE THING... WHAT A DARK HORSE THAT WAS...
Tch!
SURE THING?
Dark horse?
OH, I MEANT ... MISS SACHIE
What I meant to say was...
WHACK
SO, WHAT ABOUT THIS YEAR?
WHAT'RE YOU GUYS COMPETING IN?
WE'RE ...
I QUIT!
PANT PANT PANT
I'M DONE! FINITO!
NO WAY I'M PLAYING WITH YOU!
WHAT'RE YOU SAYING?
I JUST WANTED TO PLAY IN A DIFFERENT EVENT THIS YEAR WHEN YOU...
THOSE TWO ARE ON THE SAME VOLLEY-BALL TEAM?
2-A'S FINISHED ...
I THOUGHT WE COULD BET ON THE DARK HORSE FOR SURE THIS YEAR BUT...
IT DOESN'T LOOK LIKE IT NOW...
I'm putting mine on 3-F...
YELL YELL
I HEARD THAT 2-D HAS THE BAKET-BALL TEAM CAPTAIN.
THEN I WANT 2-D!
THEN...

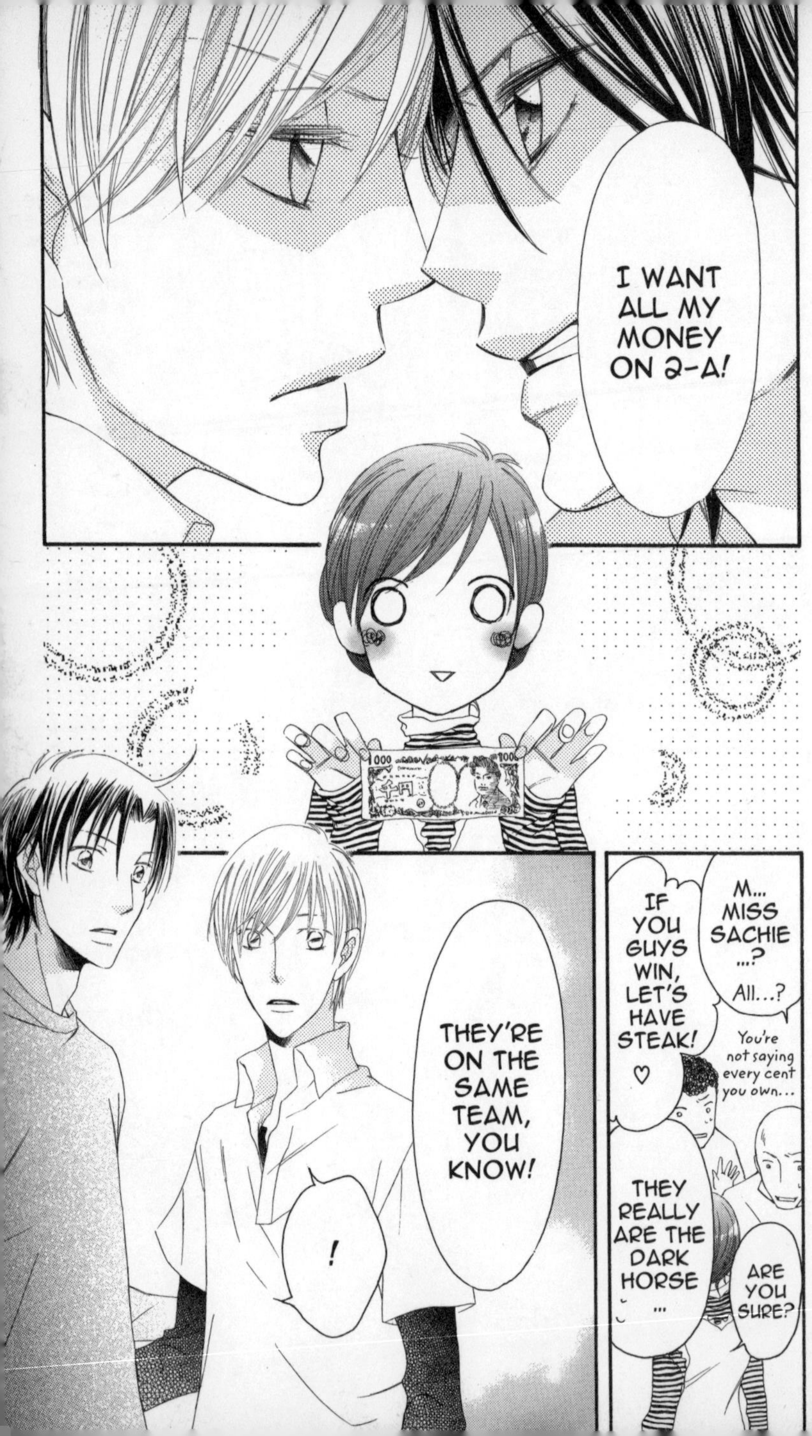
I WANT ALL MY MONEY ON 2-A!
M... MISS SACHIE ...? All...?
You're not saying every cent you own...
IF YOU GUYS WIN, LET'S HAVE STEAK! ♡
ARE YOU SURE?
THEY REALLY ARE THE DARK HORSE ...
THEY'RE ON THE SAME TEAM, YOU KNOW!
!

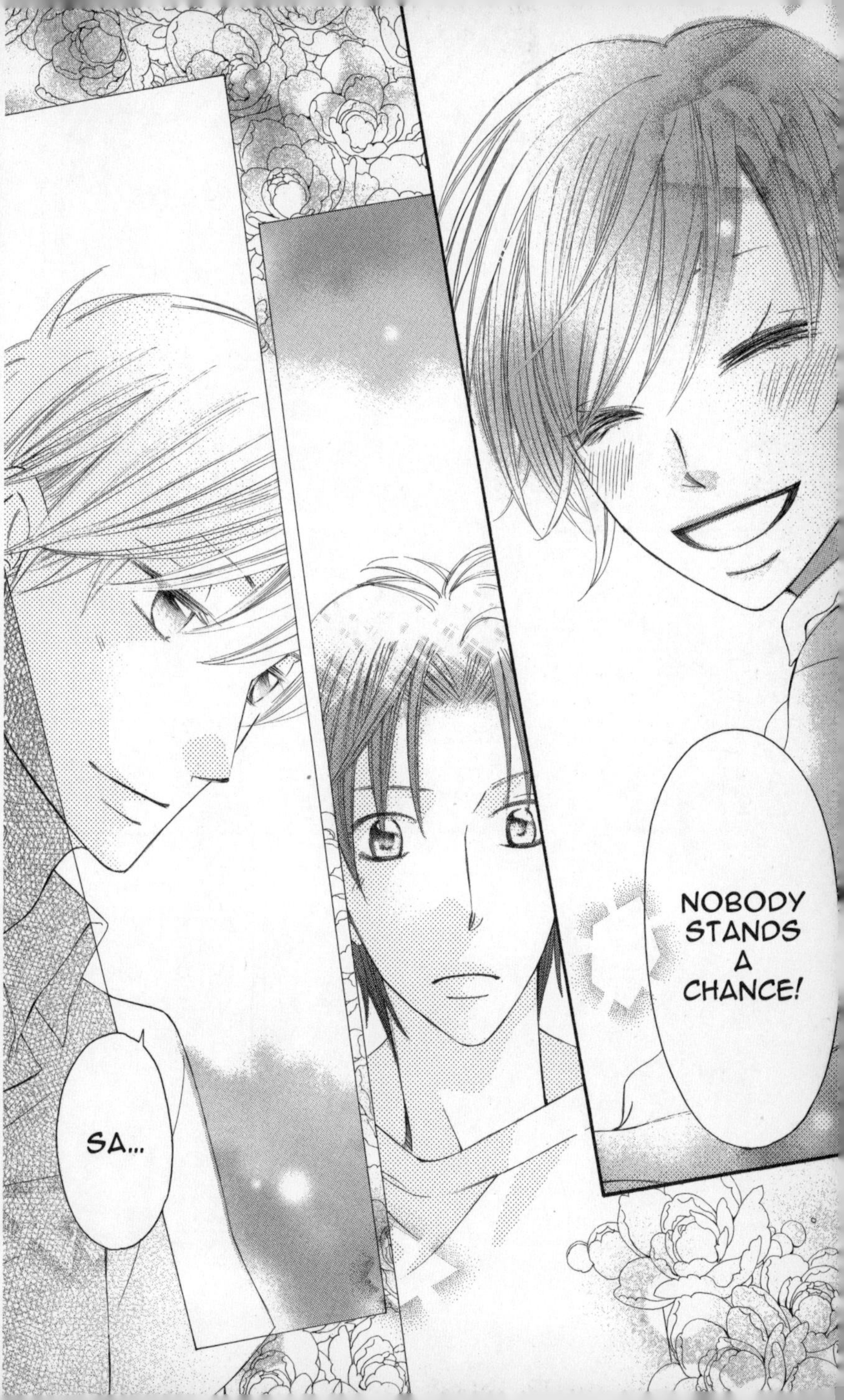
NOBODY STANDS A CHANCE!
SA...

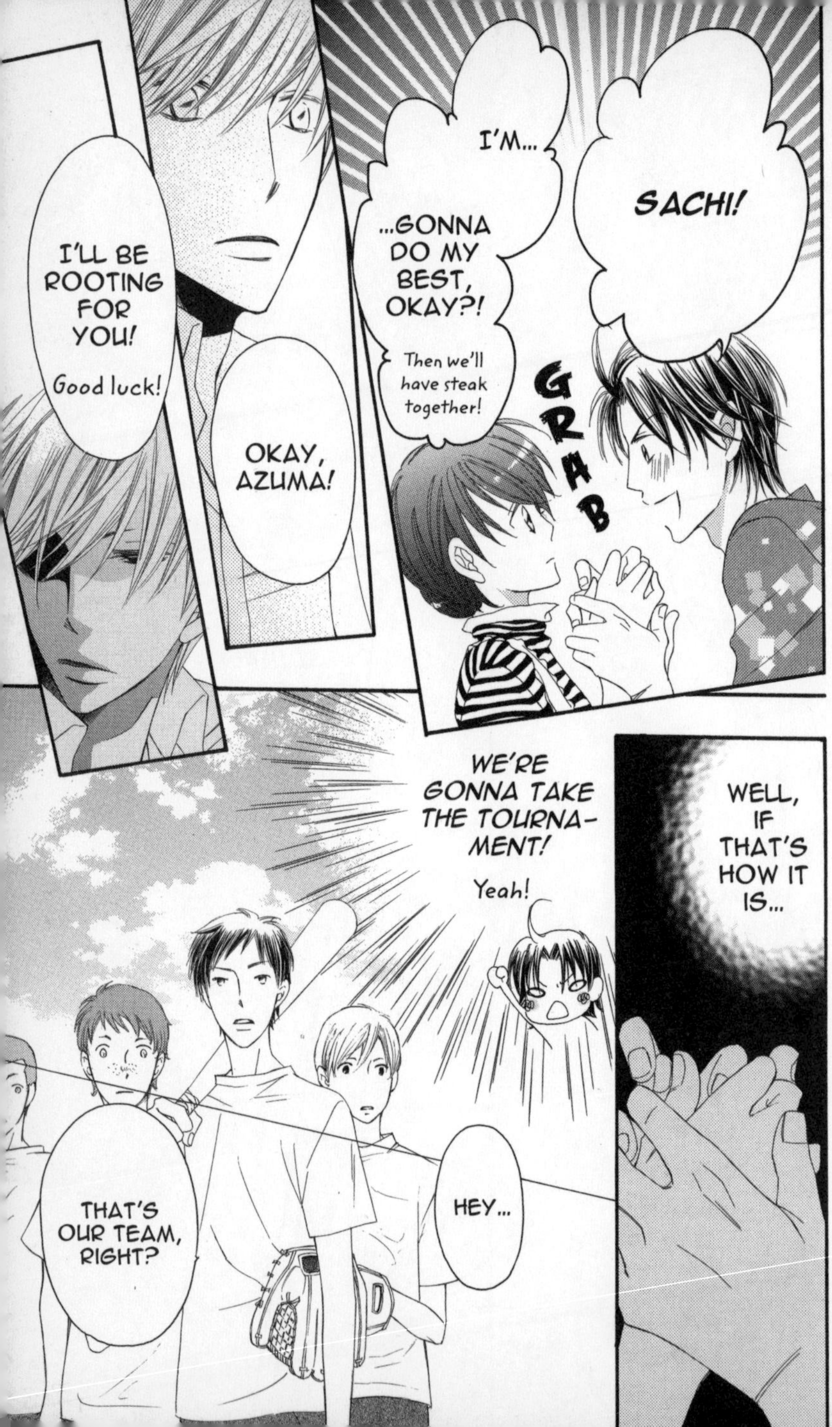
SACHI!
I'M...
...GONNA DO MY BEST, OKAY?!
Then we'll have steak together!
GRAB
OKAY, AZUMA!
I'LL BE ROOTING FOR YOU!
Good luck!
WELL, IF THAT'S HOW IT IS...
WE'RE GONNA TAKE THE TOURNA-MENT!
Yeah!
HEY...
THAT'S OUR TEAM, RIGHT?

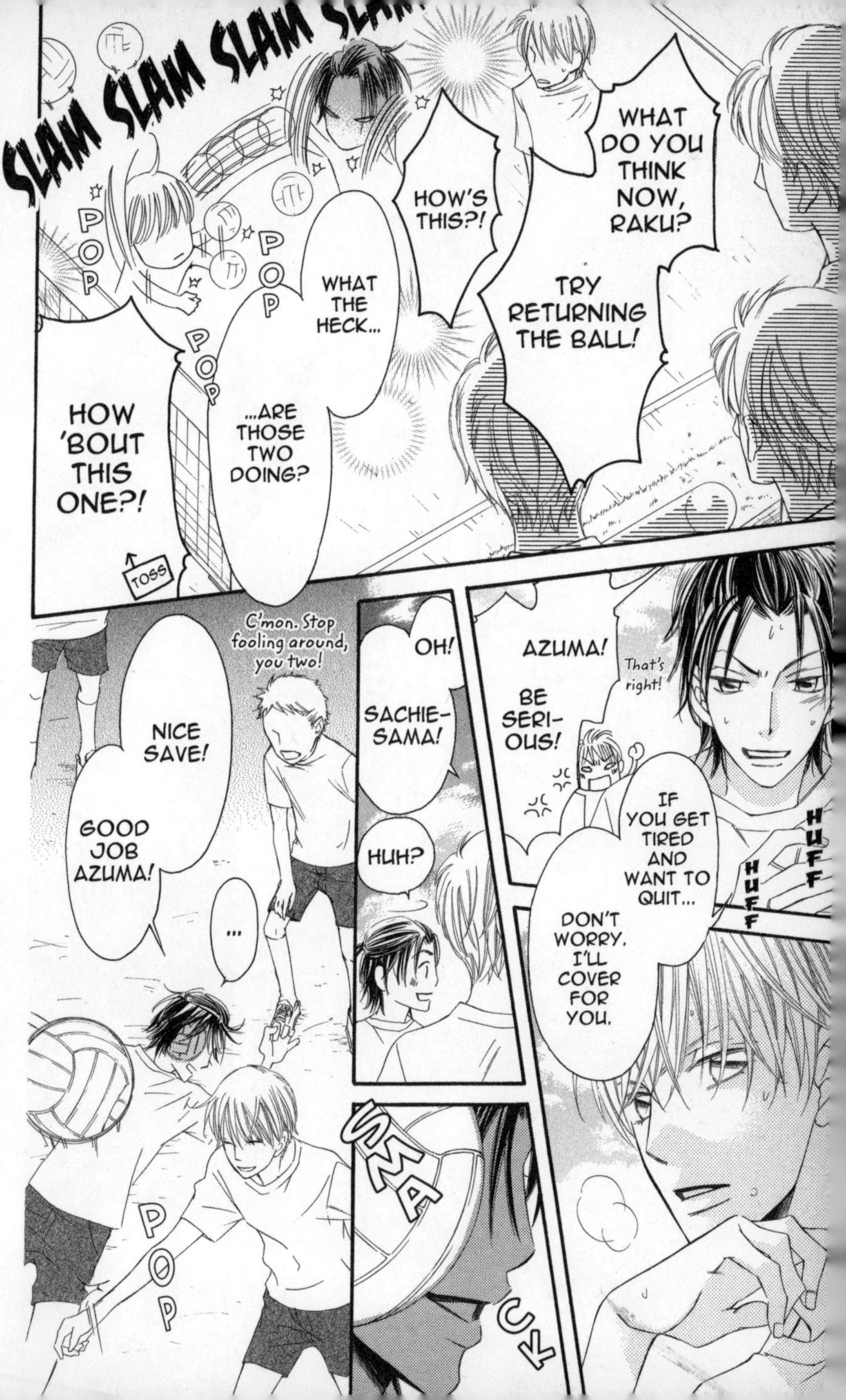
WHAT DO YOU THINK NOW, RAKU?
TRY RETURNING THE BALL!
HOW'S THIS?!
SLAM SLAM SLAM SLAM
POP POP
POP POP
POP POP
WHAT THE HECK...
...ARE THOSE TWO DOING?
HOW 'BOUT THIS ONE?!
TOSS
AZUMA!
BE SERI-OUS!
That's right!
HUFF HUFF
HUFF
IF YOU GET TIRED AND WANT TO QUIT...
DON'T WORRY. I'LL COVER FOR YOU.
OH!
SACHIE-SAMA!
HUH?
WHA
CK
C'mon. Stop fooling around, you two!
NICE SAVE!
GOOD JOB AZUMA!
...
POP POP

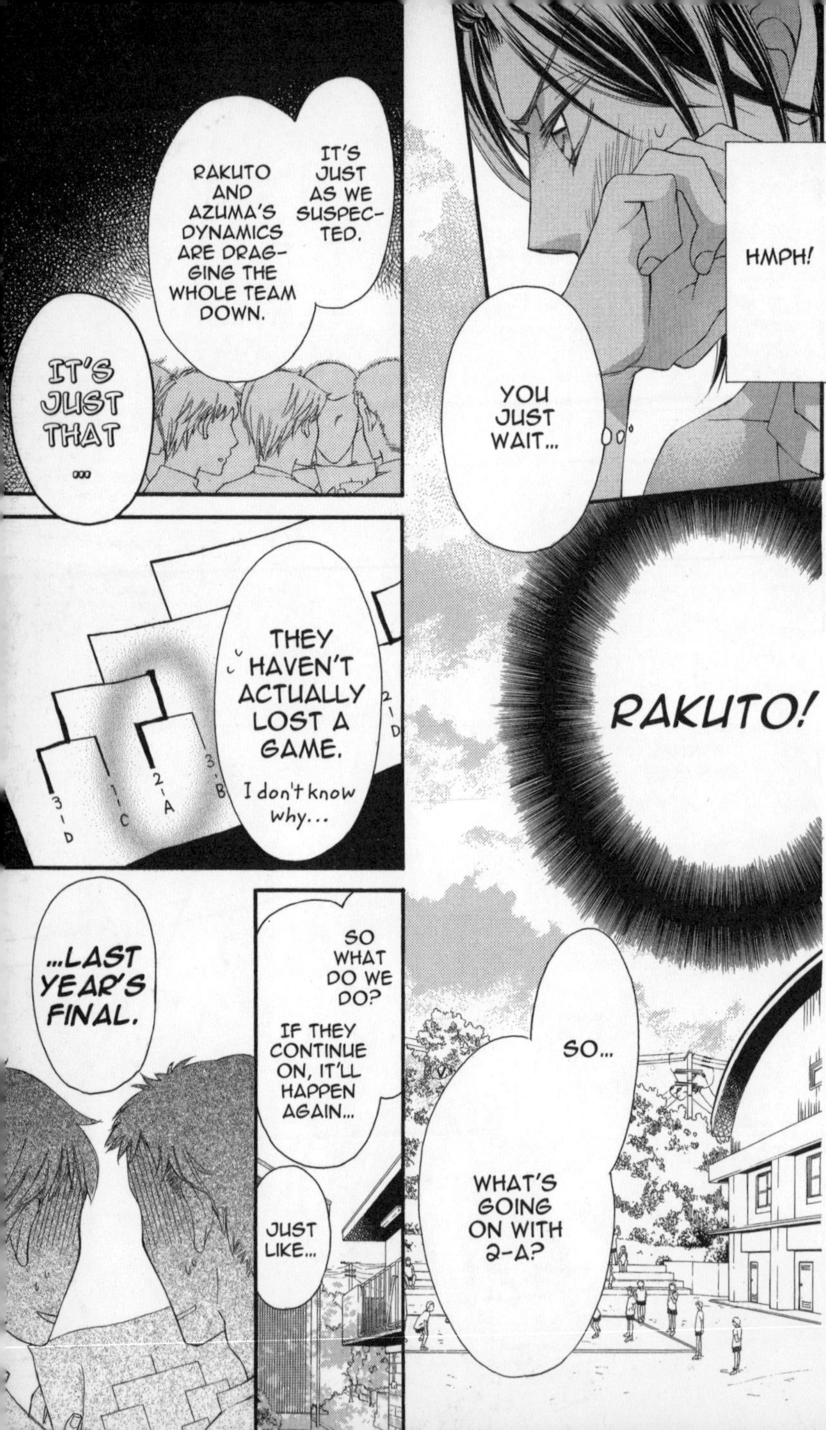
HMPH!
YOU JUST WAIT...
IT'S JUST AS WE SUSPEC-TED.
RAKUTO AND AZUMA'S DYNAMICS ARE DRAG-GING THE WHOLE TEAM DOWN.
IT'S JUST THAT...
RAKUTO!
SO...
WHAT'S GOING ON WITH 2-A?
THEY HAVEN'T ACTUALLY LOST A GAME.
I don't know why...
2-D
3-B
2-A
1-C
3-D
SO WHAT DO WE DO?
IF THEY CONTINUE ON, IT'LL HAPPEN AGAIN...
JUST LIKE...
...LAST YEAR'S FINAL.

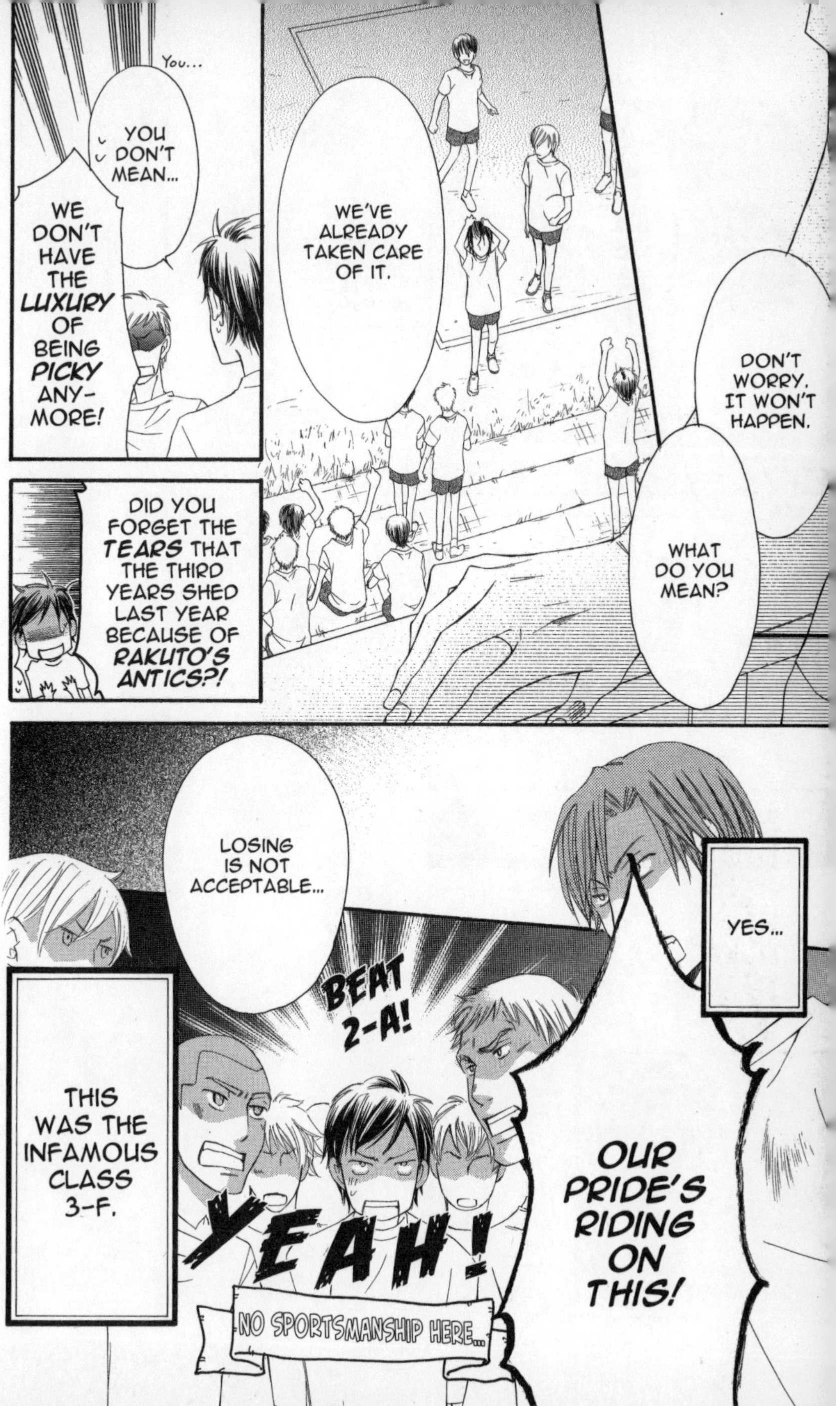
DON'T WORRY. IT WON'T HAPPEN.
WHAT DO YOU MEAN?
WE'VE ALREADY TAKEN CARE OF IT.
You...
YOU DON'T MEAN...
WE DON'T HAVE THE LUXURY OF BEING PICKY ANYMORE!
DID YOU FORGET THE TEARS THAT THE THIRD YEARS SHED LAST YEAR BECAUSE OF RAKUTO'S ANTICS?!
YES...
LOSING IS NOT ACCEPTABLE...
OUR PRIDE'S RIDING ON THIS!
BEAT 2-A!
YEAH!
THIS WAS THE INFAMOUS CLASS 3-F.
NO SPORTSMANSHIP HERE...

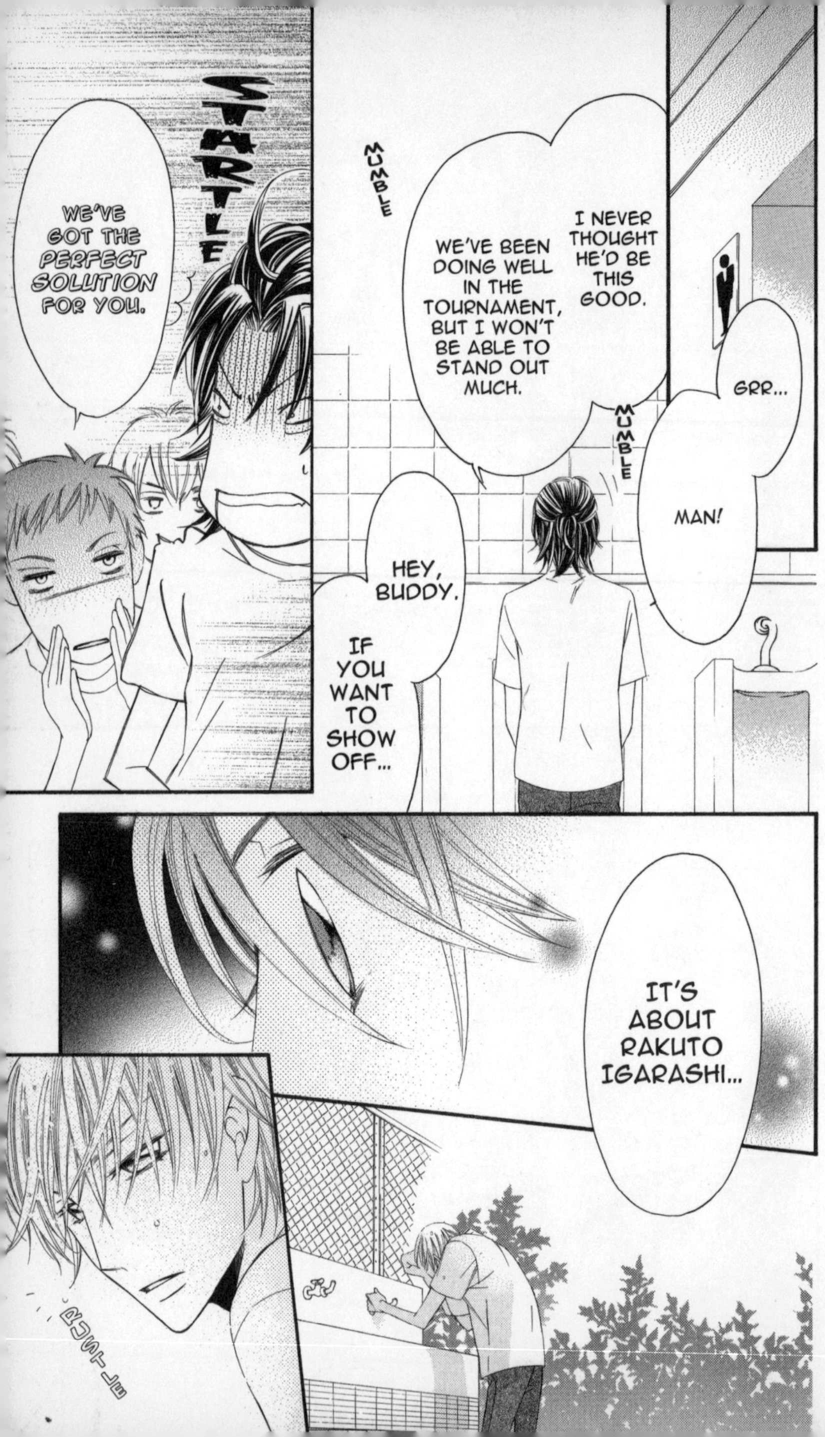

I NEVER THOUGHT HE'D BE THIS GOOD.
WE'VE BEEN DOING WELL IN THE TOURNAMENT, BUT I WON'T BE ABLE TO STAND OUT MUCH.
MUMBLE
MUMBLE
GRR... MAN!
HEY, BUDDY.
IF YOU WANT TO SHOW OFF...
STARTLE
WE'VE GOT THE PERFECT SOLUTION FOR YOU.
IT'S ABOUT RAKUTO IGARASHI...

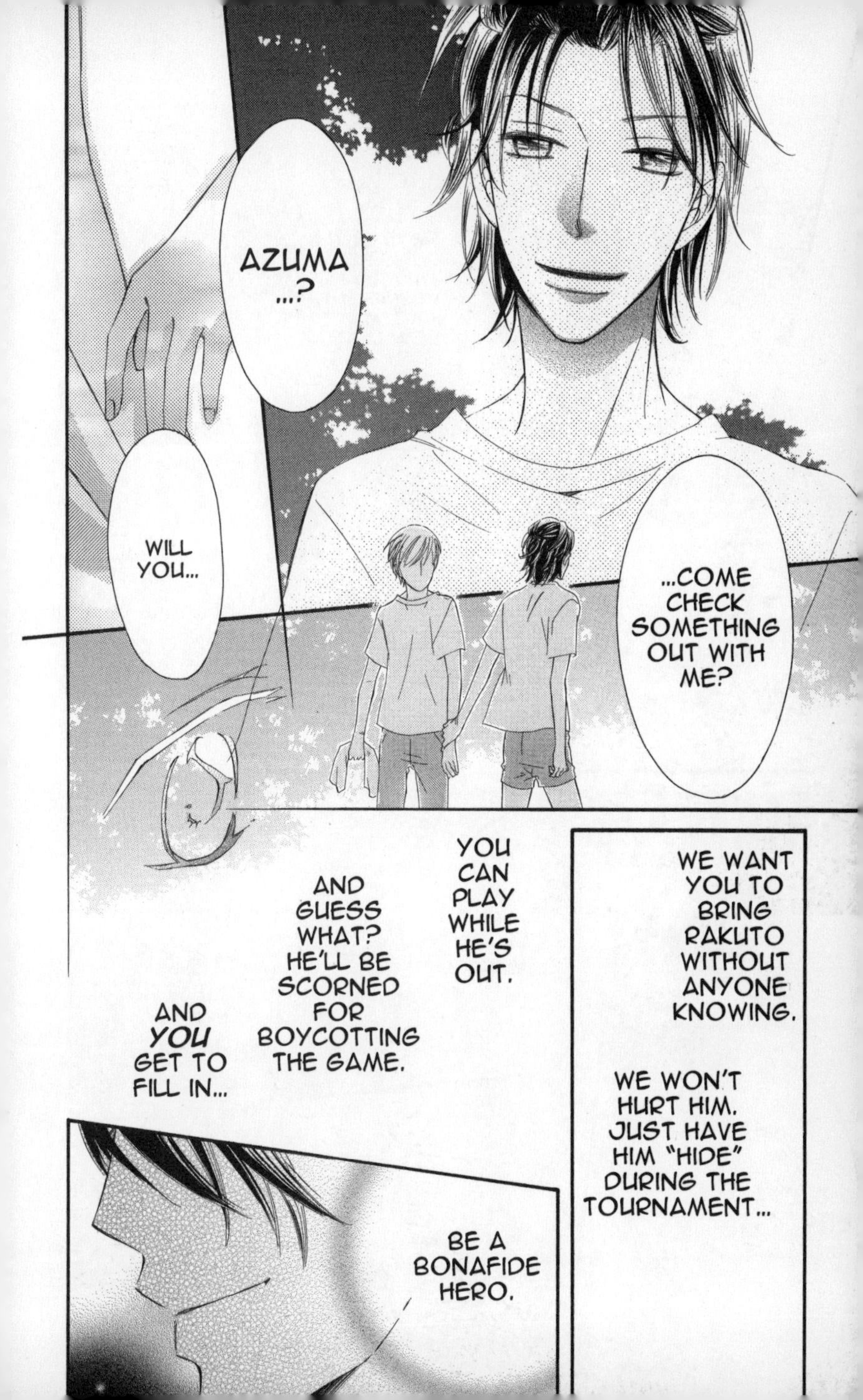
AZUMA ...?
WILL YOU...
...COME CHECK SOMETHING OUT WITH ME?
WE WANT YOU TO BRING RAKUTO WITHOUT ANYONE KNOWING.
WE WON'T HURT HIM. JUST HAVE HIM "HIDE" DURING THE TOURNAMENT...
YOU CAN PLAY WHILE HE'S OUT.
AND GUESS WHAT? HE'LL BE SCORNED FOR BOYCOTTING THE GAME.
AND *YOU* GET TO FILL IN...
BE A BONAFIDE HERO.

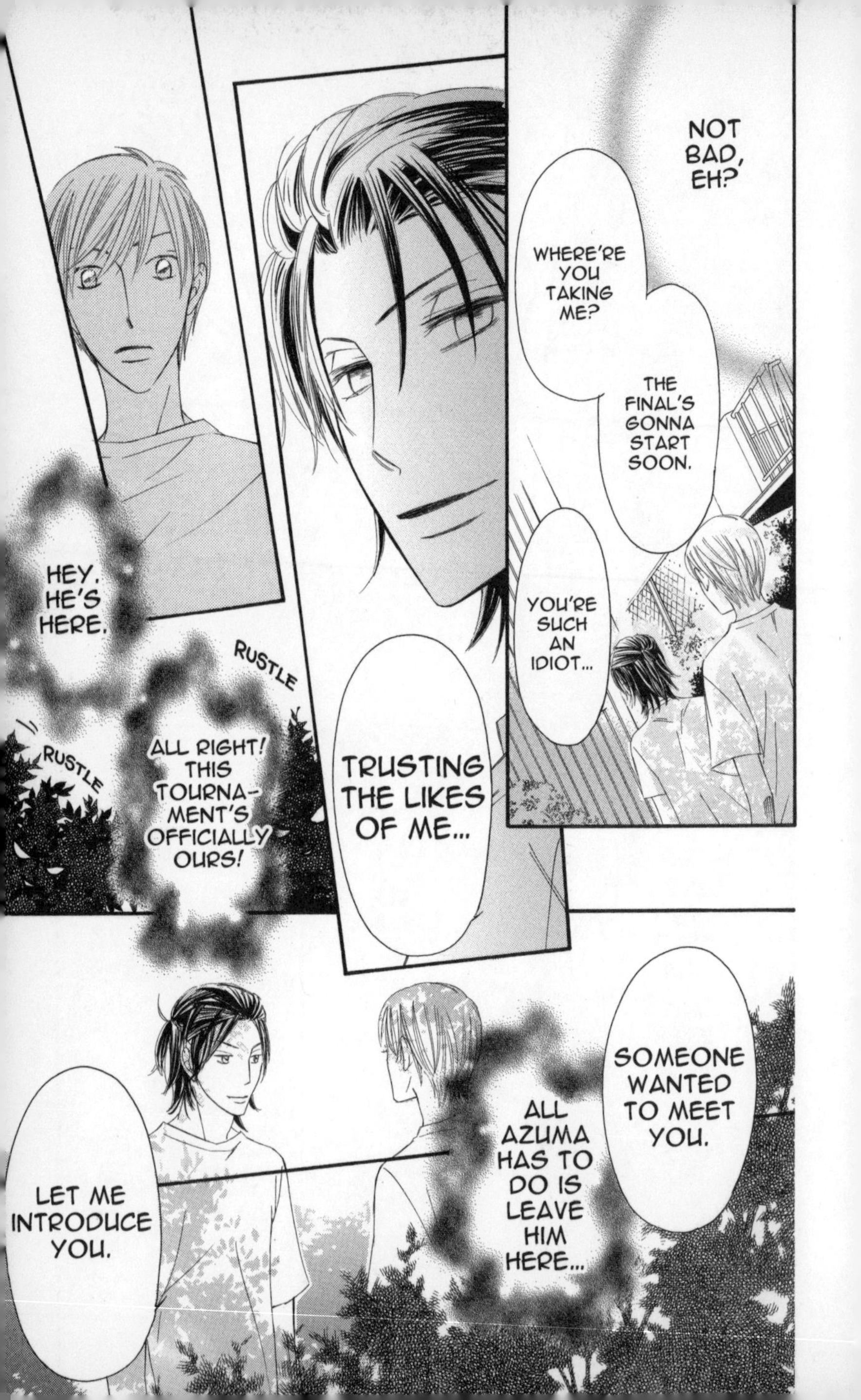
NOT BAD, EH?
WHERE'RE YOU TAKING ME?
THE FINAL'S GONNA START SOON.
YOU'RE SUCH AN IDIOT...
TRUSTING THE LIKES OF ME...
HEY, HE'S HERE.
RUSTLE
RUSTLE
ALL RIGHT! THIS TOURNAMENT'S OFFICIALLY OURS!
SOMEONE WANTED TO MEET YOU.
ALL AZUMA HAS TO DO IS LEAVE HIM HERE...
LET ME INTRODUCE YOU.

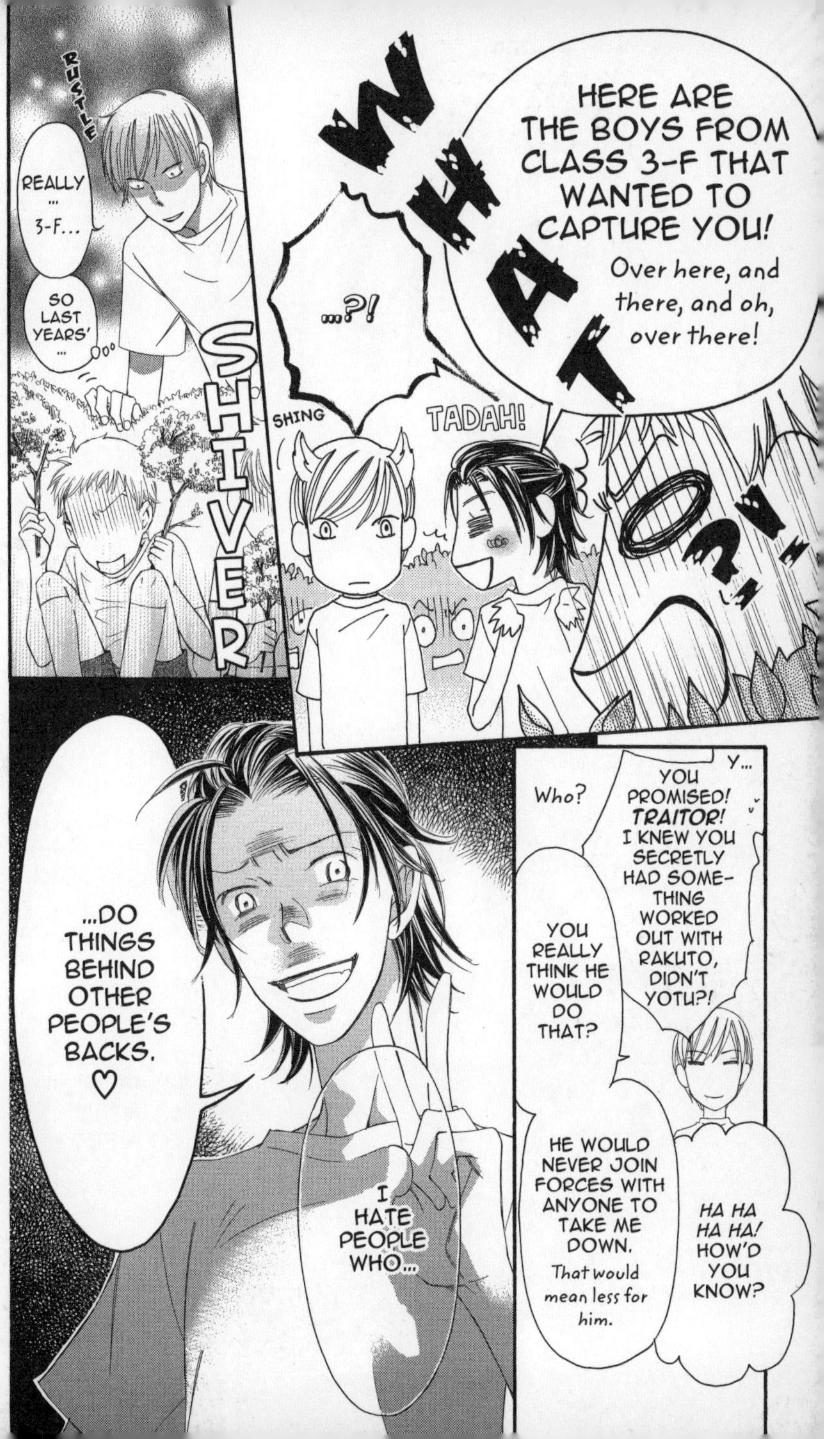

HERE ARE THE BOYS FROM CLASS 3-F THAT WANTED TO CAPTURE YOU!
Over here, and there, and oh, over there!
WHAT
...?!
TADAH!
SHING
?!
RUSTLE
REALLY... 3-F...
SO LAST YEARS'...
SHIVER
Y... YOU PROMISED! TRAITOR! I KNEW YOU SECRETLY HAD SOME-THING WORKED OUT WITH RAKUTO, DIDN'T YOTU?!
Who?
YOU REALLY THINK HE WOULD DO THAT?
HE WOULD NEVER JOIN FORCES WITH ANYONE TO TAKE ME DOWN.
That would mean less for him.
HA HA HA HA! HOW'D YOU KNOW?
I HATE PEOPLE WHO...
...DO THINGS BEHIND OTHER PEOPLE'S BACKS. ♡

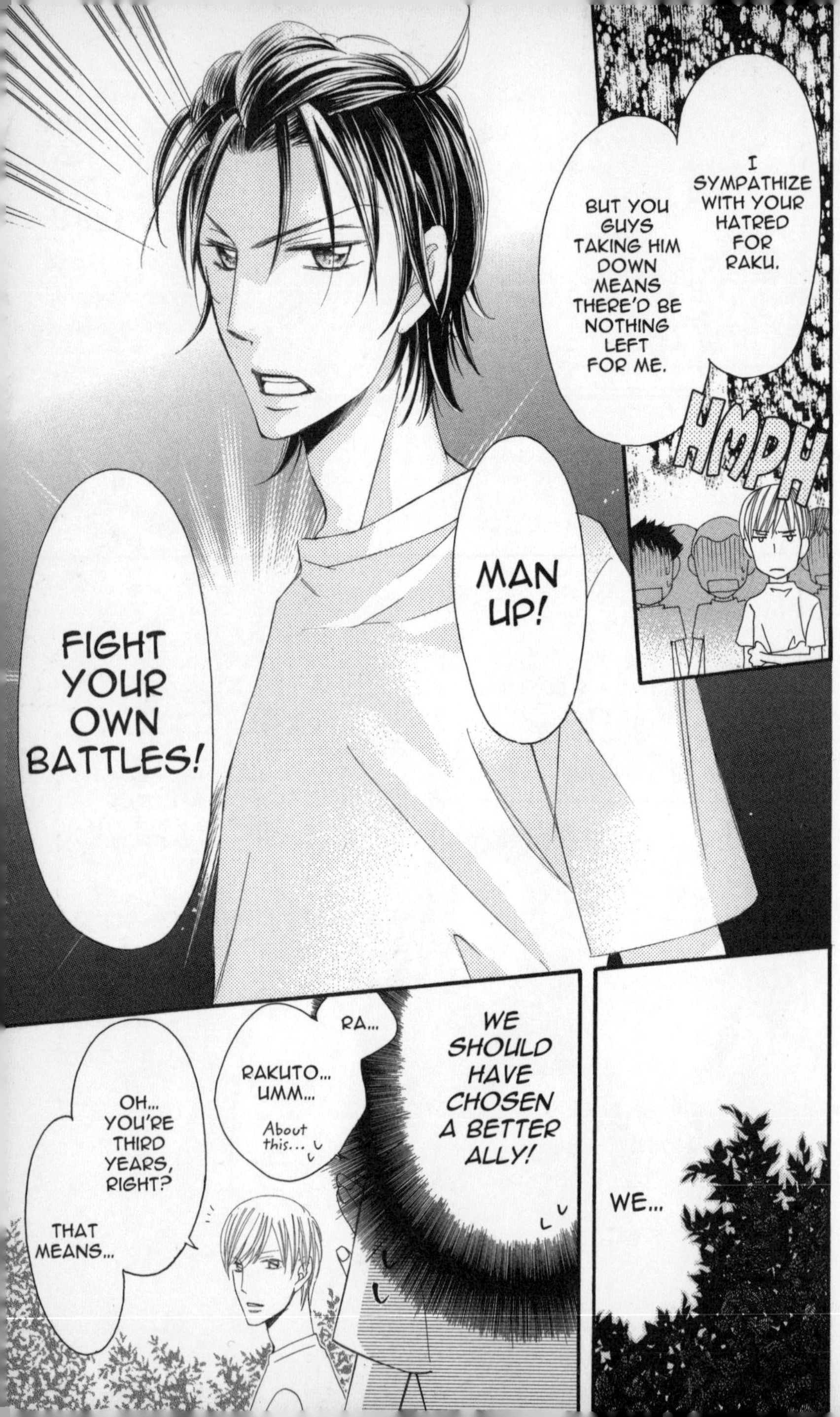
I SYMPATHIZE WITH YOUR HATRED FOR RAKU.
BUT YOU GUYS TAKING HIM DOWN MEANS THERE'D BE NOTHING LEFT FOR ME.
HMPH
MAN UP!
FIGHT YOUR OWN BATTLES!
WE...
WE SHOULD HAVE CHOSEN A BETTER ALLY!
RA...
RAKUTO... UMM...
About this...
OH... YOU'RE THIRD YEARS, RIGHT?
THAT MEANS...

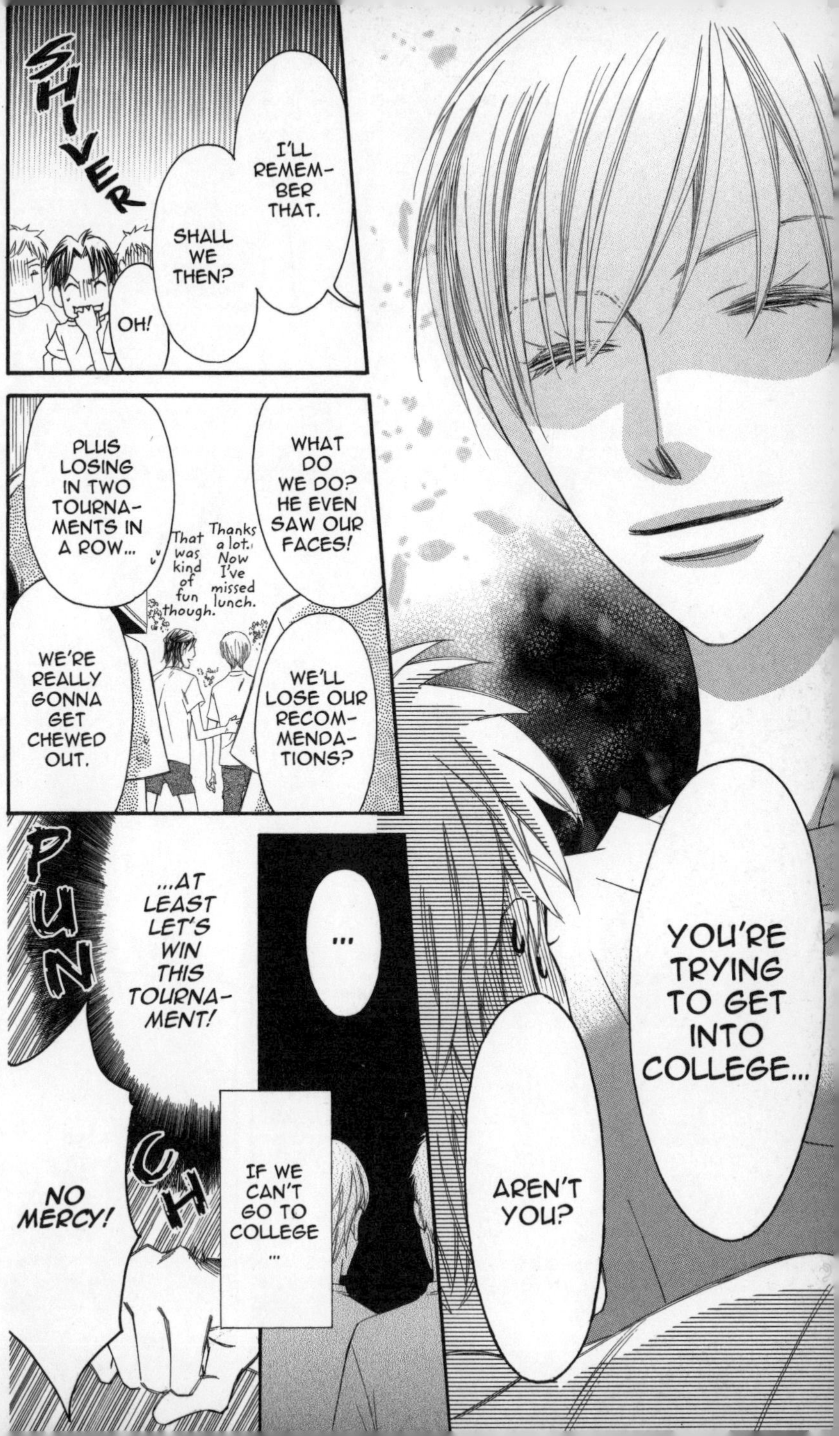
YOU'RE TRYING TO GET INTO COLLEGE...
AREN'T YOU?
SHIVER
I'LL REMEMBER THAT.
SHALL WE THEN?
OH!
WHAT DO WE DO? HE EVEN SAW OUR FACES!
WE'LL LOSE OUR RECOMMENDATIONS?
PLUS LOSING IN TWO TOURNAMENTS IN A ROW...
Thanks a lot. Now I've missed lunch.
That was kind of fun though.
WE'RE REALLY GONNA GET CHEWED OUT.
...
IF WE CAN'T GO TO COLLEGE...
...AT LEAST LET'S WIN THIS TOURNAMENT!
PUNCH
NO MERCY!

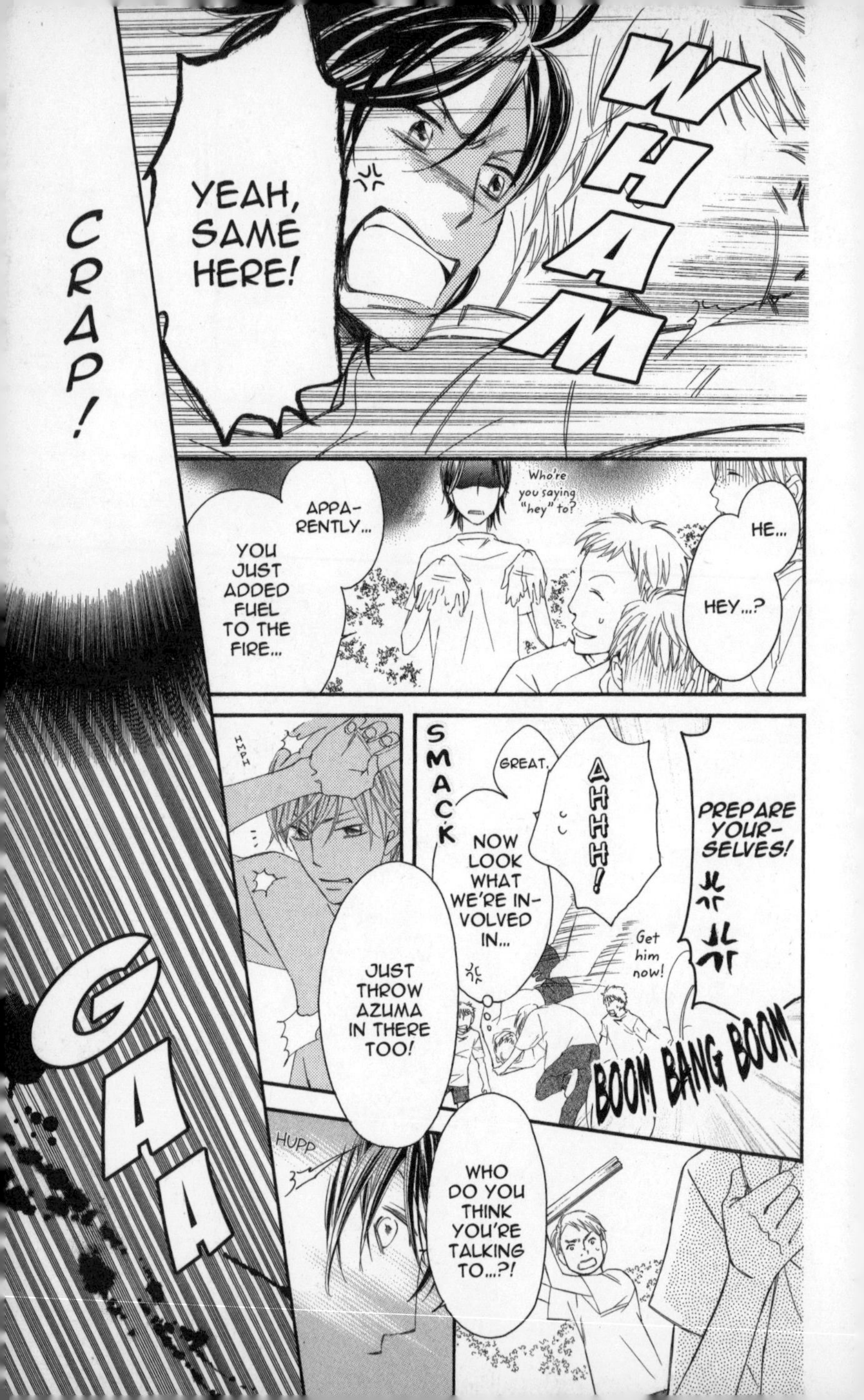
WHAM
YEAH, SAME HERE!
CRAP!
He... hey...?
Who're you saying "hey" to?
APPA-RENTLY...
YOU JUST ADDED FUEL TO THE FIRE...
PREPARE YOUR-SELVES!
AHHHH!
Get him now!
GREAT.
NOW LOOK WHAT WE'RE IN-VOLVED IN...
SMACK
BOOM BANG BOOM
HMPH
JUST THROW AZUMA IN THERE TOO!
HUPP
WHO DO YOU THINK YOU'RE TALKING TO...?!
GAAA

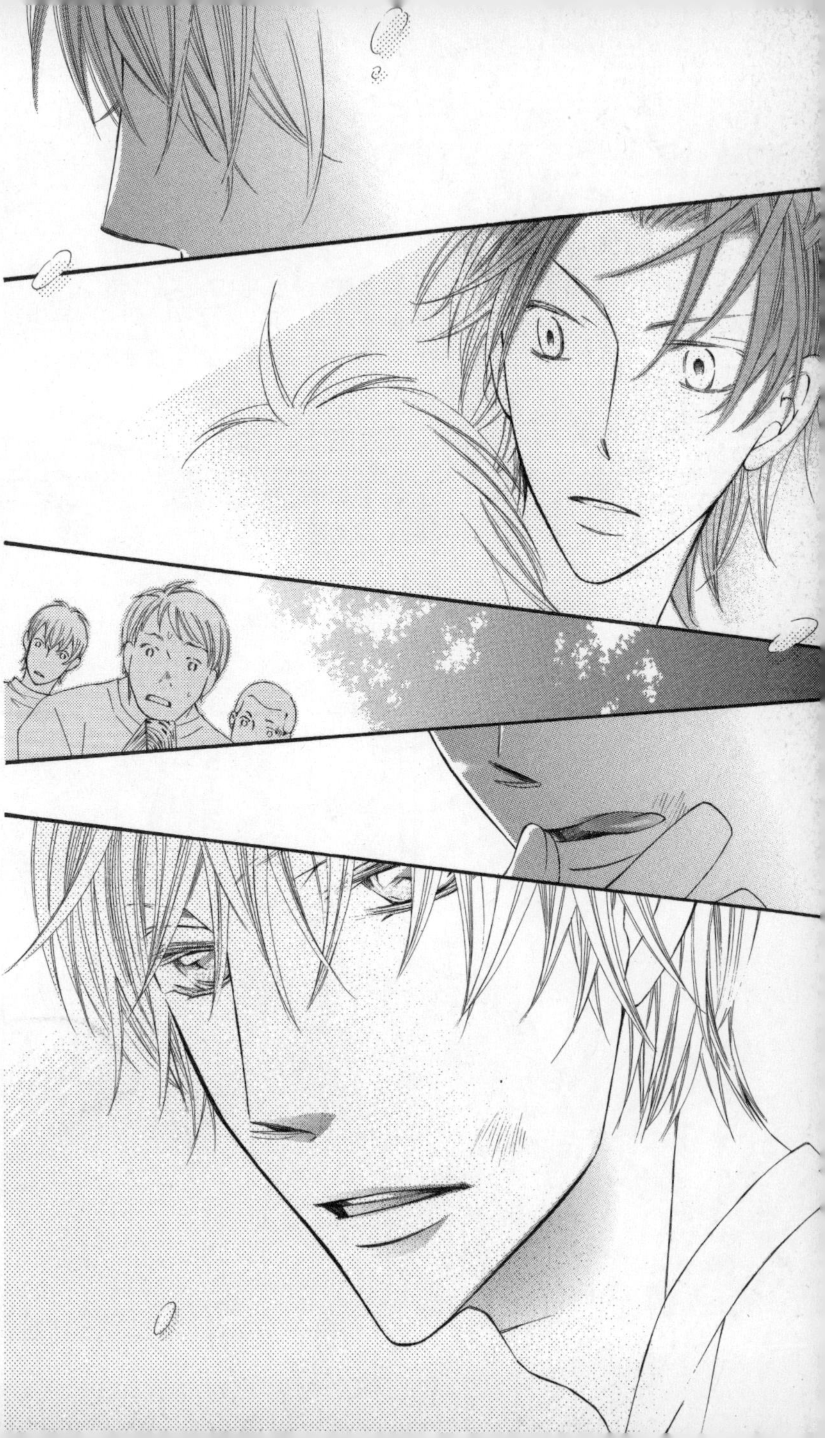

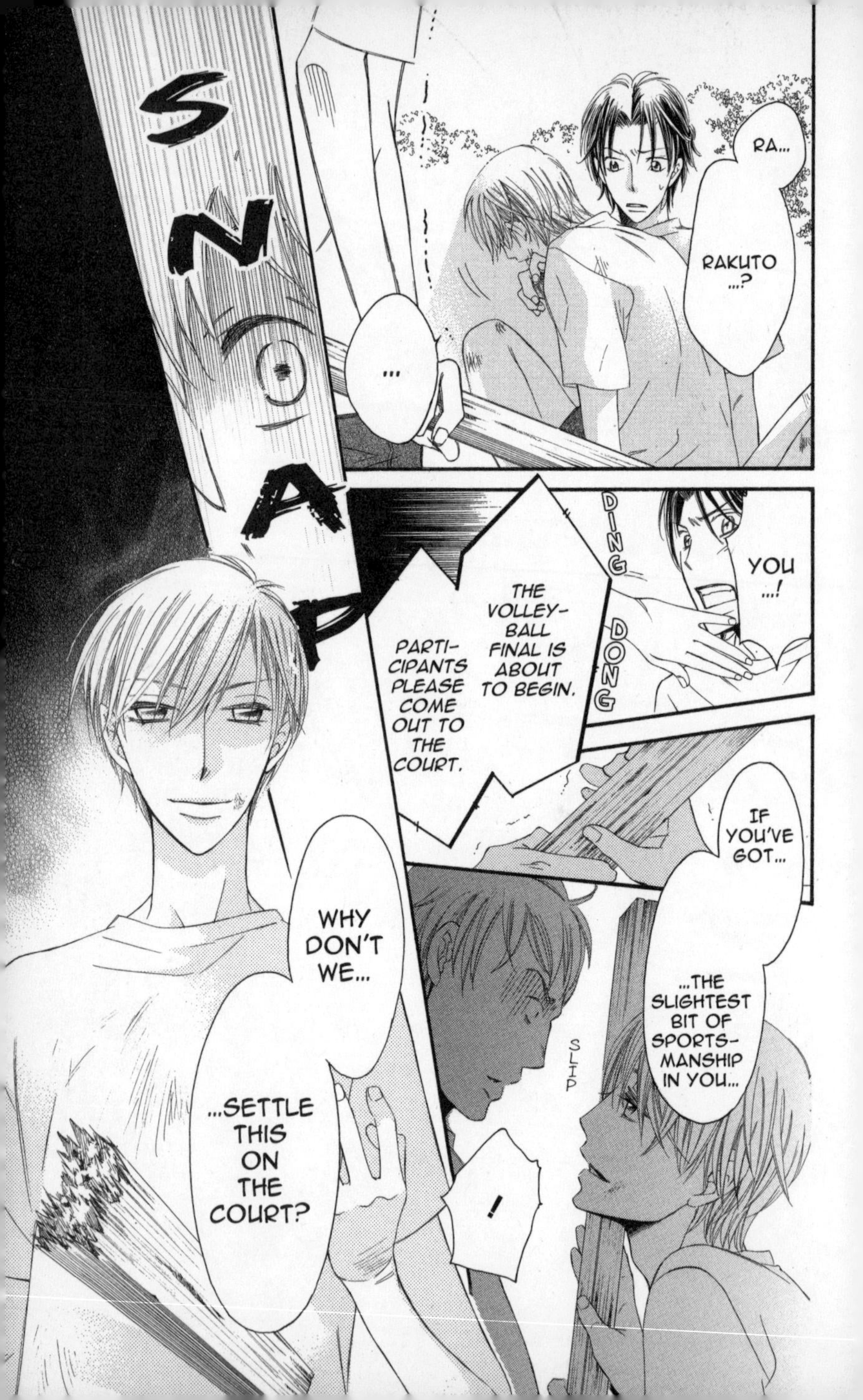
RA...
RAKUTO ...?
...
YOU ...!
DING DONG
THE VOLLEY-BALL FINAL IS ABOUT TO BEGIN. PARTI-CIPANTS PLEASE COME OUT TO THE COURT.
IF YOU'VE GOT...
...THE SLIGHTEST BIT OF SPORTS-MANSHIP IN YOU...
SLIP
!
SNAP
WHY DON'T WE...
...SETTLE THIS ON THE COURT?

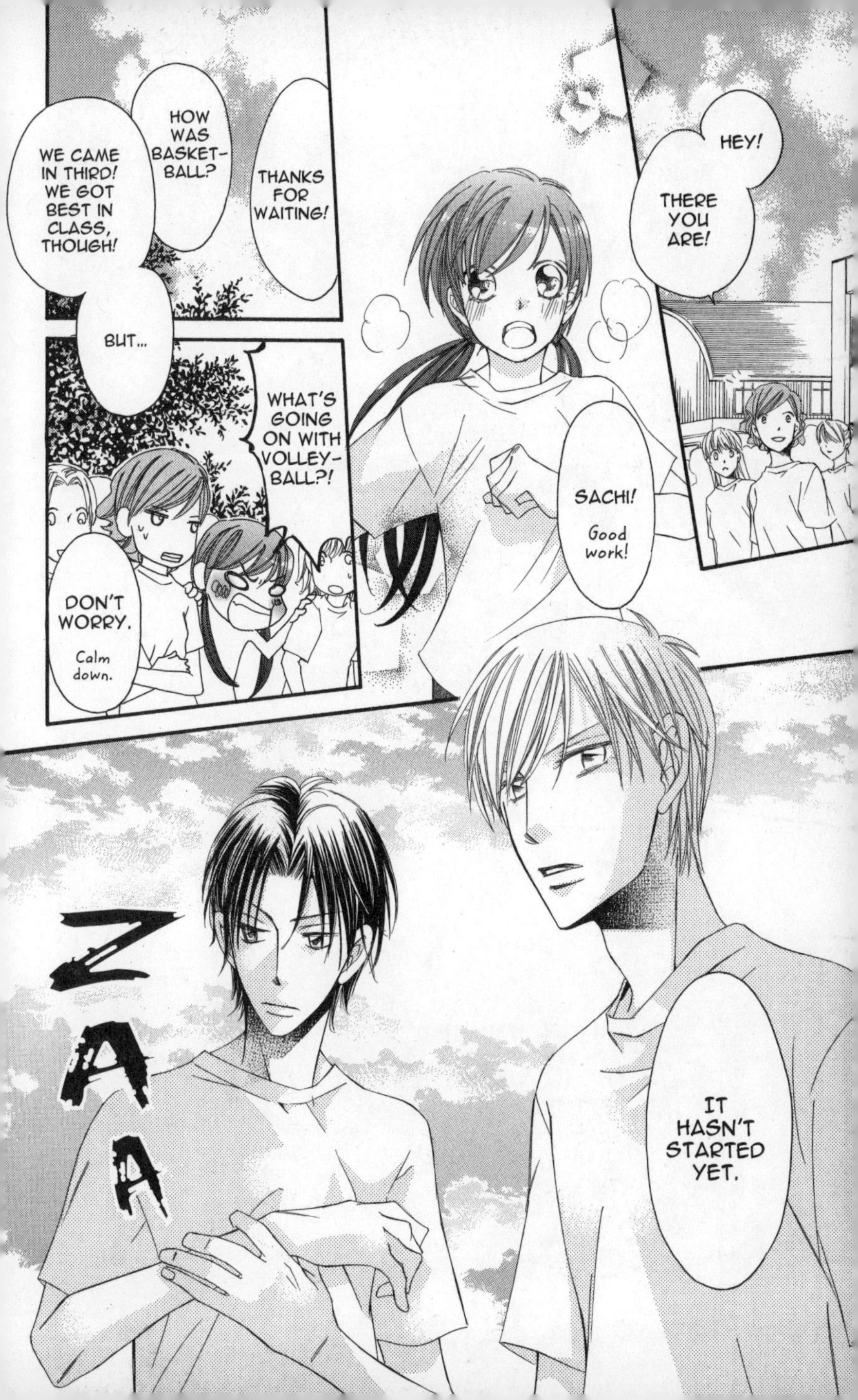
HEY!
THERE YOU ARE!
SACHI! Good work!
THANKS FOR WAITING!
HOW WAS BASKET-BALL?
WE CAME IN THIRD! WE GOT BEST IN CLASS, THOUGH!
BUT...
WHAT'S GOING ON WITH VOLLEY-BALL?!
DON'T WORRY. Calm down.
ZA
IT HASN'T STARTED YET.

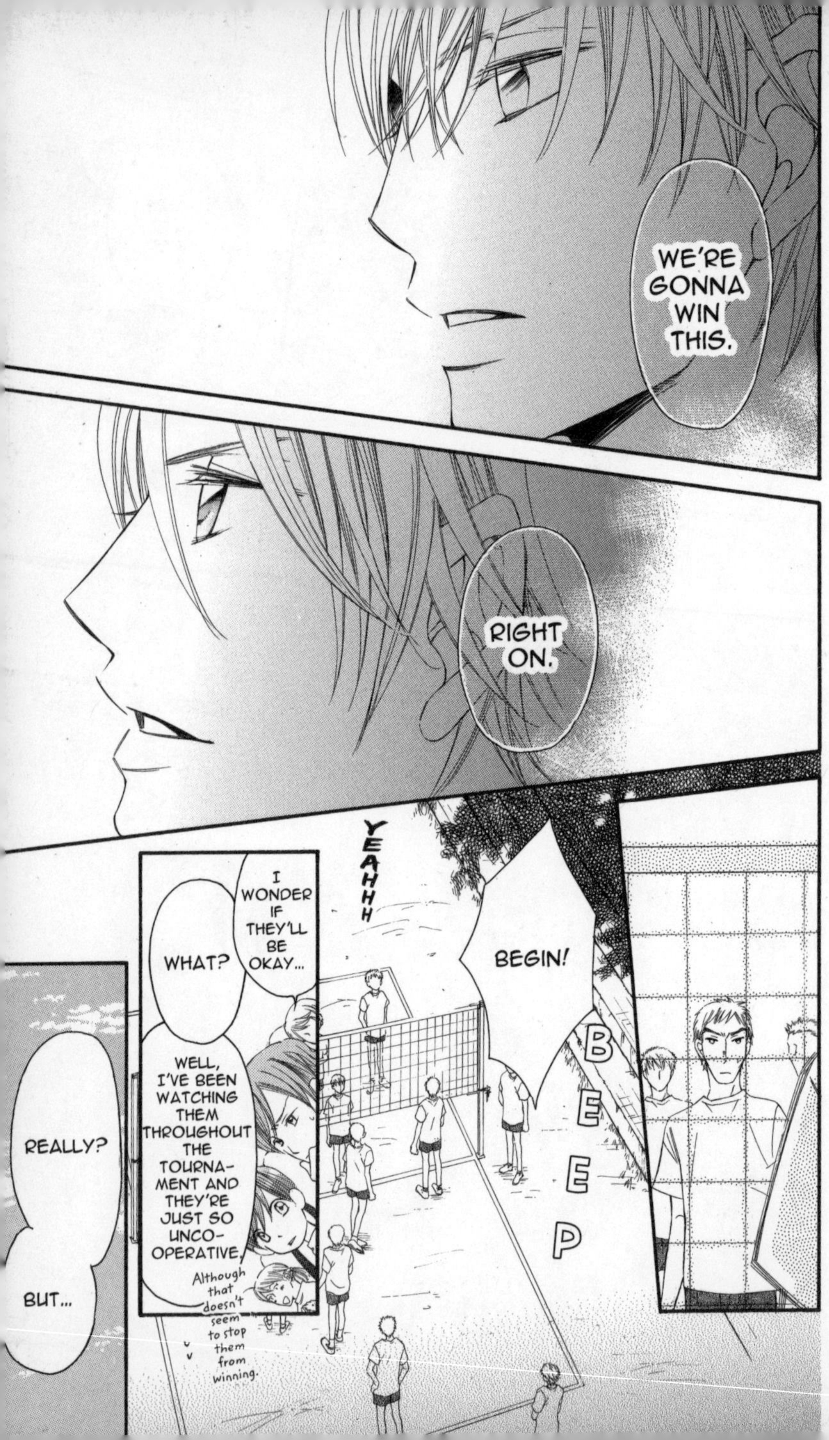
WE'RE GONNA WIN THIS.
RIGHT ON.
BEGIN!
BEEP
YEAHHH
I WONDER IF THEY'LL BE OKAY...
WHAT?
WELL, I'VE BEEN WATCHING THEM THROUGHOUT THE TOURNAMENT AND THEY'RE JUST SO UNCO-OPERATIVE,
Although that doesn't seem to stop them from winning.
REALLY?
BUT...

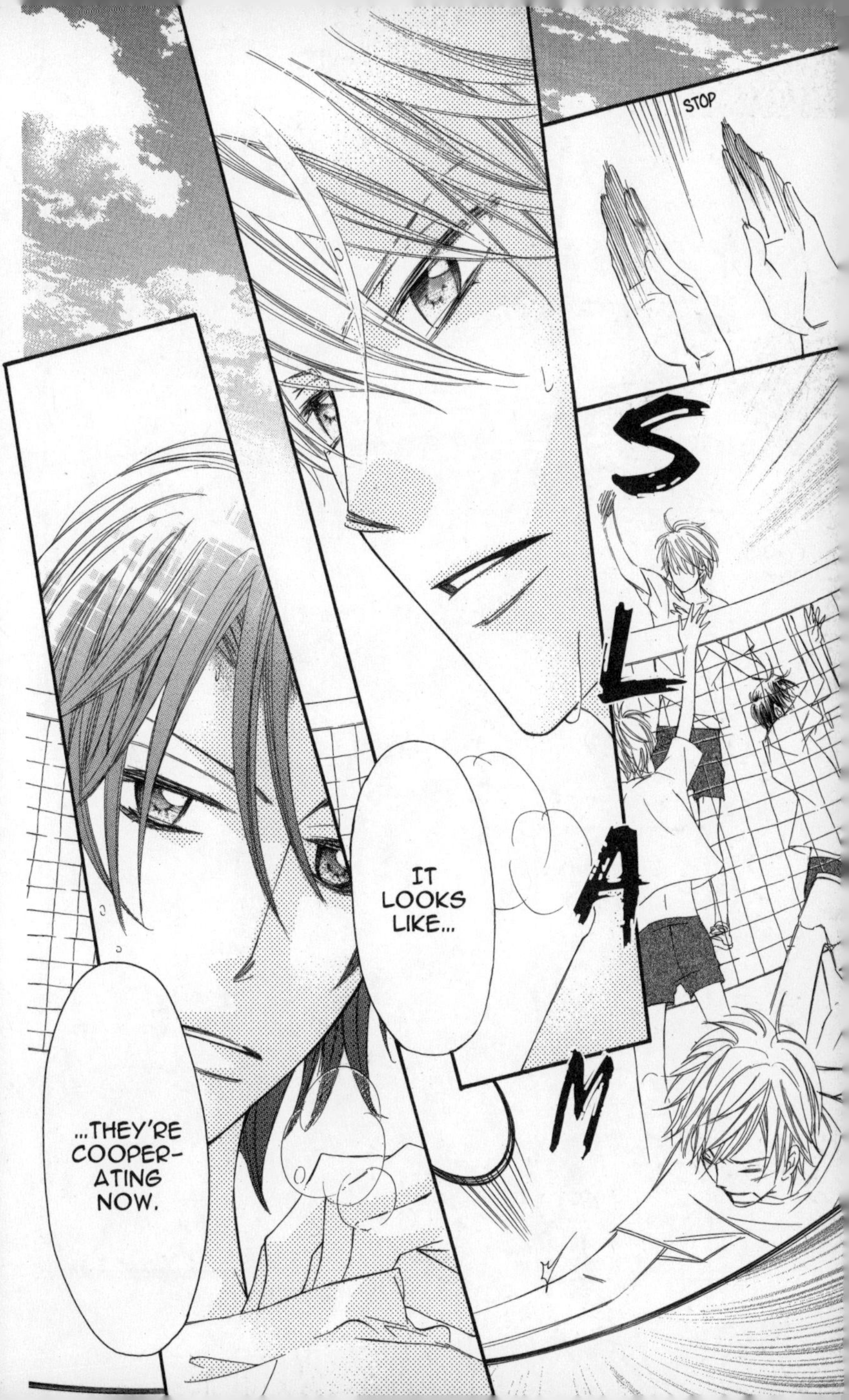
STOP
SLAM
IT LOOKS LIKE...
...THEY'RE COOPER-ATING NOW.

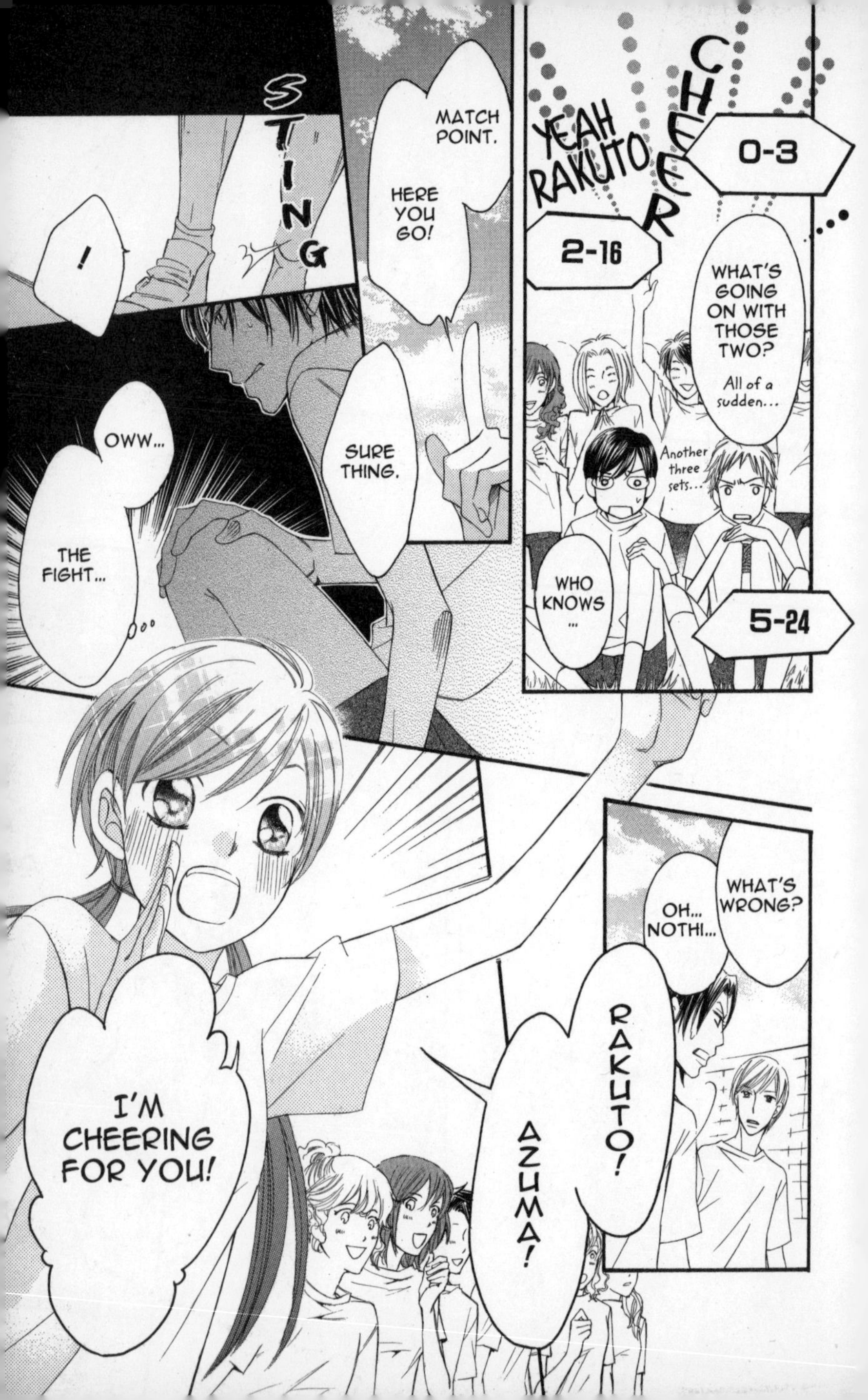
CHEER
YEAH RAKUTO
0-3
2-16
...
WHAT'S GOING ON WITH THOSE TWO?
All of a sudden...
Another three sets...
WHO KNOWS ...
5-24
MATCH POINT.
HERE YOU GO!
SURE THING.
STING
!
OWW...
THE FIGHT...
WHAT'S WRONG?
OH... NOTHI...
RAKUTO! AZUMA!
I'M CHEERING FOR YOU!

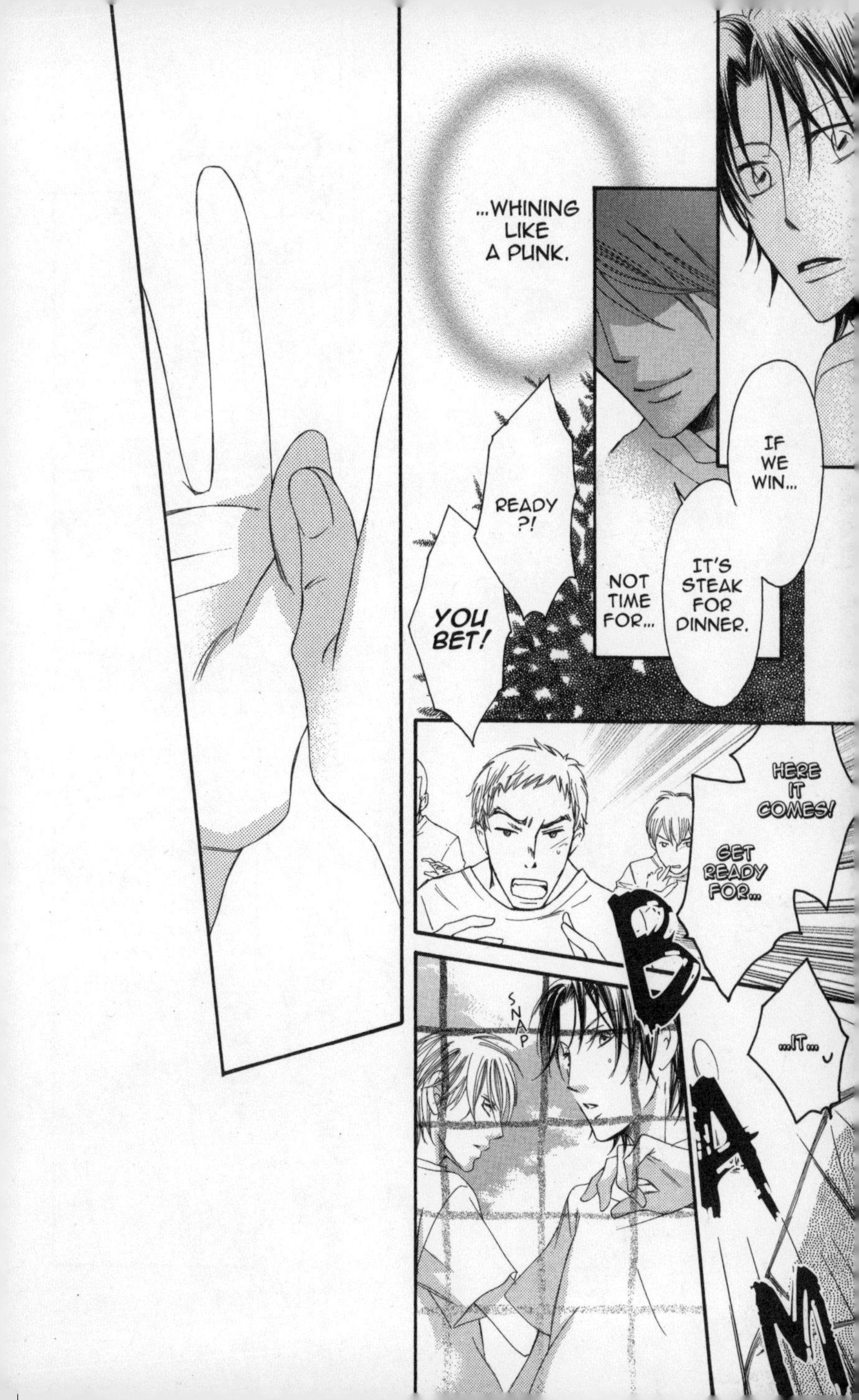
IF WE WIN...
IT'S STEAK FOR DINNER.
NOT TIME FOR...
...WHINING LIKE A PUNK.
READY?!
YOU BET!
HERE IT COMES!
GET READY FOR...
...IT...
SNAP
BAM

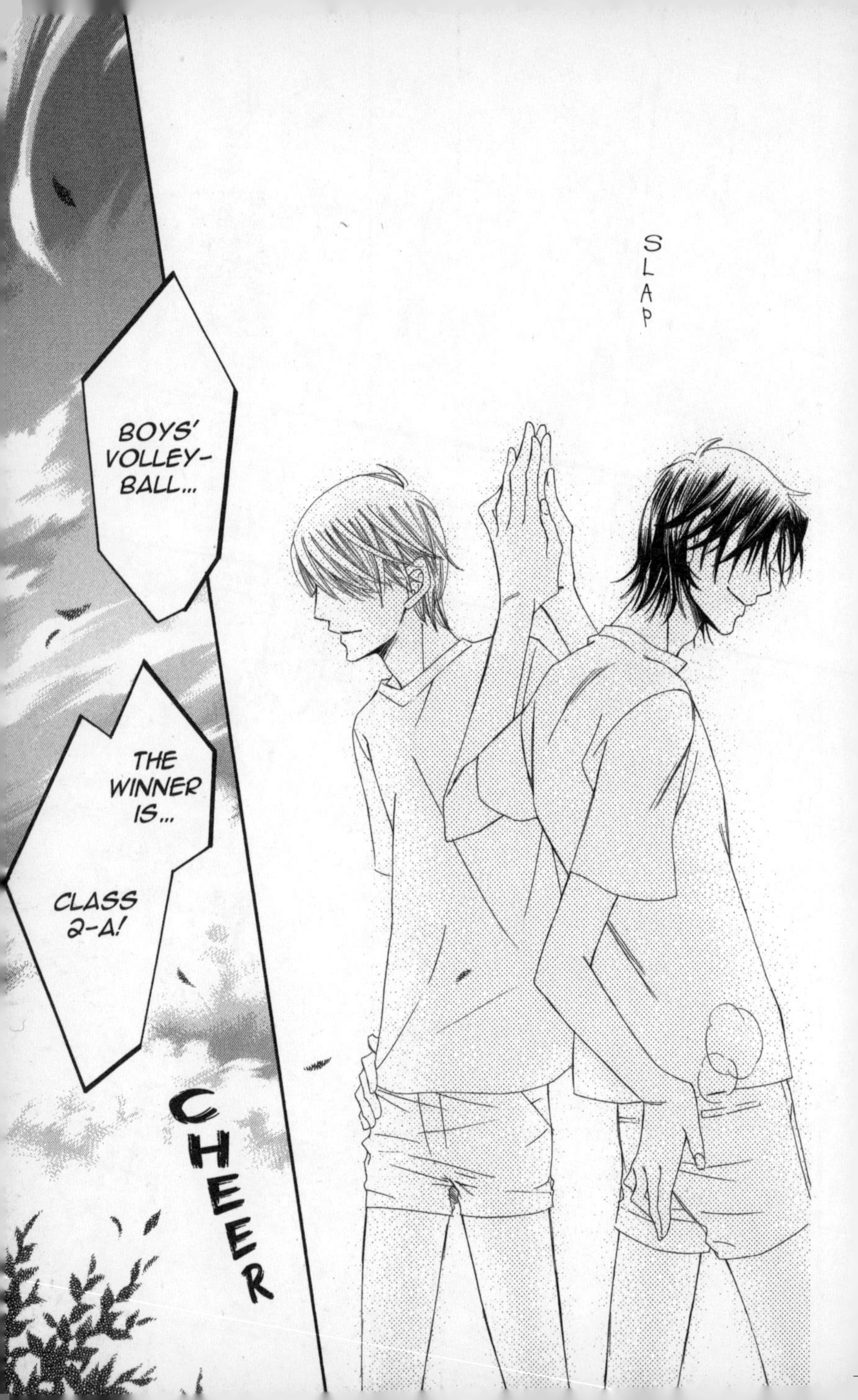
SLAP
BOYS' VOLLEY-BALL...
THE WINNER IS...
CLASS 2-A!
CHEER

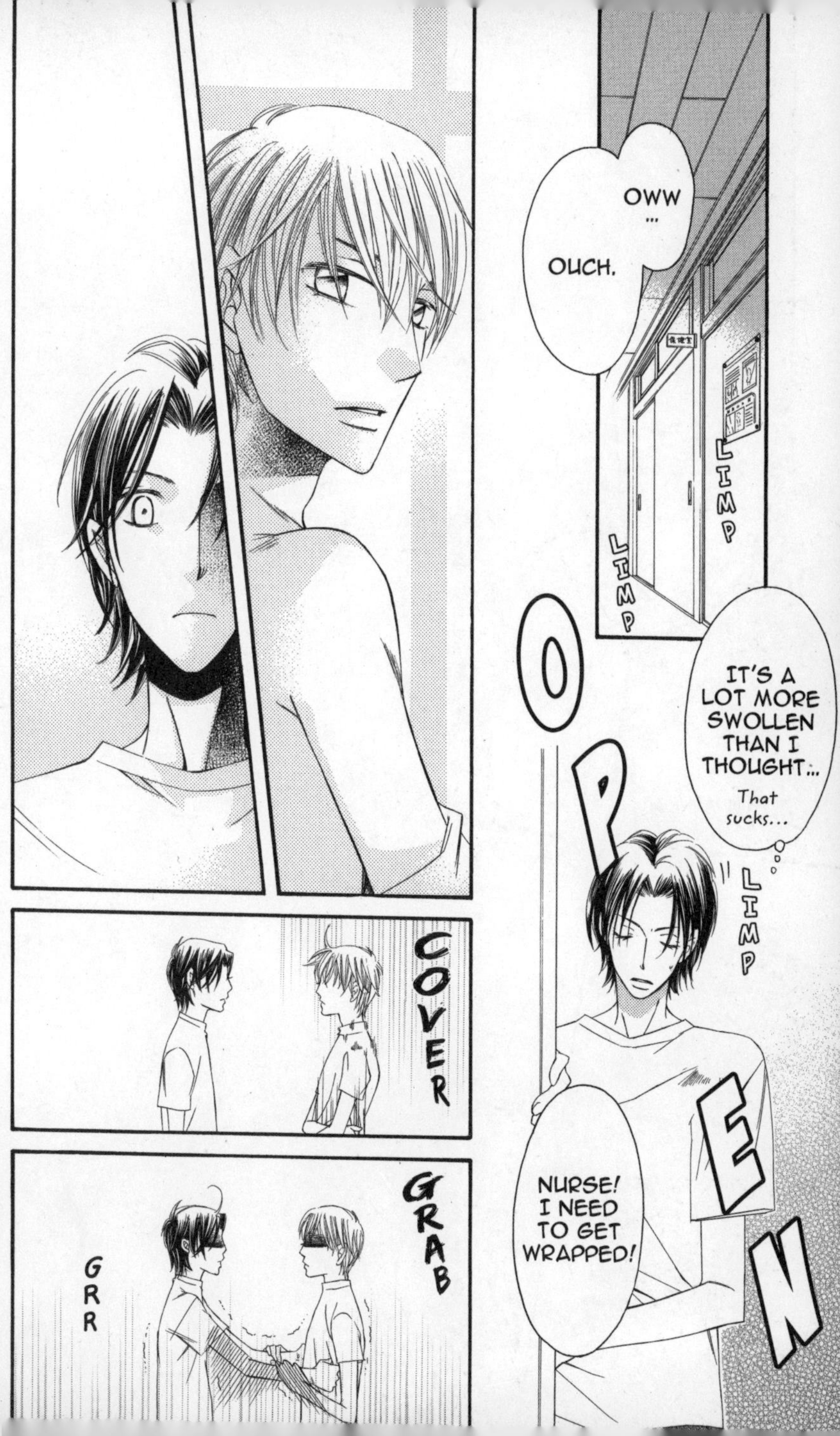
OWW ... OUCH.
LIMP
LIMP
OPEN
IT'S A LOT MORE SWOLLEN THAN I THOUGHT...
That sucks...
LIMP
NURSE! I NEED TO GET WRAPPED!
COVER
GRAB
GRR

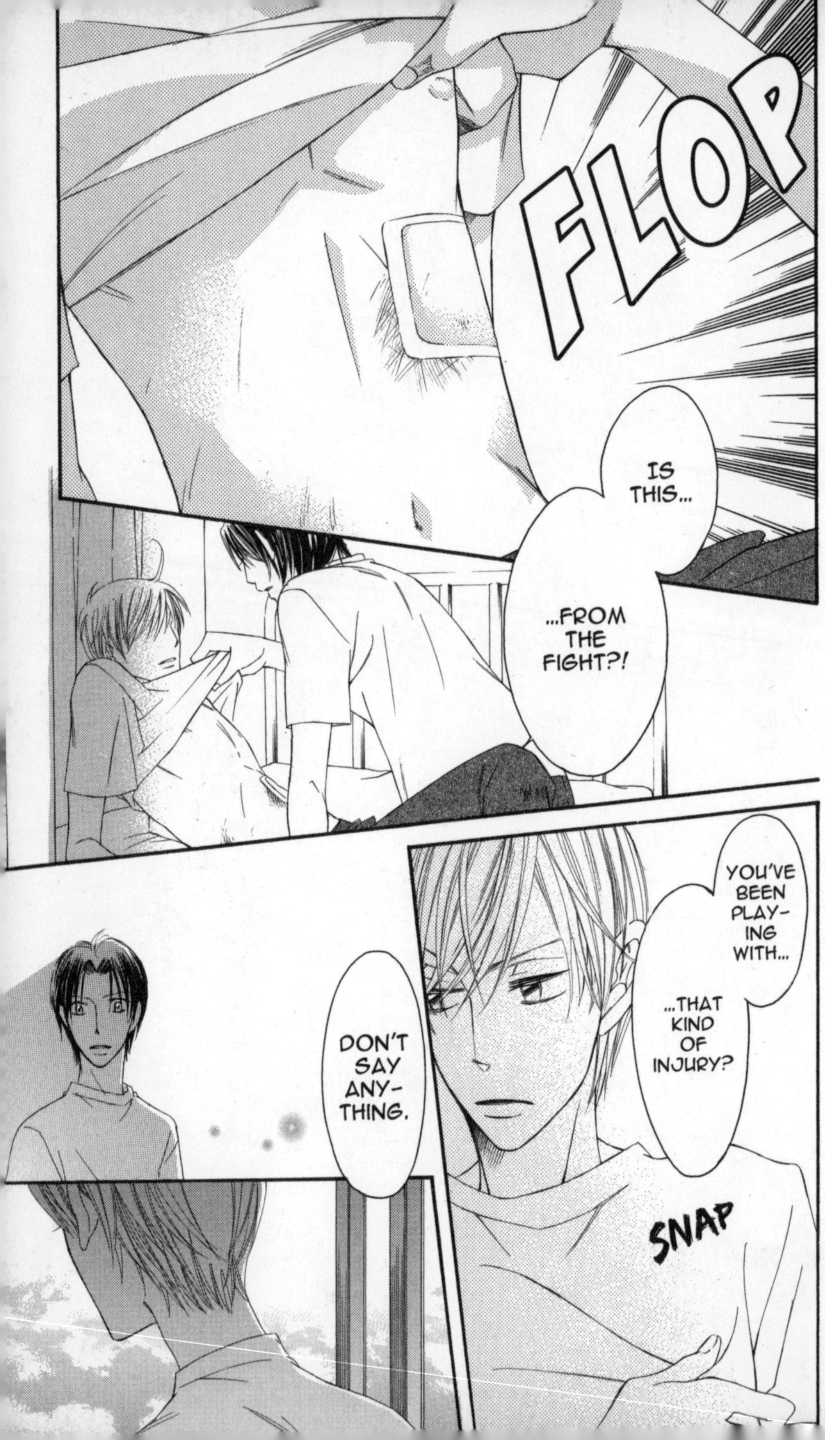
FLOP
IS THIS...
...FROM THE FIGHT?!
YOU'VE BEEN PLAYING WITH...
...THAT KIND OF INJURY?
DON'T SAY ANYTHING.
SNAP

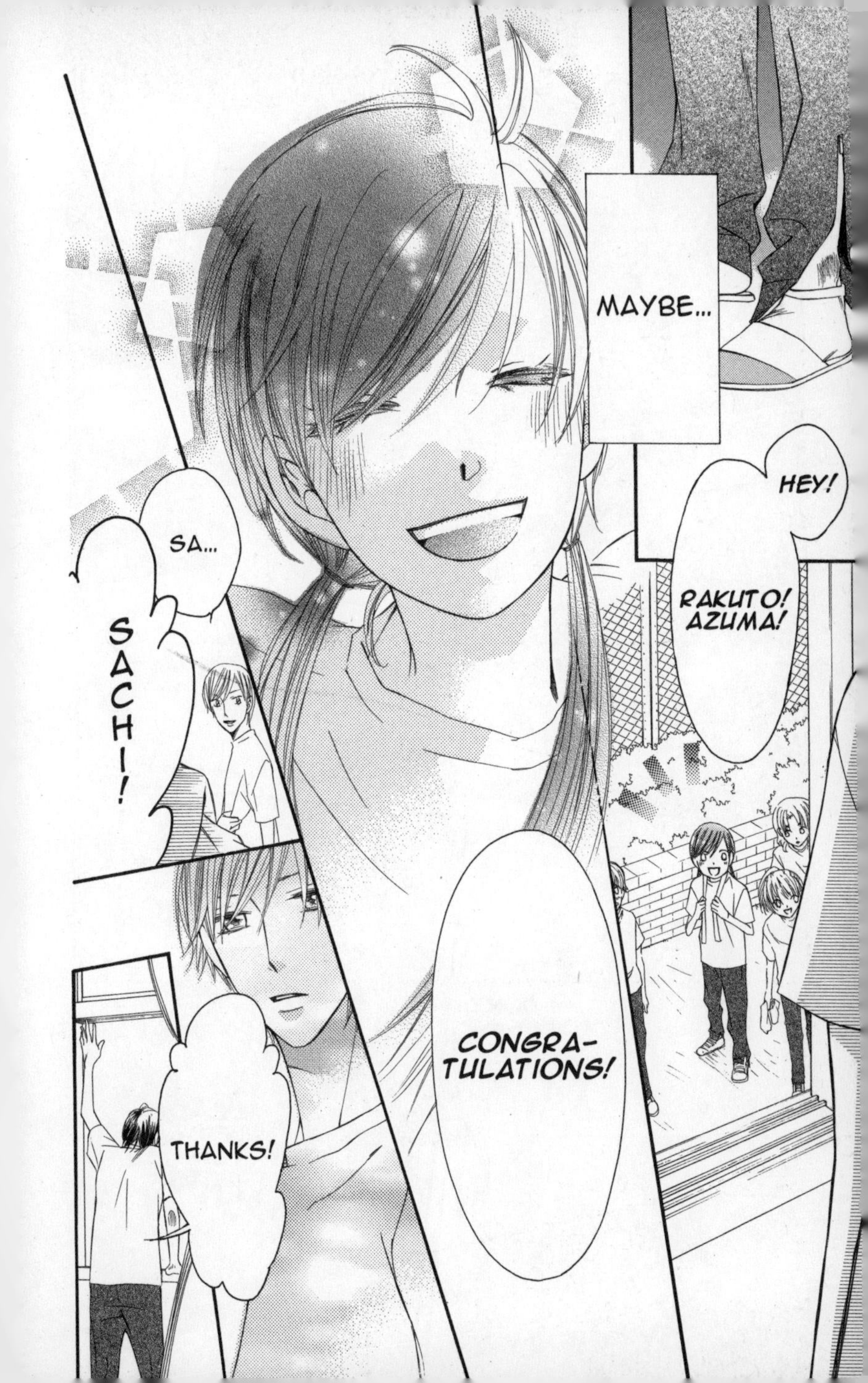
MAYBE...
HEY! RAKUTO! AZUMA!
CONGRATULATIONS!
SA... SACHI!
THANKS!

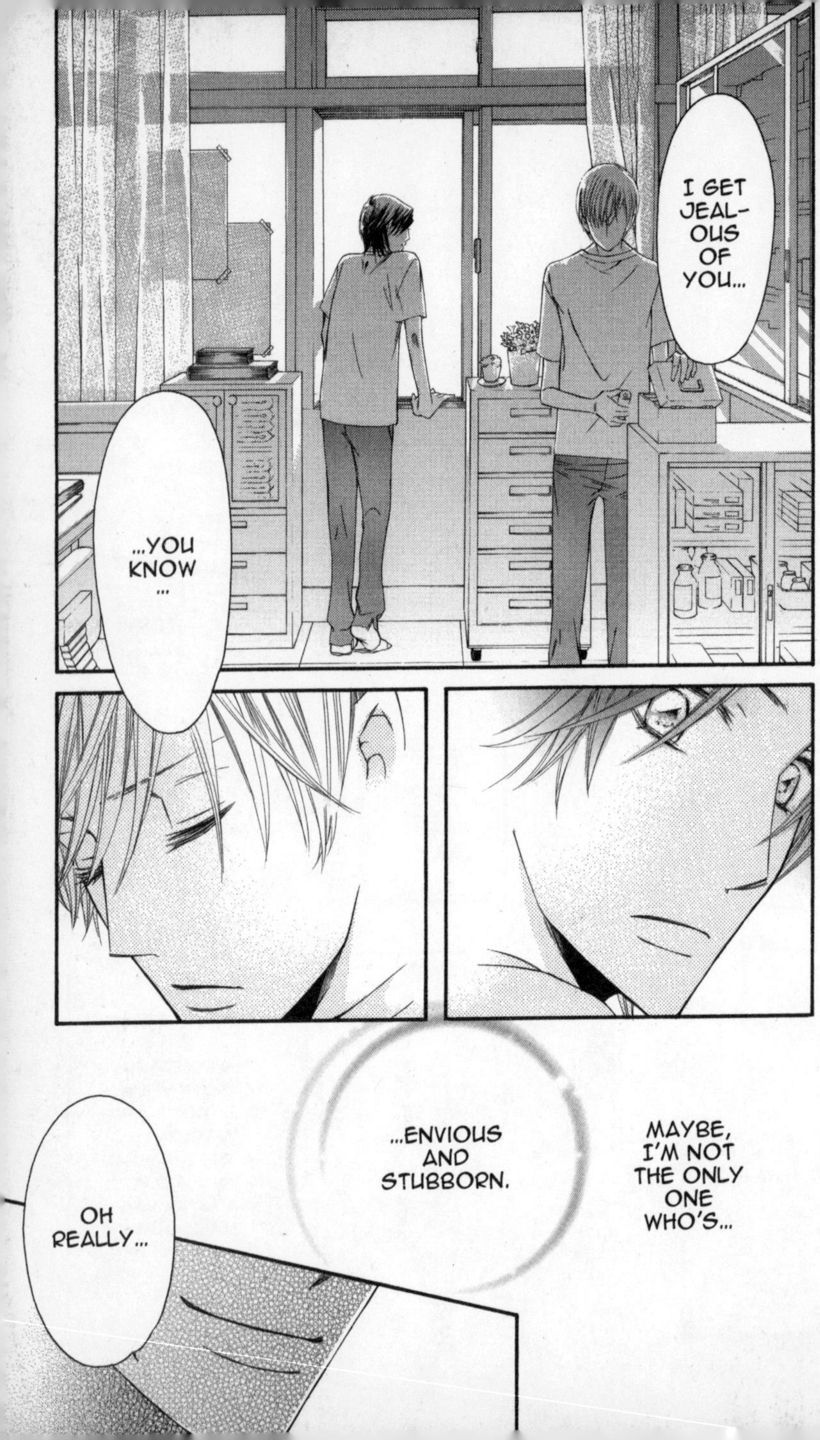
I GET JEAL-OUS OF YOU...
...YOU KNOW...
MAYBE, I'M NOT THE ONLY ONE WHO'S...
...ENVIOUS AND STUBBORN.
OH REALLY...

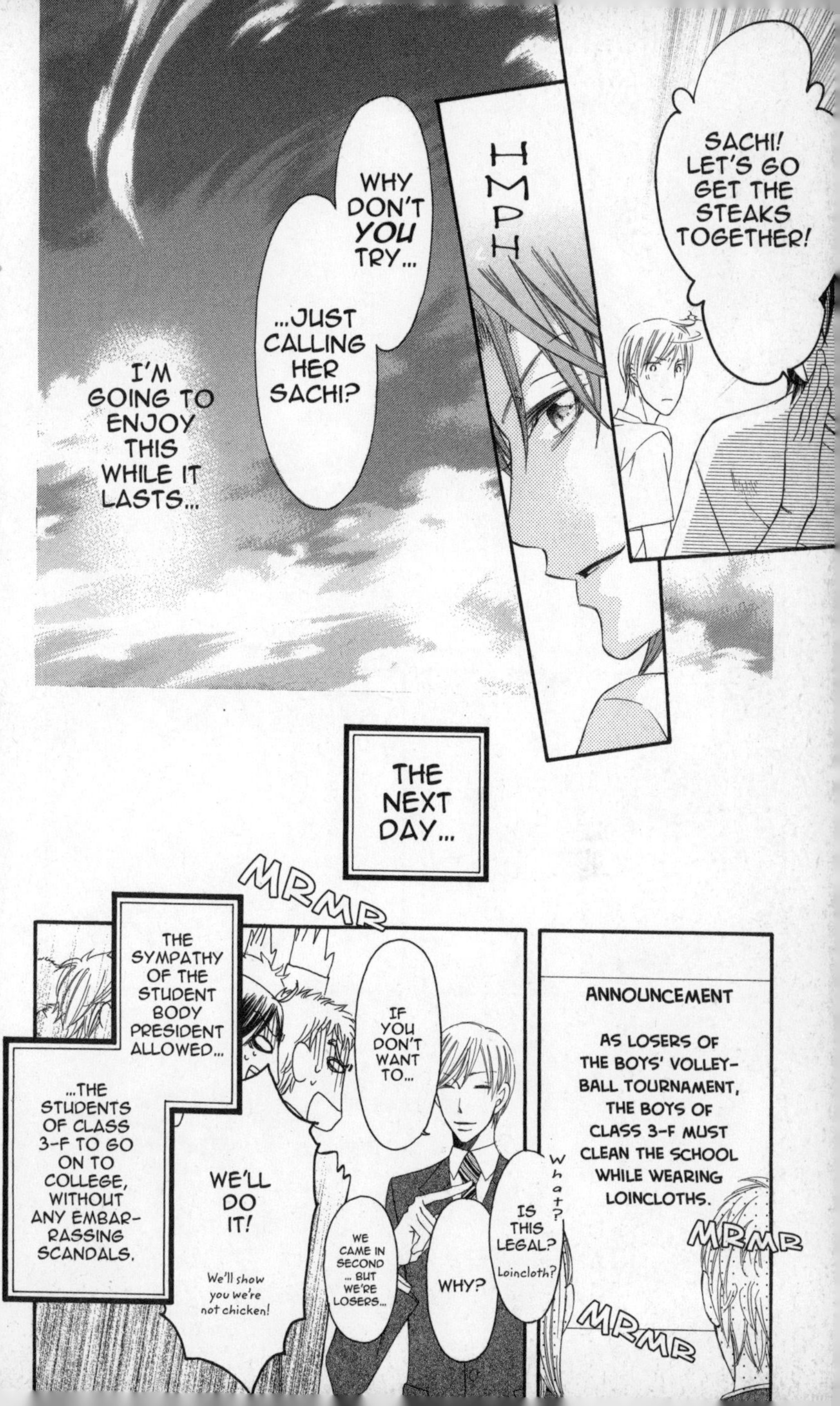
SACHI! LET'S GO GET THE STEAKS TOGETHER!
HMPH
WHY DON'T *YOU* TRY...
...JUST CALLING HER SACHI?
I'M GOING TO ENJOY THIS WHILE IT LASTS...
THE NEXT DAY...
ANNOUNCEMENT
AS LOSERS OF THE BOYS' VOLLEY-BALL TOURNAMENT, THE BOYS OF CLASS 3-F MUST CLEAN THE SCHOOL WHILE WEARING LOINCLOTHS.
MRMR
MRMR
MRMR
IF YOU DON'T WANT TO...
What?
IS THIS LEGAL?
Loincloth?
WHY?
WE CAME IN SECOND ... BUT WE'RE LOSERS...
WE'LL DO IT!
We'll show you we're not chicken!
THE SYMPATHY OF THE STUDENT BODY PRESIDENT ALLOWED...
...THE STUDENTS OF CLASS 3-F TO GO ON TO COLLEGE, WITHOUT ANY EMBAR-RASSING SCANDALS.

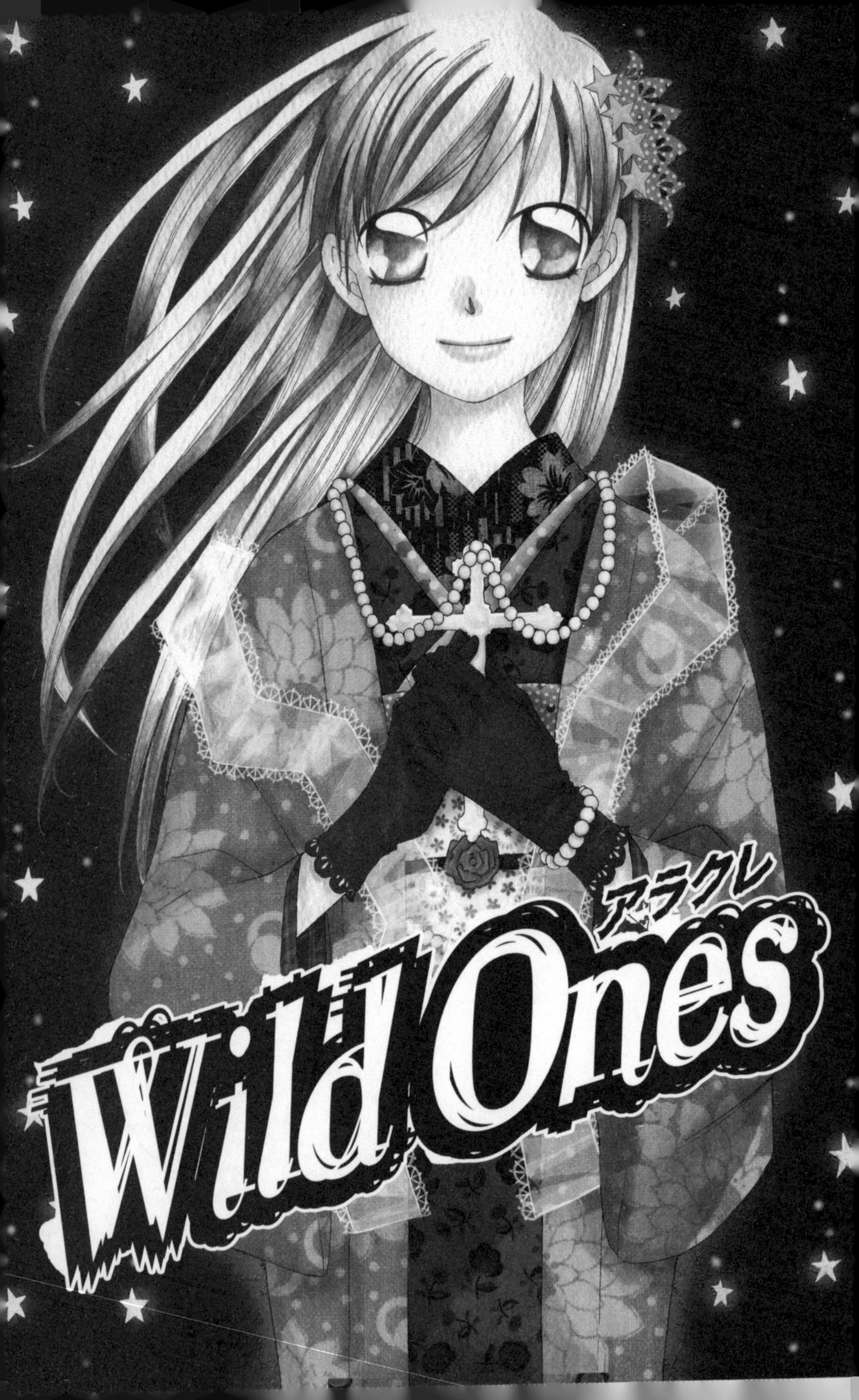
アラクレ
Wild Ones

RAKUTO AND AZUMA

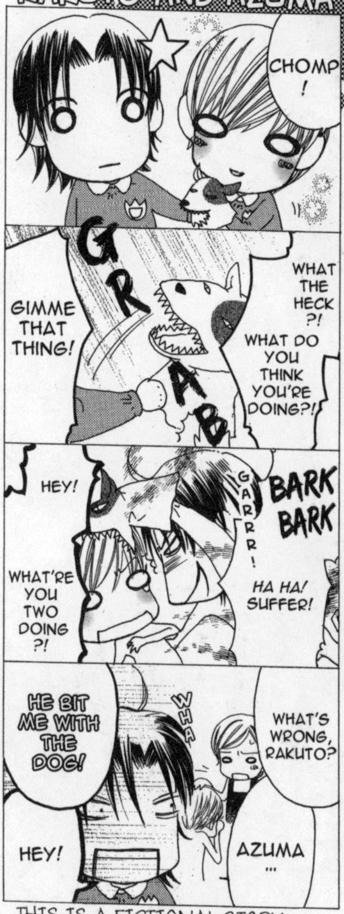
CHOMP!
WHAT THE HECK?!
WHAT DO YOU THINK YOU'RE DOING?!
GRAB
GIMME THAT THING!
BARK BARK
GARRR!
HA HA! SUFFER!
HEY!
WHAT'RE YOU TWO DOING?!
WHAT'S WRONG, RAKUTO?
AZUMA...
WHA
HE BIT ME WITH THE DOG!
HEY!

THIS IS A FICTIONAL STORY...

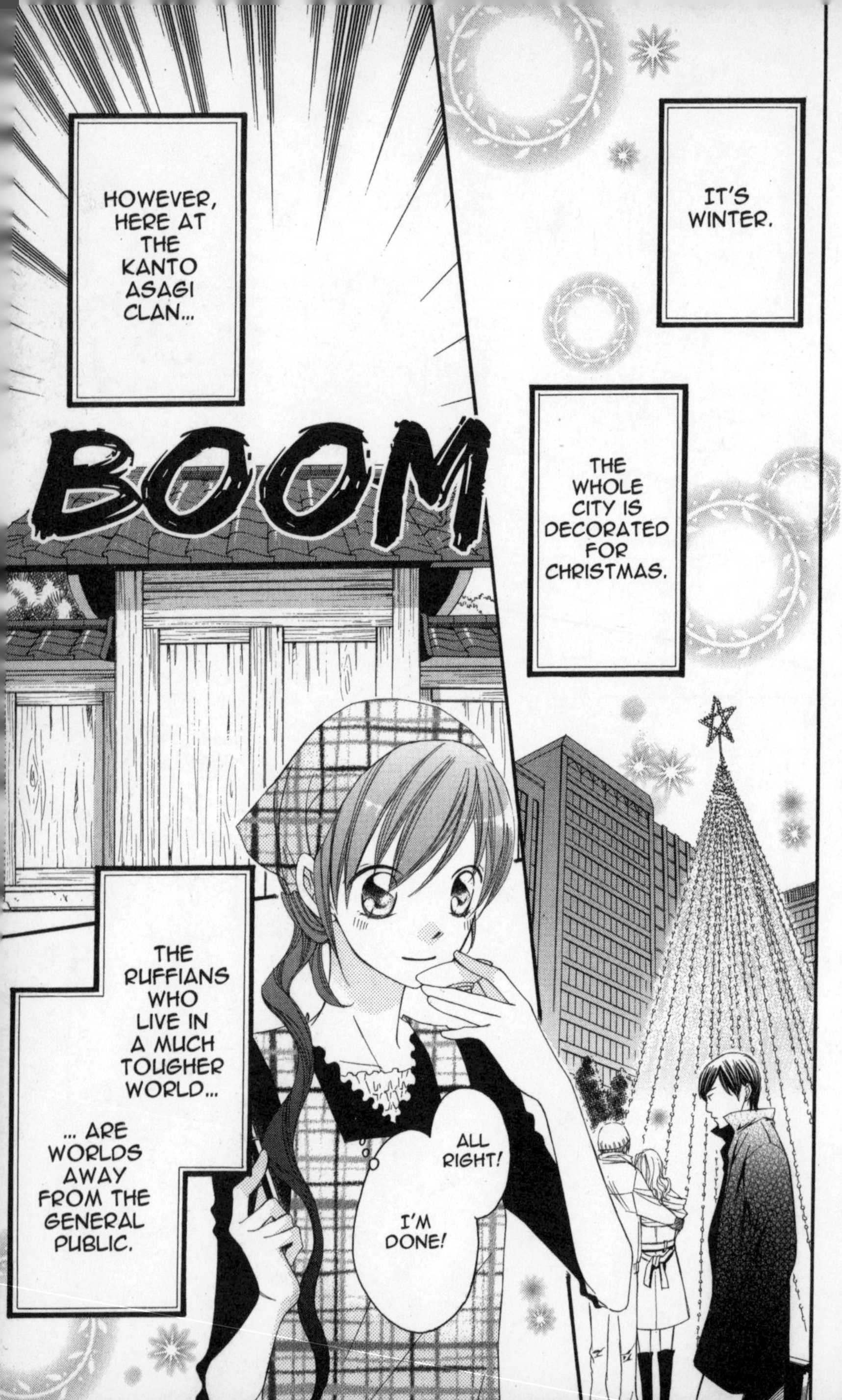
IT'S WINTER.
THE WHOLE CITY IS DECORATED FOR CHRISTMAS.
HOWEVER, HERE AT THE KANTO ASAGI CLAN...
BOOM
THE RUFFIANS WHO LIVE IN A MUCH TOUGHER WORLD...
... ARE WORLDS AWAY FROM THE GENERAL PUBLIC.
ALL RIGHT!
I'M DONE!

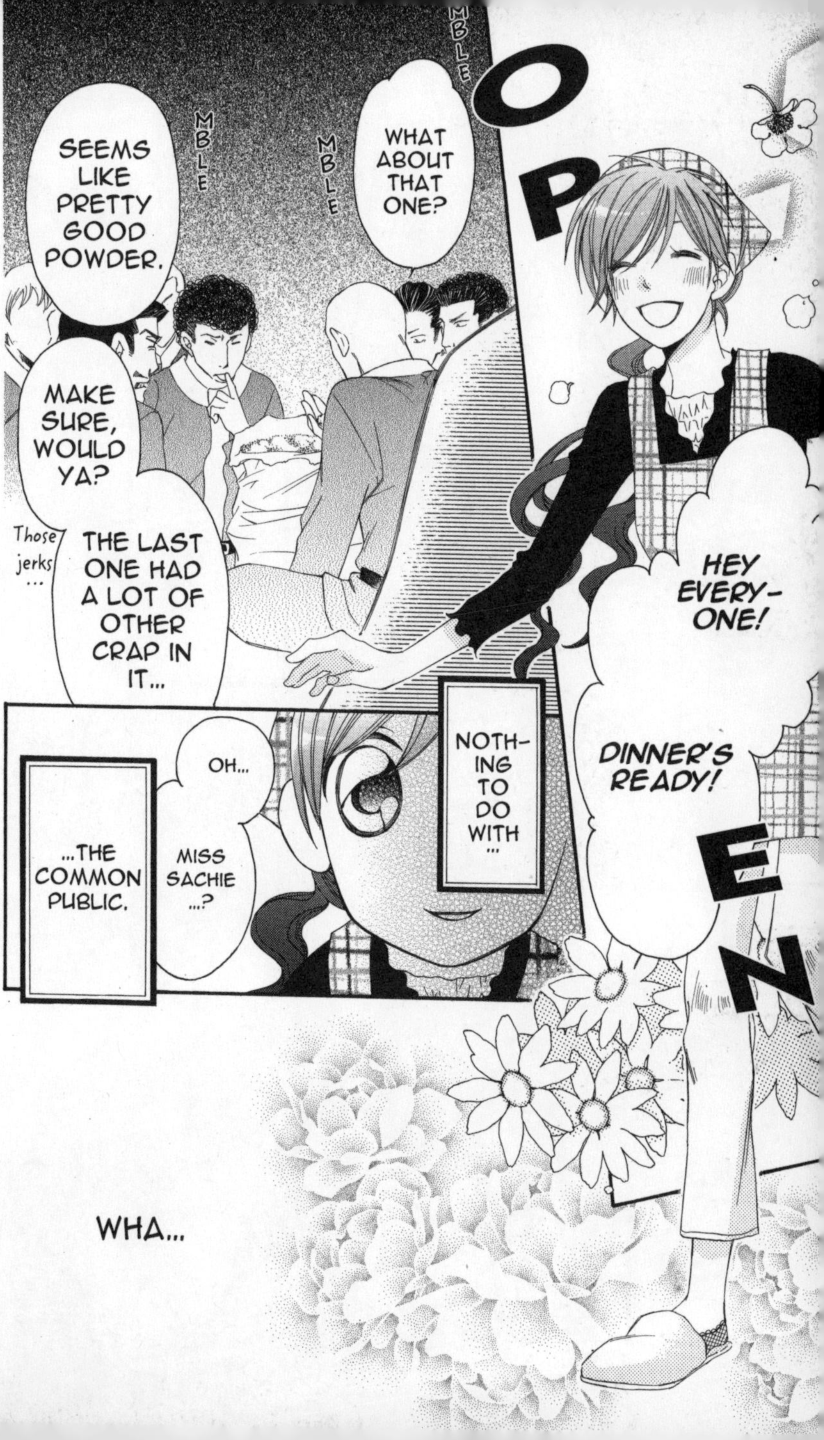

MBLE
MBLE
MBLE
WHAT ABOUT THAT ONE?
SEEMS LIKE PRETTY GOOD POWDER.
MAKE SURE, WOULD YA?
THE LAST ONE HAD A LOT OF OTHER CRAP IN IT...
Those jerks...
NOTH-ING TO DO WITH...
...THE COMMON PUBLIC.
OPEN
HEY EVERY-ONE!
DINNER'S READY!
OH...
MISS SACHIE...?
WHA...

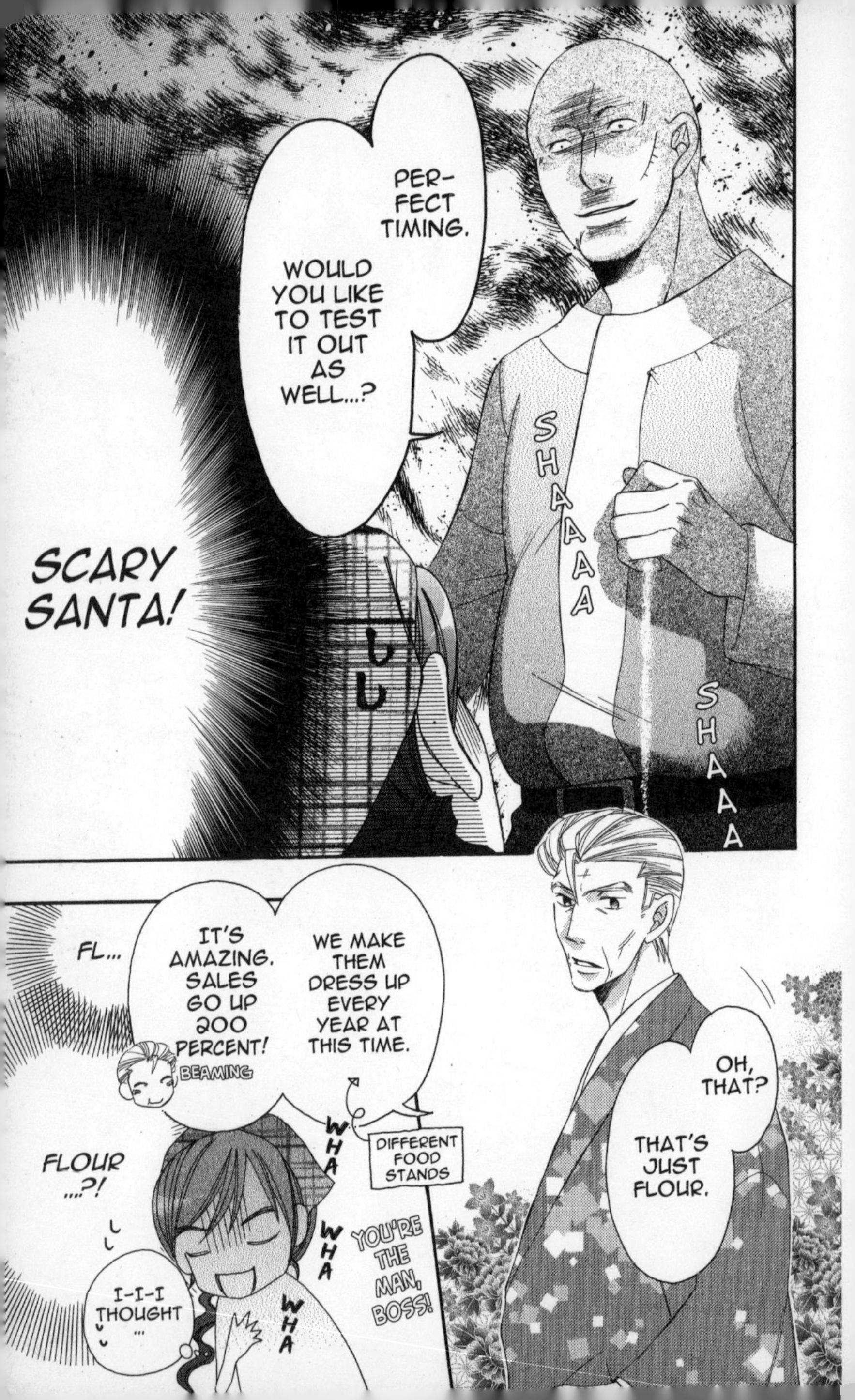

PER-FECT TIMING.
WOULD YOU LIKE TO TEST IT OUT AS WELL...?
SHAAAA
SHAAAA
SCARY SANTA!
OH, THAT?
THAT'S JUST FLOUR.
WE MAKE THEM DRESS UP EVERY YEAR AT THIS TIME.
IT'S AMAZING. SALES GO UP 200 PERCENT!
BEAMING
DIFFERENT FOOD STANDS
YOU'RE THE MAN, BOSS!
WHA
WHA
WHA
FL...
FLOUR ...?!
I-I-I THOUGHT ...

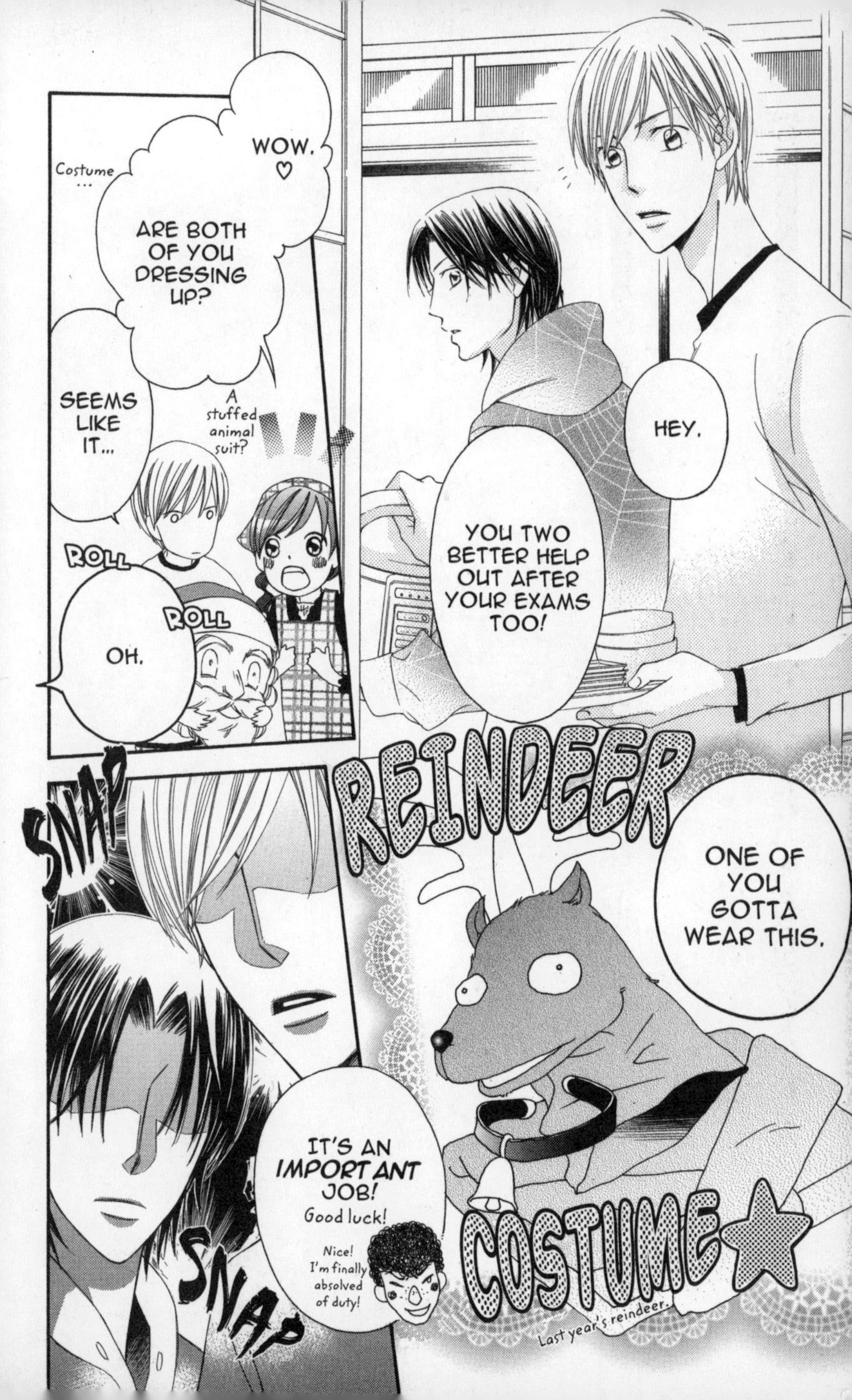
HEY.
YOU TWO BETTER HELP OUT AFTER YOUR EXAMS TOO!
WOW. ♡
ARE BOTH OF YOU DRESSING UP?
Costume...
SEEMS LIKE IT...
A stuffed animal suit?
ROLL
ROLL
OH.
REINDEER COSTUME☆
ONE OF YOU GOTTA WEAR THIS.
Last year's reindeer.
IT'S AN IMPORTANT JOB! Good luck!
Nice! I'm finally absolved of duty!
SNAP
SNAP

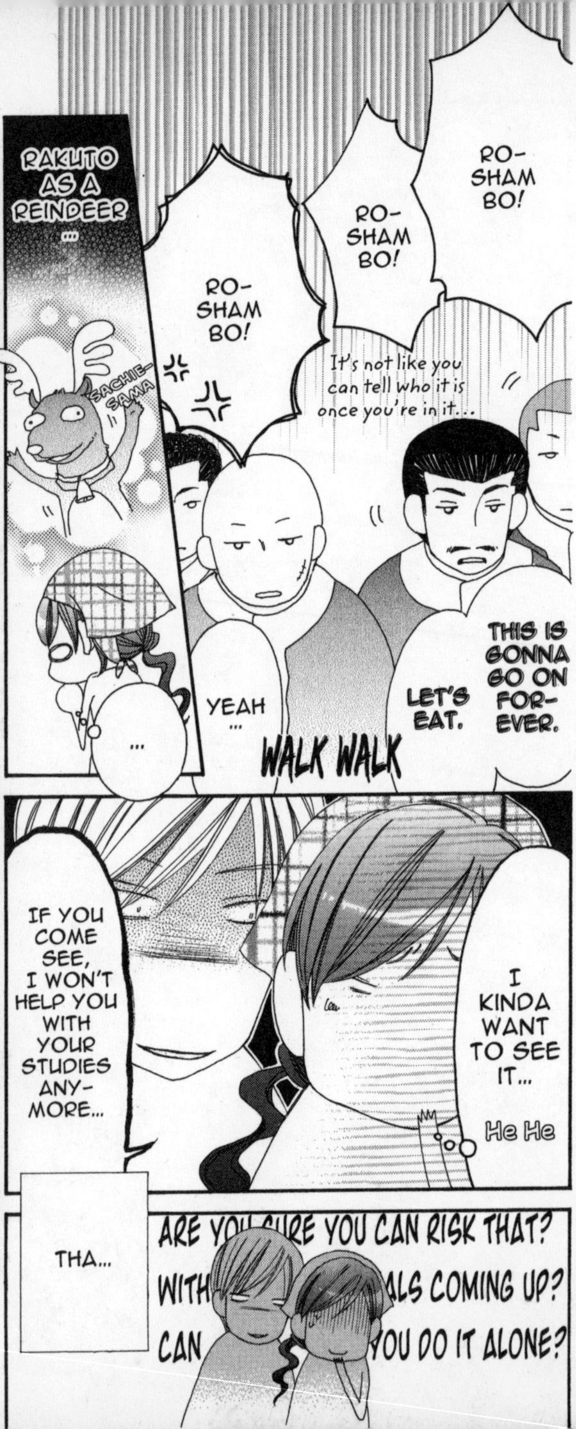
RO-SHAM BO!
RO-SHAM BO!
RO-SHAM BO!
It's not like you can tell who it is once you're in it...
THIS IS GONNA GO ON FOR-EVER.
LET'S EAT.
YEAH ...
WALK WALK
RAKUTO AS A REINDEER ...
SACHIE-SAMA
...
I KINDA WANT TO SEE IT...
He He
IF YOU COME SEE, I WON'T HELP YOU WITH YOUR STUDIES ANY-MORE...
ARE YO URE YOU CAN RISK THAT?
WITH ALS COMING UP?
CAN YOU DO IT ALONE?
THA...

THANX!

TO:
SHIBATA-SAN
SHIMOSATO-SAN
SHIKAYA-SAN
AND...
MO-CHAN!

APPARENTLY I'M ALLOWED TO HAVE A BOOK SIGNING AFTER THIS BOOK COMES OUT. I'VE NEVER MET ANYBODY WHO READS MY WORK (OTHER THAN FRIENDS), SO I'M A LITTLE WORRIED ABOUT THE SHOWING, BUT... I HOPE I GET TO MEET PEOPLE. I'M A LITTLE NERVOUS. URR... I'LL LET YOU KNOW HOW IT WENT IN THE NEXT VOLUME! TALK TO YOU THEN!

2/2007 KIYO FUJIWARA

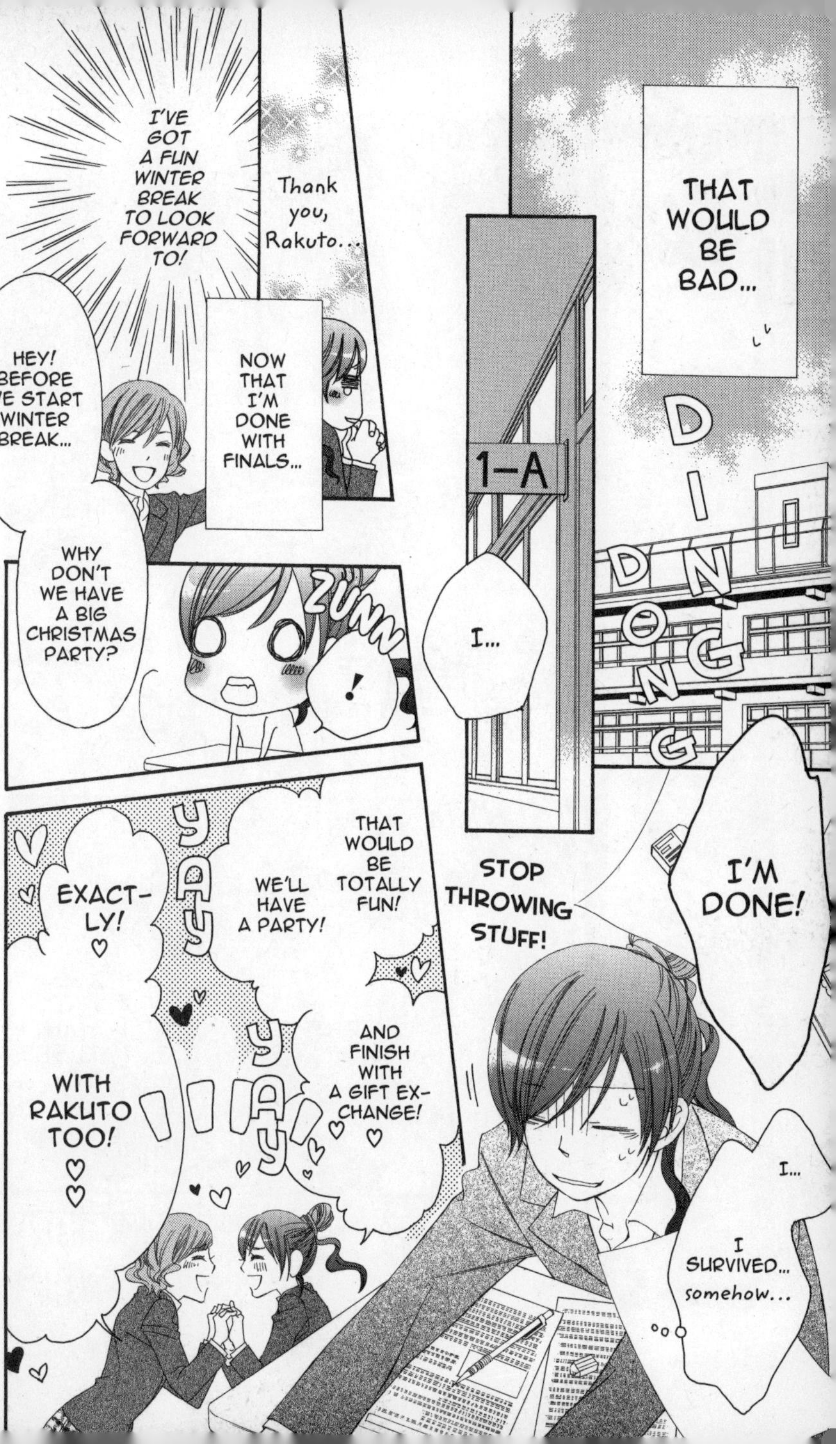
THAT WOULD BE BAD...
DING
DONG
DING
DONG
1-A
I...
I'M DONE!
STOP THROWING STUFF!
I...
I SURVIVED... somehow...
Thank you, Rakuto...
I'VE GOT A FUN WINTER BREAK TO LOOK FORWARD TO!
NOW THAT I'M DONE WITH FINALS...
HEY! BEFORE WE START WINTER BREAK...
WHY DON'T WE HAVE A BIG CHRISTMAS PARTY?
ZUNN
!
THAT WOULD BE TOTALLY FUN!
WE'LL HAVE A PARTY!
YAY
EXACT-LY!
AND FINISH WITH A GIFT EX-CHANGE!
YAY!!
WITH RAKUTO TOO!

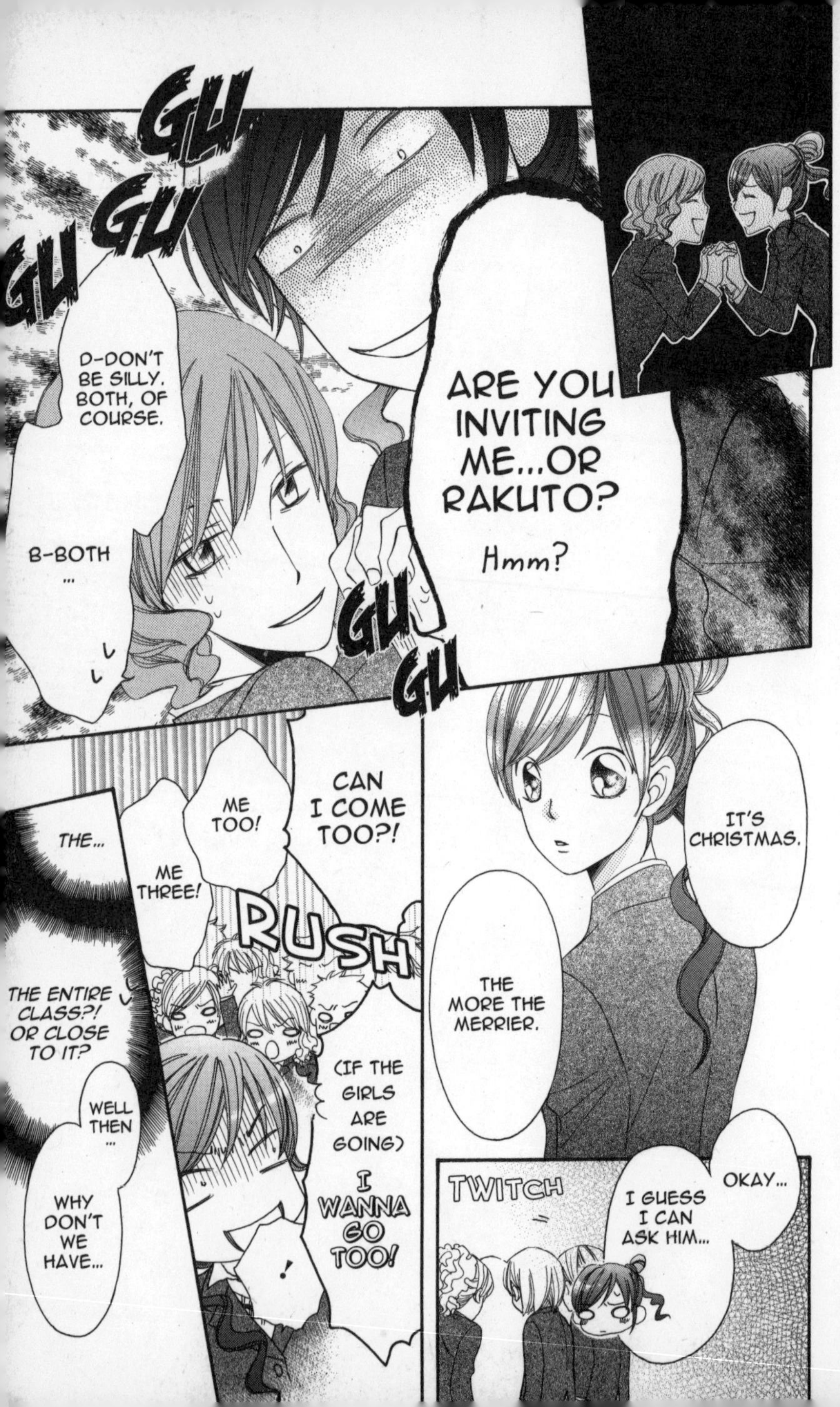
GU GU
ARE YOU INVITING ME...OR RAKUTO?
Hmm?
GU GU
B-BOTH ...
D-DON'T BE SILLY. BOTH, OF COURSE.
GU GU GU
IT'S CHRISTMAS.
THE MORE THE MERRIER.
OKAY... I GUESS I CAN ASK HIM...
TWITCH
CAN I COME TOO?!
ME TOO!
ME THREE!
RUSH
(IF THE GIRLS ARE GOING)
I WANNA GO TOO!
THE...
THE ENTIRE CLASS?! OR CLOSE TO IT?
WELL THEN ...
WHY DON'T WE HAVE...

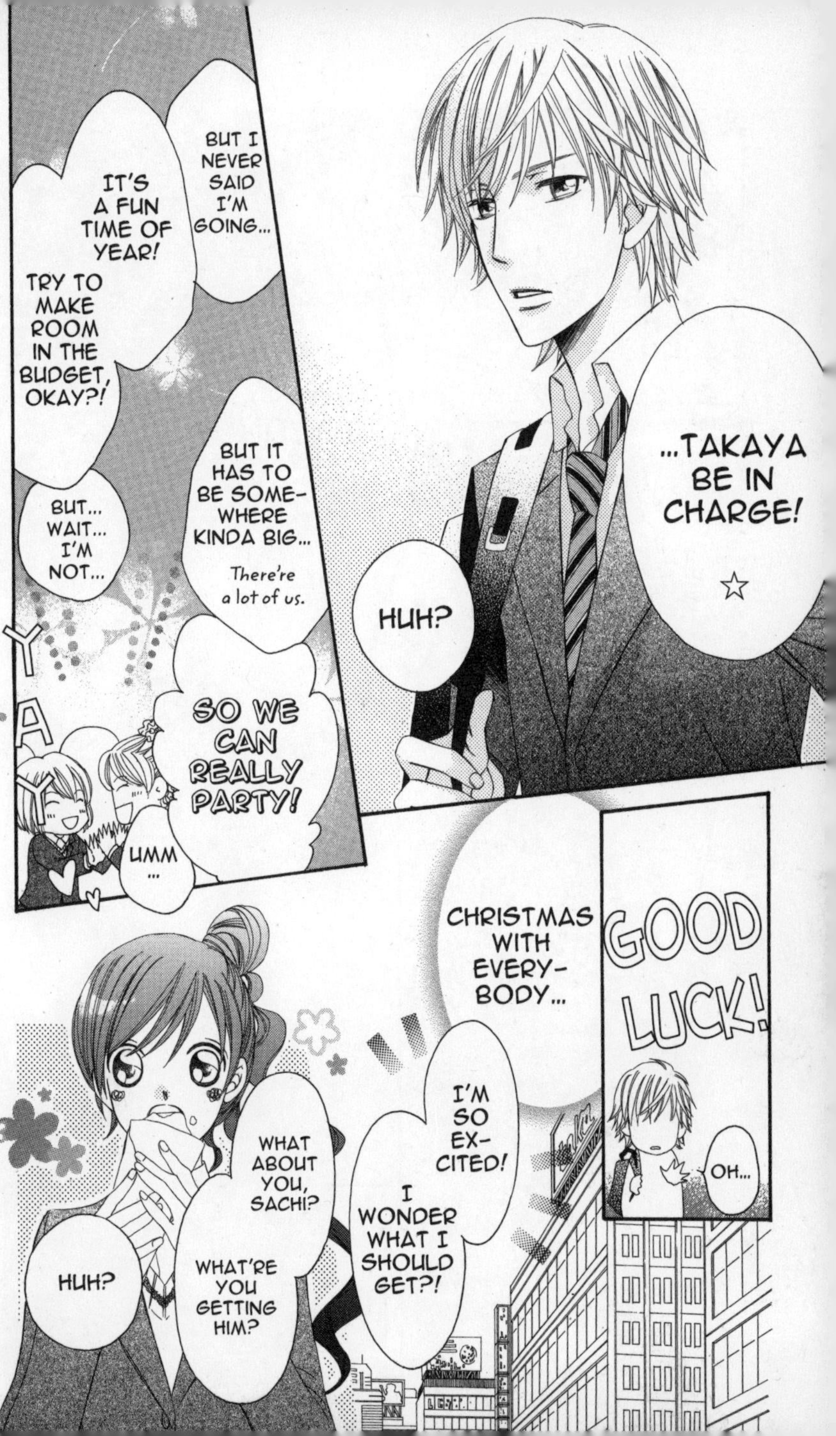
...TAKAYA BE IN CHARGE! ☆
HUH?
BUT I NEVER SAID I'M GOING...
IT'S A FUN TIME OF YEAR!
TRY TO MAKE ROOM IN THE BUDGET, OKAY?!
BUT IT HAS TO BE SOME-WHERE KINDA BIG...
There're a lot of us.
BUT... WAIT... I'M NOT...
SO WE CAN REALLY PARTY!
YAY
UMM...
GOOD LUCK!
OH...
CHRISTMAS WITH EVERY-BODY...
I'M SO EX-CITED!
I WONDER WHAT I SHOULD GET?!
WHAT ABOUT YOU, SACHI?
WHAT'RE YOU GETTING HIM?
HUH?

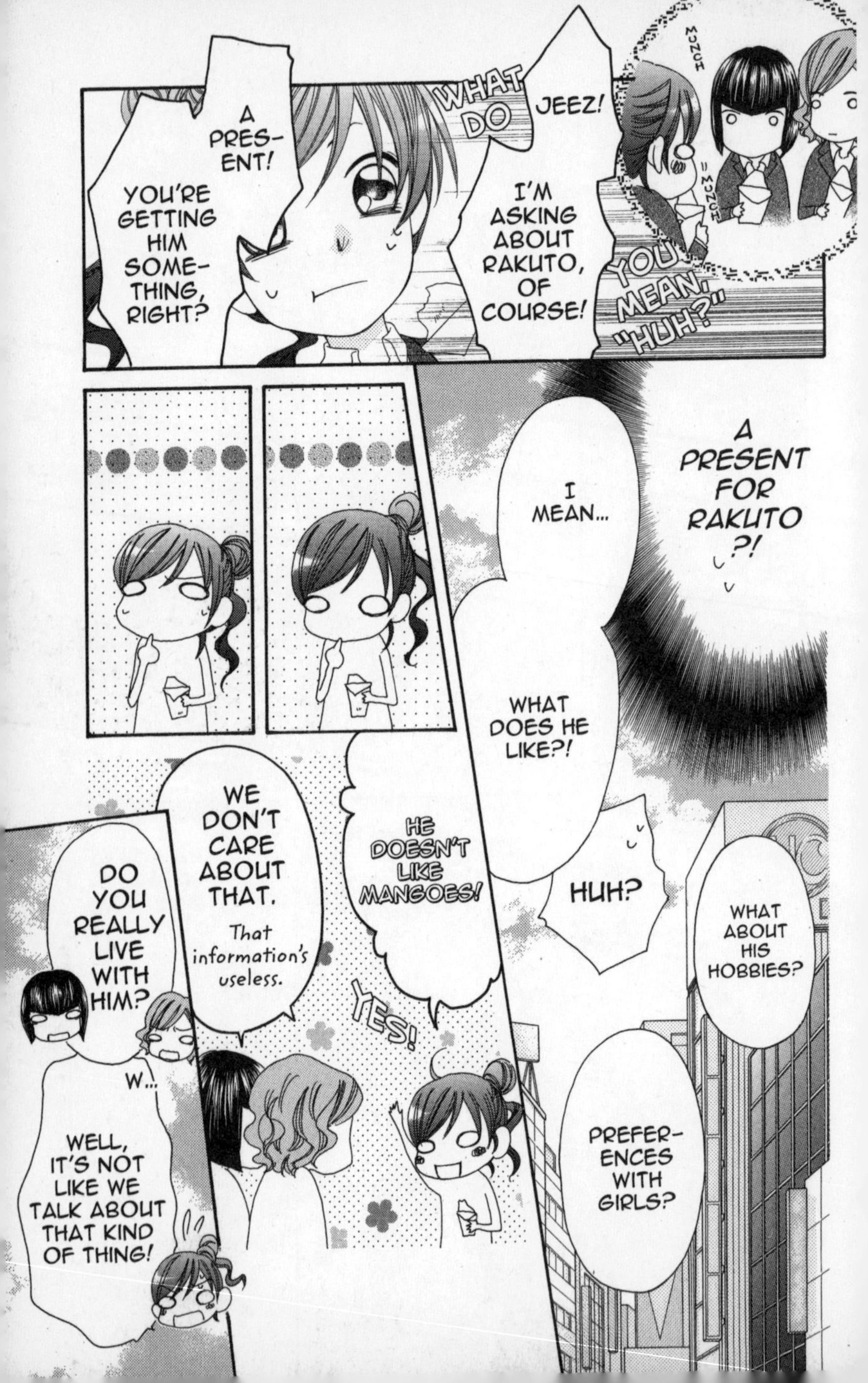

MUNCH
MUNCH
WHAT DO YOU MEAN, "HUH?"
JEEZ!
I'M ASKING ABOUT RAKUTO, OF COURSE!
A PRESENT!
YOU'RE GETTING HIM SOMETHING, RIGHT?
A PRESENT FOR RAKUTO?!
I MEAN...
WHAT DOES HE LIKE?!
HUH?
WHAT ABOUT HIS HOBBIES?
PREFERENCES WITH GIRLS?
HE DOESN'T LIKE MANGOES!
YES!
WE DON'T CARE ABOUT THAT.
That information's useless.
DO YOU REALLY LIVE WITH HIM?
W...
WELL, IT'S NOT LIKE WE TALK ABOUT THAT KIND OF THING!

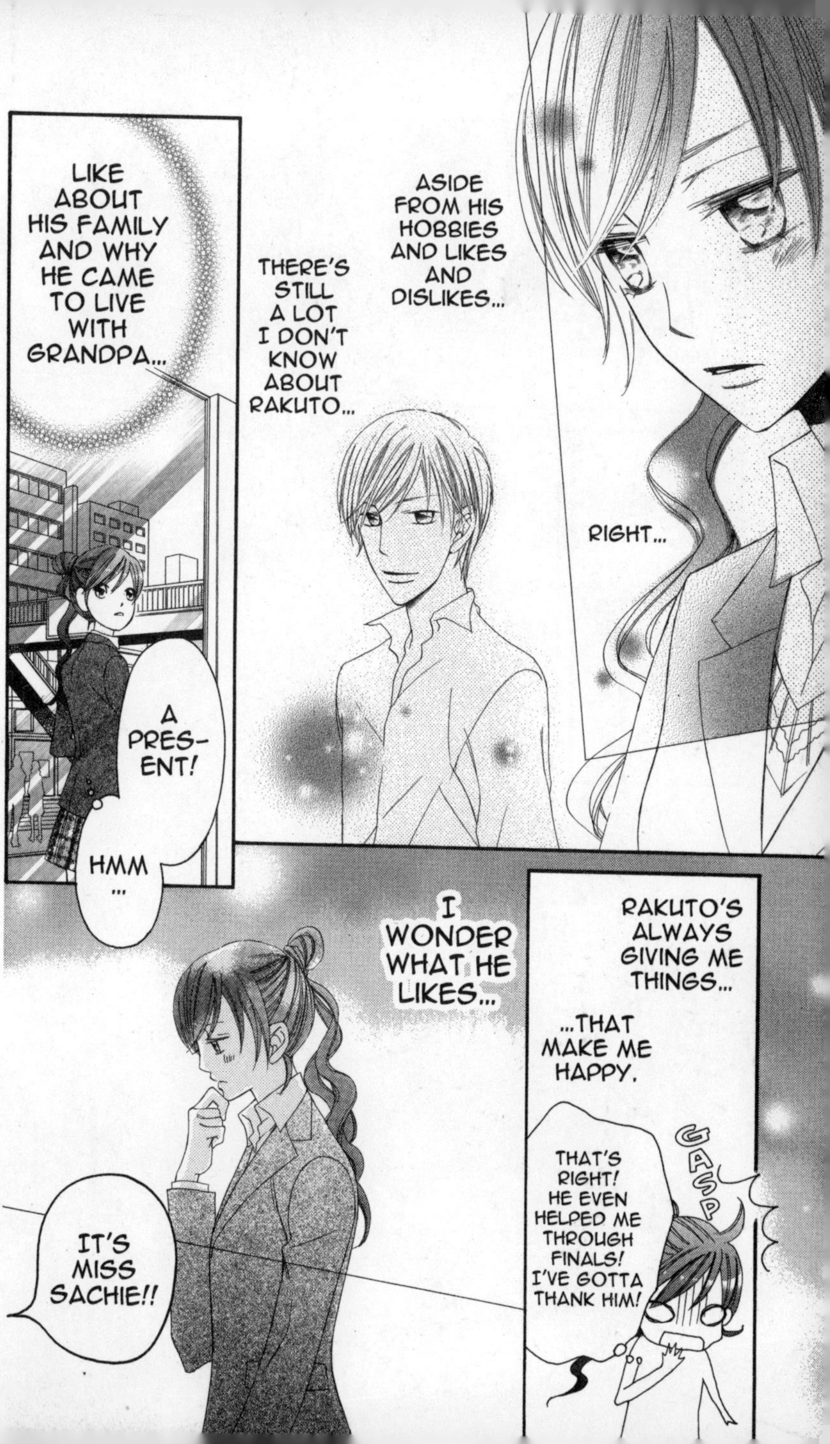
RIGHT...
ASIDE FROM HIS HOBBIES AND LIKES AND DISLIKES...
THERE'S STILL A LOT I DON'T KNOW ABOUT RAKUTO...
LIKE ABOUT HIS FAMILY AND WHY HE CAME TO LIVE WITH GRANDPA...
A PRES-ENT!
HMM...
RAKUTO'S ALWAYS GIVING ME THINGS...
...THAT MAKE ME HAPPY.
GASP
THAT'S RIGHT! HE EVEN HELPED ME THROUGH FINALS! I'VE GOTTA THANK HIM!
I WONDER WHAT HE LIKES...
IT'S MISS SACHIE!!

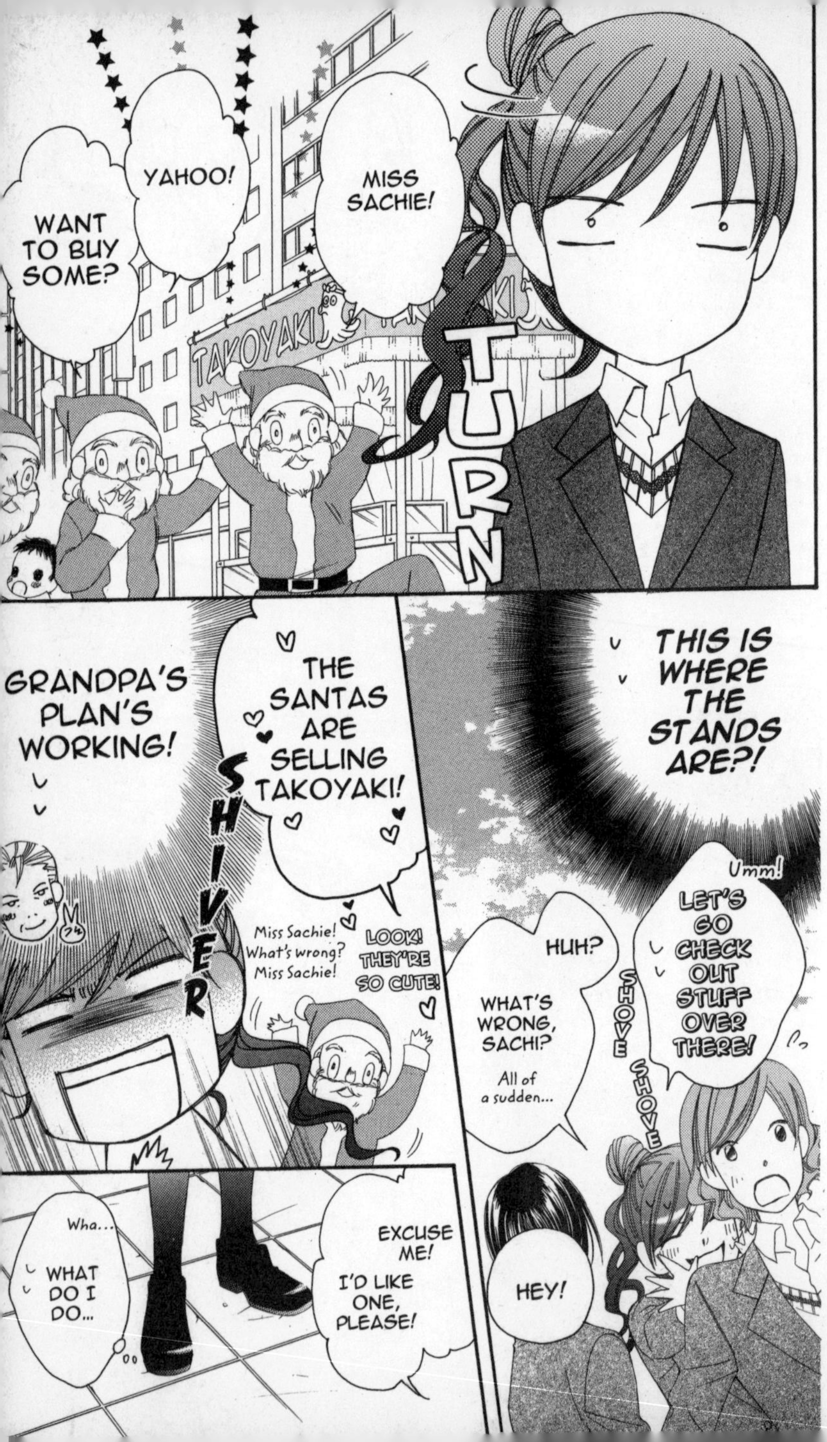
TURN
MISS SACHIE!
YAHOO!
WANT TO BUY SOME?
TAKOYAKI
THIS IS WHERE THE STANDS ARE?!
Umm!
LET'S GO CHECK OUT STUFF OVER THERE!
SHOVE
SHOVE
HUH?
WHAT'S WRONG, SACHI?
All of a sudden...
HEY!
THE SANTAS ARE SELLING TAKOYAKI!
GRANDPA'S PLAN'S WORKING!
SHIVER
LOOK! THEY'RE SO CUTE!
Miss Sachie! What's wrong? Miss Sachie!
EXCUSE ME!
I'D LIKE ONE, PLEASE!
Wha...
WHAT DO I DO...

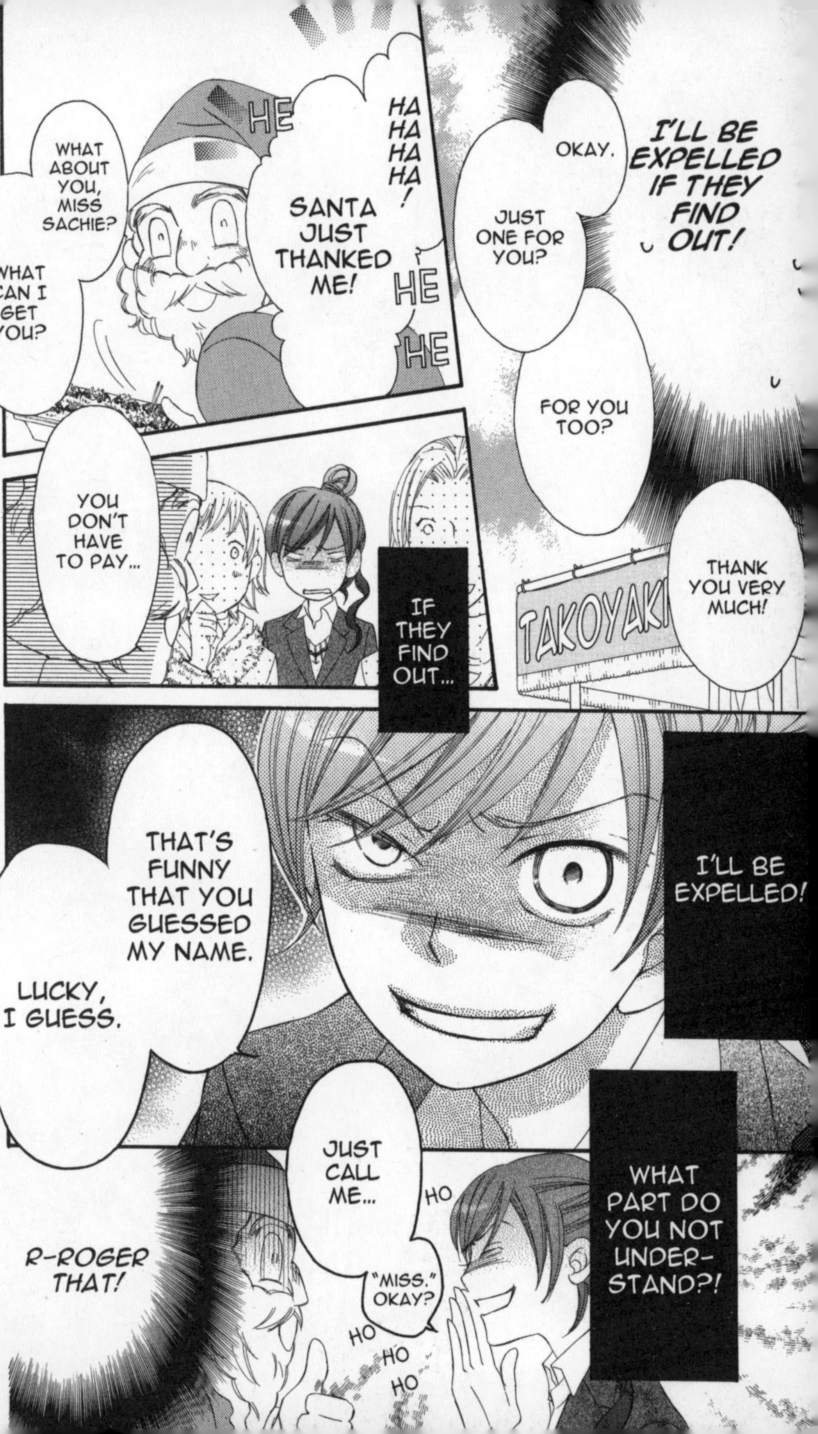

I'LL BE EXPELLED IF THEY FIND OUT!
OKAY.
JUST ONE FOR YOU?
FOR YOU TOO?
THANK YOU VERY MUCH!
HA HA HA HA!
SANTA JUST THANKED ME!
HE HE HE HE
WHAT ABOUT YOU, MISS SACHIE?
WHAT CAN I GET YOU?
TAKOYAKI
IF THEY FIND OUT...
YOU DON'T HAVE TO PAY...
I'LL BE EXPELLED!
THAT'S FUNNY THAT YOU GUESSED MY NAME.
LUCKY, I GUESS.
WHAT PART DO YOU NOT UNDER-STAND?!
JUST CALL ME...
"MISS." OKAY?
HO HO HO HO HO
R-ROGER THAT!

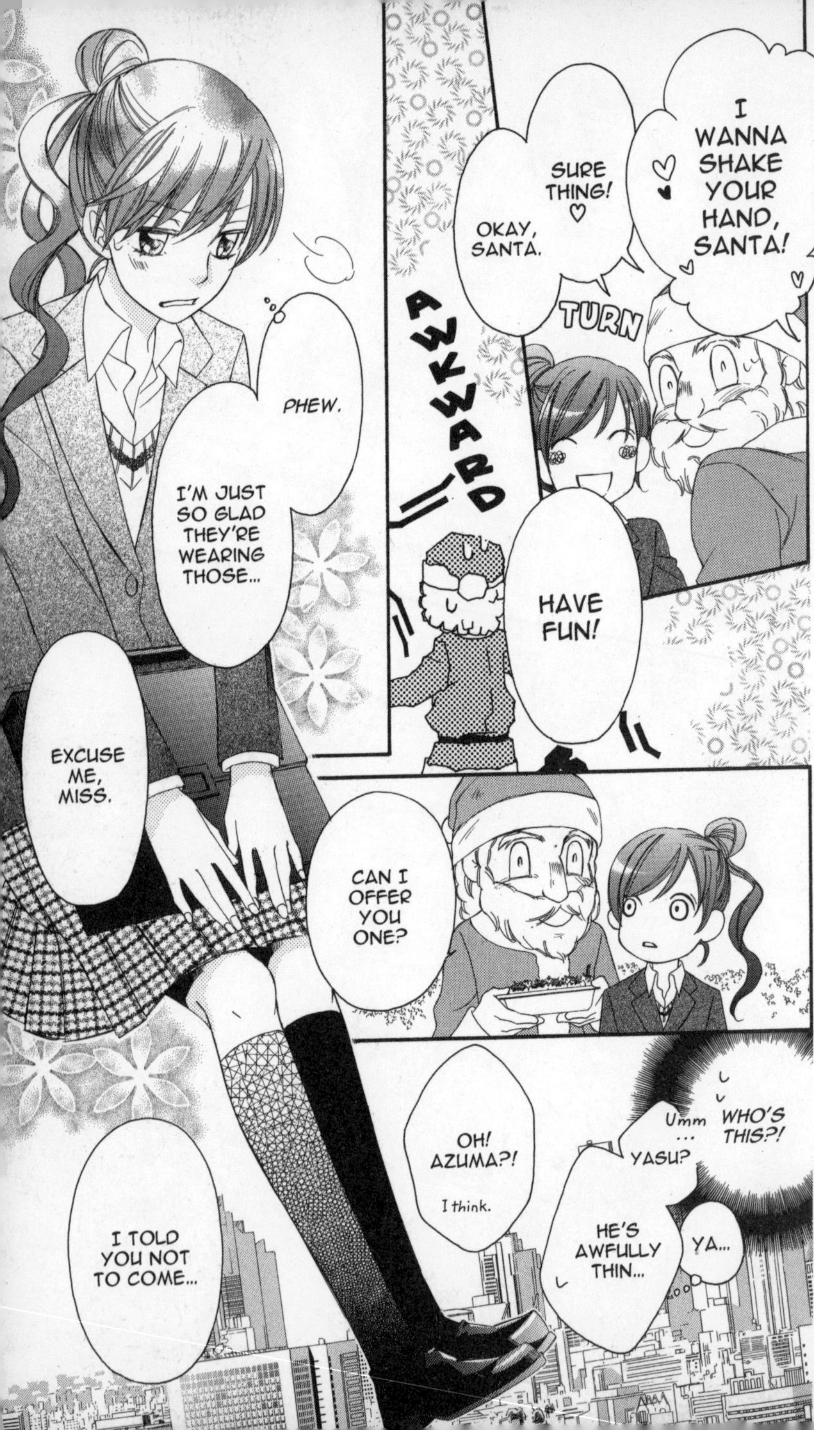
I WANNA SHAKE YOUR HAND, SANTA!
SURE THING!
OKAY, SANTA.
TURN
HAVE FUN!
AWKWARD
CAN I OFFER YOU ONE?
Umm...
WHO'S THIS?!
YASU?
YA...
HE'S AWFULLY THIN...
OH! AZUMA?!
I think.
PHEW.
I'M JUST SO GLAD THEY'RE WEARING THOSE...
EXCUSE ME, MISS.
I TOLD YOU NOT TO COME...

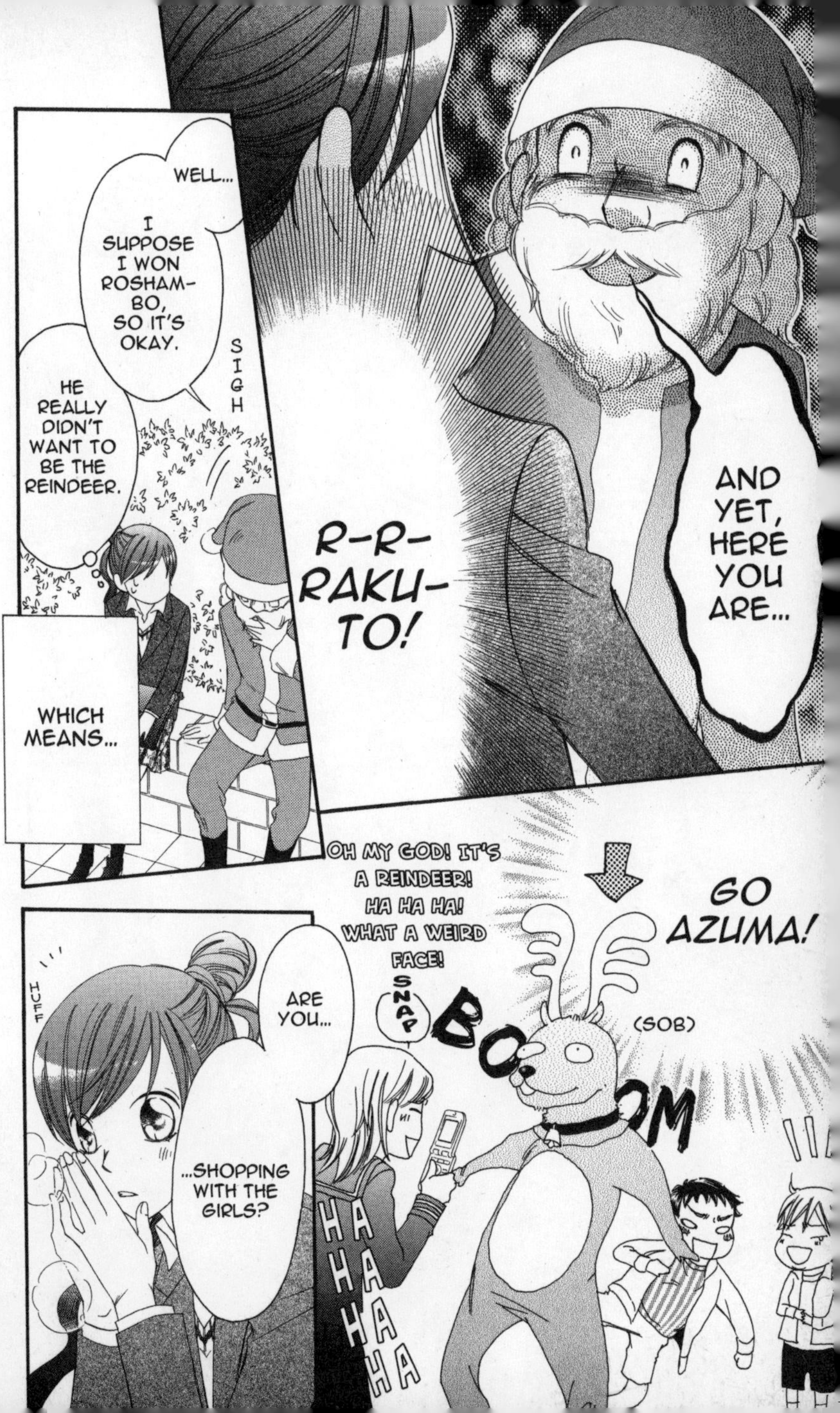
AND YET, HERE YOU ARE...
R-R-RAKUTO!
WELL...
I SUPPOSE I WON ROSHAM-BO, SO IT'S OKAY.
SIGH
HE REALLY DIDN'T WANT TO BE THE REINDEER.
WHICH MEANS...
GO AZUMA!
OH MY GOD! IT'S A REINDEER! HA HA HA! WHAT A WEIRD FACE!
SNAP
BOOM
(SOB)
HA HA HA HA HA HA
HUFF
ARE YOU...
...SHOPPING WITH THE GIRLS?

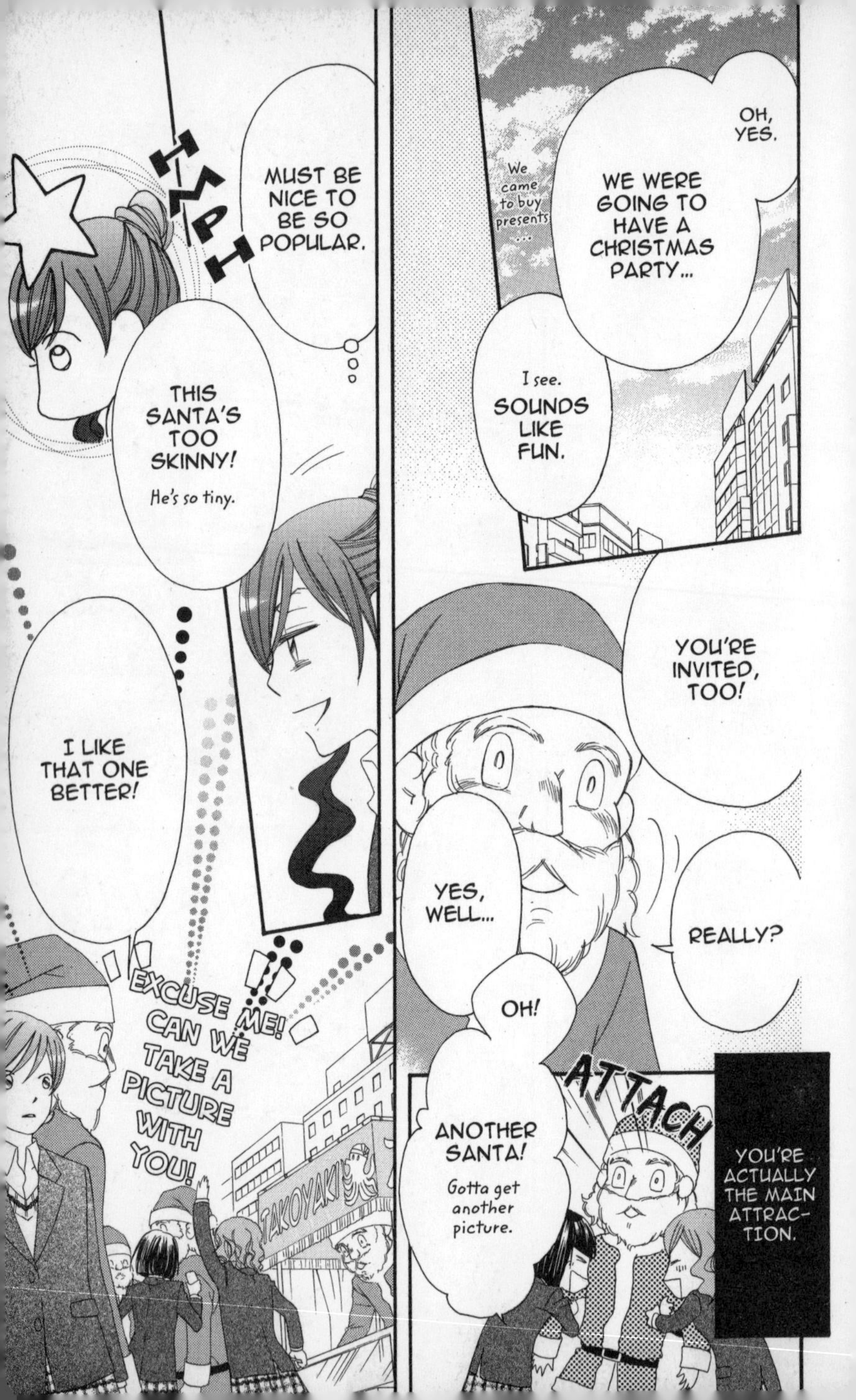
OH, YES.
WE WERE GOING TO HAVE A CHRISTMAS PARTY...
We came to buy presents...
I see. SOUNDS LIKE FUN.
YOU'RE INVITED, TOO!
REALLY?
YES, WELL...
OH!
YOU'RE ACTUALLY THE MAIN ATTRAC-TION.
ATTACH
ANOTHER SANTA!
Gotta get another picture.
MUST BE NICE TO BE SO POPULAR.
HMPH
THIS SANTA'S TOO SKINNY!
He's so tiny.
I LIKE THAT ONE BETTER!
EXCUSE ME! CAN WE TAKE A PICTURE WITH YOU!
TAKOYAKI

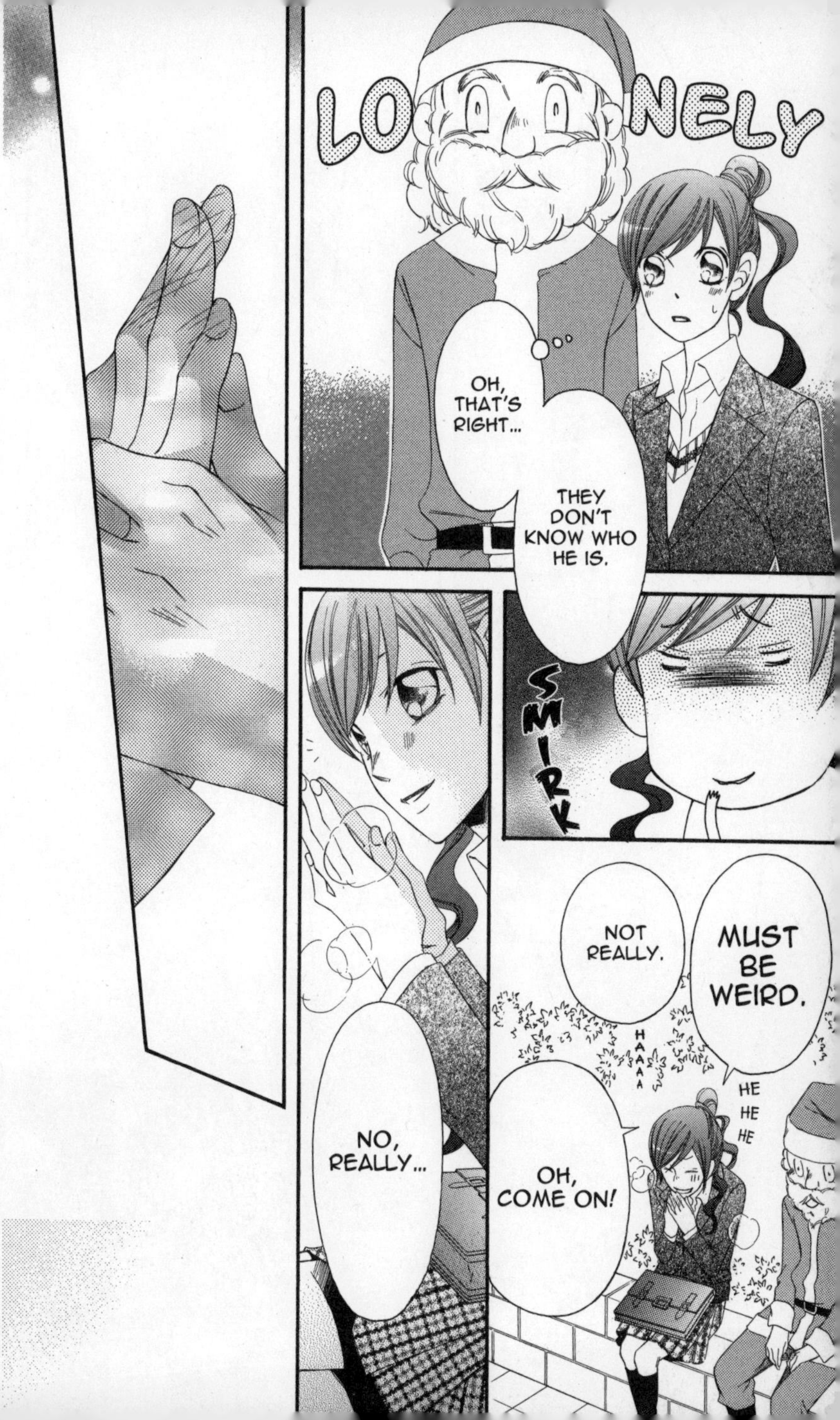
LONELY
OH, THAT'S RIGHT...
THEY DON'T KNOW WHO HE IS.
SMIRK
MUST BE WEIRD.
NOT REALLY.
HAAAA
HE HE HE
OH, COME ON!
NO, REALLY...

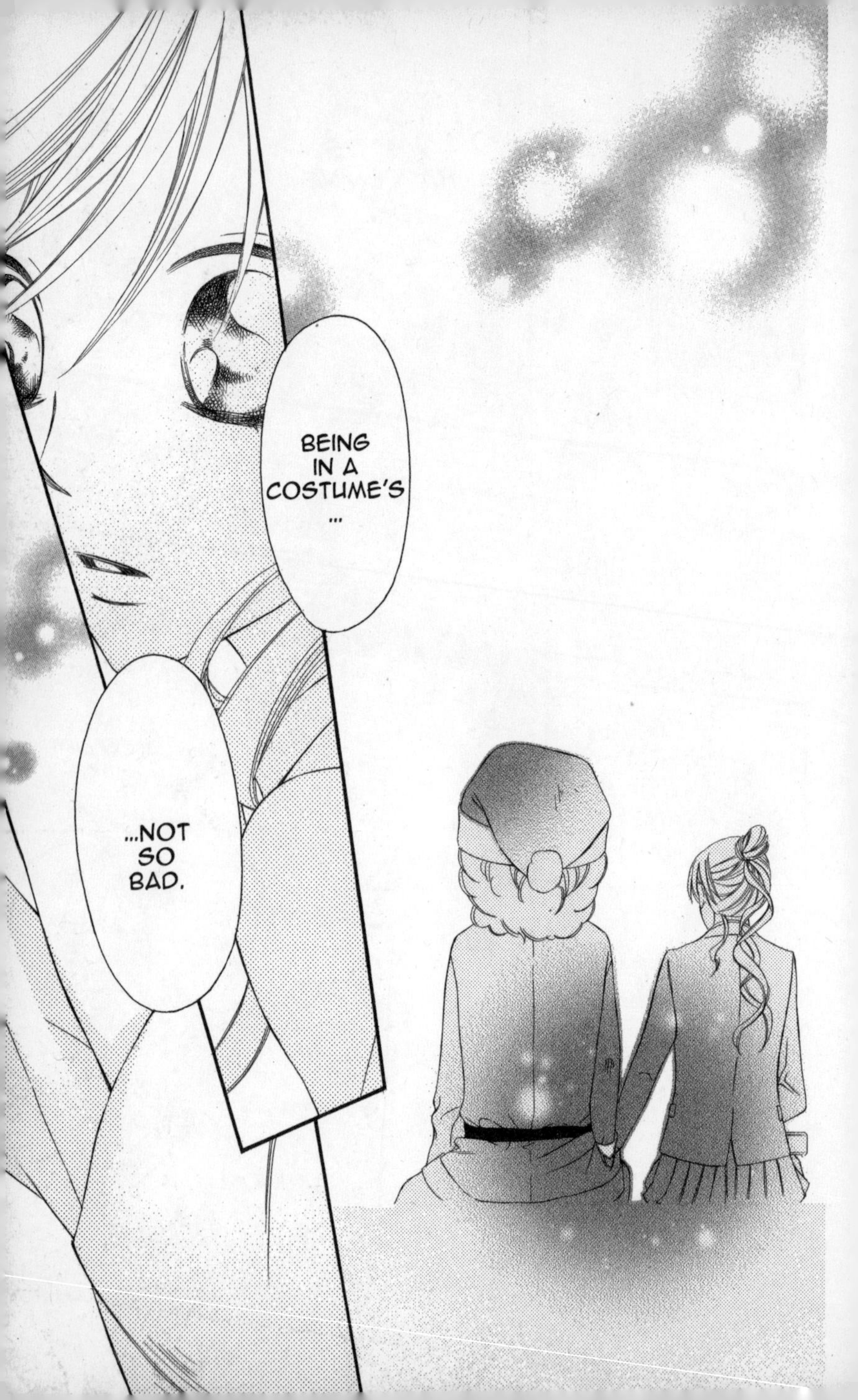
BEING IN A COSTUME'S ...
...NOT SO BAD.

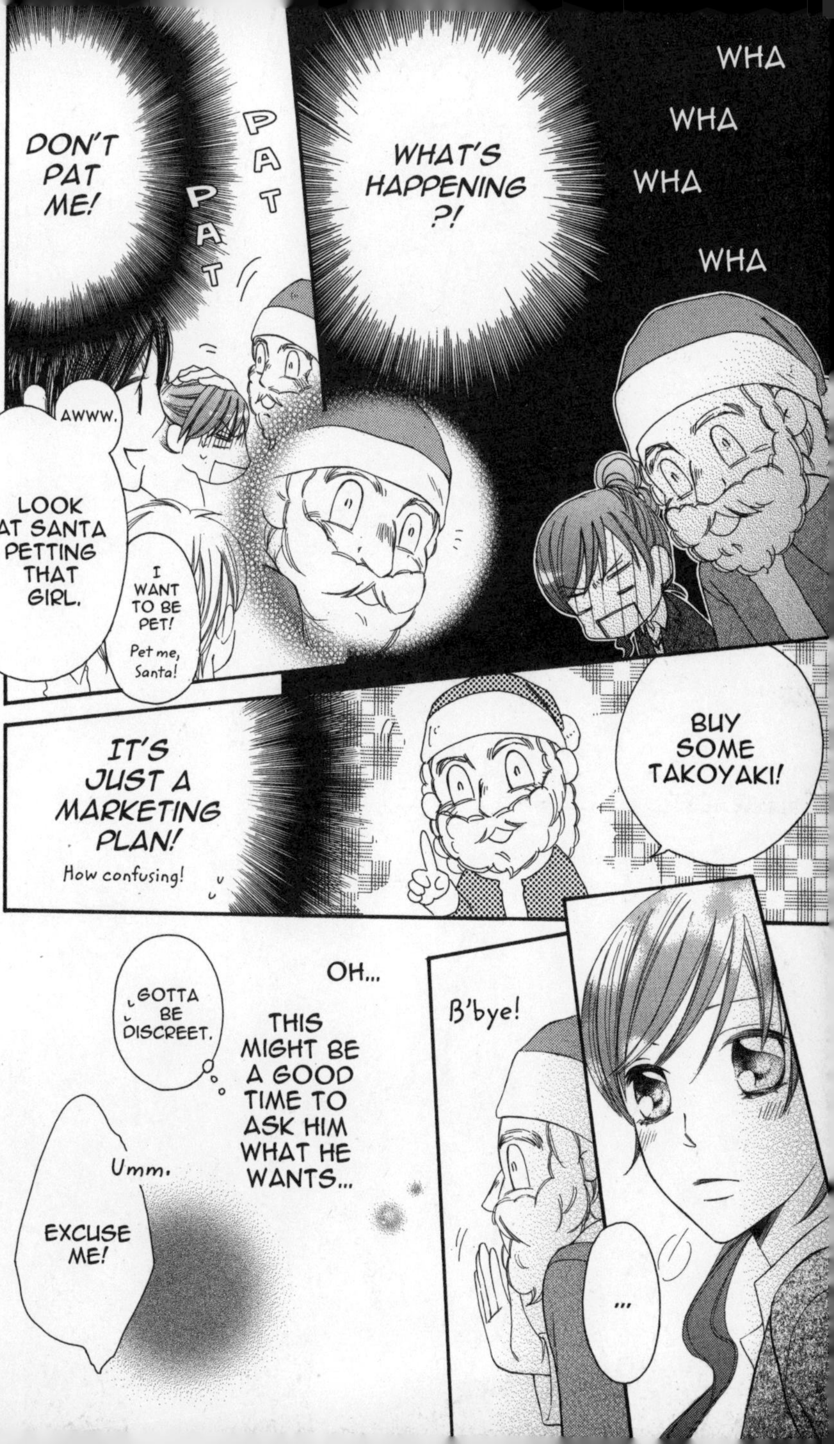
WHA
WHA
WHA
WHA
WHAT'S HAPPENING ?!
DON'T PAT ME!
PAT PAT
AWWW.
LOOK AT SANTA PETTING THAT GIRL.
I WANT TO BE PET!
Pet me, Santa!
BUY SOME TAKOYAKI!
IT'S JUST A MARKETING PLAN!
How confusing!
B'bye!
...
OH...
THIS MIGHT BE A GOOD TIME TO ASK HIM WHAT HE WANTS...
GOTTA BE DISCREET.
Umm.
EXCUSE ME!

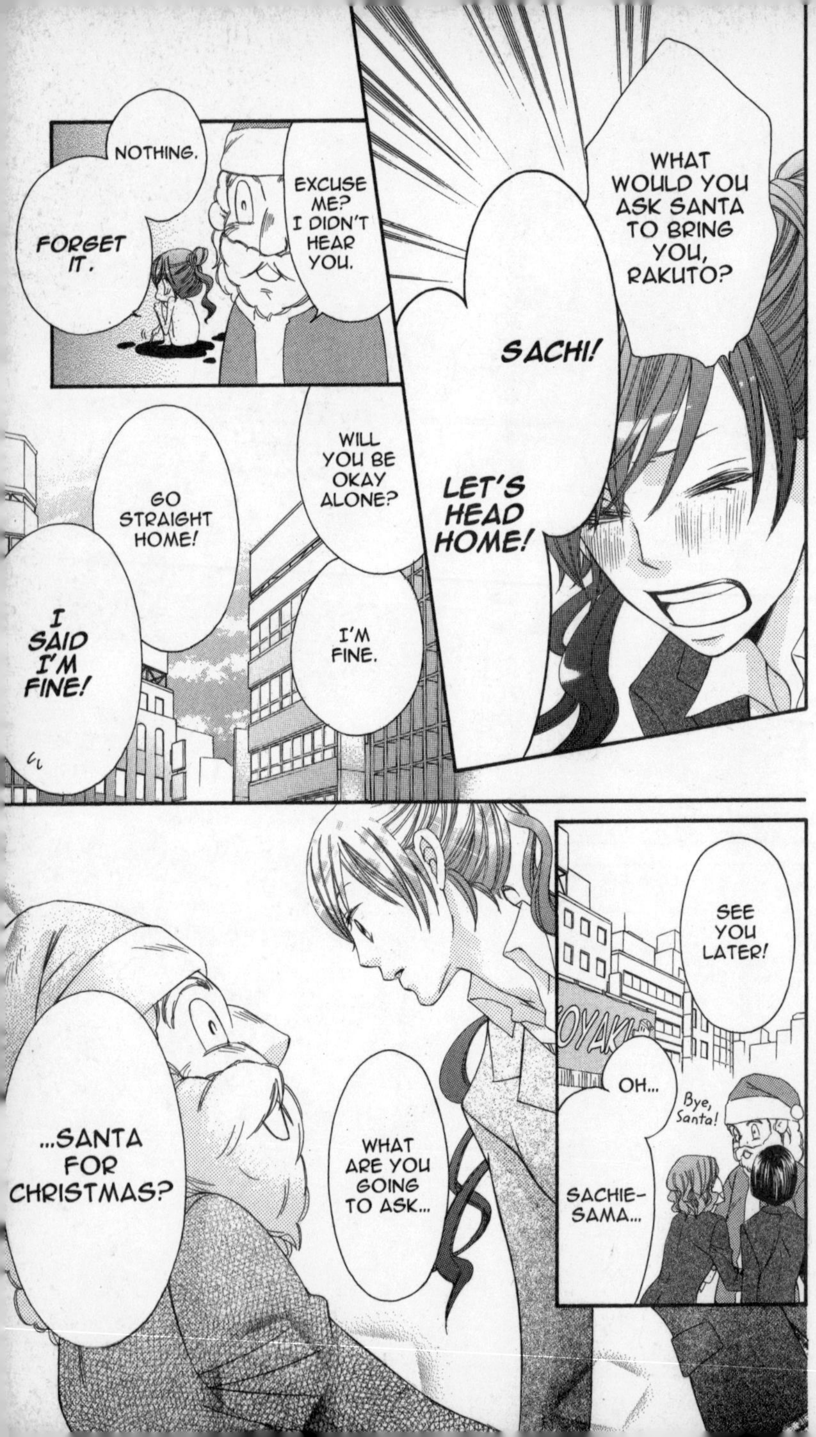
WHAT WOULD YOU ASK SANTA TO BRING YOU, RAKUTO?
SACHI! LET'S HEAD HOME!
EXCUSE ME? I DIDN'T HEAR YOU.
NOTHING.
FORGET IT.
WILL YOU BE OKAY ALONE?
GO STRAIGHT HOME!
I'M FINE.
I SAID I'M FINE!
SEE YOU LATER!
Bye, Santa!
OH...
SACHIE-SAMA...
WHAT ARE YOU GOING TO ASK...
...SANTA FOR CHRISTMAS?

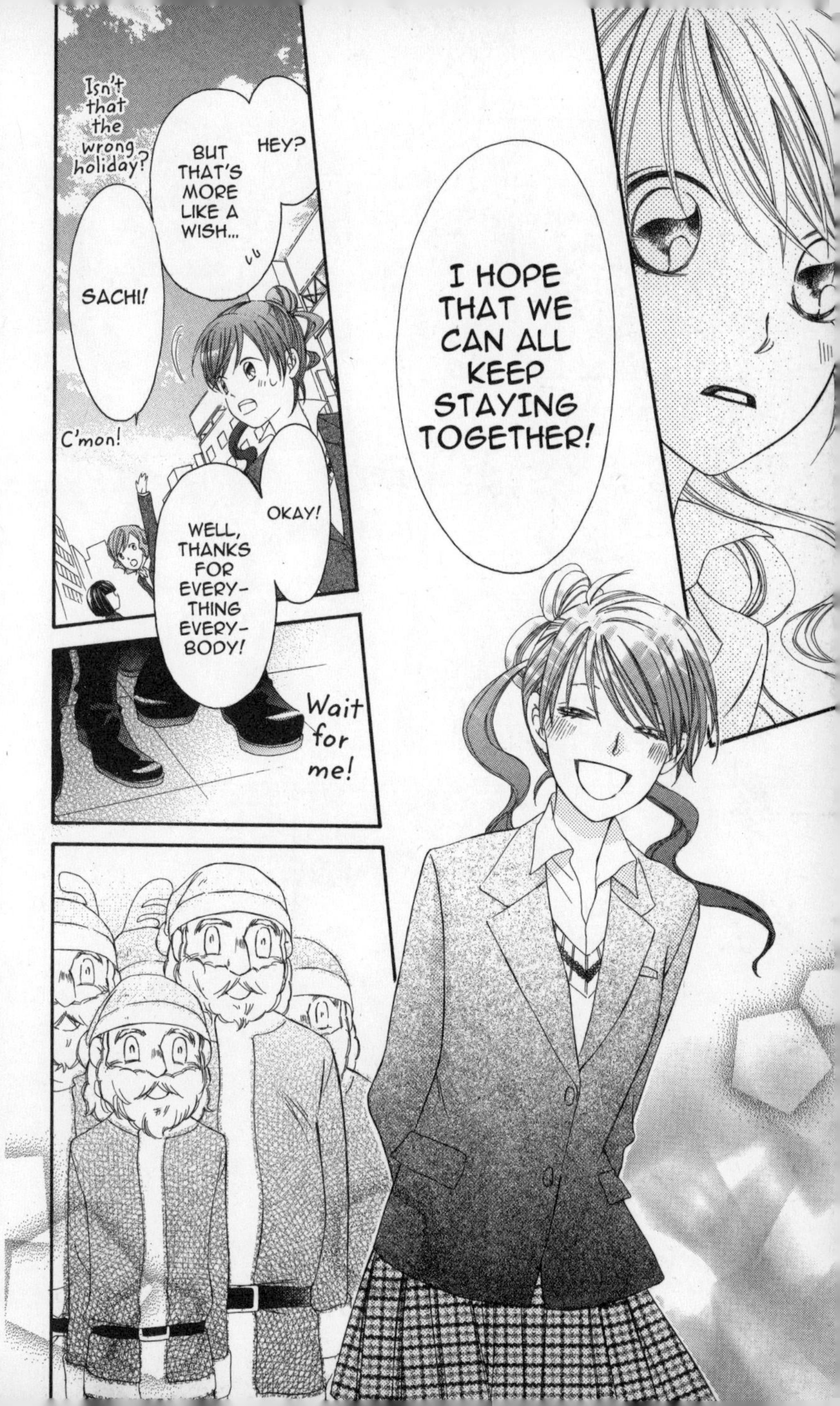
I HOPE THAT WE CAN ALL KEEP STAYING TOGETHER!
HEY? BUT THAT'S MORE LIKE A WISH...
Isn't that the wrong holiday?
SACHI!
C'mon!
OKAY! WELL, THANKS FOR EVERYTHING EVERYBODY!
Wait for me!

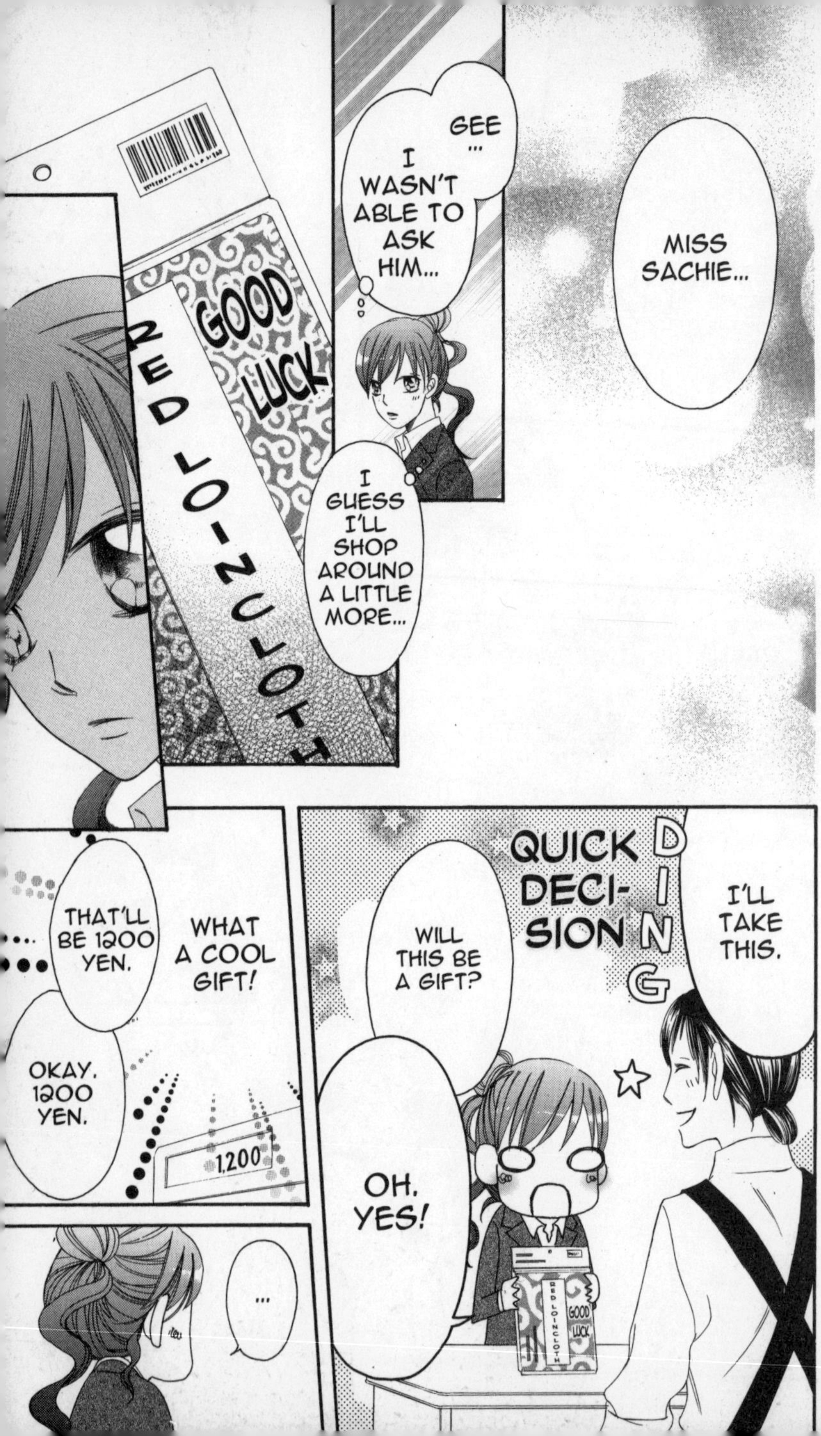
MISS SACHIE...
GEE... I WASN'T ABLE TO ASK HIM...
I GUESS I'LL SHOP AROUND A LITTLE MORE...
GOOD LUCK
RED LOINCLOTH
I'LL TAKE THIS.
DING
QUICK DECISION
WILL THIS BE A GIFT?
OH. YES!
RED LOINCLOTH
GOOD LUCK
WHAT A COOL GIFT!
THAT'LL BE 1200 YEN.
OKAY. 1200 YEN.
1,200
...

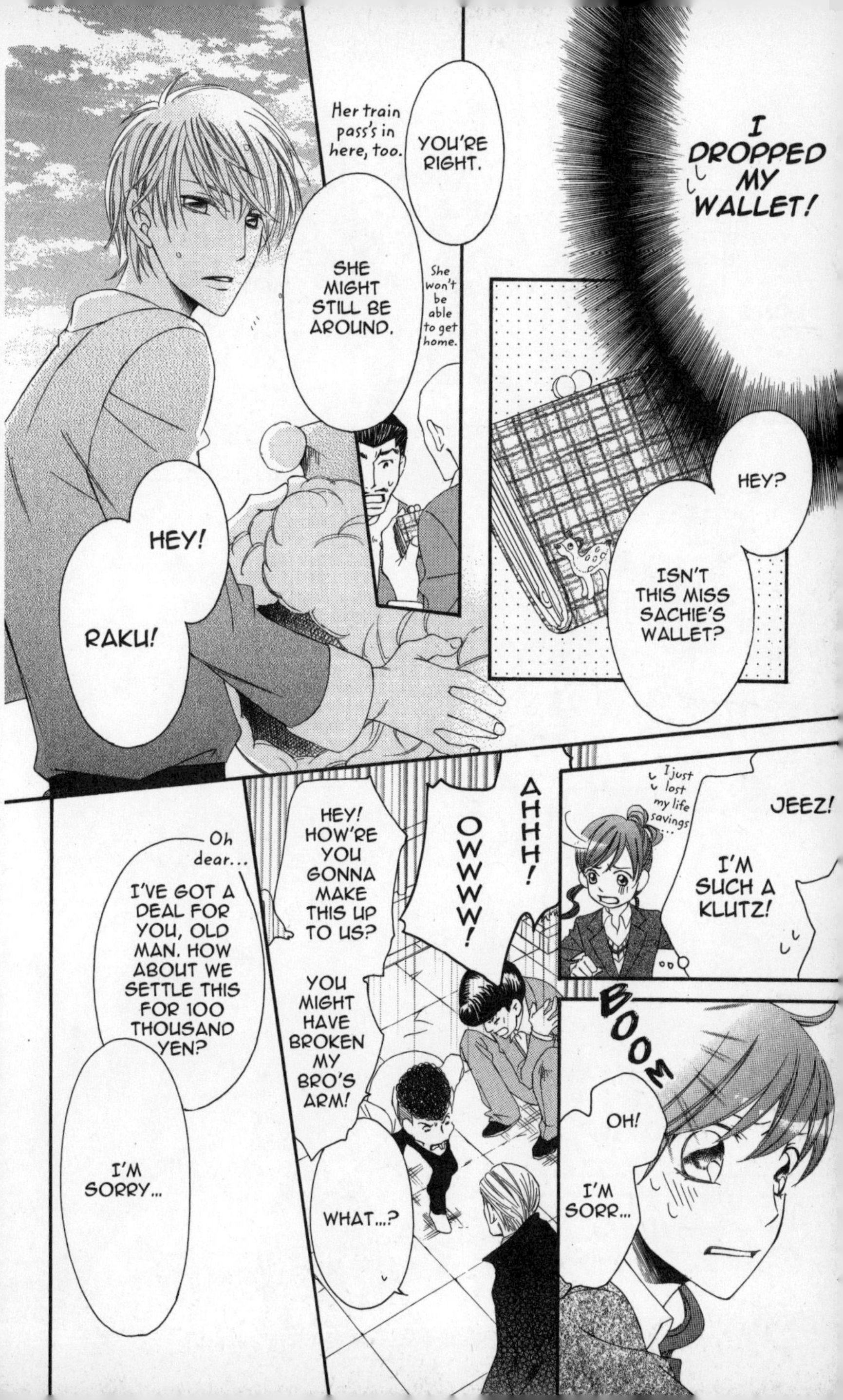
I DROPPED MY WALLET!
HEY?
ISN'T THIS MISS SACHIE'S WALLET?
YOU'RE RIGHT.
Her train pass's in here, too.
SHE MIGHT STILL BE AROUND.
She won't be able to get home.
HEY!
RAKU!
JEEZ!
I'M SUCH A KLUTZ!
I just lost my life savings...
BOOM
OH!
I'M SORR...
AHHH!
OWWWW!
HEY! HOW'RE YOU GONNA MAKE THIS UP TO US?
YOU MIGHT HAVE BROKEN MY BRO'S ARM!
WHAT...?
Oh dear...
I'VE GOT A DEAL FOR YOU, OLD MAN. HOW ABOUT WE SETTLE THIS FOR 100 THOUSAND YEN?
I'M SORRY...

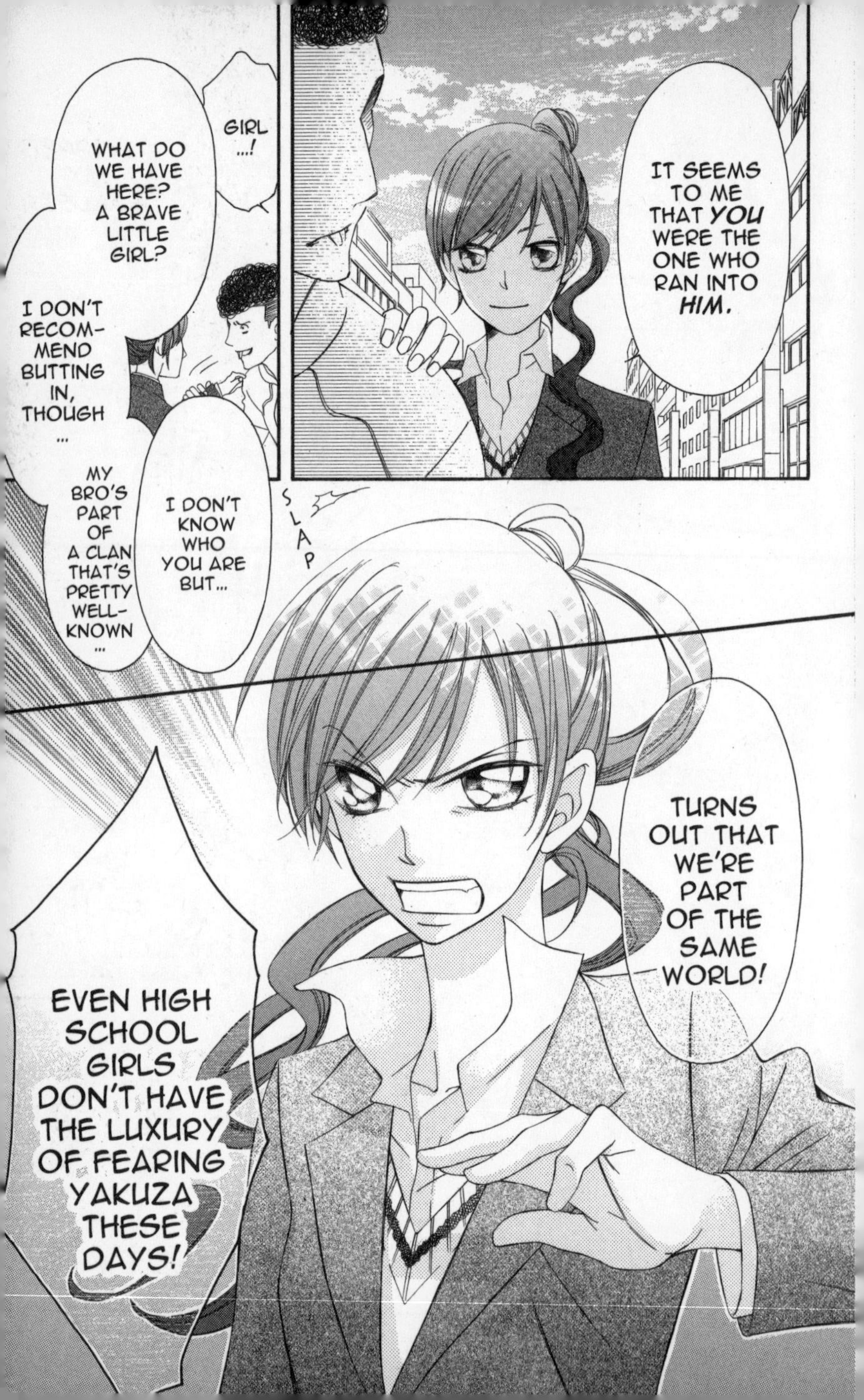
IT SEEMS TO ME THAT *YOU* WERE THE ONE WHO RAN INTO *HIM*.
GIRL ...!
WHAT DO WE HAVE HERE? A BRAVE LITTLE GIRL?
I DON'T RECOMMEND BUTTING IN, THOUGH ...
I DON'T KNOW WHO YOU ARE BUT...
MY BRO'S PART OF A CLAN THAT'S PRETTY WELL-KNOWN ...
SLAP
TURNS OUT THAT WE'RE PART OF THE SAME WORLD!
EVEN HIGH SCHOOL GIRLS DON'T HAVE THE LUXURY OF FEARING YAKUZA THESE DAYS!

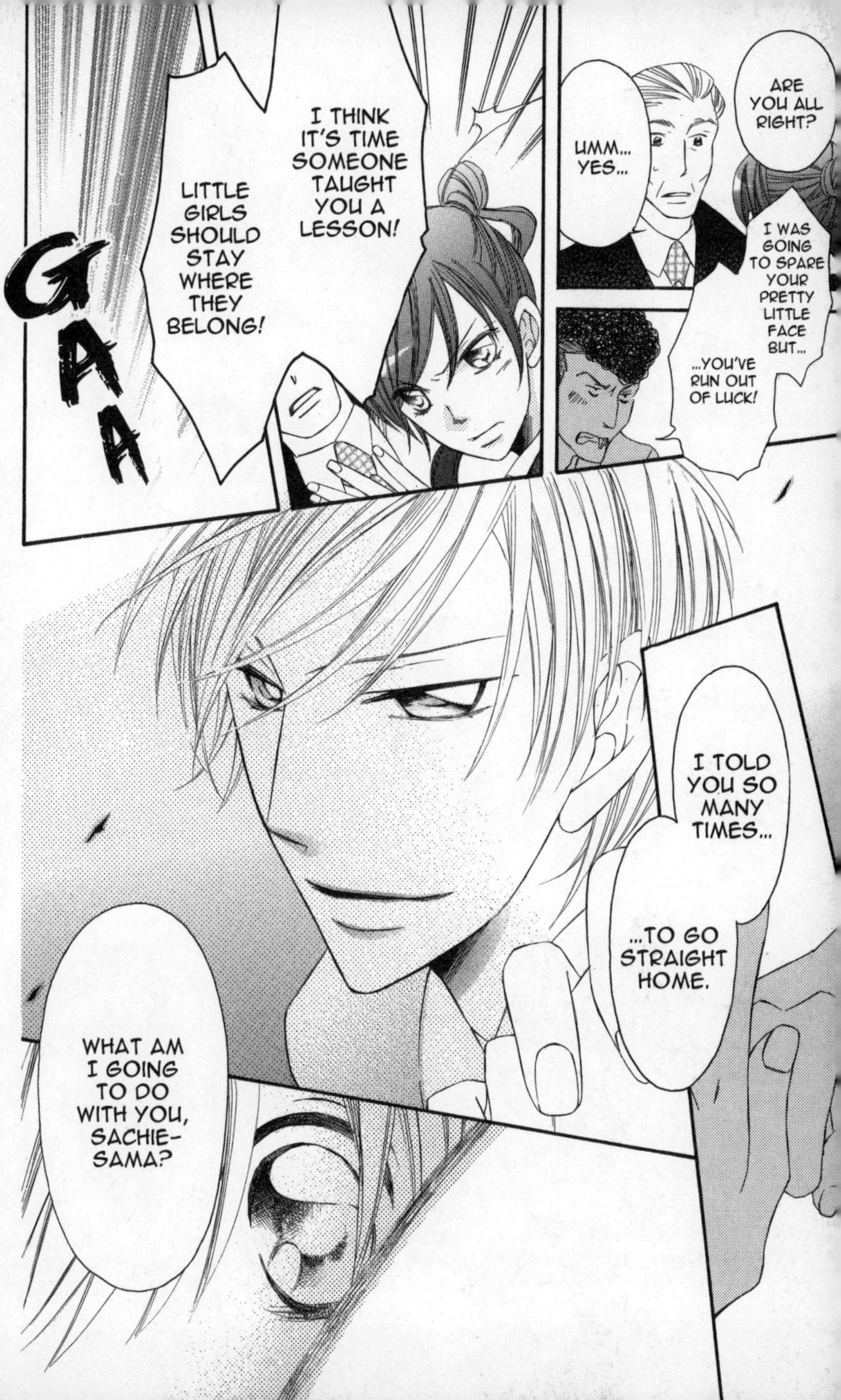
ARE YOU ALL RIGHT?
UMM... YES...
I WAS GOING TO SPARE YOUR PRETTY LITTLE FACE BUT...
...YOU'VE RUN OUT OF LUCK!
I THINK IT'S TIME SOMEONE TAUGHT YOU A LESSON!
LITTLE GIRLS SHOULD STAY WHERE THEY BELONG!
GAA
I TOLD YOU SO MANY TIMES...
...TO GO STRAIGHT HOME.
WHAT AM I GOING TO DO WITH YOU, SACHIE-SAMA?

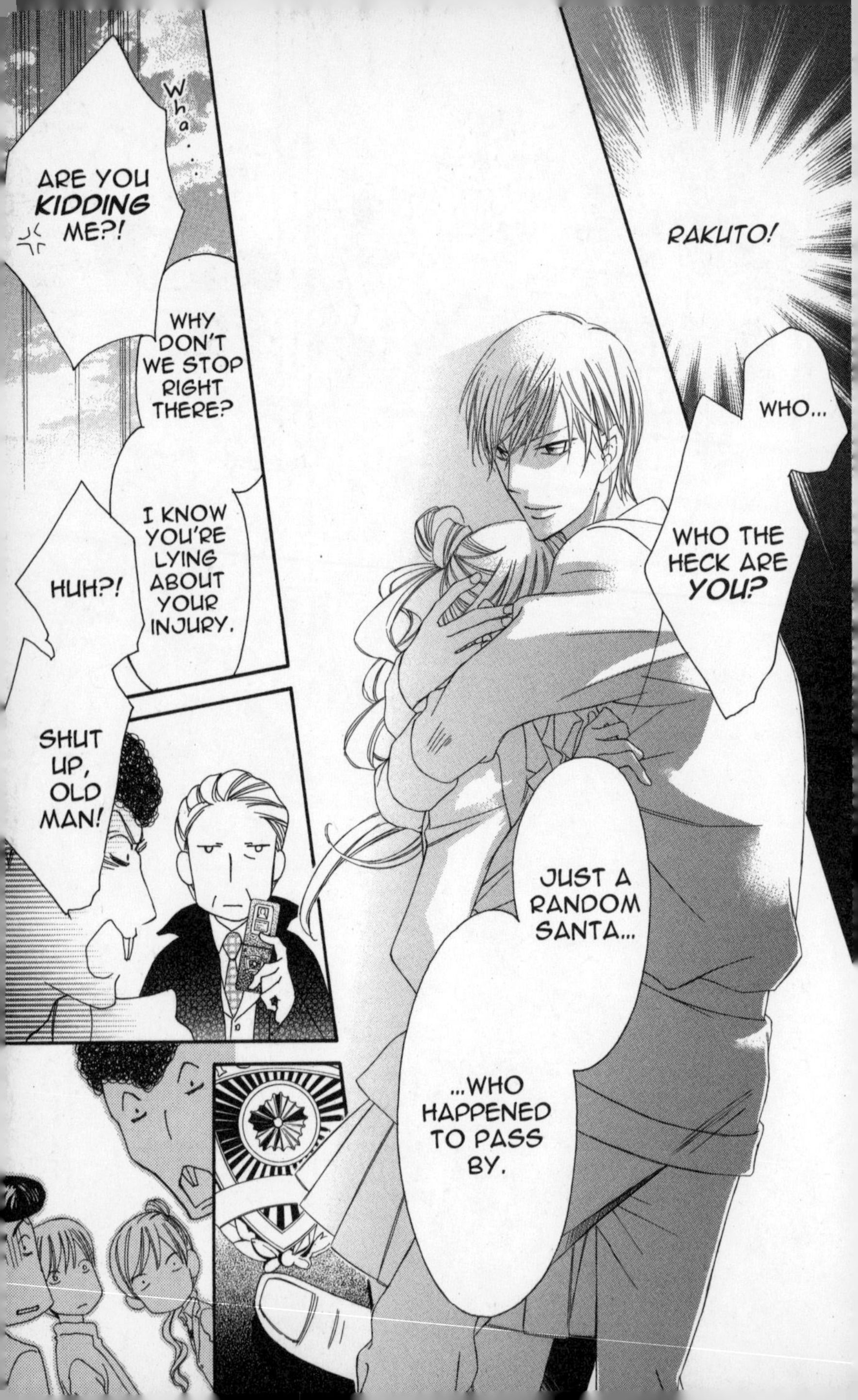
RAKUTO!
WHO...
WHO THE HECK ARE YOU?
JUST A RANDOM SANTA...
...WHO HAPPENED TO PASS BY.
Wha...
ARE YOU KIDDING ME?!
WHY DON'T WE STOP RIGHT THERE?
I KNOW YOU'RE LYING ABOUT YOUR INJURY.
HUH?!
SHUT UP, OLD MAN!

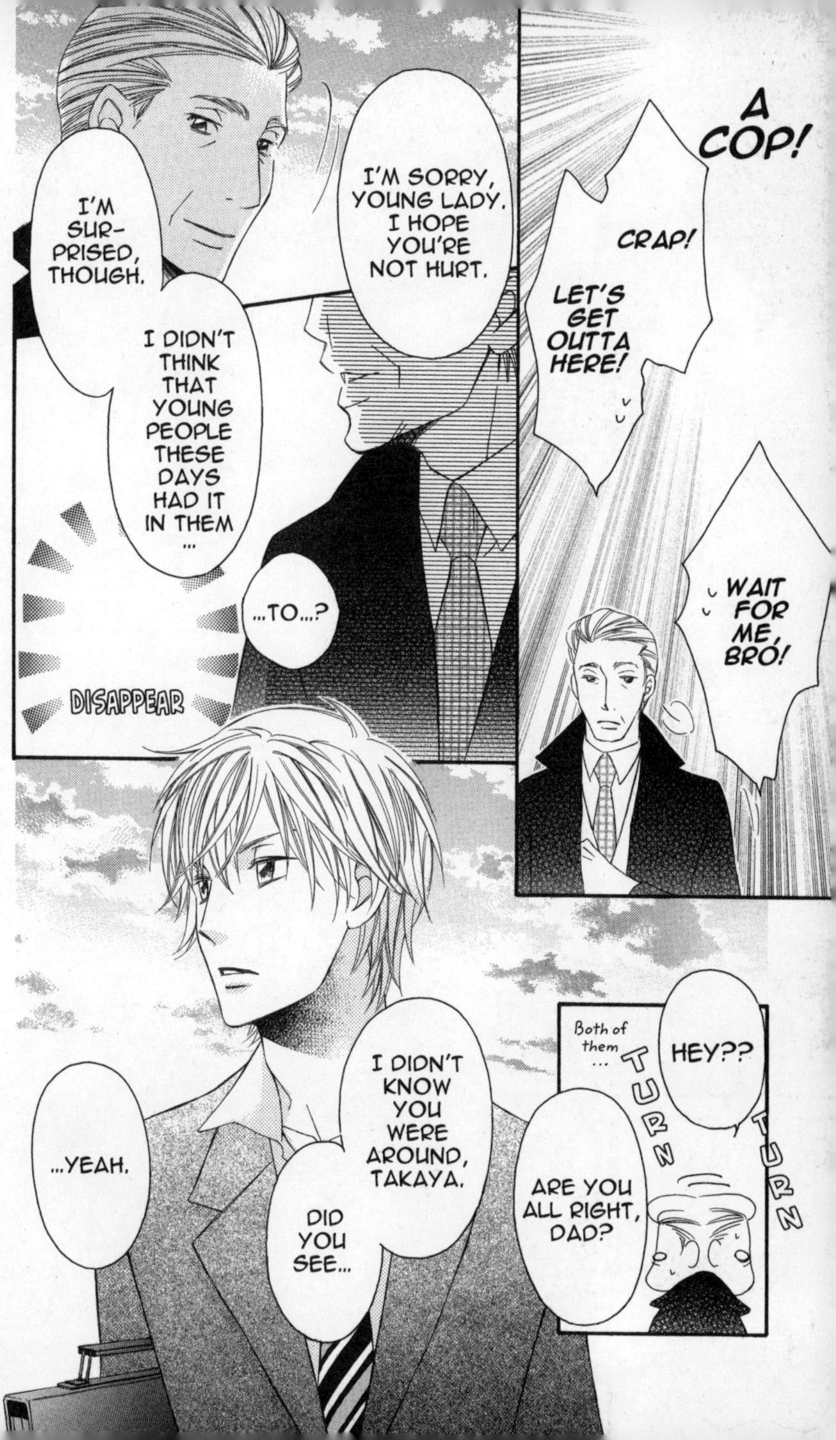
A COP!
CRAP!
LET'S GET OUTTA HERE!
WAIT FOR ME, BRO!
I'M SORRY, YOUNG LADY. I HOPE YOU'RE NOT HURT.
I'M SUR-PRISED, THOUGH.
I DIDN'T THINK THAT YOUNG PEOPLE THESE DAYS HAD IT IN THEM ...
...TO...?
DISAPPEAR
Both of them ...
HEY??
TURN
TURN
ARE YOU ALL RIGHT, DAD?
I DIDN'T KNOW YOU WERE AROUND, TAKAYA.
DID YOU SEE...
...YEAH.

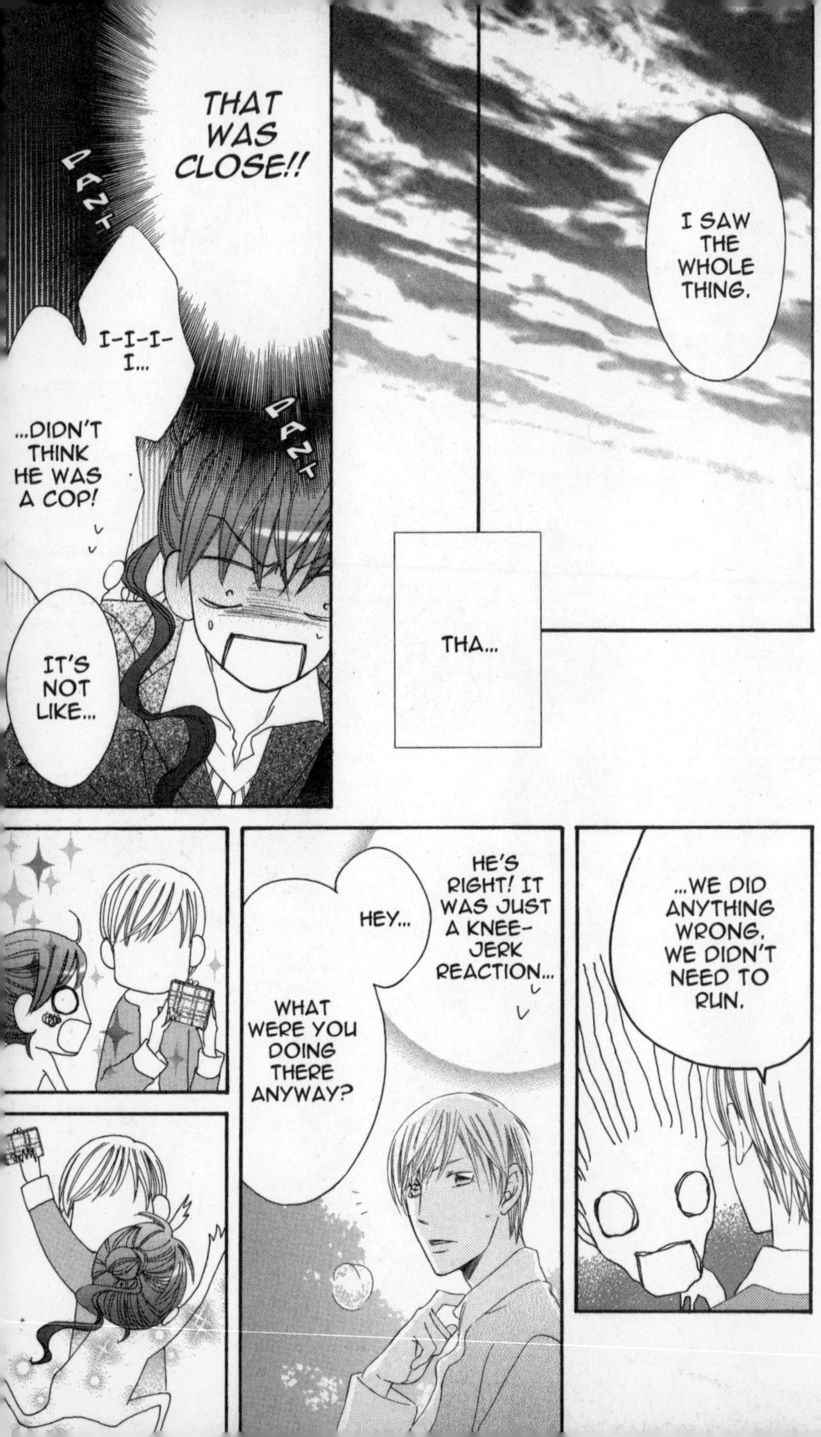
I SAW THE WHOLE THING.
THA...
THAT WAS CLOSE!!
PANT
PANT
I-I-I-I...
...DIDN'T THINK HE WAS A COP!
IT'S NOT LIKE...
...WE DID ANYTHING WRONG. WE DIDN'T NEED TO RUN.
HE'S RIGHT! IT WAS JUST A KNEE-JERK REACTION...
HEY...
WHAT WERE YOU DOING THERE ANYWAY?

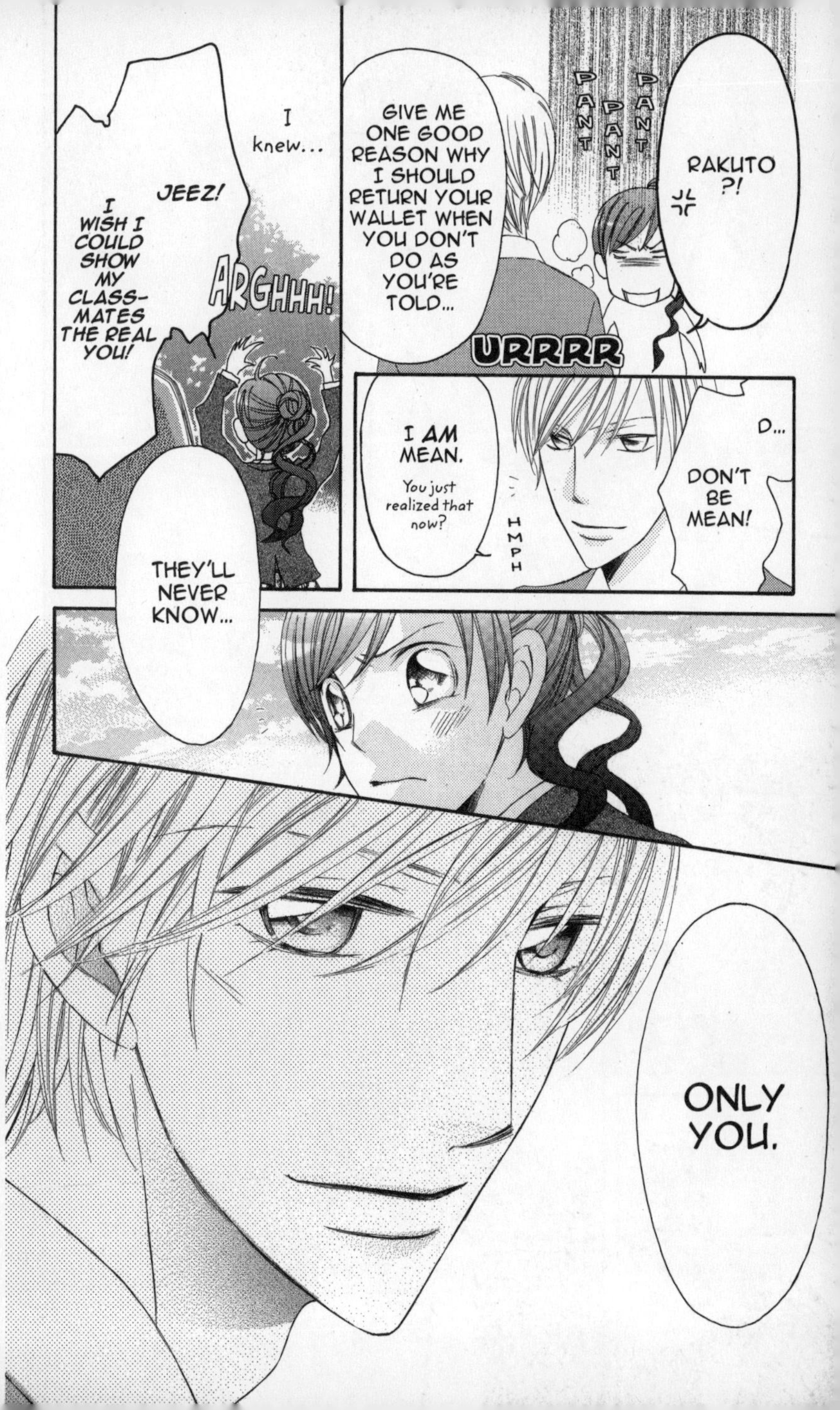
RAKUTO?!
PANT PANT PANT
GIVE ME ONE GOOD REASON WHY I SHOULD RETURN YOUR WALLET WHEN YOU DON'T DO AS YOU'RE TOLD...
URRRR
D...
DON'T BE MEAN!
HMPH
I AM MEAN.
You just realized that now?
I knew...
JEEZ!
I WISH I COULD SHOW MY CLASSMATES THE REAL YOU!
ARGHHH!
THEY'LL NEVER KNOW...
ONLY YOU.

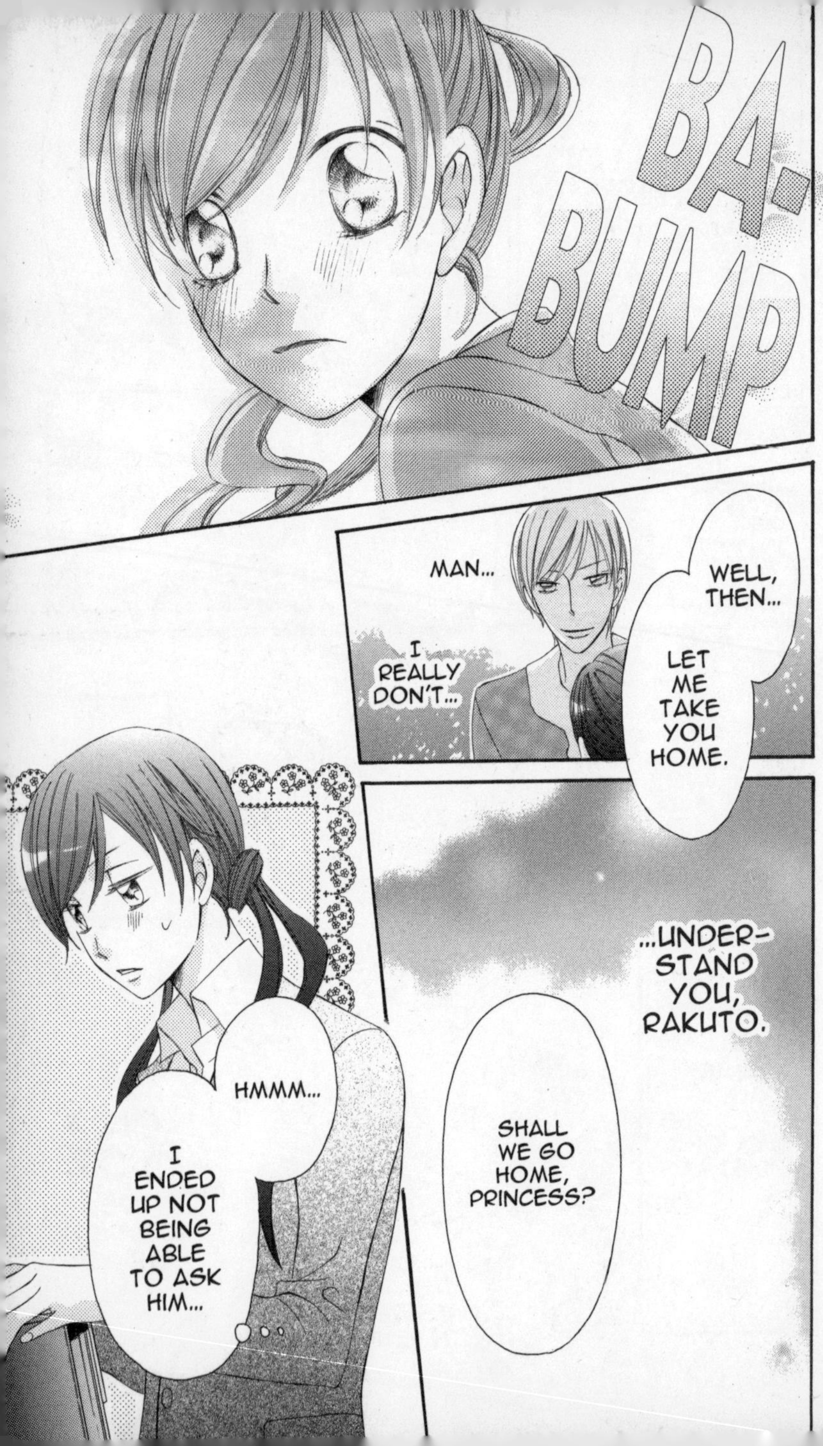
BA-BUMP
WELL, THEN...
LET ME TAKE YOU HOME.
MAN...
I REALLY DON'T...
...UNDER-STAND YOU, RAKUTO.
SHALL WE GO HOME, PRINCESS?
HMMM...
I ENDED UP NOT BEING ABLE TO ASK HIM...

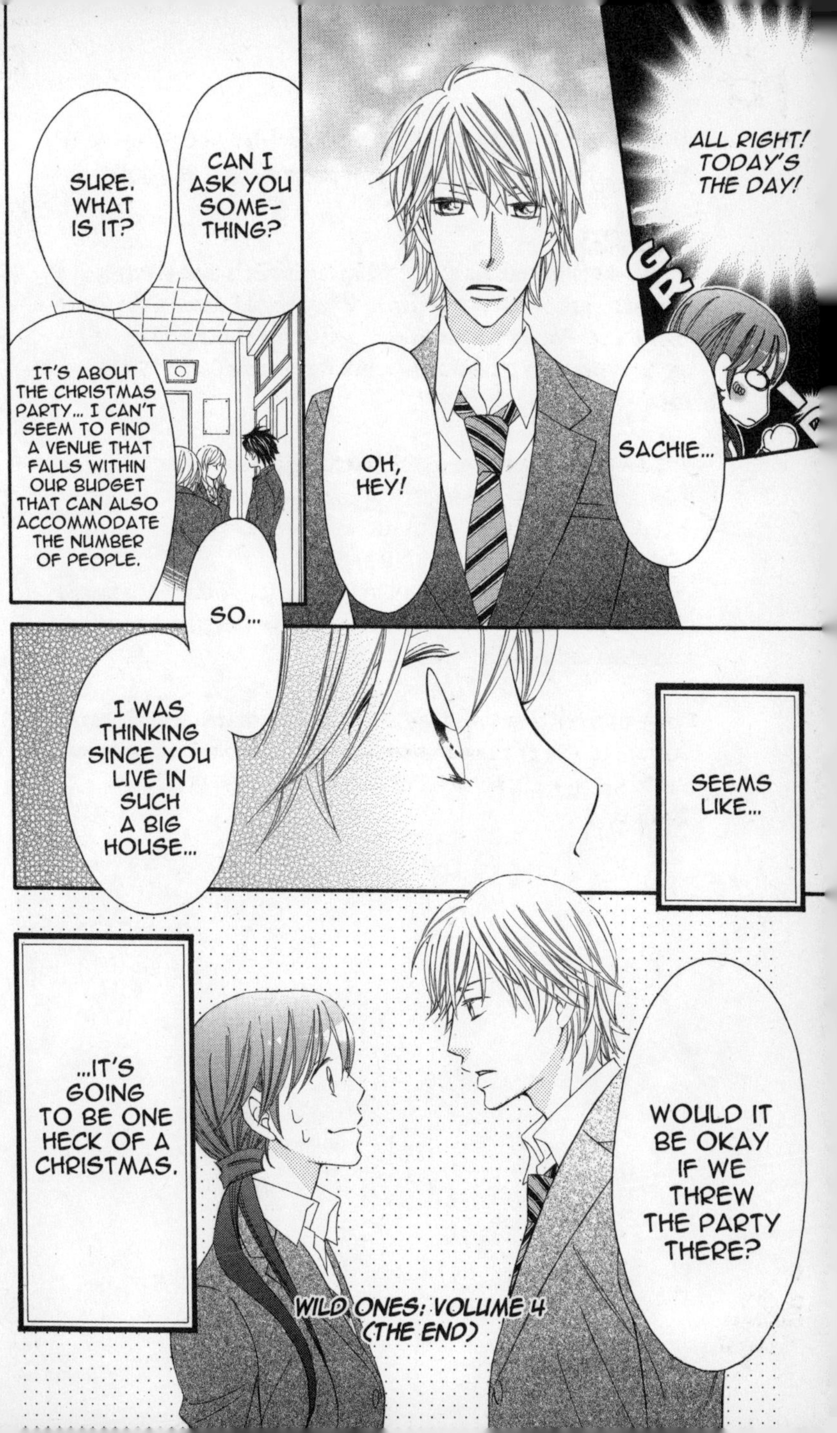
ALL RIGHT! TODAY'S THE DAY!
GR
SACHIE...
OH, HEY!
CAN I ASK YOU SOME-THING?
SURE. WHAT IS IT?
IT'S ABOUT THE CHRISTMAS PARTY... I CAN'T SEEM TO FIND A VENUE THAT FALLS WITHIN OUR BUDGET THAT CAN ALSO ACCOMMODATE THE NUMBER OF PEOPLE.
SO...
SEEMS LIKE...
I WAS THINKING SINCE YOU LIVE IN SUCH A BIG HOUSE...
WOULD IT BE OKAY IF WE THREW THE PARTY THERE?
...IT'S GOING TO BE ONE HECK OF A CHRISTMAS.
WILD ONES: VOLUME 4 (THE END)

Wanna be part of the *Wild Ones* gang? Then you gotta learn the lingo! Here are some cultural notes to help you out!

HONORIFICS

Sama – the formal version of *san*, this honorific title is used primarily in addressing persons much higher in rank than oneself. *Sama* is also used when the speaker wants to show great respect or deference. (On page 7, and for pretty much the rest of the series, Rakuto calls Sachie "Sachie-sama" in addition to "princess.")

Senpai – honorific title used to address upperclassmen, elders and seniors in the same club or school the speaker belongs to. (On page 127, the girls in Sachie's second-year class call Rakuto, a third year, "Igarashi-senpai.")

San – the most common honorific title; it is used to address people outside one's immediate family and close friends. (On page 173, the author refers to a list of her coworkers as "-san.")

Chan – an informal version of *san* used to address children and females. *Chan* can be used as a term of endearment between women who are good friends. (On page 173, the author refers to one of her assistants as "Mo-chan.")

NOTES

Page 10, panel 4 – Hamburgers
Homemade hamburgers in Japan are more like American meatloaf, containing eggs, vegetables and other fillings.

Page 19, panel 1 – Yukata
A garment that is worn in the summertime in Japan, especially to outdoor festivals and events. Though it resembles the more formal kimono, yukata are made out of cotton rather than silk.

Page 37, panel 3 – Kendo
The traditional Japanese-style sport of fencing, using wooden armor and bamboo swords. It is still practiced in Japan's public schools.

Page 43, panel 6 – Takoyaki
Fried dough balls with pieces of octopus in them. This snack originated in Osaka and is often sold by street vendors.

Page 99, panel 4 – Shin-Kobe Station
Kobe's shinkansen terminal. Some of the shinkansen stations are built in locations removed from downtown, despite having the name of that city, to facilitate construction of a high-speed intercity railway.

Page 101, panel 3 – Shinkansen
The "bullet train," a high-speed commuter railway that is a common form of transportation between Japan's major cities. It stops only at special stations.

Page 132, panel 1 – Sports Day
A national holiday devoted to sports and physical activity. On this day, many schools have sports festivals, and members of each class are chosen (often unwillingly) to represent the class in various sporting events.